SECOND E_____

ADVENTURING ON EURAIL

JAY BRUNHOUSE

PELICAN PUBLISHING COMPANY

GRETNA 1991

First edition, 1989
Second edition, 1991

This book is a revised edition of *Adventuring on the Eurail Express* © 1989.

Library of Congress Cataloging-in-Publication Data

Brunhouse, Jay.
    Adventuring on Eurail : formerly titled Adventuring on the Eurail
Express / by Jay Brunhouse.
       p.   cm.
    Includes index.
    ISBN 0-88289-834-5
    1. Europe—Description and travel—1971- —Guide-books.
    2. Railroad travel—Europe—Guide-books. I. Brunhouse, Jay.
Adventuring on the Eurail Express. II. Title.
D909.B778 1991
914.04′559—dc20
                                     90-24935
                                     CIP

Maps by Brian Clarke

Cover photo: Swedish Railroads' tilting X-2 train sweeps around curves between Stockholm and Gothenburg. Photo by Bjorn Enstrom

> *Information in this guidebook is based on authoritative data available at the time of printing. Prices and hours of operation of businesses listed are subject to change without notice. Readers are asked to take this into account when consulting this guide.*

Manufactured in the United States of America

Published by Pelican Publishing Company, Inc.
1101 Monroe Street, Gretna, Louisiana 70053

Contents

France

Iberia

Scandinavia and Finland

Germany

Austria and Hungary

Italy and Greece

Preface

You find many sensible reasons to take a train. They fire dreams of darting at a whim at safe speed from one city center to another, seeing and enjoying Europe's beautiful rivers, lakes, Alps, and hillside chateaux from freshly washed panoramic windows. You save money, you meet Europeans in congenial, give-and-take surroundings, you explore corners of the continent where scenery dazzles your eyes, you sleep and eat soundly and well, and you speed at unprecedented velocities and arrive fully ready to go. Alert travelers enjoy more than just a trip. They discover an adventure.

This book is to help adventurers who are planning to use their time in Europe confronting thrilling scenery and discovering wild and secret corners on exciting trains — the most comfortable and the most dazzling — for little money, little hassle, and much pleasure.

Mobility in Europe can be more than moving yourself here and there. It's an art. Train travelers have perfected this art to its finest form using European trains' time-warp new speed and comfort to simplify their seeing Europe's highlights. Those who have traveled by train in the past are thrilled to discover European trains' new convenience and ambience.

Take your pencil in hand. This guide tells you how to see easily all the Western European countries plus Britain. "Adventuring" draws you into eastern Germany and Hungary, too. Highlight the information you'll use and put this book in your travel bag.

This is an exciting time to adventure on the European trains. Europe's supertrains ignite travelers' sense of adventure with their magnificent, thundering "whooshes," space-age speed, and sci-fi interiors.

New and remodeled stations make trains easier to use. Newly opened Madrid's Atocha, Paris's Montparnasse, Zurich's Hauptbahnhof, Lucerne's SBB, Utrecht's Centraal, and Stockholm's Central are more than transit hubs with attached subway accesses. You use escalators and ramps instead of steps, read electronic and digital billboards, and use train station offices helping you with train travel, city orientation, and often hotel arrangements.

TGV Atlantique trains take you to 186 mph. Adventuring takes you to the North Face of the Eiger, Midnight Sun at the most northerly station of Western Europe, teetering along the cliffs of the Isle of Man, through the feudal highlands of Sardinia, and down Alpine ridges to the French Riviera.

Driven by competition from air travel, long-distance trains in Europe are clawing for survival by slashing travel times and making their trips more comfortable. Visitors are winners. With Europe's present congestion on motorways and saturation in the air lanes, traveling on Europe's supertrains means seeing Europe free of stress.

You find that adventuring on European trains gives you more time to enjoy yourself, smoother and more social rides, simpler traveling, and — with one of the new cheap rail passes — your best value in Europe.

Acknowledgments

Thank you to those who helped me gather and update information, making this edition current and complete. Thank you Kajsa Agostini, Jan Alexandersson, Hans Baumann, Duane Bellmore, Wim Binnendijk, Gerry Davidson, Marion Fourestier, George Hern, Linda Lang, Andy Lazarus, Joe Lustenberger, Anny Miller, Jan Nijboer, Armond Noble, Ulla Pakarinen, Nathan Sawyer, Dag Scher, Patricia Titley, Gwen van Essche, Barbara Veldkamp, Pilar Vico, Jens Wilhelmsborg, and Joe Zucker. Flowery bouquets to expert editor Nina Kooij.

ADVENTURING
ON EURAIL

Introduction

Here is the feeling and thrill of *Adventuring on Eurail*. The first chapter gives
you useful tips to help you make the plans you want and to get you to Europe,
well coached, with the right rail pass in your hand. You are guided aboard
your train, into your destination, and back onto your train again so carefully
a first-time adventurer will have no worries. Then it is up to you.

Experienced travelers know all national train systems have their quirks and
secret rewards. Chapters taking you through Western Europe from Switzerland
to the Midnight Sun to the Mediterranean show you how to profit from them.
Adventurous trips to everywhere Eurailpass goes, and Britain, too, are described in loving detail to enhance your travels as you ride these trains. You are
also alerted to adventurous trips that are not covered by Eurailpass.

Read the descriptions in the chapters for special trips and side options. The
"Vital Tips" sections give you special information about traveling through the
countries that most interest you.

Timetables follow each adventure to give you the latest schedules. Remember that summer and winter timetables change yearly. Times are shown using
the same twenty-four-hour clock you see in Europe. Major cities and connections are capitalized, and dots in a time column indicate that the train does
not stop at that station. Notes indicate special restrictions. Here is your first
tip: when you can punch up a twenty-four-hour clock on your digital watch,
use this mode when reading timetables.

4 ADVENTURING ON EURAIL

Other travel books tell you where to stay and what to see. This one guides you through Europe and gives you tips to make your travel time exciting, social, and offbeat — every moment a pleasure.

Vital Tips
to Adventuring on
the Trains of Europe

Arranging Your Itinerary

Study guidebooks—Milk tourist offices—Get free train information—Use the Thomas Cook timetable—Plot your train travel strategies craftily—Let travel agents fill in the blanks

Study Guidebooks

You can gather all your general and specific information about packing, hotel and hostel accommodations, air transportation, food, shopping, and sightseeing from guidebooks in your library and bookshops. Tailored for adventurers are the "Let's Go" guides edited by the Harvard Student Agencies (St. Martin's Press, 175 Fifth Avenue, New York, NY 10010) and "How to Europe" by John Bermont (Murphy & Broad Publishing, P.O. Box 3208, Newport Beach, CA 92663).

Milk Tourist Offices

After you have a general idea of your plans, write to the national tourist office of every country you think you might possibly visit. Their addresses are in Appendix A. Don't simply ask for "information" or you will receive broad-brush propaganda. Ask specifically for details about your special interests, e.g., discount programs for hotels, subway savings and maps, castles to see, scenic bicycle routes, city "keys" or discount programs for museum admissions and city tours, regional maps and sightseeing in specific cities and areas.

Get Free Train Information

Even when you are not considering buying a Eurailpass, write for their free information. Ask for all the following:

• "Through Europe by Train," a 160-page, pocket-sized timetable for the best European InterCity trains.

• "Eurail Traveler's Guide," a thirty-six-page illustrated booklet of wise tips to all aspects of train travel in Europe and an indispensable large foldout Eurail train map of Europe.

• "See Europe by Train," the promotional brochure giving you Eurail prices and rules.

Send your postcard to Eurailpass, P.O. Box 325, Old Greenwich, CT 06870-0325. In Canada write Eurailpass Distribution Centre, C. P. 300, Succursale R., Montreal, Quebec H2S 3K9. Also contact BritRail, GermanRail, and FrenchRail for additional information (see Appendix A).

Use the Thomas Cook Timetable

Check to see whether the reference desk of your public library has a copy of the Thomas Cook European Timetable. Should your library fail you, look for it in bookstores specializing in travel literature. If there is no travel bookstore near you, order the timetable from Forsyth Travel Library, P.O. Box 2975, Shawnee Mission, KS 66201-1375 (Tel. 1-800-FORSYTH). (Write ahead for a free price list and order form.)

The Thomas Cook European Timetable helps you with detailed advance planning. When you buy one, carry it with you, or tear out the pages covering the countries you are visiting and take them with you, but in many train carriages filled with adventurers in Europe you will see one or more copies of the bright, orange-colored timetable, and the owner will be more than happy to let you look at it.

All European railroads publish complete timetables, but they are generally too bulky to carry around. In some countries they run into many volumes. You sometimes find complete sets on the reference tables in the railroads' information offices in Europe. Agents in the information offices will look up details for you.

Most railroads also publish pocket-sized timetables for their most heavily used routes and leaflets listing connections between popular city pairs or regions. These are available, free for the asking, in the information offices of the railroads (not the tourist office) in train stations. Pocket timetables are also occasionally available free in North America. Request them from the railroads' offices (see Appendix A) before you leave.

Plot Your Train Travel Strategies Craftily

Consider several travel strategies depending on where you decide to go and what you want to do. Adventurers traveling long distances prefer the circular trip plan. Start and end your train travel at your airline's European gateway and cover your stops with a circular plan that brings you back to your gateway city. (You can sometimes arrange an "open-jaw" airline ticket that allows you to return from a different city than the one in which you arrived.) When you want to see Europe extensively, you can see more using this plan.

You have best results when you plan at least one overnight following your arrival at your airline gateway city to allow for jet lag and familiarization, and at least two when you return there. This gives you flexibility to change your plans or cope with any unexpected delays during your trip.

Before you leave home, make a working itinerary. Using your timetables, select the best trains. Outline your day, city, and train connections. Carefully note the days of the week because some trains do not run on weekends or local holidays.

Make your itinerary loose enough so you can vary it depending on circumstances. Keep backup and alternative plans in the back of your mind. You can usually count on reliable train connections, but — for example — when you travel farther and farther south in Italy, trains run later and later. Strikes and natural disasters such as washouts can (and do) devastate split-second plans.

Some travelers save money by alternating nights in hotels and aboard trains. They travel on an overnight train, check into their hotel in the morning, shower, etc., do their sightseeing in the afternoon, and see the city by night. On the following day, they check out of their hotel, leave their luggage with the receptionist, top off their daylight sightseeing, dine, pick up their luggage, and leave on the late-evening overnight train for their next destination.

The second strategy involves locating in one city and taking day trips to nearby places of interest. You double your time on the train and return to your bed at the mercy of the train schedule, but you won't waste time packing, unpacking, and checking in and out of hotels. When you want to see an area intensively, this is the plan you follow.

When you are visiting both Britain and the Continent, schedule Britain either first or last. However, Eurail Flexipasses and the BritFrance Pass (see below) let you sandwich some days in Britain into the middle of your itinerary.

Let Travel Agents Fill in the Blanks

The right travel agent will save you a lot of time and effort and surprise you with good advice. Their computers handle rail passes. Many railroads' products are not sold directly to consumers. Appendix A lists the consumer telephone number for Rail Europe, the FrenchRail subsidiary that issues BritFrance, Eurail, European East, FrenchRail, GermanRail, Greek, Hungarian, ScanRail, Spain, and Swiss Rail passes.

Let travel agents buy for you your Eurail, regional, and national rail-pass products, hotel packages, and airline tickets. They also make reservations (up to two months in advance) for seats, overnight sleeping cars, and couchettes in the trains. Make these seat and sleeping reservations at the same time you buy your rail pass, as soon as you can, to avoid electronic glitches. You must pay telex fees for these reservation services, but in times when the dollar is weak, the lower price when you pay in dollars offsets the telex fee.

Be sure to pester your agent with questions on inexpensive charter flights, discount seats made available by consolidators, special promotional air transportation/rail pass combinations, and hotel "checks" or vouchers. (Confirm this by telephoning the airlines' 800-number international tour desks.)

It's not worth agents' time to write your letters for inexpensive hotels or pensions, and you are better off handling this yourself before you leave or, even easier, when you get there. Most adventurers like to have a confirmed place to stay for the day they arrive and then make their subsequent arrangements as they travel along.

Choosing the Right Pass for You

Eurailpass—Eurail Flexipass—Eurail Saverpass—Eurail Youthpass—
National and regional rail passes—Rail/Drive passes

Eurailpass

Eurailpasses are airline-style tickets covering unlimited travel on the national train networks of seventeen countries: Austria, Belgium, Denmark, Finland, France, Germany (including the eastern states), Greece, Hungary, Republic of Ireland, Italy, Luxembourg, the Netherlands, Norway, Portugal, Spain, Sweden, and Switzerland. You buy versions for use on consecutive days or on a flexible basis where you choose the number of days you wish to travel within a given time limit.

BritRail and some private lines are not affiliated. When Eurailpass does not cover a route in this book, you will read about it.

It is true that when you pay for all your transportation in one lump sum, Eurailpasses seem like a lot of money, but nothing approaches their value when you take total advantage of them.

• It is convenient. By buying rail passes before you leave home, adventurers avoid standing in lines at counters they sometimes can't find to purchase tickets or surcharge coupons in unfamiliar currencies from foreign agents who often do not speak English (this problem is acute in Hungary). This frees you to board any train you choose, thus making it easier for you to travel on impulse, especially on the more popular lines with trains departing hourly.

• It is easy to use. You don't have to sort through stapled and loose tickets and coupons to show the conductor. Just flash your pass.

• You can change your mind. When an acquaintance convinces you to go to Rome instead of Vienna, just board the next train. When it's flooding in Venice, get off the train in sunny Salzburg.

• It's cheap. You pay in low-inflation dollars. Fixed prices reflect last year's exchange rate.

• You pay at home and know in advance to the cent exactly how much your transportation will cost.

• Free Eurailpass information gives you a planning edge. Their map and pocket timetable guide you through Europe. Their booklet of tips smoothes your way.

• If your pass is lost or stolen on the road, you can replace it at one of the forty-nine Eurail Aid offices nearby (see Appendix B).

Eurailpasses cover fast-train surcharges. You sit in first-class sections of the best trains of Europe without having to go to the trouble and expense of paying for that second charge.

Further, you have access to the handful of elite trains that are limited to buyers of first-class tickets, such as Italy's high-speed Pendolinos, the Super Panoramic Express in Switzerland, business TGV (fast train) connections between Paris and Lyon, and EuroCity trains between Paris and Brussels.

In addition, you receive 50 percent discounts on selected Europabus trips and 20 percent off Pullman and Altea hotels.

Your travel agent provides your Eurailpass with a tear-off coupon and the line blank where your passport number is to be entered. Before you board your first train, you must have staff at the train station (any train station in Europe) validate the pass by entering your passport number and hand-stamping it or validating it with the agent's validator. Keep the validation coupon separate, perhaps with your traveler's checks receipts. You need it to prove your purchase for replacement if you lose your pass. When traveling, you should keep your passport handy so the conductor can check it against the passport number on the Eurailpass. In practice this happens very rarely, except in the Netherlands where rumor has it that forgeries have been found.

Reservation fees, special business train supplements for meals, and charges for sleeping accommodations on trains or aboard ships are not covered by the pass.

Treat a consecutive-day Eurailpass like a cow. Milk it every day. Eurailpass gives you free the kinds of things you would want to do even if you had no other reason to buy the pass itself. The bonuses cover some six pages in the "Eurail Traveler's Guide." Read how best to use them in each section of this book.

Now with the new, full range of Eurail and national flexipasses available that you can use at your discretion, it makes sense to conserve the high-scale travel pass for long-haul travel days and buy local tickets for inexpensive, short excursions.

Buy your pass through your travel agent or any of the Eurailpass-issuing offices listed in Appendix A. Buy them just before price hikes, which usually occur on January 1, because you have up to six months to validate them in Europe.

Eurailpasses are most easily purchased from your nearby travel agent at home. But—contrary to popular notion—they may also be purchased in Britain and Eurailpass countries at any of the forty-nine Eurail Aid offices listed in Appendix B by permanent residents of North and South America, Asia, Australia, New Zealand, and most of Africa who have been in Europe less than six months. In addition to being less available in Europe, they are sold at a premium over the price you pay at home and you must pay in local currencies. This latter restriction is less onerous than you would think because most Eurail Aid offices accept MasterCard and Visa but the premium is considerable because Eurailpass's dollar equivalent sales price varies with the relative exchange rate. At a comparison made in Switzerland just before this guide's press time, Eurailpasses there were 29 to 44 percent more expensive than in the U.S.

Eurail Flexipass

Adventurers do best buying consecutive first-class Eurailpasses when traveling extensively across Europe, but those visiting only a few international destinations save money buying Eurail Flexipasses or Eurail Youth Flexipasses. These provide travel for the specific number of days required, and allow a reasonable time in which to use them.

There was a time when European trains were blooming with flower children holding Eurailpasses and knocking about carefree from Narvik to Naples. Those days are by and large past. Modern rail pass purchasers are known to be more likely to stop longer at a single destination.

Eurail Flexipasses give you new options in planning. You stay as long as you want in one place without squandering money you invest in a pass. Concentrate your time in fewer locations and range less far afield with your travel adventures. Break your train traveling to rent a car, spend some time with relatives in the old country, sunbathe on a Greek isle, ski in Switzerland, or even take time to visit England or an eastern European country that doesn't honor the Eurailpass.

Flexipasses are do-it-yourself passes. Your airline-style pass includes a separate, yellow coupon with spaces to date in ink on the days you travel. Enter the date when you decide to board the train—or aboard the train quickly when the conductor starts to pass through—and travel that entire day as much as you want until midnight.

Flexipass's cover is the validation slip which you have a validating officer stamp, enter the first and last days of validity, and detach for you to keep separate. The second coupon is a red-carbon copy of the first for you to carry with you when traveling.

When you start your trip between 7 P.M. and midnight, date the box with the following day so your validation continues until the following midnight. Some adventurers ride overnight and use up only one validation date while avoiding the cost of lodging.

Traveling on one of the overnight international sea crossings covered by Eurailpass uses up only one validation date because you enter either the date of departure or the next day's date to take advantage of connecting trains at both ends.

There is a difference you need to know: replace a Eurailpass if lost or stolen by taking the validation coupon to one of the forty-six Eurail Aid offices in Europe. You cannot replace Flexipasses.

Eurail introduced international first-class Flexipasses on a trial basis in 1988. The nine-day pass proved so popular that in 1990 Eurail produced additional first-class Flexipasses for five and fourteen days. In 1991, Eurail introduced Eurail Flexi Saverpasses and Eurail Flexi Youthpasses.

Eurail Saverpass

Eurail gives a bargain for three or more adventurers traveling together on a first-class consecutive or Flexipass basis during the summer (only two are required during the rest of the year). The problem is traveling together. Your group can't break up and go traveling off in separate directions and still qualify for the discount, which is about 30 percent.

When you tailor your traveling to these restrictions, you qualify for the good deal.

Eurail Youthpass

When you are younger than twenty-six, buy a second-class Youthpass valid for one or two months or a Flexi Youthpass for fifteen or thirty days of travel within three months. You save money of course, and you find it easier to meet Europeans of your same age, who almost always will be traveling at the lower fares.

Second-class travel is more crowded, but every bit as scenic as first-class travel. Only in Italy is first class markedly superior.

Eurail Youthpasses cost about two-thirds as much as Eurailpasses. You get even more value from Flexi Youthpasses when you combine them with inexpensive national and regional passes according to your travel plans. They give you the same benefits and bonuses as first-class Eurailpasses, except that you must pay to upgrade to first-class-only trains and express steamers on the Rhine River. You would only ride these anyway when you travel with parents or older adults (especially when they need you to qualify for a Eurail Saverpass) or when you want extra comfort and greater flexibility with a full-fare Eurailpass.

National and Regional Rail Passes

So many American travelers use Eurailpasses on long European express trains that conductors' eyes sometimes blur checking the passes. When a conductor sees you flashing the colorful rail pass of his homeland, he knows you have an interest in his country. He adjusts his eyeglasses, smiles, and mentally snaps to attention.

Most national railroads of Europe have their own all-purpose rail passes valid for unlimited travel within their borders. Some are good deals you buy in advance in U.S. dollars. The most popular ways to save money—and have lots of fun—are the best-selling passes of Britain, Finland, France, Germany, Italy, the Netherlands, Spain, and Switzerland. Regional passes for Scandinavia, the Benelux countries, BritFrance, European East (Austria, Hungary, Poland, and Czechoslovakia), Greek Railpass, and Spain/Portugal combine travel on several networks and extend the coverage you receive with a Eurailpass. You visit Britain with a BritFrance Pass, travel east with a European East Railpass, or use the ferries in Greece with a Greek rail and sail pass.

Such passes save you money in several ways. You pay less per day, adults can travel second-class at lower prices, you take juniors with you and pay as little as half for their tickets (free with a Swiss Pass), and you receive useful side benefits that are different from Eurailpass's bonuses.

National passes and regional passes do not let you travel across unlimited national boundaries like the continent-wide Eurailpass, but when you plan to travel in a single country or region these passes will usually save you money compared to a Eurailpass. Residents have their own promotional pass programs for which you are ineligible.

Adventurers in a single country or region use the same guidelines when choosing rail passes. When you want to travel extensively, you choose consecutive rail passes. When you want to travel selectively, you take Flexipasses.

Rail/Drive Passes

A Rail/Drive pass can be an ideal marriage, but leave the driving to your spouse.

Some of your friends report good results driving through Europe in rented cars. They argue fiercely with others who advocate train travel. Both cite the relative convenience, cost, and ability to learn about and appreciate Europe while traveling by their favorite means.

Rental auto advocates insist that you can visit villages not served by trains, and thus take advantage of cheaper lodging; that you can drive to the front door of your destination and make detours on a whim.

The most common reason that you hear for not traveling by train is that train travel doesn't let you see the countryside and reach remote areas. Renting a car, just like at home, seems to be a solution, but Europe is different than home. Visiting Europe gives you the viable option of traveling by train.

Annually, there are four times as many fatal accidents on European roads as on North American ones. Renting a car means fighting congestion and watching the road ahead — and that's not why adventurers visit Europe. The cost can also be higher than expected, considering the high cost of gasoline, taxes of 6 to 33 percent, and tolls.

Trains carry visitors to remote towns as well as rental cars. Unlike the train system in North America, the European rail system spreads out like a series of connecting webs between major cities, and local trains take you to most of the same areas as cars. When you visit friends, they expect to meet you or the taxi waiting in front of the station will take you to them.

Everyone who has traveled by train will tell you that you get on and off just as easily, cut a great deal of red tape and bother, and see more than when you are behind a wheel cursing crazy drivers or buried in a road map sorting out lines that don't seem to exist. You don't have to stuff the back seats of small automobiles with your luggage or worry about it or the car getting ripped off. You don't suffer the quirks of foreign automobiles or strange and sometimes dangerous rules of the road. You don't have to search out parking places and walk even greater distances through pedestrian malls from a parking place than from the train station. You can stay in cheaper suburbs and commute by train, and — this is important — you learn much useful information and insight from the Europeans you meet in your train compartment.

Eurailpass, BritRail Pass, France Railpass, German Railpass, and Swiss Pass sell combination Rail/Drive programs you prepay in dollars.

The brainchild offered by Eurailpass/Hertz (through your travel agent/ French National Railroads) might combine the best of both worlds. The Eurail-Drive Pass gives you three individual days' unlimited use of an economy-class car in all Eurailpass countries (except Hungary) added to the features of a four-day Eurail Flexipass, the option of buying at a preferential rate up to five additional train and/or car travel days, and free drop-off within the country where you take possession.

Rail passes give you the freedom to travel easily over long distances. Your car gives you local transportation, delivers you to doorsteps of relatives, and takes you to special, secluded hideaways.

BritRail's (Hertz), GermanRail's (InterRent/Europcar), French Railroads' (Avis), and Swiss Railroads' (Hertz) plans in connection with their national rail passes work similarly. These companies have locations throughout Europe, many in or near train stations. On average their European fleets are less than six months old and English-speaking personnel are on call twenty-four hours a day.

Boarding Your Train

Using subway and rapid-transit services—Finding your departure platform—Locating your proper carriage

Using Subway and Rapid-Transit Services

All of Europe's major cities have either a subway or a rapid-transit connection to their principal train stations—and usually both. Subways save you steps by bringing you directly into the platform areas in many stations ("Bahnhof," "Estacion," "Gare," "Pu," "Stazione"). Rapid-transit trains from the suburbs (which in all cases you ride free with a Eurailpass except for Paris's regional electric trains, the RERs) sometimes let you off on platforms parallel to the one from which you leave.

Almost all major cities have two or more train stations. Be absolutely certain you go to the correct one. You don't want to carry your luggage into Paris's Gare d'Austerlitz only to find out your train is boarding at the Gare de Lyon.

Finding Your Departure Platform

When you arrive, especially when you are in a hurry, immediately look for departure information. This could be in the form of numeric signs, clacking digital signs, huge electronic BritRail displays, or most common, yellow posters— "Abfahrt," "Avgaende," "Avgang," "Depart," "Lahtevat," "Partenze," "Salida," "Vertrek" (not the white ones, nor the ones printed in red in the Netherlands; those are for train arrivals)—which confirm your departure time and tell you the number of the departure platform or track ("Anden," "Bahnsteig," "Binario," "Gleis," "Plattaforma," "Quai," "Raide," "Spar," "Spoor," "Spor," "Via," "Voie").

Locating Your Proper Carriage

While you are walking to your platform, look for posters or glassed-in bulletin boards ("Composition des Trains," "Composizione Principali Treni," "Indulo Vonatok," "Kaukojunien Vaunujarjestys," "Var i Taget gar Vagnen," "Vognenes Placering i Perron Afsnit," "Wagenstandanzeiger") with color-coded cutouts of lined-up locomotives and train carriages (couchettes, dining, first- and second-class, etc.). You may see these anywhere, but most often right in the center of your departure platform. It is easiest to pick out your train by its departure time.

On these posters you identify the carriage in which you have a reservation by its carriage number. Often, vertical lines or strings are superimposed to form a grid, and a "sector" letter *(A, B, C,* etc.) indicates where your carriage now stands or will stand. When your long InterCity (domestic), EuroCity (international), or TGV train arrives, you will avoid rushing down the platform when you are already standing at the stopping sector for your carriage. When you have no reservation and are traveling by Eurailpass — and don't care which carriage you board — still determine where the first-class ones to your specific destination come to a stop.

While you are looking at the train make-up, look to see whether your train is carrying a buffet or restaurant car and where it is located relative to your carriage.

In French-language Swiss stations, instead of composition boards, the digital departure signs above the platforms give you the entire train make-up at the bottom: an arrow indicates the direction the train travels, a "1" indicates each first-class carriage, a knife-and-fork dining symbol indicates the restaurant car, and a "2" indicates each second-class carriage. Below this shorthand is a note in French telling at which sector the car for children will arrive. (These carriages are marked with a teddy bear and a "Kinderwagen" sign.) Zurich's Hauptbahnhof's digital signs contain lists of destinations, type of train, departure time, and digits showing how the carriages stand in sectors A, B, and C.

When your train sweeps in, watch for striping above the window line. A yellow stripe indicates first class (blue dashes on some Dutch trains, none on most Spanish and German trains). When your train slows to a stop, begin walking to your carriage — but be sure to check that your destination matches the signboard fixed to the outside of the carriage (Finnish Railroad's new InterCity trains have LED displays on the outside showing destinations and times of arrival). Another signboard is usually posted in the vestibule. TGV Atlantique trains have LED displays in the vestibule showing their destination, train number, and carriage number, so it is difficult to go wrong.

When you are carrying heavy luggage, leave it in the space usually provided at the entryways of salon carriages, but guard it carefully at station stops. When it is light, hoist it onto the overhead rack above your seat.

When you sit in a compartment, you have overhead privileges. Etiquette requires that you pile your suitcases in the space in the overhead rack directly above your seat and not distribute them randomly. This makes it easy to see that your seat is occupied even when you leave for a moment.

With a reservation, you have an assigned seat. Without one, you must be careful not to sit in one already reserved. These are marked with paper or plastic strips (usually yellow) inserted in seat backs or on hallway doors. On the other hand, when there is no slip or it says "non reserve" or "nicht reserviert," it is available. When the seat is reserved from Hamburg to Cologne, you are welcome to sit in it between Mainz and Basel.

In a compartment, try to sit next to the window facing forward. In a salon car, you can appreciate the scenery better by sitting next to a window at the back of the carriage.

Arriving in Your City

Luggage carts—Changing your money—Locating a hotel room—
Reserving your train connection—Getting to your hotel

Luggage carts

While your train is slowing for your destination and you ready your luggage to exit your train, watch the passing platform to see where abandoned luggage push carts are standing. Most larger train stations have them and when you know where they are you can take them before someone else appropriates them. In some stations maintenance workers or porters stack them in out-of-the-way corners.

Luggage carts are free for you to use, but the trend is to link them together so that to release one you must have a coin of the proper denomination (one Mark at Munich's Hauptbahnhof, five Swedish crowns at Stockholm's Central, ten francs at Paris's Montparnasse, ten Danish crowns at Copenhagen H.). Diagrams show you how, but they are tricky to follow. These annoying mechanisms refund your coin when you lock up your cart, but it means you must have a correct coin when you arrive.

When you leave your train you often pass into an underground passageway. The direction toward platform one leads you to the main hall. Here you usually find a change bank, train information office, and—in most countries—a tourist office nearby.

Changing Your Money

The very first thing to do upon arrival is to change for local currency. Most adventurers use traveler's checks and most have some currency from the country they just left.

In most large train stations, the change banks are open long hours and give you the same rate you find at large bank offices on the street. Even when you receive a slightly less advantageous rate, you need enough local currency to get around until you visit a larger branch. Beware of any office of a nonbank. You can expect poorer rates and/or a heavy service charge.

Look for these signs: "Bank," "Cambio," "Change," "Valuutanvaihto," "Vaxel," "Wechsel," or "Wissel." Sign your traveler's checks (changing one $50 check instead of two $20s and a $10 is usually cheaper) when you reach the counter and pass it to the teller with your passport or a photocopy of your passport. Changing currency usually requires no passport. (Some stations have machines to do this.) Coins are seldom accepted. Avoid getting caught with very high denomination coins by changing them into paper before you leave. Spend the lower-denomination coins for provisions.

Bank credit cards are accepted everywhere. Get cash advances at banks with those logos posted.

Locating a Hotel Room

Your second order of business is locating a room for the night. Some tourists scrupulously follow hotel recommendations in travel guides, but the rule is simple: the more you pay the more you get, and vice versa. Competing hotels on the same block with equal amenities charge virtually the same. In fact, ones recommended in best-selling guides may be able to charge slightly more because of their popularity with guidebook-reading disciples. Beware of hotels that guidebooks describe as "clean." When writers say nothing more positive, look elsewhere.

It's often worth a few minutes after your arrival just to go outside the train station and look around. Frequently you see an attractive or suitable hotel nearby. Some railroads own and operate hotels in or near their train stations. From 500 major train stations in Germany you can book ahead InterCity hotels in Hanover, Heidelberg, Mannheim, Munich, Stuttgart, and Ulm. In Cologne and Zurich, you will see clusters of hotels outside the back entrances.

In many large train stations there are two information offices—one operated by the railroads ("Auskunft," "Information," "Inlichtingen," "Neuvonta," "Oplysninger," "Reise Zentrum," "Renseignements," "Travel Centre") and one by the city tourist office. The personnel in the train information office won't be happy answering your questions about hotel rooms. Those in the city tourist office send you across the station for train information.

You often find the city tourist office ("Bureau de Turisme," "Tourist Information Centre," "Turismo," "Syndicat d'Initiative," "Verkehrsverein," "Verkehrsburo," "VVV") by looking for the information sign: **i**. You may see it adjacent to the train information office, a few doors down the street from the exit of the train station, across the street, in a kiosk in the plaza in front of the train station, or nearby but indicated by an arrow. When the city tourist office does not have a location serving the train station, often a commercial, profit-making organization performs the function of finding you a room. In many Swiss train stations you find electronic consoles with photos of hotels, their prices, indications of whether they are filled, a city map showing you their locations, and automatic, free telephone connections with their room clerks to make reservations.

The best time to arrive at the tourist office for a hotel booking is about 10 A.M. When you arrive at popular or convention destinations late in the afternoon or in the evening, you will find it very difficult or impossible to find a good room unless you have made reservations in advance. You may have to reboard a train just to find a soft place to sleep.

At the tourist office counter, specify how much you want to pay and the area you want to stay in. Staying near the train station is often convenient, but sometimes an off-color neighborhood is also nearby. The tourist office personnel advise you. You are usually charged a nominal service fee. Sometimes you must also leave a reasonable deposit, which is later deducted from your hotel bill, and are told to check into your assigned hotel within a specified period of time. This time is negotiable when you have errands to accomplish first.

Reserving Your Train Connection

Before you leave the train station, go back to make your reservation for your next train. Reservations are not required for slower trains, but you must make reservations for better trains, except in Germany and Switzerland (except the Glacier Express) where Eurailpass holders don't pay the surcharge and travel without reservations.

For long-distance travel, always select EuroCity (EC) or InterCity (IC) trains. EuroCity's 74 trains promise you English-speaking personnel to help you on the departure platform and serve you on the train; dining cars, cafeterias, or at least a refreshments trolley; a free timetable; and minimal wasted time at intermediate stops and border crossings. For your own peace of mind, you should reserve seats on international express trains during busy travel seasons on Fridays, Sundays, and local holidays, especially from Amsterdam and through Scandinavia.

Not all booking agents can or want to be bothered speaking English. You save yourself many headaches by giving to the reservations agent a piece of paper showing your date of travel (numerals for the day, month, and year, in that order), the time you want to leave (using the twenty-four-hour clock), departure city with arrow pointing to destination city, whether you prefer a smoking or a nonsmoking ("Nicht Raucher," "Niet rokers," "Non-fumar,"

"Non-fumeurs," "Non fumatori") compartment or section, and present your note simultaneously with your Eurailpass and — if you wish — your bank credit card. (To conserve cash, consider using your bank credit cards to make as many Europe-wide advance reservations as possible in these countries which accept bank cards: Austria, Britain, Finland, France, Ireland, Spain, and Sweden.) Present all three at once. The minimum credit-card charge in France is thirty francs.

Agents in some countries require train numbers. In these cases, go first to the train information desk to find the number of your train and then to the reservations counter.

Usually reservations counters are separated into domestic ("Binnenland, "In-land," "Inrikes," "Interieur," "Paikkalippuja") and international ("Ausland," "Buitenland," "Matkapalvelu," "Utrikes") reservations. Make sure you don't stand in a long line at the wrong counter.

Getting to Your Hotel

Many large train stations are served by rapid-transit trains and/or subways. There are almost always discounts available on the subways ("Metro," "Metron/Metroon," "Underground," "U-Bahn," "T-Bana") including multiride, magnetically encoded tickets, strip-tickets, and passes for a day, a week, or longer.

Rapid-transit but not subway trains are usually covered by your Eurailpass. In the Munich Hauptbahnhof you find parallel "S-Bahn" and "U-Bahn" lines. Eurailpass covers only the former.

Sleeping and Eating throughout Europe

Adventures in Train Lodging

One of the great pleasures of train travel in Europe is waking up in a brand-new city, yawning, stretching, and peeking expectantly out of the train window at bright, quaint, and different surroundings that promise fresh, new adventures. Feeling vigorous and eager after a good night's sleep, you are ready to conquer exciting new worlds.

Europe's long-distance trains offer you a worthwhile saving of vacation time and dollars usually spent sleeping in hotel rooms. Overnight express trains with famous names weave convenient international webs through western European countries. Respected names such as Wiener Walzer, Nord Express, Viking Express, Arlberg Express, and Sud Express pull seemingly endless strings of first- and second-class coaches, sleeping cars, and couchettes.

Fully equipped sleeping cars ("Bedplaats," "Makuuvannu," "Place-Lits," "Schlafwagen," "Sovvagn") are designed for demanding business travelers, but couchettes ("Liegewagen," "Ligplaats") give you an excellent value for your money. These mini-dormitories with four or six bunks are usually your best buy for overnight train travel. Their popularity with adventurers and European families is well deserved.

You sleep two to a side in first-class couchettes and three to a side in second-class couchettes. The lodging cost is the same in both classes. The difference is the train fare. You receive more room in first class because you pay more for your ticket (or pass).

Reserve sleeping compartments on EuroCity Night and most international trains first- or second-class. The most expensive is the "Single" (S), available in first class. This is a twin-bedded first-class compartment with only the lower bunk used. A first-class "Special" (Sp) is a smaller one-bed-only compartment. The larger first-class compartment is also available as a "Double" (D), with the top bed folded down. When you are traveling on a second-class ticket, the compartments are called "Tourist 2" (T2) with two beds, either one above the other or two upper beds, across from each other, and "Tourist 3" (T3), with three beds in a tier, one above the other.

Nordic and British railroads offer inexpensive domestic sleeping-car accommodations instead of couchette accommodations. Three-berth sleeping compartments in Nordic countries cost very little. Compared to hotel prices, two-berth compartments on BritRail are a steal.

When you want to save even more by not reserving a couchette, you still sleep very well. Most trains' seats slide forward so that you can pull them together and change a day compartment into a bedroom.

Such a large fraction of adventurers spend their nights sleeping in day-coach compartments on the long-distance expresses that a certain etiquette has evolved. Most seats recline partially or collapse together by pulling forward at the bottoms. It takes no practice to make three parallel beds by pulling forward at the bottoms. This is so practical the whole passenger list does it, but it's a nuisance when the claustrophobic person nearest the window crawls over two sleeping people to get off the train at 3:30 A.M.

Wise overnight adventurers sit nearest the corridor so they can step out to visit the washrooms or snack bar, or even get off to buy a sandwich from a platform vendor during a lingering, middle-of-the-night stop. Overnight trains are usually in no hurry.

When you are only two riding in a compartment overnight, it is more comfortable to fold up the arm rests, stretch full-length along the seats, use a parka or even unsnap the padded headrests for pillows, and sleep soundly until morning.

However, when the train is crowded and the compartments filled, you won't be able to stretch out. You spend the night uncomfortably avoiding your fellow adventurers' space. It's not pleasant on crowded trains; your best bet is a couchette or sleeping compartment.

Couchettes can be reserved and paid for up to two months in advance through a travel agent in America. When the dollar is weak, this will often cost less than buying it in Europe, even when you must pay a telex fee. In Europe, you make reservations at most large train stations. All national railroads but Portugal's and Greece's have connected, computerized reservations systems, but the Nordic system does not interface with the one to the south. When couchettes are not completely sold in advance, you usually see a railroad agent selling couchettes at a portable reservations counter set up next to the train to accommodate last-minute arrivals. When making a couchette reservation, specify which level bunk you prefer. Some adventurers prefer top bunks because they are most private and give them space for their carry-ons; some prefer bottom bunks because they are most convenient. No one prefers middle bunks.

The glamorous Wagons-Lits sleeping-car system is a thing of the past, although you occasionally see a sleeping carriage still carrying an old Wagons-Lits logo. These have more or less been replaced by nationally owned trains and eight international trains classified as EuroCity Night Trains.

Be on the lookout for the EC Alfred Nobel between Hamburg and Stockholm or Oslo, the EC Galilei between Paris and Florence, the EC Komet between Hamburg and Brig or Chur, the EC Palatino between Paris and Rome, the EC Rialto between Paris and Venice, and the EC Stendhal between Paris and Milan. These are the EC Night Trains.

EuroCity Pablo Casals carries "Gran Clas" sleeping cars between Barcelona and Bern, Zurich, and Milan. The EC Barcelona Talgo between Paris and Barcelona, the EC Paris-Madrid Talgo, and the Barcelona-Madrid Talgo are upscale trains carrying only deluxe sleeping cars.

All the various sleeping-car configurations are not always on a given train or even in every country. Even international couchettes can be a surprise. A couchette originating in Zurich, Switzerland, for Amsterdam, the Netherlands, runs mostly through Germany, but uses an Italian Railroads' carriage staffed with a Danish porter.

When you board carriages fitted with couchettes, depending on the time of night, the standard bench seats usually have already been converted into bunks. Otherwise, passengers agree when it is time for them to convert them. All Europeans know how. Bright and early in the morning, train employees clear the bedding and reconvert the couchettes to regular seating for daylight travel.

Your porter leaves a plastic-wrapped package containing a blanket, a sheet-bag, and a pillow for every bunk. The sheet-bag is partially fitted like a bottom sheet to keep it from slipping, but there is no way to tuck in the blanket. It is always a tug of war between you and gravity to keep your blanket from dropping to the floor. You stretch out quite comfortably, but undressing is discretionary in mixed company.

You would not expect such a difference in comfort between air-conditioned, first-class couchettes, and second-class ones (which may or may not be air-conditioned). The extra space created by removing two bunks and two people is astonishing. When you travel on a first-class pass or ticket on a French or Italian train (these two railroads offer first-class couchettes), the couchettes are a dream. On the other hand, many adventurers find it more comfortable to sleep in an air-conditioned first-class sitting compartment than a second-class, six-passenger, natural-ventilation couchette—unless the sitting compartments are crowded.

Couchette porters (who hold the passports to show at frontier crossings so you need not be disturbed) often have a case or two of cold beer and soft drinks they are happy to sell when the journey begins. Many make their private compartments available for a pickup party of talkative international adventurers.

Budget adventurers in France should also investigate an innovation called "Cabine-8." These specially configured sleeping carriages provide eight semi-reclining contoured bunks, four per side, per compartment.

Dining on Wheels

Large train stations have some sort of travelers provisions or grocery store you should visit. One of the more important things to buy for long trips is a liter or two-liter plastic bottle of mineral water with a resealable cap. Some people bring canteens with them. A Swiss army knife with a bottle opener and corkscrew is even handier.

Dining on European trains ranges from white-tablecloth service on the best EuroCity trains, Switzerland's Glacier Express, InterCity trains in Germany, Italy, and Switzerland, and business trains in Scandinavia and Finland; to well-presented cafeterias on Scandinavian, Finnish, and German trains; to meals served at travelers' seats on BritRail's InterCities, French TGVs, Spanish Talgos, Italian Pendolinos, and Switzerland's Gottardo; to wheeled refreshment trolleys (called "mini-bars") overflowing with local specialties, sandwiches, pastries, and refreshments on most long-distance trains. Starting in May 1991, McDonald's will operate two family restaurant cars serving Big Macs and chocolate shakes on trains between Basel and Geneva.

As you would expect, prices are higher aboard trains than in stations and higher in stations than in local supermarkets.

Avoiding Problems

For simplicity, this book has dropped all the umlauts, accents, and other pronunciation marks you see as you travel. The Thomas Cook timetable retains all local spellings.

Will you have language troubles in Western Europe? None. Most of the words you need to know to travel by train are obvious. Pictographs (illustrated in the free rail pass reference materials you send for) are used throughout Europe — and you won't need them in Britain. You have found already most of the important word translations in this book.

City names are generally the same as in English. Just a few baffle: Copenhagen is Kobenhavn; Florence is Firenze; Venice is Venezia in Italian, Venedig in German; Antwerp is Anvers in French, Antwerpen in Dutch; Geneva is Geneve in French, Genf in German; Munich is Munchen in German, Monaco in Italian; Vienna is Wien; Helsinki is Helsingfors in Swedish; the Danube is the Donau; Monaco is known as Monte Carlo; Hauptbahnhof is German for main train station and Bahnhof refers to any train station.

It's advisable always to travel as though you were trekking through New York's Times Square, but it is never so dangerous. Except for areas of high drug activity and unemployment, most adventurers report smooth and safe travel. Paranoia is not worth your mental effort, but caution is. (One publicized incident where travelers on a night train were reputedly gassed and robbed sounds as likely as flying saucers.) Carry little cash, use traveler's checks, and keep separate the pink copy of your traveler's checks, the detached Eurailpass stub, and a photocopy of your passport and credit cards.

Switzerland

Vital Tips for the Trains
of Switzerland

*EC Gottardo—Airport trains—Zurich regional transit—Swiss
pass—Swiss card—Using Eurailpass bonuses—Swiss Rail'N Drive—
Regional passes*

Swiss trains are best, according to travelers' votes. Adventurers ride them for
their unsurpassed views of the Alpine country, taking them places automobiles
can't, their frequent service, punctuality, impeccable maintenance, helpful
personnel (who often speak English), comfort and cleanliness, and service to
the tiniest and most colorful villages.

Switzerland comes close to being a train travelers' kingdom and certainly
Swiss travelers are kings. Every Swiss averages more than 1,000 miles a year
traveling by train, making them European leaders in train travel.

Keeping track of the Swiss train companies is like tabulating a can of alphabet soup. The Swiss Federal Railroads has nine initials—three for each of the
three largest language groups: SBB (Schweizerische Bundesbahnen) for the
German-speaking region, CFF (Chemins de Fer Federaux Suisses) for the
French, FFS (Ferrovie Federali Svizzere) for the Italian. Coaches carry all three
designations but you'll see "SBB" in this book. Nearly a hundred additional
companies operating private railroad lines, funiculars, ships, and cable cars
advertise their particular initials in one or more languages.

You need not worry. Swiss planners have efficiently coordinated all schedules (usually with hourly departures), posted them for you to see in every station, and grouped them in a single official timetable ("Indicateur," "Kursbuch," "Orario"), which for your convenience is revised only once a year at the beginning of June in two volumes, one for trains (with a winter supplement for international connections) and one for buses. You can buy them from Aros Travel, 608 Fifth Avenue, Suite 410 New York, NY 10020 (Tel. 212-245-1150) and Roberts Travel Service, 260 Stockton Street, San Francisco, CA 94108 (Tel. 415-433-1991).

When you trace the outline of Switzerland on a map, it's all bulges and squeezed-out extrusions. Vertically, it's even tougher—and the Swiss have crisscrossed it with adventurous trains. In addition to adventuring on the four described here, don't overlook riding the Brunig line between Lucerne and Interlaken (SBB's only narrow-gauge line), the Gotthard route between Lucerne/Zurich and Lugano, the Lotschberg and Simplon Tunnel routes, the narrow-gauge RhB (Rhaetian Railroads) connections to Arosa, Scuol, and other mountain resorts, and the Centovalli line between Locarno and Domodossola, mostly on Italian soil but covered by the Swiss Pass (see below).

SBB has three kinds of domestic trains: regional, fast, and InterCity. SBB's entire IC train fleet is outfitted with "noiseless" carriages (50 percent less interior noise). They accelerate to 100 mph between Martigny and Sion, 87 mph near Baden. When you ride them you find they are utilitarian, but not flashy. All carry orange-colored, sit-down restaurant carriages with white linens, tables for two or four, waiters in white jackets, and excellent cuisine prepared in onboard kitchens.

A crossroads of Europe and a popular destination, thirty-three EuroCity trains take you to, or across, Switzerland. They include seventy SBB air-conditioned, salon carriages built in 1990-91 for use on 125 mph EuroCity routes to Munich, Stuttgart, Milan, Brussels, Ventimiglia, and the Netherlands.

You can tell these carriages from SBB's InterCity carriages because SBB's EuroCity carriages are light gray with dark gray striping while their IC carriages are forest green with dark gray striping. Their entrance doors are painted red.

The forty second-class carriages feature individual halogen reading lamps, folding tables, toilets for handicapped, and innovative mirrors.

French TGVs from Paris arrive in Bern, Lausanne, and Geneva, with ongoing Swiss connections to Milan. The upscale Pablo Casals overnight train serves Geneva, Lausanne, Bern, and Zurich from Barcelona. The EC Helvetia between Hamburg and Zurich and EC Mont Blanc between Hamburg and Geneva feature elegant restaurants.

EC Gottardo

The EC Gottardo is a gray-and-black electric railcar, the pride of the SBB system. SBB's flagship, it is your best choice between Winterthur, through Zurich's airport and main train station, to Milan daily.

Gottardo's interior has art deco fixtures, carpets, black-print plush seats, electrical Venetian blinds between double windows, halogen reading lamps, a diaper room, and for the first time in Europe: separate men's and women's toilets. Meals are served at your seat.

Handsomely equipped, the former Trans Europe Express train is now a modern EuroCity train. Its new livery carries the lettering "EuroCity"—but the shining chrome TEE symbol remains to connect its grand history with its second childhood.

Airport Trains

You find it very convenient to use SBB's excellent airport trains in Zurich and Geneva. Stations at both airports are integrated into the Swiss railroad network by long-distance IC trains not only to city centers but also directly to international destinations. At Zurich and Geneva airports, first stop by train information (i) to have your Swiss Pass or Eurailpass validated. At Zurich proceed via escalators (direction: "Bahn/Railway") using the escalator-friendly luggage carts. At Geneva, you merely push your cart on ground level across to the adjacent terminus to catch your train.

Check your luggage through to your destination at special "Welcome Luggage" counters. This can be a convenience when you must change trains. Luggage checked at airport stations is given preference. You usually pick it up when you arrive at your destination. The cost is ten Swiss francs per piece. This is an exception; normal checking of your luggage from city to city will take more time than you expect.

Swissair allows their departing passengers to check in, receive boarding passes, and check their luggage at over one hundred train and postal bus stations.

Zurich Regional Transit

The escalators you find in the direction of the Limmat river on the east side of Zurich's main train station take you to the underground center of Zurich's environmentally friendly S-Bahn system, which opened in May 1990 and accepts Eurailpasses and Swiss Passes. Adventurers travel to every village in canton Zurich and many excellent places in the greater Zurich region in a reasonable time on hourly or half-hourly intervals.

Many of these trains consist of double-decker carriages and electric locomotives. Their main corridor takes you from Winterthur, through Effretikon (with a branch to the Zurich airport), to Zurich's main station and along the west bank of Lake Zurich through Thalwil and Wadenswil. On Lake Zurich's east bank, S-Bahn's "Gold Coast Express" runs to Rapperswil.

Some of the other scenic places to visit that adventurers now reach easily by S-Bahn include Stein am Rhein, Schaffhausen, Bremgarten, Zug, Einsiedeln, Baden, and Brugg. Travelers without rail passes encounter a patchwork of price zones, but the automatic ticketing machines do the calculations for you. Twelve-trip strip cards and six-day S-Bahn Flexipasses give travelers a 16 percent discount.

Swiss Pass

Swiss Passes are versatile. You receive travel on the SBB, most of Switzerland's privately owned railroads (more than the Eurailpass), most of the lake steamers, and all of the Swiss postal buses. In addition, you receive discounts on many mountain funicular and private lines. Further, you may ride public transportation (streetcars and buses) in twenty-four cities including Basel, Bern, Geneva, Biel, Zurich, Winterthur, Baden/Wettingen, Lausanne (including the funicular to Ouchy), La Chaux-de-Fonds, Fribourg, Lugano, Locarno, Neuchatel, Olten, St. Gallen, Schaffhausen, Solothurn, Aarau, Thun, Lucerne, Zug, and Montreux/Vevey.

You buy Swiss Passes for eight or fifteen days' or a month's consecutive travel or a Swiss Flexipass valid for three travel days in fifteen, either for first- or second-class travel. Children from six to sixteen pay half-price. First class costs about 60 percent of a Eurailpass. You save still more when you buy the cards for shorter periods or second-class travel (still quality travel in Switzerland). You also obtain a free "Family Card," which allows youngsters under age sixteen to travel free with a parent and unmarried youths aged sixteen to twenty-five to travel at half-price with a parent.

You often see parked in front of train stations yellow-and-white buses with bold red stripes and posthorns front and side. These are the famous Swiss postal buses that you ride free with a Swiss Pass. Of the thousand or so routes you may wish to use, the most exciting include the transit of Italy from Lugano/Menaggio/Chiavenna/St. Moritz and the dazzling routes over the Susten, Furka, Neufenen, and Gotthard passes from Meiringen and Andermatt.

You may also take free cruises on Lakes Geneva, Constance, Zurich, Lucerne, Thun, Brienz, Neuchatel, Biel and Murten, on the Untersee, that segment of the Rhine River between Schaffhausen and Kreuzlingen, and on the Aare River between Biel and Solothurn. You will find it very enjoyable to break your travels with restful day outings on these big white steamers. The most beautiful way to enter Geneva is by lake steamer.

Swiss Card

The Swiss federal government subsidizes (on grounds to reduce air pollution) a card valid for half-fare travel on all public transportation (not city buses or streetcars) at extremely reasonable prices. One in three Swiss adults owns one. You buy them, valid for one month, in U.S. dollars. Holders are eligible to use the "Family Card" for their children's travel.

Although you pay half-fare for some trips that Eurailpass or Swiss Pass holders ride free, you will frequently come out ahead when your travel is lighter than it would take for a Swiss Pass to pay for itself or when you travel on routes not fully covered, such as to the Jungfraujoch, Schilthorn, and Gornergrat.

When you buy them in the U.S. (through FrenchRail, see Appendix A), Swiss Cards cover your trip from a Swiss airport or border point to your destination in Switzerland and return (you are allowed to use different Swiss airports or border stations).

Swiss Cards cannot be purchased in Switzerland. You buy in Switzerland the "Swiss Half Fare Card," which costs about two-thirds of the Swiss Card and gives you all the advantages of a Swiss Card except for free round-trip tickets to the airports or border crossings. When you plan to fly to Switzerland and base your first and last days near Zurich or Geneva, you save a few dollars buying a Swiss Half Fare Card in Switzerland. Otherwise the transportation to your destination in Switzerland covered by a Swiss Card bought in North America saves you money.

For longer stays or multiple visits to Switzerland, buy a Swiss Half Fare Card in Switzerland valid for a year. Analyze your itinerary before making a purchase, but it is a good bet that a half-fare card will save you money.

Using Eurailpass Bonuses

Most of the railroads and the same lake and river steamers listed above (50 percent off for crossings of Lake Constance) honor the Eurailpass, but with certain exceptions. Not participating in the Eurailpass program (but in the Swiss Pass arrangement) are the Furka-Oberalp Railroad (FO)—which you need to use on the Brig-Disentis segment on the Glacier Express and the Goschenen/Andermatt connection with the Gotthard line—the BVZ Railroad between Brig and Zermatt, and the Bernese Oberland Railroad (BOB) between Interlaken Ost and Grindelwald/Wengen. Nor are Eurailpass holders eligible to use the Swiss "Family Card" for their children.

Swiss Rail'N Drive

Swiss Rail'N Drive passes give you three days of train travel and two days of Hertz car rental for you to use within fifteen days. Extra days of car rental may be paid.

You may drive the car through neighboring countries provided you return it to an agency within Switzerland within the fifteen days. You are not charged for dropping the car off at an agency different than the one where you took possession.

An annual road toll, called "Vignette" (sticker), is levied on autos for use of the Swiss superhighways. Cars rented in Switzerland already come with it. When you pick up a car outside Switzerland, you must purchase the Vignette, costing thirty Swiss francs when crossing the border or at any Swiss post office.

Regional Passes

When you are interested in traveling in only one particular region, it is worth investigating Regional Passes. These summer-season passes are valid for fifteen days of which you choose five for unlimited travel and ten days for travel at half-fare.

Regions featuring these discount programs include: Montreux/Vevey, Vaudois Alps, Bernese Oberland, Graubunden, and Central Switzerland. In Central Switzerland, you may also buy a ten-day pass including two days of free travel. Locarno/Ascona and Lugano regions offer unlimited seven-day passes.

You receive a 20 percent discount on the purchase of Regional Passes when you already hold a Swiss Pass or Swiss Half Fare Card purchased in Switzerland. Purchase them at train stations of the regions you are visiting.

Now that you have your travel pass or ticket in hand, your train leaves on time for these four Swiss train adventures: the Glacier Express from Zermatt, the Bernina Express to the Italian border, the railroads of the Jungfrau Region, and the Panoramic Express from Montreux.

Glacier Express
Flowering with Adventurers

Glacier Express train service between Zermatt and Chur or St. Moritz has flowered since tourism officials discovered, with surprise, that an adventurous train trip could attract visitors without their having to invest additional Swiss francs or spoil the landscape.

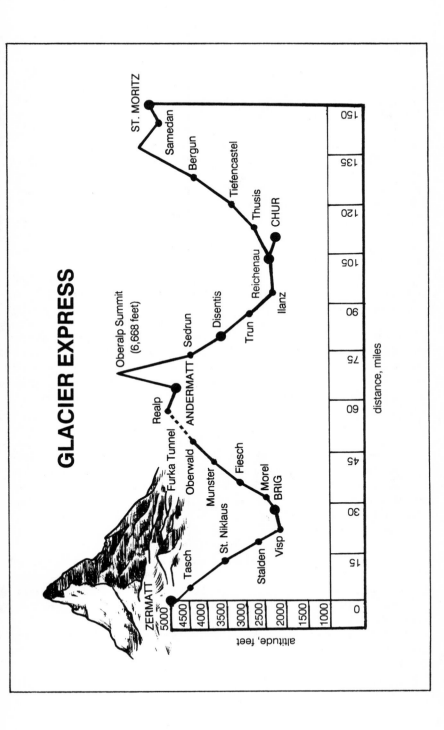

One train a day since 1930 was sufficient until adventurers discovered the excitement of traveling above the Rhone and Rhine rivers along their valleys to their sources at the Furka Pass. The newest timetable shows Glacier Expresses *B, C, D, F, G,* and *K,* three a day in each direction. Glacier Expresses *A* and *H* are reserved for travel groups and feature three specially built panoramic dome cars similar to the ones on the Panoramic Express.

This train curiously has always been named "Glacier Express," in English and French, although you pass through three language regions (French, German, and Romansch). When the Furka tunnel was opened in 1982, the Glacier Express moved from summer-only service to a year-round delight.

Make reservations in advance, unless you only use the segments east of Disentis carried by the Rhaetian Railroads (RhB). Obligatory seat reservations cost six Swiss francs. They may be made in most large train stations throughout Europe.

Glacier Express trains *B, C, F, G,* and *K* carry a belle epoque dining car, all wood paneled with heavy brass fixtures and yellow-brown petit point upholstery (the newest one seats sixty). White jacketed waiters serve lunch, but you should make dining reservations in advance. There are never enough seats to accommodate all travelers. The conversation piece is the Glacier Express wineglass (for sale) with a bent stem so that, in theory, you face it one way uphill and reverse it downhill. In fact, you worry more about your wine sloshing over when you are traveling horizontally. Train *D,* the late departure from Zermatt, carries a dining car from Andermatt to Chur, with service beginning at 3:34 P.M. This is sufficient for afternoon tea and drinks.

When you arrive at the Zermatt train station, you are immediately drawn into that magical square in front of it bubbling with enchantment and leading to the fairy-tale main street lined with hotels and shops designed in the characteristic architecture made fashionable by the Seilers, the family of hoteliers who established Zermatt in 1855. The Bahnhofplatz is dominated by horse-drawn carts and is filled with charm. You are welcomed by parties of bell captains and drivers in black hotel caps, ready to lead you in a horse-drawn carriage to your nearby hotel. In winter, riding in horse-drawn sleighs gives you the feeling of being in a winter wonderland.

When you clear the sparkle from your eyes, you see that Zermatt's modern Gornergratbahn station stands opposite the train station on one side of the Bahnhofplatz and a Swiss chalet housing the tourist bureau stands on the other. The tourist office is open 8 A.M. to 8 P.M., Monday to Saturday, and 4 to 8 P.M. on Sundays.

While you are in Zermatt, take a journey up the world's first electrified rack railroad, the Gornergratbahn, for one of the most rewarding mountain train adventures in Switzerland. The Matterhorn (and there is no competition) is one of the world's most-photographed natural wonders. It dominates the scene throughout most of your journey and you see increasingly magnificent views of the surrounding peaks as you climb.

From the Gornergrat (10,132 feet), extend your excursion still more by climbing farther to the east on the 2.8-mile cable line to Stockhorn (11,588 feet) on the highest open-air transport in the Swiss Alps.

Leaving Zermatt, the Glacier Express retraces your cogwheel train up, because there is no other way to Zermatt, but it is worthwhile revisiting the 1½ hours of smashing scenery, passing cataracts, rushing waters, and tall, wooden Valais houses and storage barns, or Spychers, protected from rats by stones.

A powerful red BVZ railcar, required for the steep upward climb, pulls your Glacier Express train out of Zermatt. (The BVZ accepts Swiss Passes, but not Eurailpasses.) The red carriages are narrow, because of the slim gauge, but still offer ample space to first-class passengers riding two-opposite-one. Their interiors are bright, warmed by Scots-plaid, vinyl upholstery — red in the smoking section, green in nonsmoking.

You follow your path on diagrams inserted in the utility table below your window showing altitude relative to distance to St. Moritz. St. Moritz (5,822 feet) and Zermatt (5,261 feet) surmount each end, but on the way you climb to 6,668 feet at the summit, Oberalp Passhohe.

At Randa, seven miles down the Glacier Express route, you see the Dom rising up one side and the Weisshorn up the other. These are the highest peaks in the Alps after Mont Blanc and Monte Rosa. Descending another eight miles, you pass through Brattbach tunnel, 428 feet long, and a series of concrete avalanche shelters. Officials realized these were necessary to maintain Zermatt as a winter sports center when the winter avalanche of 1931-32 buried the line.

The BVZ lives in mortal fear of road building. Rail travel is profitable here. The BVZ is one of the few narrow-gauge railroads turning a profit. Renewals and reconstructions were undertaken on guarantees from federal and cantonal authorities that no road would be built up the Visp valley above Stalden, but this promise lapsed in 1952. A highway from Tasch to St. Niklaus was authorized in July 1961.

When your train stops in Tasch, the point closest to Zermatt accessible by car, you look out on the parking lot. It is said that this is the largest parking lot in Europe. Since 1965, the BVZ has maintained hourly bus service between St. Niklaus and Visp and even runs a school bus between Stalden and Visp.

In Visp, your BVZ train stops in the street in front of the SBB station. Your final 5¼ miles of the meter-gauge BVZ parallel the tracks of the SBB. The BVZ segment makes it possible for you to travel by meter-gauge lines from the top of the Gornergrat, 211 miles to Tirano in Italy, with only two changes, at Zermatt and St. Moritz.

Brig is a major railroad junction of north-south and east-west trains. Your BVZ train runs into the south side of an island platform in front of the SBB station with road traffic rushing past on both sides. You can easily connect here between the narrow-gauge BVZ and Furka-Oberalp Railroad (FO) trains and those of the standard-gauge SBB and BLS (Berne-Lotschberg-Simplon Railroad) to Italy.

The FO takes over in Brig, but you do not need to change trains. You travel to Oberwald through the scenic and broad upper Rhone valley at 3,300 to 4,300 feet. The valley supports farms and farmhouses on both sides of the line. There is always one snowcapped peak at the end which is replaced by another when you reach there. Dense pine forests clothe the lower slopes of the mountains. Above, you make out high Alpine pastures and still higher summits covered with snow the year around.

Your train climbs steadily from Brig except for abrupt steps typical of glacial valleys, at Grengiols, above Fiesch, and below Gletsch. Above Grengiols, the valley is known as the Goms. At these steps, the valley also narrows, forcing your train to use loops, spirals, or a rack, or even all three, to overcome the height.

After you pass through the chestnut forests surrounding the village of Morel, you feel the cogwheels chattering as you climb to Fiesch.

Leaving behind the Rhone valley's picturesque villages, you reach the reddish-brown Oberwald station (4,480 feet) where your train swings into the all-weather Furka tunnel, the longest narrow-gauge train tunnel in the world, which permits the Glacier Express to operate all year round. However, it deprives you of views of the Rhone glacier that awed early travelers. You must now take the postal coach over the Furka Pass to approach this azure glacier.

Special flatcars transport automobiles through the Furka tunnel in winter, when the Furka Pass is closed—a great convenience for skiers—but unfortunately corrosion of the rails in the humid tunnel is proceeding twice as fast as expected. This is partially due to salt-containing snow melting from the automobiles onto the rails. Engineers are watching the rails closely, installing measures to prevent galvanic corrosion, and washing them regularly.

After climbing through the tunnel for seventeen minutes, you emerge at Realp (5,045 feet). From here you serpentine downward through six U-turns with a view down on Andermatt (4,701 feet), the famous ski resort which bristles even more in summer with Swiss soldiers on their compulsory annual military service maneuvers. Andermatt's 1972 depot and spacious, modern station also connect to a 2.3-mile-long, double-rack railroad which gives you the option of descending the mountainside in fifteen minutes to Goschenen on the north side of the Gotthard tunnel to change to trains along that line.

Past Andermatt, you begin climbing sharply to the Oberalp Pass, the highest point on the line, but you feel the cogwheels under the train chattering, so you know your climb is under total control. When you leave, Andermatt appears almost vertically below your train, first on one side and then on the other. You trace out your train's path ahead by the ribbon of rail zigzagging above you. "Curves" on the Glacier Express mean nearly right-angle turns.

Beyond the Oberalp Pass, you have some fine views over the Outer Rhine valley as you descend to Sedrun on a ledge high above the river. It is said that Sedrun is where the Rhine spends its vacation.

Nineteen minutes later you come to a stop in Disentis, but don't look for inspiration in the eye-catching onion-shaped dome of the baroque church on the valley floor. Look up to the left (north) to the imposing Benedictine Abbey on the mountainside, which is the place of prayer for the rich folks. The poorer folk attend the church on the valley floor. Disentis used to be divided into two villages: one by the Abbey, one by the river.

Disentis is the geographic center of the Alps. On the north (Germanic culture), the mountains have German and Romansch names; on the south (Italian culture), they have Italian and Romansch names.

In Disentis, your FO train joins the Rhaetian Railroads (RhB) system, where your first segment, to Ilanz, was laid specifically to connect the RhB with the FO. This is the least challenging of all the narrow-gauge sections, although you pass over the lofty Val Rusein and Val Lumpegna viaducts shortly out of Disentis.

You descend steadily all the way from Disentis to Ilanz, with good views of the valley in the first four miles as you run high above the left bank of the Outer Rhine on a rock ledge. As you approach Ilanz, the lower slopes of the valley are thickly wooded with conifers. The typical farmhouses you see on the mountainsides, in the Valais style, are quite a change from the Engadine houses you will soon see.

Ilanz (2,289 feet) is the first big city on the Rhine, and is the beginning of Switzerland's Romansch-speaking region. Yellow and red postal buses stand by ready to take passengers up the twisting Vals valley to the health resort of Vals, where the mineral water, Valser, is bottled. (You might also see a tanker car labeled "Valser" transporting the water.)

Past Ilanz, on the Ilanz line (opened in 1903), you see spectacular limestone scenery. The major obstacle to construction was the deep gorge that the Outer Rhine had carved through prehistoric landslides of rubble more than 2,000 feet deep. A second handicap was that high villages along the route were remote and inaccessible. Steeply graded roads had to be built between the stations and the villages.

In Reichenau, you meet the Albula line. Glacier Express trains *B* and *D* turn north here for the final nine miles to Chur. Glacier Express train *C* is divided here, with the Chur section continuing and the St. Moritz section directed south through the Albula tunnel. (The Glacier Express *B* section for St. Moritz first goes to Chur and then returns south.) Please turn to the section describing the Bernina Express, which departs from Chur.

Summer Glacier Express Service

B	C	D				F	G	K
0854	1010	1210	dep.	ZERMATT	arr.	1445	1645	1845
....	....	1223	dep.	Tasch	arr.	1433	1632	1833
0929	1047	1247	dep.	St. Niklaus	dep.	1410	1610	1810
1002	1121	1321	arr.	Visp	dep.	1336	1536	1736
1003	1122	1322	dep.	Visp	arr.	1335	1535	1733
1015	1134	1334	arr.	Brig	dep.	1323	1523	1723
1025	1148	1348	dep.	Brig	arr.	1311	1515	1653
....	....	1400	dep.	Morel	dep.	1301	....	....
....	....	1405	dep.	Betten	dep.	1255	....	....
....	....	1420	arr.	Fiesch	dep.	1236	1446	....
....	....	1421	dep.	Fiesch	arr.	1235	1445	....
....	1259	1455	dep.	Oberwald (Furka Tunnel)	arr.	1201	....	....
1156	1336	1524	arr.	Andermatt	dep.	1132	1330	1520
1158	1340	1534	dep.	Andermatt	arr.	1130	1323	1511
....	....	1554	dep.	Oberalppasshohe	dep.	....	....	....
....	1425	1618	dep.	Sedrun	dep.	1046	1236	1417
1257	1445	1635	arr.	Disentis/Muster	dep.	1029	1215	1400
1313	1455	1650	dep.	Disentis/Muster	arr.	1023	1202	1344
....	....	1705	dep.	Trun	dep.	1006	....	....
....	....	1713	dep.	Tavansa-Breil	dep.	0958	1140	....
1350	1528	1727	arr.	Ilanz	dep.	0945	1127	1307
1351	1530	1730	dep.	Ilanz	arr.	0944	1126	1306
....	1552	1752	dep.	Reichenau-T.	dep.	0917	1104	1241
1420	1602	1802	arr.	CHUR	dep.	0904	1053	1230
1450	1543		dep.	CHUR	arr.		....	1210
1500	1600		dep.	Reichenau-T.	dep.			1201
1536	1636		arr.	Tiefencastle	dep.		0952	1123
1537	1637		dep.	Tiefencastle	arr.		0951	1122
1637	1737		arr.	Samedan	dep.		0846	1020
1640	1740		dep.	Samedan	arr.		0844	1013
1648	1748		arr.	St. Moritz	dep.		0835	1005

Glacier Expresses *B* and *K* join and separate at Chur.
Glacier Expresses *C* and *G* join and separate at Reichenau.

Connections with Basel/Zurich/Zurich Airport

1425	1625	1825	dep.	CHUR	arr.	0851	1043	....
1550	1750	1950	arr.	Zurich (Hbf.)	dep.	0733	0910	....
1616	1816	2016	arr.	Zurich (Air.)	dep.	0703	0843	....
1705	1905	2105	arr.	Basel (SBB)	dep.	0627	0756	....

Bernina Express
The Impossible Takes a Little Longer

You roar into the cliff of the black Landwasser tunnel, your Bernina Express throttled wide open, soaring high above the stream and over the treetops, riding the summit of an unseen viaduct without guard railings. It is like flying — or falling.

This climax of the 6½-mile section from Tiefencastel to Filisur follows your crossing of two famous viaducts. First you pass the Schmittentobel viaduct, 6.1 miles out of Tiefencastel. Its seven arches rise 118 feet. Then, out of a 164-foot tunnel, you quickly glimpse ahead the five classic arches of the 1903 Landwasser viaduct curving to the right and the river far below. The viaduct's 400-foot span rests on 213-foot piers, and its celebrated southern arch plunges you directly into the Landwasser tunnel.

The Albula line is a triumph of creative railroad engineering. Your powerful, green, electric locomotive "Rhaetia" climbs through so many extraordinary spirals and tunnels up the Albula valley that it resembles a model engine racing through every complicated loop, tunnel, bridge, cloverleaf, and dramatic overpass that an ingenious toy shop display can conjure.

Your locomotive's speed of 30 to 35 mph seems heady, given the acrobatics, but your narrow-gauge coach swings around tight corners so smoothly that you don't feel frightened — even at the edges of sheer cliffs. You are too preoccupied watching the extraordinary views.

The Rhaetian Railroads (RhB) introduced the best train on this line, your Bernina Express, in 1973, for a one-day excursion through a rarely visited corner of Switzerland. It is also used for passage to Italy.

There are two Bernina Expresses southbound. Bernina Express *A* departs Chur at 8:55 A.M. in the summer only, stopping at just a few stations and not serving St. Moritz. Forty-five minutes earlier, Express *B* leaves with cars for St. Moritz which are separated in Samedan, so you must be sure to be on the right

cars for Tirano. Past Pontresina, *B* makes more stops, which adds about half an hour to your travel time but also to the enjoyment of your trip.

Northbound, Express *C* runs only during the summer and makes every stop from Tirano to St. Moritz, but does not run past St. Moritz, where you must change to a regular train for Chur. Express *D*, also summer-only, runs the faster timetable, traveling directly from Tirano to Chur.

Passengers on Bernina Express trains *A* and *D* are charmed by English-speaking hostesses with information about the area outside, but travelers must pay a surcharge of six Swiss francs which includes a seat reservation. Make your reservation in advance at any train station in Switzerland, Germany, or Austria. (Trains *B* and *C* may be reserved at a cost of four Swiss francs, but this is optional.)

The red cars of the RhB leave from the front of Chur's SBB station. On the first stretch from the mountain capital of Graubunden canton, you will be traveling on the Albula line. Between Pontresina and the Swiss border across from Tirano, Italy, you will be riding on the Bernina line.

RhB is a private company serving the mountainous cantons of eastern Switzerland. It celebrated its 100th birthday in 1989. Your seats in its first-class spic-and-span salon cars are comfortable, two-opposite-one, and highlighted by red (for smoking) or green (nonsmoking) Scots-plaid seat covers. RhB accepts Eurailpasses and Swiss Passes for free passage.

During your 2¼-hour, fifty-five-mile trip from Chur to Pontresina, you pass through forty-two well-engineered tunnels or galleries totaling more than ten miles (well over a quarter of the mountain segment). The line's 108 bridges and towering viaducts of arched rock and stone come to nearly two miles.

You leave Chur down a broad flat valley with forested mountains on both sides. You see corn; cows; big, busy factories; and churches with onion-shaped steeples.

Hikers push the panoramic windows down from the top to admit fresh mountain air. Photographers lean out, snapping photos nearly the whole length of the trip. In winter, skiers and beautiful people traveling to St. Moritz are warmly dressed. The train passes through the most agreeable summer and winter mountain climate in Europe.

The tracks paralleling your train's line are three-railed. This is so both the narrow-gage RhB and the standard-gauge SBB cars can share the same works and electric lines.

You first follow the Rhine valley to Reichenau where the Inner Rhine (Hinterrhein) comes from the south to join the Outer Rhine (Vorderrhein) beneath the Castle of Reichenau. The two rapid rivers churn together, mixing their chalky blues and cloudy whites of melted snow and glacier runoff.

You pass steep and thickly wooded slopes with villages and ruins of feudal fortresses secluded in green foliage. Bends are so sharp that you can see both the locomotive and the end of the train. Past the gray-plaster Thusis station house you travel eight miles through the Schyn gorges to Tiefencastel, one-third in tunnels and one mile over early twentieth-century viaducts. The sturdy, hand-built stone bridges complement the wonderful scenery rather than cheapen it.

The view here is very good from the left side, but the back seats of the carriage give a better panorama of the unfolding landscape outside. The non-smoking section is longer and offers wider views. The murky tints of the blue-white waters of the Albula River run far below your twisting train on the mountainside.

The valley widens again and you see the Tinzerhorn mountain group ahead. Change to the right side for better views of the breathtaking scenes you are approaching. Past Tiefencastel, the Albula River runs fast and the valley becomes more and more wooded with fir trees, larches, and arolla pines. At this point you cross the Schmittentobel viaduct and roar into the Landwasser tunnel, as described at the beginning of this section.

Like many admirers of the Landwasser viaduct, break your journey at Filisur station (boarding a local train later on) to walk down the footpath and inspect the dramatic structure from below.

The most difficult terrain of your trip is on the 5.8-mile segment from Filisur to Bergun. You climb one foot for every twenty-eight traveled. The Albula valley becomes narrower and you become more steeply walled-in. In this short section, you pass through fourteen tunnels and over eight viaducts.

The next section to Preda is the highlight of your trip. "Slow but sure" is the watchword you appreciate during this stretch.

The direct distance to Preda from Bergun is 4 miles. Engineers have bent your line into such extraordinary contortions of loops and spirals that you actually travel 7.6 miles, including 1.7 miles through seven tunnels. If you climbed directly, you would climb one foot for every sixteen, but the expensive spirals and reversals of direction safely reduce your grade to one in thirty.

Plan to change from side to side to watch the elegant contortions. Look back for at least three extraordinary sights of the pleasing village of Bergun while your train climbs higher and higher.

You enter the Engadine region. Engadine architecture is so unique and bright that it sets the region off from the rest of Switzerland more distinctly than if you had crossed a frontier. The houses you see are white and thick-walled, with small, irregularly spaced windows widening outwards. Their most distinctive feature is their "sgraffito" (now you know where the word "graffiti" came from). Masons covered rough, gray plaster with coats of white limewash and then artfully scraped away the wash to bring out charming gray scrolls, interesting geometries, and fascinating embroideries.

From Preda, your Rhaetia picks up speed through the 3.6-mile Albula tunnel. It seems to go on forever. It is the highest (6,242 feet) principal tunnel through the Alps and the most expensive and difficult engineering work of the RhB.

When you emerge from the Albula tunnel at Spinas, clumps of larch have reappeared and your train is pointed downwards. You cross and recross the Beverin River at Bever and then run down the flat floor of the Inn valley above the Inn River. The colors of the glorious peaks of the Bernina massif ahead through the Pontresina Gap are vivid. The air is electrified with natural radiation.

Railroad hands separate Bernina Express B in the large, modern Samedan station at 9:53 A.M. One portion goes to St. Moritz. Your half goes to Pontresina and onto the Bernina line, the highest in Europe without cogwheel assistance.

Both St. Moritz and Pontresina — all the villages of the Engadine region, in fact — welcome tourists. The inhabitants speak Romansch, Switzerland's fourth national language, but the area is so international that English is widely understood. Bring extra money if you can, especially to St. Moritz, but if you can't, inexpensive lodging catering to adventurers is easy to find.

Besides more aerial acrobatics, the Bernina line presents you with another distinction: it is a joy to photograph. You are able to focus on the magnificent scenery through pulled-down panoramic windows while traveling along at only a snail's pace. Trains south of Pontresina average only 20.5 mph, including stops, which is slower than the Glacier Express.

Beyond Pontresina, the valley becomes wider with every mile. Panoramas open on every side while your train runs high on the mountainside on tracks that were laid to avoid spoiling the beauty of the Taiser Forest. Past the Berninabach Falls bubbling with froth in early summer, you turn your lens to the right for a splendid picture of the magnificent Morteratsch glacier and the most glorious peaks of the Bernina range, especially Piz Bernina itself, a double rocky summit of 13,261 feet.

High above the timberline, your Bernina Express reaches the summit at Bernina Hospiz (7,403 feet), where winter lasts seven months. You have climbed 5,973 feet by simple adhesion — even more than any Swiss rack railroad with cogs — and reached the highest station in Switzerland served by adhesion railroad.

Lago Bianco to your right, covered by ice until late May, was originally four lakes but it was dammed to form a reservoir for Brusio power station, forcing the railroad to be moved some thirty feet higher. From here you descend through the 630-foot Scala tunnel, the Pozzo del Drago tunnel (the dragon is rumored to lurk in the nearby lake), and an avalanche gallery to reach Alp Grum (6,858 feet).

It is time for lunch. Your Bernina Express carries a refreshments trolley where most passengers buy snacks, but travelers on Bernina Express *B* have a chance to disembark at the brownstone Alp Grum station (an amazing place for lunch) and then continue on one of the four later trains. You enjoy vast views over the Palu glacier and its surrounding peaks. There is also an Alpine garden. Most thrilling of all is the view from above the tracks on the terrace of the upper restaurant down the Poschiavo valley to blue Lake Poschiavo, 4,231 feet below and only 6.8 miles away. The trains calling at the toylike station below look like those on a scale-model railroad.

Your train's climb from Pontresina has been relatively easy. Descending follows a route that required surveyors to perform near miracles. To reach Poschiavo, your train has to drop 4,034 feet through larch and spruce forests in a horizontal distance of only 4.7 miles. Engineers solved this problem by designing a series of cautious, cascading cuts, circular tunnels, sharp zigzags and astonishing loops.

First you descend to the right in a semicircle, passing below Alp Grum station to the 833-foot Palu tunnel, in which you make a three-quarter turn and emerge down the mountain. For a second time you pass below the restaurant terrace into the 948-foot Stabline tunnel, emerging on the back slope of Alp Grum before doubling back through the 745-foot Pila tunnel and returning below the terrace for a third time.

In less than ten minutes, you look up from Cavaglia (5,553 feet) to see the restaurant at Alp Grum, now 1,305 feet above you. The forests have turned to deciduous trees: hazel, aspen, alder, and birch.

Your coming descent to Poschiavo is the most miraculous of all. Your train makes four more zigzags and tunnel turnarounds. You see Poschiavo first on the left and then four more times on the right while your train loops above the towers of the city. Photographers race back and forth across the carriage in order to capture all of the kaleidoscopic scenery.

Past Miralgo (whose name, "Look at the Lake," refers to your view), you again descend steeply to Brusio. Here your train's crossing of the raised, looping stone viaduct having only a 164-foot radius—an open spiral—brings highway traffic to a stop.

Italian passport control at Campocologno is performed on the train. Then your Bernina Express continues down the valley past vineyards, fig trees, and tobacco plantations, across a steel bridge over the pressure pipes of the Brusio power station (which generate electricity powering the line), and past the Renaissance pilgrim's church of the Madonna di Tirano to the Italian frontier at Tirano, a pleasant little town of mountain houses and terraced vineyards.

Adventurers either return on the Bernina Express, or continue on Italian trains to Milan's Centrale station. Try not to arrive at Milan's inconvenient Porto Garibaldi station—you will have to ride the subway to Milan's Centrale station for onward connections.

Summer Bernina Express Service

Connections with Basel/Zurich/Zurich Airport

	0554	dep.	Basel (SBB)	arr.	2205
0604	0643	dep.	Zurich (Airport)	arr.	2116
0630	0710	dep.	Zurich (Hbf.)	arr.	2050
0801	0848	arr.	CHUR	dep.	1917

Bernina Express

B	A				C	D
0810	0855	dep.	CHUR	arr.	1910	1855
0820	....	dep	Reichenau-Tamins	dep.	....	....
0838	....	arr.	Thusis	dep.	*	*
0840	....	dep.	Thusis	arr.	1842	1827
0856	....	arr.	Tiefencastel	dep.	*	*
0857	....	dep.	Tiefencastel	arr.	1822	1807
0910	0949	arr.	Filisur	dep.	1808	1753
0911	0950	dep.	Filisur	arr.	1807	1752
0923	....	dep.	Bergun (Bravuogn)	dep.	....	....
0939	....	dep.	Preda	dep.	....	....
0953	....	arr.	Samedan	dep.	....	....
0955	....	dep.	Samedan	arr.	....	....
1002	1035	arr.	PONTRESINA	dep.	1707	1700
1020	1044	dep.	PONTRESINA	arr.	1628	1654
1032	....	dep.	Morteratsch	dep.	1617	....
1043	....	dep.	Bernina Diavolezza	dep.	1608	....
1056	....	dep.	Ospizio Bernina	dep.	1553	....
1106	1126	arr.	Alp Grum	arr.	1543	....
1140	1200	arr.	Poschiavo	dep.	1503	1540
1142	1201	dep.	Poschiavo	arr.	1457	1538
1151	1209	dep.	Le Prese	dep.	1448	1531
1202	....	dep.	Brusio	dep.	1436	1519
1212	1229	arr.	Campocologno	dep.	1426	1508
1213	1230	dep.	Campocologno	arr.	1418	1503
1221	1237	arr.	TIRANO	dep.	1410	1455

*No new passengers allowed to board.

Connections with Milan

1241	1338	dep.	TIRANO	arr.	1144	1442
1317	1418	dep.	Sondrio	dep.	1110	1416
1509	1535	dep.	Lecco	dep.	0952	1248
1610	....	arr.	Milan (P. Garibaldi)	dep.	....	....
....	1618	arr.	MILAN (Centrale)	dep.	0900	1205

Railroads of the Jungfrau Region
Top of Europe

The North Face of the Eiger

After burrowing through the solid rock of the Eiger for several miles, Eigerwand station is startling. You hear "Ahs" as your train passes portals glowing with reflected white light. Folk music plays on the platform. It gives you an eerie feeling to be at this treacherous location where climber after climber tried and failed to scale the wall outside until finally, in 1938, the sheer face was conquered for the first time.

Passengers surge from the train to a set of twelve plate-glass picture windows—enough for everyone—revealing an amazing view of the Grindelwald valley, some 6,000 feet below. From the portals you look out onto the very center of the Eiger North Face.

The Railroads of the Jungfrau Region carry you to a land of snow and ice you cannot possibly reach otherwise unless you are a competent Alpine climber accompanied by guides.

Interlaken Ost (for "east") train station is your stepping stone to the Jungfrau region, although beginning in June 1991 you can board through carriages originating in Lucerne. Narrow-gauge BOB (Bernese Oberland Bahn) trains departing from platform 2 take you to the region famous for the highest train station in Europe, a score of great mountaineering centers, and the spot where James Bond confronted his archenemy in *On Her Majesty's Secret Service*.

When you travel from Interlaken Ost to the Jungfraujoch, the highest train station in Europe, BOB's route takes you through Grindelwald to Kleine Scheidegg, where you board the Jungfrau Railroad. Returning to Interlaken Ost, descend through Wengen on the Wengernalp Railroad (WAB).

Traveling from Interlaken Ost to the Schilthorn (of James Bond's Piz Gloria notoriety) takes you on four spectacular modes of travel. You leave the WAB at Lauterbrunnen, board the funicular to Grutschalp, transfer to the mountain Murren Railroad, and top your adventure with a dramatic gondola ride to the mountaintop restaurant crowning the Schilthorn (9,748 feet).

When you have taken both the Schilthorn and the Jungfraujoch trips, you

RAILROADS OF THE JUNGFRAU REGION

SCHILTHORN

JUNGFRAUJOCH

Eismer

Eigerwand

Eigergletscher

Kleine Scheidegg

Murren

Grutschalp

WENGEN

Lauterbrunnen

Zweilutschinen

GRINDELWALD

INTERLAKEN

0   10   20
MILES

N

judge the question: "Which is the more adventurous?" The Jungfraujoch is more famous and gives you things to do at the top—a museum, ice palace, "Toporama," and more. The Schilthorn gives you a stunning panorama, a thrilling ascent, and Bond's Piz Gloria. Try to visit both.

Your climb to the Jungfraujoch is expensive (the Schilthorn adventure is less expensive). Eurailpasses are not accepted past Interlaken Ost and Swiss Passes will take you only as far as Grindelwald (although the cards come in handy again during the Schilthorn trip). Although trains are second-class only, do not invest in this trip when it is cloudy at the summit. The tourist office next to the extravagant Grand Hotel Victoria Jungfrau, a ten-minute walk from the Ost about halfway to the West station, will give you reliable advice before you set out. At the same time, check to see if there is currently an early-morning departure (before the connecting trains from Zurich and Geneva arrive) at reduced prices.

The new (1990) brown-and-tan BOB cars marked for Grindelwald take the Grindelwald valley. Those in front marked for "Lauterbrunnen" travel up the Lauterbrunnen valley for Wengen, Lauterbrunnen, and the funicular to Grutschalp.

Your first stop is Wilderswil. Several Swiss with walking boots and Alpine walking sticks get off for the rack-and-pinion railroad to Schynige Platte.

Shortly before making your second stop, you get your first teasing view of the great white Alps in the distance. You feel a surge of anticipation.

Crossing the first frolicking branch of two Lutschinen torrents, the White Lutschine and the Black Lutschine, you arrive in Zweilutschinen, where they meet. The two sections of your train are separated.

To the Jungfraujoch

Your car to Grindelwald runs along the raging Black Lutschine, carefully banked with flagstones on the left. Contrary to its name, it is white with melted glacial runoff.

Climbing the Grindelwald valley, you see tall chalets scattered on the left. On the right you hear bell-tolling cows. Outside your pulled-down window you can almost pick a dazzling horticultural bouquet of delicate white wild flowers. A river on your right charges down over huge boulders and the waterfall dropping from above makes a rainbow arc from the sun.

Now you come round a bend, revealing a vision. The magnificent Eiger towers like a giant wall, its peak hidden in flying clouds. You look to the left and there is the Schweizerhof hotel with its red shutters. Now your train coasts to a stop in the brown-shuttered Grindelwald station (3,392 feet).

On an unforgettable site, Grindelwald, the "Glacier Village," is the center of the eastern Jungfrau Region, and looks like a Swiss village should look. Each chalet is neatly arranged and tucked under a tree, balconies are swept, geraniums are in full bloom and fuchsias flower from every window box. Firewood is corded neatly and stored symmetrically under the eaves. In the fields, hay is carefully stacked.

Grindelwald has changed with the times by adding a few key hotels and a modern indoor swimming pool, but it has not lost its essential mountaineering charm or its good mountain air. The tourist office (open 8 A.M. to noon and 2 to 5 P.M., closed Sunday) is three to four minutes to the right up the main highway from the station.

You quickly change to the waiting, thirty-one-inch-gauge, green-and-yellow striped, 1990 WAB train carriage which starts out down the mountainside past gardens filled with fruit and great dahlias of all colors before stopping at Grund station. Then it zigzags up the opposite mountain slope for its approach to Kleine Scheidegg.

This is a playground for long camera lenses. You see model farms, summer houses, hotels, chalets, churches, and cows with bells swinging on their necks.

At the Brandegg stop (4,272 feet), your ears pop. The clang of cowbells wafts through the lowered windows. The animals look uncomfortable on the steep mountainside as they take the last clumps of green grass.

Past Alpiglen (5,252 feet), your train enters a snowshed and then clanks through a double-tracked passing-point. The landscape has scattered trees, stubborn shrubs, and a marshy look. You pass through more snowsheds with extruded steel uprights for strength.

Kleine Scheidegg (6,762 feet) comes into view. From a distance, the big hotels look like those found on a game board. A lilting alphorn serenades you as you climb off into a semicircle of hotels and restaurants. On this ledge connecting the Lauterbrunnen and Grindelwald valleys, you can cross to one of several large restaurants facing the station. Crowds of adventurers bask in the sun and enjoy the outdoor service on sunny days. Usually you will see a man in full Swiss folk costume playing an alphorn. You can order a nice lunch, a pair of sausages with potato salad, or just a beer while you listen to the melodious sounds of the alphorn and relish the incredible view of the Eiger, immense before you like a wall.

Kleine Scheidegg's shingled train station stands before the turnstiles where you board a thirty-nine-inch-gauge, Jungfrau Railroad's (JB) carriage for your trip to the summit. In addition to their chocolate-livery carriages, JB is proud of their "Rowan" carriages with natual rowan-wood sidings.

So formidable were the difficulties of working at this great altitude that sixteen years were required to complete the 5¾ miles upward from Kleine Scheidegg. Even then, the track ended at the Jungfraujoch, 1¼ miles and more than 2,000 feet below the summit of the Jungfrau, its intended goal.

Immediately after you start to climb, you have wonderful views back on Kleine Scheidegg and the Eiger glacier close on the right glaring brightly at you. When you near the glacier you see its detail, the scalloping and furrows caused by runoff, and you appreciate the vastness of it even more.

Your climb is so steep that those facing forward are thrown against their seat backs and those facing backwards brace themselves to keep from sliding out of their seats. Be sure to choose a forward-facing seat on the right side.

Your first stop is the Eigergletscher (Eiger glacier) station (7,612 feet), which was faced with granite in 1990. This is where the construction crew in 1898 established a colony of 150 workers just below the perpendicular North Face. Now you see the repair shop for the Jungfrau Railroad just below the entry to the long tunnel ahead.

Surging ahead, you enter the 4.4-mile tunnel gallery where you will spend some forty-one minutes in darkness. Travelers exclaim and push up the windows because of cold air suddenly blasting on them. Heat percolates from under the seats. You sit two-opposite-two in one-class, fancy seats more spacious than the other narrow-gauge trains of the Jungfrau region.

You climb so steeply that when you pass the horizontal sign "Open all year round," it appears cocked at an angle. The maximum gradient would be one foot in four on a direct route, so a corkscrew tunnel had to be constructed. The curved course allows you to stop at two intermediate stations with extraordinary views.

A gong sounds. Now you hear yodeling. Then an impersonal, recorded greeting in German and then French and English announces a five-minute stop at Eigerwand, the "Face of the Eiger" (9,400 feet).

From Eigerwand your train curves slightly more than ninety degrees in order to continue its climb. It runs through a tunnel scarcely big enough for one train only. You wouldn't dare walk alongside.

Less than a mile farther, now below the southeastern face of the Eiger and 10,368 feet high (a job which took the tunnelers two years to excavate), you reach the Eismeer (Sea of Ice) station. A hollow has been carved out of the rock big enough to hold a double track, so that ascending and descending trains pass one another. Once again you hear yodel music and an announcement for a five-minute stop. Here you see a view over the ragged surface of the glacier toward the Wetterhorn, the Schreckhorn, the Fiescherhorner, and the great crevasse under the Monchsjoch.

Your final segment lifts you only 970 feet, so the designers flattened the gradient from one in four to one in sixteen feet (except for the last 1,640 feet). For many years this stretch was carried by ordinary adhesion, at just more than eleven miles an hour, but now the line is rack-and-pinion throughout.

The Alpine world of the Jungfraujoch (11,336 feet) is on view at the "Top of Europe" complex, where five levels of modern architecture blend harmoniously with the surroundings. Take the elevator to the Sphinx panoramic platform; visit the scientific exhibit. When you get hungry, dine in a restaurant or cafe. This is a wonderful complex of mountain restaurants, ice sculptures, husky dogs, mountaineering, and the "Toporama" slide show.

Departures are half-hourly during the summer. If you miss one there is always another carriage waiting for you. You will be warm and satisfied after your magnificent day, and you won't be alone dozing on your way down.

To the Schilthorn

For this adventure, board a BOB car at Interlaken Ost station marked for Lauterbrunnen, or take the WAB to Lauterbrunnen from the Jungfraujoch. Remember that Eurailpass is not valid here. In Lauterbrunnen, disembark and cross the highway to the sign over the "cave" opening: "Bergbahn Lauterbrunnen-Murren." Your climb in the stepped, sixty-passenger funicular will surprise you with its steep incline and length.

When you reach the upper terminus you immediately board the waiting Murren Railroad, a four-car brown-and-white electric tram which takes you 2¾ miles horizontally to Murren. You will see one of the grandest views of the world here. The magnificent presence of the Jungfrau seems only a stone's throw away across a precipitous chasm. On your return, a casual walk from Murren to Grutschalp will long remain one of your fondest memories.

When this tram reaches Murren, disembark and walk through the village fifteen minutes to the Schilthornbahn — there is only one street through Murren so you can't get lost. You pass every shop conceivable for a small village and carefully tended, flower-covered chalets as pleasant as any. Benches along the way offer places to break your walk.

You join the Schilthornbahn at its second stage. The first stage brings riders from the valley floor (free with the Swiss Pass) in 100-passenger gondolas from a postal bus connection at Gimmelwald.

Your second-stage, swinging, eighty-passenger red gondola with white "Schilthorn Bahn" lettered in front (reduction with a Swiss Pass) glides over the spacious Blumental ("Flower Valley") in a cable span of 3,038 yards supported by only two intermediate pylons. You appear simply to glide up a threatening rock face to a stop at the top of a towering bastion. First you look down on unbelievable rock formations sculpted by snow and glaciers. Then you look down on the glaciers.

At Birg, you change gondolas. Birg (8,781 feet) has a restaurant and sun terrace. Your second gondola is a single-cabin for 100 persons. Between Birg and the summit, you see the scenery unfolding in all directions until you see Mont Blanc and Germany's Black Forest appearing in the distance and the

Jungfrau Alps face you. This span is 1,931 yards long—the longest unsupported span in the country. You notice even the gondola operators look exposed and weatherworn and wear dark glasses and sun creams. Finally you see some venturesome, hearty Swiss outside clambering down the snow. Your gondola swings to a final stop and you feel as daring as James Bond himself when he took those last few steps here to meet his archenemy in *On Her Majesty's Secret Service*.

As you saw in that film, Piz Gloria is a round building. The restaurant revolves in fifty-minute cycles past a continuous circle of picture windows that show off sectors of the 360-degree panorama. There are revolving restaurants and other revolving restaurants, but none have prepared you for the sense of the Swiss Alps rotating around you while you enjoy hearty Swiss specialties to the melodies of a mountain accordionist. Below, there is a self-service cafeteria with modest prices.

On the sun terrace, deck chairs are especially valued by travelers who have trouble with the high altitude. The red-and-white Swiss flag fluttering overhead seems planted as a backdrop for your photographs.

Railroads of the Jungfrau Region *
Typical Service

Interlaken—Grindelwald—Kl. Scheidegg—Jungfraujoch

0931	dep.	INTERLAKEN OST	arr.	1626
0936	dep.	Wilderswil	dep.	1621
0946	dep.	Zweilutschinen	dep.	1613
0953	dep.	Lutschental	dep.	1606
0959	dep.	Burglauenen	dep.	1559
1002	dep.	Schwendi	dep.	1555
1009	arr.	GRINDELWALD	dep.	1548
1015	dep.	GRINDELWALD	arr.	1525
1025	dep.	Grindelwald Grund	dep.	1520
1054	arr.	KLEINE SCHEIDEGG	dep.	1432
1102	dep.	KLEINE SCHEIDEGG	dep.	1422
1112	dep.	Eigergletscher	dep.	1412
1158	arr.	JUNGFRAUJOCH	dep.	1330

Interlaken—Lauterbrunnen—Wengen—Kl. Scheidegg—Jungfraujoch

0931	dep.	INTERLAKEN OST	arr.	1630
0936	dep.	Wilderswil	dep.	1626
0945	dep.	Zweilutschinen	dep.	1618
0954	arr.	LAUTERBRUNNEN	dep.	1608
1010	dep.	LAUTERBRUNNEN	arr.	1600
1024	arr.	WENGEN	dep.	1543

1030	dep.	WENGEN	arr.	1535
1046	dep.	Wengernalp	dep.	1511
1055	arr.	KLEINE SCHEIDEGG	dep.	1502
1102	dep.	KLEINE SCHEIDEGG	arr.	1447
1112	dep.	Eigergletscher	dep.	1438
1158	arr.	JUNGFRAUJOCH	dep.	1400

Interlaken — Lauterbrunnen — Murren — Schilthorn

1031	dep.	INTERLAKEN OST	arr.	1530
1036	dep.	Wilderswil	dep.	1526
1045	dep.	Zweilutschinen	dep.	1518
1054	arr.	LAUTERBRUNNEN	dep.	1508
1102	dep.	LAUTERBRUNNEN	arr.	1458
1113	dep.	Grutschalp	dep.	1447
1130	arr.	MURREN	dep.	1430
1140	dep.	MURREN	arr.	1420
1155	dep.	Birg	dep.	1410
1159	arr.	SCHILTHORN	dep.	1401

*Beginning June 1991 through carriages will run between Lucerne and Grindelwald.

Panoramic Express
A Taste of Gold

Your blue-and-white electric power car curls back and forth, up through terrace after terrace of lush vineyards. You look down on Montreux's freshly whitewashed hotels, patina-green copper roofs, and brown wooden chalets getting smaller and smaller. The little strip of town set upon the only place the Swiss could find for it between the steep Vaudois Alps and the "Vaud Riviera" on the shores of Lake Geneva never loses its charm.

You have powerful views from the Panoramic Observation Car of the narrow-gauge Montreux-Oberland-Bernois Railroad (MOB). Daily Panoramic Express trains carry four panoramic cars with rooftop windows at forty-five degrees.

The Super Panoramic Express train will surprise you even more. It also carries a "chalet" car and a spectacular "Grande Vue" car in which twelve lucky passengers in three rows sit in front of, and below, the driver, with nothing between them and the rushing scenery but wraparound glass. The experience is the only one of its kind in Europe—but these seats cannot be reserved. You must arrive early to find a choice front-row seat.

When you ride the Super Panoramic Express from Montreux you ride in one of the best trains in Europe (and one of the few remaining first-class-only ones). These glassed wonders show you beautiful scenery in a way no other carriage can.

Lenk

To Interlaken

ZWEISIMMEN

Gstaad

Chateau-d'Oex

PANORAMIC
EXPRESS

Les Avants

0   5   10   20
MILES

MONTREUX

The "Super" runs only on weekends and holidays. If you can't fit the Super into your itinerary, the observation cars of the wonderful daily Panoramic Express still give you an outstanding show.

Although you can also start the Panoramic Express in Lenk or board it in Zweisimmen, the shimmering glare off Lake Geneva during a westward afternoon descent to lakeside blinds your view. It is always more scenic to make this trip going eastward from Montreux.

There is no better place to stay before beginning or after ending your Panoramic Express trip than Montreux. The flower-scented promenade here is one of Europe's most beautiful. Montreux occupies a lovely site sheltered from the wind on the eastern end of Lake Geneva and known for the mildest climate north of the Alps. Tourists enjoy excursions, water sports, tennis, and just strolling along the promenade. Snow in winter falls only a few hundred feet above the town.

Montreux's train station is arranged oddly on the side of a mountain. You reach platform No. 1 for the SBB to Lausanne/Geneva/Geneva Airport by climbing stairs or by elevator. Platform No. 5, where you board the Panoramic and Super Panoramic, is next to the MOB office. Climb the stairway to the left.

The tourist office is down the stairs in front of the train station; go to the promenade and 1,000 feet to the left (south). The steamers circling the Lake of Geneva dock nearby before proceeding around Chillon Castle. (They, too, are free on Eurailpasses and Swiss Passes—even for landings in France.)

To reach the train station from the lake steamers, walk left and up the steps. Agents at the tourist office will give you a free Panoramic Express color brochure and map to increase your pleasure. Of course, they will also make hotel arrangements.

Board your Panoramic Express in Montreux and enjoy this next adventure. As your train weaves farther up the mountainside, Lake Geneva shrinks and becomes dwarfed by gray, snow-streaked French Alps towering in the background. With a view like a satellite in the sky, you can pick out the casino and the red-and-white Swiss flag over the Montreux Palace Hotel. The tall building you see near the lake was built in 1964, when high-rises were the rage. It is a condominium boasting a twenty-sixth floor restaurant. The Eurotel to its right was built the same year. It is the second-tallest in town. You see lake hamlets like Vevey and Lausanne to the north, and the Rhone River valley to the south stretching toward the Simplon Pass.

The Panoramic Express has two first-class cars and two second-class cars. Traveling first class, passengers sit two-opposite-two with nine rows per carriage. Second-class passengers sit the same in fourteen rows per car. The difference is the amount of legroom and the comfort of the upholstery. SBB recommends reservations but does not make them obligatory, but when you want to ensure window seats, make reservations. The hillside above Montreux is famous for its trees and flowers. You pass through grape arbors to an altitude of nearly 2,000 feet, past walnut trees to 2,300 feet, and among fruit trees to 3,250 feet. Wild narcissus sparkle in springtime.

On your left you see the first of the charming chalets like those in the Bernese Oberland; they give you a warm first impression of the celebrated Golden Pass route, which rivals the Glacier Express for the most spectacular east-west route in Switzerland. Looking up through the oblique windows reveals the crests of the Alps and gives you great depth of perspective. You feel inspired by the devastating height of the Alps above you. Because about 90 percent of your car is glass, be thankful for the air-conditioning which overcomes the greenhouse heating.

Your final memory as you cross the crest is a long view down the valley to Chillon Castle, with a white Lake Geneva steamer gliding into dock.

Over the summit and through a long tunnel you enter the wholly different Sarine valley. Your Panoramic Express Observation Car picks up speed on the single, narrow-gauge track. The conductor with a blue-and-white MOB winged emblem pinned to his black cap (patent leather visor) accepts your Eurailpass or Swiss Pass with a smile. The MOB is one of Switzerland's private railroad companies honoring both.

Now you are riding through cuts in the limestone mountainsides past Les Scieres. Brown-and-white contented-looking cows graze in the tall, green grass. Families harvesting hay wave at you with green handkerchiefs, glad of an excuse to lean on their wooden rakes. Most passengers wave back. The brown-and-white cows shake their heavy bells and more or less ignore them.

The valley is wild and green, but above, the limestone Vaudois Alps form flat-topped ridges and throw long shadows you see through the oblique windows. You regret that your train seems to rush. You wish it would slow down so you could study the rugged mountain crests, the peaceful valleys, and the randomly scattered, typical houses with broad, graceful eaves, intricate woodwork, and flower boxes overflowing with bright yellow and blue blossoms.

Looking at the homes, the dress, and the work, you form an impression of the way of life of these mountain people who speak French, are generally Protestant, and decorate their farmhouses profusely. They live in tidier versions of those you will see only a half-hour ahead in the Bernese Oberland, the region that gave our language the word "chalet" and this form of house synonymous with Switzerland the world over. They have low-pitched roofs and wide eaves on four sides.

Your Panoramic Express stops next in Chateau-d'Oex (say "Chateau Day"), at 3,083 feet. The traditional architecture here is magnificent. This is the typical family resort of the Vaudois Alps, with public pool and skating rink and a high lift to La Braye on the summit above.

You pass through Rougemont station (3,254 feet), remarkable for its carved wood decorations. The huge sloping roof below the train that catches your eye covers an early Romanesque church built on the site of an eleventh-century, Cluniac priory. Swiss from all over the country travel here to visit the church and the adjacent sixteenth-century castle.

The quaint Saanen station (3,364 feet) marks the point where you leave the Sarine valley and enter German-speaking Canton Berne. Some houses here, now adorned with climbing plants, date from the seventeenth century. Saanen's old-fashioned character makes a good contrast with that of its booming neighbor, pricey Gstaad, only three minutes ahead.

In Gstaad, buildings get bigger. The hotels do well here in this smart village, one of Switzerland's premiere winter resorts and a quiet summer destination.

When your express train winds up the mountain overlooking Gstaad, the view back is ideal for photographers. Passengers cluster to the windows to take advantage.

Saanenmoser's train station (4,043 feet), with green shutters and cutouts in the shape of hearts, must be the most filigreed in the world. The station's dark brown wood sets off the white detailing and lace curtains on the windows.

Picking up speed, you sweep down the Saanenmoser depression. Spiky Alpine peaks stand in the distance and farmhouses defy the pull of gravity on both slopes of the valley.

Your trip is nearly over when you arrive on the valley floor at Zweisimmen (3,090 feet). This is your junction for Lenk and Spiez/Interlaken, the route known as the "Golden Pass" leading onto the Brunig line to Lucerne. Tracks 1 and 2 (forty-two-inch gauge) are devoted to your blue-and-white narrow-gauge train from Montreux. Tracks 3, 4, 11, and 13 (sixty inches) lead SBB trains to Spiez/Interlaken.

Construction is planned to add a third rail for narrow-gauge trains to the standard-gauge line connecting Zweisimmen with Interlaken's East station. When this is completed in 1995, Panoramic Express trains will roll right through Zweisimmen and your travel time to Lucerne via Spiez/Interlaken over the narrow-gauge Brunig Line will be cut by thirty minutes.

As it exists, almost everyone changes for the dark-blue-and-white carriages of the Bern-Lotschberg-Simplon Railroad (BLS) for the twenty-seven-mile run to Spiez. This private line also accepts Eurailpasses and Swiss Passes.

Those adventurers to Spiez are back on big rails, but how disappointed they must feel when they look up for the view and realize they no longer have windows to see the high scenery.

Panoramic Express observation cars sit with the air-conditioning dead. After about five minutes, workers finish coupling on a new electric locomotive, the dispatcher waves his signal wand, and you go—but in a surprising direction: not back up the mountainside. You travel twelve miles laterally, up the Simmental ("Tal" meaning valley) and arriving in Lenk fifteen minutes later.

The Simmen Valley is a showcase for beautiful farmhouses. Every year a panel of judges selects the most beautiful farmhouse in Switzerland and every year a farmhouse in the Simmental either wins or ranks high.

The village of Lenk (3,500 feet) is another of those wonderful summer and winter mountain resorts of which Switzerland seems to have no end. Whether you visit for lunch before continuing or take an extended vacation here, Lenk is a pleasant stay.

Super Panoramic and Panoramic Express Service

(A)	(B)	(A)	(B)				(B)	(A)	(B)	(A)
0856	1000	1400	1420	dep.	MONTREUX	arr.	1136	1230	1702	1902
....	....	....	1430	dep.	Chernex	dep.	....	....	....	....
....	1024	....	1444	dep.	Les Avants	dep.	....	....	1642	....
....	....	....	1503	arr.	Montbovon	dep.	....	....	....	....
....	....	....	1504	dep.	Montbovon	arr.	....	....	....	....
0953	1058	1457	1519	arr.	Chateau-d'Oex	dep.	1039	1135	1604	1804
0954	1100	1459	1521	dep.	Chateau-d'Oex	arr.	1037	1134	1602	1802
....	1108	....	1531	dep.	Rougemont	dep.	1029	....	1553	....
....	....	....	1537	dep.	Saanen	dep.	....	....	1547	....
1010	1116	1516	1540	arr.	Gstaad	dep.	1020	1116	1544	1744
1011	1118	1518	1542	dep.	Gstaad	arr.	1018	1113	1542	1742
....	....	....	1551	dep.	Schonreid	dep.	1010	....	....	....
....	....	....	1555	dep.	Saanenmoser	dep.	....	....	....	....
1036	1145	1545	1610	arr.	ZWEISIMMEN	dep.	0950	1043	1515	1715
1049	1150	1550	1649	dep.	Zweisimmen	arr.	0928	1018	1508	1708
1107	1205	1608	1707	arr.	LENK i. S.	dep.	0910	1000	1453	1653

Connections

*1105	1221	1621		dep.	ZWEISIMMEN	arr.	0939	1039	1455	1655
1151	1251	1657		arr.	Spiez	dep.	0903	1003	1408	1608
1201	1301	1701		dep.	Spiez	arr.	0859	1000	1359	1559
1221	1321	1721		arr.	INTERLAKEN (Ost)	dep.	0839	0939	1339	1539

*Local train.
(A) Super Panoramic Express (Weekends and Holidays Only).
(B) Panoramic Express (Daily).

Britain
and Ireland

Vital Tips for the Trains
of Britain and Ireland

*British trains—Irish trains—The London Underground—Euro-
tunnel—Airport trains—Sleepers—Pullman lounges—Sealink—
Hovercraft—BritRail passes—BritFrance pass—Rail Rover and
regional tickets—Scottish Travelpass—Senior Citizen Railcards—
BritRail/Drive—Tours and day trips—Using Eurailpass bonuses in
Ireland—IrishRail passes*

British Trains

To appreciate how easy and "civilised" it is to get around Britain by train just
realize that Britain has more track per square mile than any other country.
More than 15,000 trains a day traveling over an 8,887-mile passenger network
take you to more than 2,400 stations throughout England, Scotland, and
Wales. London has eight mainline stations accessible by Underground. London's Underground takes you to and from Heathrow Airport. British Railroads'
(BritRail) Gatwick Express train speeds you to and from Gatwick Airport.

Travel in Britain centers on BritRail's core InterCity lines. The electrified West
Coast line takes you from London to Glasgow (and to Edinburgh in May 1991)
and the East Coast Line, newly electrified, between London and Edinburgh.

All of BritRail's name and InterCity trains carry first-class (look for the yellow stripe) and standard-class (BritRail calls its second class "standard class") carriages. Most of the locals consist of standard-class carriages only. You can still find a few quaint, old ones, with separate doors leading to each compartment.

You are able to reserve seats on InterCity trains up to two months in advance, and usually two hours before departure. Reservations costing about $3.75 are obligatory on trains marked in the timetable with a white *R* in a black box. Those marked with an *R* in an outline box are busy, and BritRail recommends reservations.

Computer-issue reservations coupons are wallet-size and contain all the usual departure information plus coach letter and seat number. Ask for "F" (for "facing") or "B" (for "backwards") seats, which refer to the direction of travel.

BritRail's premium trains are Pullmans, IC trains with tables preset with linens and bright flowers. Advantages include meals and light refreshments served at your seat, few stops, convenience, and punctuality.

New blue-and-gray, 90 mph trains with "Express" livery are the flagship of the BritRail's fast, modern regional fleet that includes high-tech 75 mph Sprinters, Super Sprinters, and electric trains.

Trainphones are common on BritRail's IC and regional "Express" trains. You pay for your calls, national and international, by using a "Phonecard," which you buy in advance at train stations and elsewhere.

Irish Trains

With a Eurailpass, it is not expensive to make Ireland your gateway to Europe. IrishRail, which honors the Eurailpass, is an arm of the Irish Transport Company, "Coras Iompair Eireann" (CIE), which also runs the CIE intercity buses, DART (Dublin's state-of-the-art electric regional transportation), and all city buses.

IrishRail is the most convenient way to go into the country for Eurailpass holders. Make Dublin your rail hub to reach all popular tourist centers. Dublin has three main train stations: Connolly, Pearse, and Heuston. Connolly and Pearse are connected by DART, which is free with your Eurailpass and IrishRail pass. Bus line No. 90 runs between Heuston and Connolly stations.

Travel times are short on IrishRail's modern, fully dieselized trains. Train journeys never take more than four hours—which is about the time it takes you to get from Dublin in the east to Tralee in the southwest. On mainline service you relax in comfort and watch the green Irish countryside. Waiters serve snacks or full meals—or even pints of Guinness—on the first-class service between Dublin and Cork.

To see completely the Republic of Ireland, supplement your train travel with the red-and-yellow CIE Expressway buses also covered by Eurailpass. Buses link every city and hamlet with mainline trains from stops usually in front of the train stations. Buy not only a train timetable but the Provincial and Expressway Bus Timetable.

The London Underground

London's train stations, and Heathrow Airport too, are connected by London's busy subway system known as the Underground. When you buy individual tickets, remember to keep them to operate the automatic turnstiles when you exit.

London Travelcards are reasonably priced. When you buy them by the day, no photograph is required. You can even buy them for about $4.50 from the vending machines located in Underground stations for unlimited travel over a 650-square-mile area, but with a catch: you can't buy them before 9:30 A.M., Mondays to Fridays. This is fine for late-rising visitors, but makes them unsuitable for business travelers.

Travelcards are valid for unlimited travel by Network South East trains, the Underground, Docklands Light Railway, and on most of London's buses (not the Airbus). For about fifty cents less, you buy a Travelcard valid for a day only in central London, which is usually sufficient.

You can buy longer-term Travelcards with a minimum of seven days for any period (including odd days). Generally, when you will be traveling in London for five or more days, buy a seven-day Travelcard. For these, in London you will need to obtain a free photocard, requiring a passport-type photograph either brought with you or bought from a machine.

When you want the convenience of paying in dollars and the security of having a Travelcard voucher in hand before you leave, BritRail in North America markets "London Visitor Travelcards" valid for three, four, or seven days.

Eurotunnel

Construction of the Eurotunnel beneath the English Channel to connect Britain and France is underway in both countries. During 1993, you will be able to ride by train between London and Paris in three hours and between London and Brussels in two and a half using the TGV-Nord network through France.

The high-speed British link from the Eurotunnel to London is scheduled to be completed in 1998, running to Swanley, just outside of London, and then continuing into London's Kings Cross station.

An international consortium of British, French, and Belgian companies is also building thirty shuttle trains for use in the new tunnel. The trains, each with eighteen coaches including 210 first-class and 584 second-class seats, will travel nominally at 100 mph.

Airport Trains

The Piccadilly line on London's Underground is your access to Heathrow Airport (the London Underground has eleven lines). Travel to either of two stops: use the first stop for Heathrow terminuses 1, 2, and 3 (make sure you know which). The loop at the end of the line takes you to the second stop, terminal 4.

Wheel your luggage carts right up to Heathrow's train entrance. A straight trip between Heathrow and Piccadilly Circus takes about forty-five minutes, but when you must change from one subway line to the Piccadilly, your trip will take longer, especially on Sundays when service is less frequent.

To reach Gatwick Airport from London, board the Gatwick Express at Victoria station's modern Rail/Air check-in facilities on platforms 13 and 14. This area is equipped with elevator, escalator, and special escalator-friendly luggage carts. British Airways maintains a terminus lounge above the platform.

The Gatwick Express is a gray-and-white, red-striped IC train specifically designed for air travelers. You ride in air-conditioned carriages, enter through wide doors, store your luggage on convenient shelves, and walk between compartments through automatically opening doors. You may telephone from the train and charge it to your credit card.

The Gatwick Express carries you nonstop at speeds up to 90 mph, cutting your travel time between Gatwick and Victoria station to thirty minutes. Quarter-hourly service begins at 5:30 A.M. from Victoria. After 10 P.M., standard train service continues around the clock. Use your BritRail pass or the South East Rail Pass you receive in buying a "Capital Travel Pak" from BritRail, or of course, buy a single ticket.

A new high-speed rail link, taking you between Heathrow Airport and London's Paddington station, will be a reality in 1993.

Called the "Heathrow Express," construction of the new rail link began in 1990 so you can travel the fifteen-mile trek between central London and Heathrow Airport in only seventeen minutes. Trains will leave from each location every fifteen minutes.

Sleepers

BritRail's InterCity Mark III sleepers take you over all sleeper routes. First-class sleepers accommodate one passenger; second-class cabins accommodate two in an upper and a lower berth.

You can remain on your early-arriving trains in your sleeping compartment until at least 7 A.M., sometimes later, depending on the train. Your porter asks you whether you wish to be awakened early for arrival or after sleeping late. His call is always accompanied by the welcome coffee or famous English tea. Most trains have sleeper lounge service for first-class passengers. BritRail converted first-class salon cars into pubs with bars, twenty-six lounge seats, and a public telephone. Located mid-train, this is where first-class passengers buy drinks, light meals, and snacks before and after their trip.

Pullman Lounges

Terminuses of BritRail's InterCity trains have corners of quiet luxury for you to enjoy. You need a first-class ticket (a first-class BritRail or BritFrance pass will do) to enter salons filled with soft chairs and served by a host offering free coffee.

Use the string of Pullman lounges extending to Leeds (in the station concourse, open 6:30 A.M. to 9 P.M.), Newcastle (station concourse, 7 A.M. to 8 P.M.), Edinburgh Waverley (first floor opposite platforms 7 to 10, 7 A.M. to 11:30 P.M.; 8:30 to 11:30 P.M., Sundays), and Glasgow Central (first floor, above main concourse, 7 A.M. to 11 P.M.; 8:30 to 11 P.M., Sundays) stations.

Ring the buzzer to enter, show your ticket or pass to the welcoming host, lounge in the comfortable chairs, and enjoy free coffee or tea, Mondays to Fridays, and Sunday nights.

At the Pullman Lounges in London's Kings Cross (at platform 8, open 7 A.M. to 9 P.M.) and London's Euston (on the first floor concourse adjacent to "Carriages Restaurant," open 7 A.M. to 11 P.M.; 8:30 to 11 P.M., Sundays), you also need an American Express card.

Sealink

Sealink operates more ships to more places (France, the Netherlands, Germany, Ireland, the Channel Islands) from Britain than any other company. It offers restaurants, shipboard pubs, comfortable lounges, spacious duty-free "Seashops," and even feature films on some ships. Make your reservations and buy your tickets in North America through BritRail Travel International (see Appendix A) or at the International Rail Centre at London's Victoria station.

You have a choice of travel across the English Channel from London's Victoria station via Dover to Ostend, Belgium: Jetfoil or ship. The train/Jetfoil typically takes 5¼ hours; the train/ship, 7¾.

Travel on the British "St. Nicholas" or the Dutch "Koningin Beatrix" via Harwich from London's Liverpool Street station to Hoek of Holland usually takes 11 hours by day, 13 hours by night.

From London's Liverpool Street station via Harwich to Hamburg, Germany, via Scandinavian Seaways takes 22½ hours.

Sealinks to Ireland take you across six routes: Fishguard-Rosslare, Holyhead-

Dun Laoghaire, Holyhead-Dublin, Liverpool-Dun Laoghaire, Liverpool-Belfast, and Stranraer-Larne. On certain dates you must have free ship reservations (a sailing control ticket), so obtain your control tickets as early as possible.

Hovercraft

Your fastest way across the English Channel is by flying Hovercraft between Boulogne and Dover. It is supported by a cushion of air over the waves of the channel and propelled by enormous propeller blades rotating high over the vehicle.

The flight of the brightly hued red, white, and blue Hovercraft can be bumpy. Some passengers become queasy during tough seas. Hovercraft frequency depends on season and may be suspended during windy or stormy weather.

On the Hoverspeed Reception Centre on platform 8 at London's Victoria station, stewardesses check in your luggage airline style (you collect it on arrival in Boulogne), leaving you free to ride BritRail's Kent Coast diesel train, not a pride and joy of BritRail, and cross the channel without struggling with luggage. At Dover, you transfer by free shuttle bus to the Hoverport, where there is a bank and duty-free shopping available. Similarly, at the Boulogne Hoverport you find banking and shopping opportunities.

FrenchRail runs excellent yellow-striped turbotrains served by refreshments trolleys between Boulogne Hoverport and Paris's Gare du Nord.

In London's Victoria station's South Hall look for international departures information on the extreme right side of the huge departures board. In Paris's Gare du Nord's main hall, Hovercraft ("Aeroglisseur," in French) departures are clearly shown on the "Depart Grandes Lignes" signboard.

BritRail Passes

BritRail Passes are your basic go-everywhere, see-everything travel convenience. They are your ideal way to adventure in Britain by train. You travel free on every BritRail train in England, Scotland, and Wales, save the narrow-gauge private railroads in Wales and the Isle of Man trains.

Eurailpasses are not valid in Britain, so BritRail compensates by selling such an array of tempting train values that your head begins to swim. Write for their free color brochure, "Go BritRail," take it slow, and find the right combination for you.

BritRail sells consecutive and flexipass versions of first-class ("Gold") passes for rates about one-sixth more than Eurailpasses, but buy passes for second-class (the brochure prefers "standard-class") travel ("Silver") for more than one-fourth off the prices of the Gold passes. Buy consecutive passes for eight, fifteen, twenty-two days or one month.

BritRail makes their passes especially attractive to those over sixty and those between fifteen and twenty-five by offering about 10 percent off for Senior first- and second-class passes and 20 percent off second-class Youth Passes. There are no first-class Youth Passes. Children five through fifteen pay about half.

BritRail also offers BritRail Flexipasses which allow you leisure time, like Eurail Flexipasses. By paying for four days of travel out of eight, eight days out of fifteen, or fifteen out of one month, you save about 15 percent of the cost of a standard first- or second-class BritRail Pass. Senior and Youth BritRail Passes are also available with the same Flexipass option and equivalent savings, except that Britain's fifteen-day Youth Flexipass is valid for two months.

You buy BritRail Passes on the Continent, in Germany and France, for example, and in the Republic of Ireland, but you pay in local currencies, so it is more convenient to buy them before leaving America.

BritFrance Pass

BritRail and FrenchRail are collaborating on an excellent, convenient flexipass way for you to travel in both countries and connect between them by Hovercraft.

BritFrance Passes provide unlimited train travel in Britain and France (you decide how many days you want to travel in each country), plus two coupons allowing you to travel round trip across the English Channel by Hovercraft.

Buy first- or second-class or Youth versions for any five travel days out of fifteen, or ten out of one month at BritRail and FrenchRail offices (see Appendix A).

Like a France Railpass, you pay no high-speed surcharges on FrenchRail travel. Reservations are essential for your Hovercraft crossings. They are free when you make them in Paris at any International ticketing counter or cost $3 per person in London at a BritRail Travel Centre.

The passes consist of a master ticket containing your name, passport number, and signature, which (before or on your first day of use) you must have validated at one of the "Orientation" kiosks in the Paris train stations or at any BritRail Travel Centre. On each day you use them, you date the computer-printed boxes on the second coupon by hand. The two Hovercraft coupons are detached as you use them.

Rail Rover and Regional Tickets

In Britain you purchase, in pounds sterling or by Visa or Master Card, Rail Rover tickets valid for seven or fourteen days, first- or second-class, on most BritRail timetable trains, or a range of regional and local Rail Rovers in the regions of England's North West and North East, Coast and Peaks/Wales, South West, East Midlands, Anglia, Heart of England, and Scotland (plus five Scottish Area Rovers).

Flexible Scottish Rover tickets are your most economical buy when you want to choose the days you travel. You buy them for four travel days in eight, or ten in fifteen.

For Scottish Travelpass information contact Travelpass, Hi-Line, Hi-Line House, Dingwall, Ross-shire IV15 9JE.

Scottish Travelpass

When you travel extensively in the Scottish Highlands and Islands (Kyle of Lochalsh, for example), a seven of eight- or thirteen of fifteen-day Scottish Highlands & Islands Travelpass not only covers second-class travel on BritRail (called "ScotRail" there) within the region, but includes Caledonian MacBrayne's ferries to the islands off the west coast, P&O's Scrabster to Stromness, and gives you one-third off Scottish Bus Group and Citylink buses. Buy it in Scotland (Glasgow and Edinburgh gateways) or from Scot-American Travel Advisors, 26 Rugen Drive, Harrington Park, NJ 07640 (Tel. 201-768-5505). It is not available through BritRail in America.

Senior Citizen Railcards

Adventurers over sixty, regardless of nationality or residence, are eligible to buy Senior Citizen Railcards costing about $30 a year (payable by cash or credit card). It provides at least one-third off on most British rail and London Underground fares and discounts on several ferry services. You can even take along up to four children, at one pound sterling per head, second class.

The upgrade to European-wide discounts is not available to U.S. residents.

Show your passport to obtain them at any major British Rail Travel Centre in Britain.

BritRail/Drive

The BritRail/Drive plan combines a BritRail Flexipass for four or eight days' or one month's train travel with a Hertz rental automobile with unlimited mileage also for four, eight, or twelve days, respectively.

Hertz has some one hundred pickup stations at major BritRail stations, at eleven airports, and eighty-nine more at practically any place you might venture.

You keep the car for blocks of twenty-four-hour periods. You can pick up a car in one station and drop it off in another. In between, you have use of the rail pass portion of the option. For long hauls, you use the train, and for short hauls and exploring the countryside you have the car.

You pay for the package in dollars and receive all instructions before you leave, making it very easy to use.

Tours and Day Trips

BritRail offers a convenient and economical way to book a selection of luxury day trips and tours from London. These are detailed in "Go BritRail." They include day trips on the historic Pullman carriages of the Venice Simplon Orient Express like those used on the English leg of VSOE's opulent trip to Venice, a Britainshrinkers train/bus sightseeing calendar (BritRail Pass holders save up to 42 percent), and the escorted "Great Britain and Great Wales Expresses."

Using Eurailpass Bonuses in Ireland

Eurailpass gives you two bonuses that are valuable — essential — to seeing enjoyably the Republic by Eurail.

You can travel free on Expressway buses owned and operated by CIE (except the services to and from Northern Ireland operated jointly with the northern administration).

You can also connect with the trains on the Continent just by paying port taxes. The Irish Continental Line (ICL) gives Eurailpass holders free deck passage and Irish hospitality on its two car ferries, the *Saint Patrick II* and the *Saint Killian II* serving the Irish ports of Rosslare and Cork and the French ports of Le Havre and Cherbourg. You travel between Rosslare and Le Havre (21 hours) on four round-trip sailings per week during the summer and two to three per week during off-season. ICL's Rosslare-Cherbourg sailings (17 hours) take you twice weekly during the summer; once a week from October to February. Its Cork-Le Havre sailings (21½ hours) occur once a week during the summer only.

ICL's ferries are large and comfortable — the equivalent of mini-cruises. You dine in a dining room or cafeteria, shop duty-free, gamble, go to the movies, and socialize in the bar-lounge and disco. You must pay extra for cabin accommodations, but by the time your Eurailpass credit is deducted from the overall charge, your costs for these are quite reasonable. For prices and reservations, contact CIE Tours International (see Appendix A).

IrishRail Passes

Adventurers to Ireland buy an Emerald Isle Card, which is a flexipass good for eight travel days in fifteen or fifteen travel days in thirty. You use it throughout the Republic of Ireland and Northern Ireland for unlimited travel on all scheduled IrishRail and Northern Ireland Railroads trains, plus all scheduled long-distance bus services and city bus services in Dublin, Belfast, Cork, Limerick, Galway, and Waterford.

Buy your Emerald Isle Card from your travel agent or CIE tours (see Appendix A).

Adventurers aged sixteen to twenty-six should be sure to pick up from any Republic of Ireland InterCity train station a free "FaIR" Card entitling them to discounts between 45 and 55 percent off the adult fares for one-way and six-day round-trip IR tickets.

With a FaIR card, adventurers also can buy a Citibonus Ticket valid for a weekend round-trip from Dublin to any InterCity station in the Republic including unlimited travel on Dublin Bus and Dublin Suburban Rail from a Friday to the following Thursday.

Adventuring in the British Isles takes you aboard BritRail's new supertrain, on Scotland's Kyle line from Inverness, on the Isle of Man trains, along the coast of Wales and through slate-mining Welsh countryside, and on an electric odyssey along Bay of Dublin.

Flying Scotsman
New Superswallow

The swallow, logo of BritRail's diesel speed-record-holding InterCity trains since 1966, has accelerated — taking adventurers with it to Scotland — on the livery of BritRail's new electric InterCity 225 supertrains.

Speed? InterCity 225 gives it: "225" (kilometers an hour) converts to your speeding through green British countryside at 140 miles an hour.

Call these trains, "Superswallows." Adventurers are riding aboard next century's trains now, sitting in stunning "Mark 4" passenger carriages and riding behind BritRail's most powerful ever locomotives, Electra power units, with driving vans/trailers.

For a fast and luxurious trip on BritRail's electrified East Coast Line, take BritRail's new InterCity 225 trains, such as the Flying Scotsman to York and Edinburgh and the Yorkshire Pullman to Leeds.

Remember May 1991 as the milestone first running of the InterCity 225 passenger trains that cut your travel time between London and Edinburgh to less than four hours. Adventurers are already bragging about winging InterCity 225's branch to Leeds in less than two hours when that first segment was electrified in late 1989.

You hear that the regularly scheduled Flying Scotsman train has left London's Kings Cross station daily at ten sharp since 1862. The Flying Scotsman, BritRail's flagship on this route — lacking nameplate — still leaves "Kings X" (as British travelers affectionately know Kings Cross) at ten sharp, but now makes your trip faster and seats you in the lap of luxury.

Everywhere that Electras with new class 91 serial numbers stop, you see tow-headed youngsters crowding platforms, pursuing their peculiarly British hobby: "train spotting." The instant that they recognize a never-before-seen Electra coming into view, they add it to their lists by jotting into their copybook its serial number, date, and where they spotted it.

On the nameplate of one Electra, they see a mouse.

Having long since exhausted the roster of benevolent kings, queens, and major royalty to christen their locomotives, BritRail honored Terence Cuneo, their artist celebrated for illustrating forty years of BritRail history, who always marks his art with a small mouse.

At a glance, InterCity 225's livery appears similar to BritRail's diesel Inter-City 125 trains—gray and white with red striping—but 225's head-turning Mark 4 carriages stand apart, as a new generation's should, because their sleek walls cant aerodynamically inwards.

When you press the push buttons to slide open the external doors (which are wider than before) and board, the first thing you observe is "Metro-Cammell" milled into the serrated aluminum steps. These Mark 4 carriages are the first to be designed and built outside BritRail's workshops by competitive bidders.

When you board, tables through the first-class sections are set with Dudson fine china cups and saucers, pink napkins, cream and sugar packages. Staff look efficient wearing BritRail-issue red ties, gray vests, red-striped white shirts, and black skirts or trousers.

While your Electra locomotive pulls your Superswallow out of Kings Cross station you sense a rocking motion as your Superswallow feels its way to the mainline tracks. Your ride feels modern and efficient yet comfortable.

Into the countryside, the swallow skims quickly atop elevated trestles. You see straw rolled into bundles for farm animals. Wooden picket fences mark off green fields. It stops first at small, brick Peterborough station, already seventy-six miles up the line in forty-six minutes (100 mph). On departure the conductor announces over the intercom, "We would like to welcome those passengers who have just set atrain at Peterborough."

Toward Grantham your Electra locomotive glides through the rolling, green English countryside populated by nibbling, black-faced sheep and snug, tile-roofed brick row houses nestled far away from motorways peppered with commerce. Above Grantham's Georgian houses, you see one of Britain's noblest church spires. This miracle of medieval achievement, built just before 1300, towers 300 feet with its sculptures intact.

Up the East Coast line, golden fields of rapeseed grown for monounsaturated oil brighten one side and bored-looking, brown-and-white dairy cows opposite make a striking contrast to the occasional industrial site.

York, the best-preserved medieval city in Britain, provides your Flying

Scotsman's primary stop. Try to visit York's famous Railway Museum (open daily), which houses a history of the railroad.

Your Flying Scotsman runs through a cutting into Edinburgh's Waverley station (say "Weaver-ly") exactly like a determined fish swimming upstream with a gleam in its eye. When you look down from above, the cutting's banks are so similar to a river's that you are astonished to see rails instead of water below.

Edinburgh's Waverley station is a candidate for one of the world's most beautiful train stations. Its location places it amidst visible highlights of Scotland and below Edinburgh Castle. Waverley is a rambling affair, with tracks on four sides of the covered middle area which is bisected by auto, bus, and taxi traffic.

In the station, you find the Pullman Lounge, Buffet, Railbar, Tourist Accommodation Bureau, City Transport Information, Festival Office (for the Edinburgh Festival), and the "Travel Centre," a wonderful period room with Renaissance walls, a glass cupola with golden cherubs, and pleasant ironwork flattering the skylights.

You also find the elevator entrance to the North British Hotel, a "Shopping Parade" of kiosks, and one of the nicest waiting areas in Europe. Waverley's smooth floors are ideal for suitcases with wheels because you must walk long distances. Look for pushcarts hidden away in the corners.

In front you see the memorial erected by the queen's own Cameron Highlanders to their comrades fallen in Egypt. It shows a man in a kilt.

The Yorkshire Pullman is InterCity's name train between London and Leeds. Here you make reservations either in a normal salon or in the dining room where a complete English breakfast is served. Because of its early, 7:50 A.M. departure time from London, few stops, high velocity, and two catering cars for breakfast, the nine passenger carriages of Yorkshire Pullman are usually sold out with business travelers. First class is crammed with briefcases.

Adventurers have to admit that compared with some of the views they see through the window of a train, their approach to Leeds is not that arresting. But as your Superswallow approaches Leeds station, the familiar preamble to virtually any northern industrial city becomes more interesting.

In the midst of railroad cuttings and warehouses, passengers note an extraordinary tower. During West Yorkshire's heyday a Victorian industrialist modeled a factory chimney after Giotto's campanile for Florence Cathedral — in brick, not marble — and his industrial folly still stands.

From what you hear about Leeds these days, comparing it with a Renaissance city would not be out of place. It is, according to its champions, the new capital of England's revived and assertive North. Its magnetism is expected to increase now that business travelers commute to Leeds from London aboard the Superswallow in less than two hours.

After learning of Leeds' revival, it comes as something of a disappointment for an adventurer to stroll down its main business streets. Buildings like the magnificent Town Hall and the Corn Exchange show an undeniable grandeur, but Leeds also has more than its fair share of bleak and discolored office blocks. Leeds station, in the center of town, is a covered, efficient, medium-sized station. On the concourse to your left when you arrive, you find telephones, the Pullman Lounge, luggage checking, ticketing and train information. Arrows point to city information nearby outside.

Leeds' station's best feature, facing City Square, is the 1937 Queens Hotel (now operated by Trusthouse Forte) with its art deco Portland stone facade.

Mark 4's spacious interiors surprise first-time passengers with their radical departure from the standard train look that they expect from BritRail. Designers created a restful ambience with decorative shiny chrome-plate tubing, soothing gray fabrics, diffused ceiling lighting, indirect light spilling down the wall, pink linen gardenias and Dudson china set upon permanently anchored gray tabletops, and overlapping black and white box designs in the woven carpet.

Variations in seating layout and full-height tinted glass screens disguise the length of the salon and create an intimate first-class interior. In the middle of the carriage, files of 1 + 2 seats change to 2 + 1, offsetting the aisle and creating an interesting focal point, or key.

Tip: For individuals or pairs, the roomiest seats are those facing pairs at the key: numbers 12F and 12B; 13F and 13B. (*F* for front-facing and *B* for back-facing.)

The gray plush seats, with antimacassars embroidered with ivory swallows, recline a few inches with a tug on the black release. Put your soft-sided luggage in the overhead racks; store your hard suitcases and backpacks in the ample space near the entryways.

The bar/buffet (say "buffey") section is situated between first- and second-class sections. You find pay telephones in both.

The decor in the second-class carriage is rosier, not gray. Adventurers sit two-opposite-two throughout, which prevented designers from staggering the files. Decorators instead staggered tinted glass partitions and inserted occasional tables to achieve a social atmosphere with denser seating.

In second class, service personnel push snack trolleys through carpeted aisles (what a surprise to find rough-wearing synthetic tweed carpeting in second class!). Adventurers use tables folding down from seat backs.

Although the 225s boast a step-change in comfort over predecessor InterCity carriages marked "125" (for mph), Mark 4 carriages are not stenciled "225." Some think this may be because additional 225 carriages may be used for the future acceleration of Britain's West Coast Line to 250 kilometers per hour (155 mph) scheduled for 1994.

Weekday InterCity 225 Service, London to Leeds

	London (Kings Cross) dep.	Peterborough dep.	Grantham dep.	Newark N'gate dep.	Retford dep.	Doncaster dep.	Wakefield W'gate dep.	Leeds arr.
	0700	0751	0813	0825	0840	0857	0916	0938
(Y)	0750	....	....	....	....	....	....	0957
	0820	0911	0933	0944	....	1011	1030	1052
	0910	0956	1018	....	1039	1056	1120	1137
	1010	1056	1118	1129	1144	1156	1220	1237
(Y)	1110	1201	1223	1234	....	1301	1320	1342
	1210	1256	1318	1329	....	1356	1415	1437
	1310	....	1413	1424	1439	1456	1515	1537
	1410	1501	1523	....	....	1556	1615	1637
	1510	1556	....	1625	1640	1656	1716	1738
(Y)	1550	....	....	....	....	1727	1746	1807
	1625	1711	1733	....	1754	1811	1830	1852
(Y)	1710	....	1811	....	....	1845	1904	1922
(Y)	1750	....	1856	....	....	1930	1947	2011
	1825	....	1929	1941	1955	2012	2031	2053
	1910	1956	2018	2030	2045	2102	2127	2143
	2010	2056	2118	2129	2145	2156	2226	2237

Weekday InterCity 225 Service, Leeds to London

	Leeds dep.	Wakefield W'gate dep.	Doncaster dep.	Retford dep.	Newark N'gate dep.	Grantham dep.	Peterborough dep.	London (Kings Cross) arr.
	0500	0512	0531	0546	0601	0613	0635	0731
	0610	0622	0641	0656	....	....	0740	0836
	0640	0652	0711	....	....	0742	....	0853
	0710	0722	....	....	....	....	....	0909
(Y)	0730	0742	....	0810	0824	....	....	0948
	0850	0904	0924	....	0947	0959	1021	1115
	1010	1022	1041	1057	1112	1123	1145	1243
(Y)	1110	1122	1141	....	1205	1217	....	1335
	1210	1222	1241	1257	1311	1323	1346	1444
	1310	1322	1341	....	1405	1417	1439	1540
	1410	1422	1441	....	....	1513	1535	1637
(Y)	1435	1448	1509	....	....	1541	1603	1706
	1510	1522	1541	....	1605	1617	....	1735
	1610	1622	1641	....	....	1713	1735	1837
	1710	1722	1741	....	1805	1817	....	1936
	1810	1822	1841	1856	1911	1923	1945	2047
	1915	1927	1946	....	2013	2025	2047	2145
	2027	2040	2103	2118	2132	2144	2206	2309

(Y) Yorkshire Pullman.

The Gutsy Kyle Line
Wild and Romantic

While your Kyle train's gutsy Class 156 Super Sprinter diesel railcar, its face painted safety-yellow, climbs steeply into the sparsely settled northwest corner of Scotland, your fellow passengers prepare for the wildest and most romantic passage in all of Great Britain. For best results, sit on the right.

The Highlands' wild landscape and sparse population make building difficult and expensive, yet Kyle was ultimately served. Riding the Kyle line from Inverness to Kyle of Lochalsh reveals the essence of Scotland, exposing tough new images every moment. Your eighty-two-mile run shows peaks, headlands, forlorn islands and skerries, lochs and glens — and yet cries of protest from the local people were needed in 1974 to save this line much admired by train-lovers and adventurers.

When your train pulls in at one of the fourteen lonely stations along the line, villagers climb aboard, marvel at the new train, and greet friends. Postal workers collect the mail while passengers board from creaky wooden footstools still used because there are few boarding platforms.

Your Kyle train is designed for longer-distance, cross-country journeys. Five sets of panoramic windows, each with about six feet of anti-glare, tinted, and double-glazed glass, show you a changing picture of Scotland's Highlands.

You never lose sight of the views. The line twists so tightly that you see both the driver ahead and the carriages trailing you as you round the many curves.

Kyle line trains run every day of the week from the brightly remodeled Inverness station. BritRail Passes and Scottish Travelpasses are welcome. Be sure to pick up a free Kyle line color brochure at the Travel Centre. Maps and cameras are required equipment on this line.

Passing over the nine arches of the 1990-rebuilt stone viaduct over the river Ness, you travel half an hour to Dingwall. In the green fields past Dingwall, try to picture one of the bloodiest clan battles in history, pitting the Mackenzies against the MacDonalds in 1429. It took place on Knockfarril (579 feet), near the vitrified fort built by King Brude of the Picts.

Now you climb steeply past Raven Rock, hunching 250 feet over the line to your left. At the summit of your first climb you see the dramatic contrast between the quieter green countryside dotted with cattle that stretches back below your train to Dingwall and the harsh Highlands ahead. Over the crest you approach brown, lifeless hills, wild woodlands, and rocky landscapes. Until the beginning of June, snow hugs mountains you see on your right.

Your modern Sprinter picks up speed on the downhill slope, crosses the Blackwater, and races beside Loch Garve on your right. Loch Garve, which means "Rough Lake," is mirror-smooth on calm days, and you see the reflection

KYLE LINE

KYLE OF LOCHALSH

Duirinish
Plockton
Duncraig
Stromeferry
Attadale
Strathcarron
Achnashellach
Achnasheen
Achanalt
Loch Luichart
Garve
Dingwall
INVERNESS

N

0   5   10

in the lake of pine-covered Little Wyvis (2,497 feet). The greater bulk of Ben Wyvis (3,297 feet) hulks behind it.

Your diesel coasts to a stop at Garve beside the tiny, tan, plaster station house surrounded in summer by cut wheat cropped in the fields. You see the pink Garve Hotel nearby. Garve, in the mountains of Wester Ross, is a camping center during the summer.

From Garve you pass through rolling countryside and past reforesting plantations. Passing over the Corriemoillie Summit (429 feet), you see heather-clad Loch Luichart with birches lined along its shores. The sky is incandescent with blue. The six miles of Loch Luichart join the weather systems east and west.

Loch Luichart was the first lake in the Highlands used to generate electricity in 1952. The hydroelectric project lifted the water twenty feet and submerged two miles of land, including the former track and station. Your train has been rerouted to the hastily built stone station house replacing the one sitting underwater.

You enter Strath Bran on the south side of Loch a Chuilinn, then cross quickly to the north side of sparkling Loch Achanalt (the two lakes are practically continuous) past marshy fields to Achanalt station.

Continuing along Strath Bran through wet, green grasslands, with desolate mountains in the distance, the scenery hardens. When you approach the tiny village of Achnasheen, meaning "Field of Rain," you have reached the bleakest bit of the line.

Your Sprinter comes to a stop. Post-office workers unload mail. Then your car climbs again. The treeless and rocky hills are especially attractive to a certain breed of moutaineer. Looking westward toward Glen Docherty you see the Torridon Mountains, old even in geologic terms. Liathach is the great barrel peak to the left, banded with hoops of sandstone and rising shear. To its right you see high-ridged Ben Eighe, looking white as snow but really covered with pale quartzite fragments for much of its height.

The summit of the line, Luib summit, lies only 700 feet above sea level between Loch Scaven and Loch Gowen, which drain into different seas. It is not high, but wild. You hear the crying of curlews and the loud, fluting calls of European sandpipers. Sometimes you see herds of deer, and golden eagles soaring on broad wings. In September, you may well hear great stags roaring at one another.

You almost hear your heated diesel sighing with relief as it heads downhill. At the Glencarron halt, some of the passengers with packs, ropes, and pickaxes climb off, planning to scale the cleft peak of Fuar Tholl (2,968 feet) on your right.

You then enter the deer-haunted Achnashellach Forest, thick with spruce, willow, birch, and holly. Watch for the splendid view of Glen Carron on your left before you glide into Achnashellach station.

Out of Achnashellach you pass Loch Dhugaill, surrounded with spruce. This is the country of the oldest rocks in the world, Archean gneiss forming its floor and Cambrian quartzite its walls, so that the predominant colors are pinks and grays.

At Strathcarron, the second double-tracked station, you pass the return train. Your driver must stop to pick up a token to continue. You lean out the window and listen for the train coming from Kyle.

Impatient train-lovers and camera hawks rush outside to the head of the train and climb onto the iron overpass to snap photos of the imminent meeting. You cheer and applaud when the drivers meet. Then the photographers race back to their seats for fear of being abandoned at this remote stop. It is possible to take the train halfway to Kyle and then immediately travel back on the return train, but were you to do so you would miss the more spectacular half.

Past Strathcarron, a warm burst of air prompts you to remove your parka. You leave behind cold hills and enter the softer Gulf Stream climate.

Across the lake to your right, you see the whitewashed cottages of Loch Carron village gaily bedecked with roses. Loch Carron had good herring and salmon fishing before fishing failed about 1850, too early for the Kyle line to be of any help.

Loch Carron widens on your right, and the pressing question of the moment, as you look back at Fuar Tholl, is whether you really make out the famous profile of George Washington in the outline of the mountain.

You stop next at Attadale, meaning "Valley of the Fight." Here you try to imagine Vikings dueling and sporting. You run side by side with the highway between Attadale and Stromeferry through tall spruce forests on dangerously steep slopes.

Stromeferry, at the narrowest part of Loch Carron, was a short-lived terminus of ships to the Hebridean Islands, but piracy and shipwrecks abruptly terminated trading.

This last part of the Kyle line, past Duncraig, is the most spectacular. Look sharply, for the scenery dashes by faster than words. On level ground you race past the village of Plockton before finally slowing for Plockton's train station on the western outskirts.

Plockton is the gem of the Kyle line. Your train curves along the shore revealing gleaming white cottages across azure water and the striking, pink-rock Applecross peaks in the background. Plockton owes its size to the days when its schooners traded as far away as the Baltic. It looks like an island from your view but is actually on a thin promontory.

You see it best from across the water, a classic picture that sells well. You see paintings of this scene, complete with romantic yachts decorating the foreground, hanging in parlors and pubs throughout Britain.

When you run along the lakeside between tall mountains past Plockton, you become more excited than during any other section of the line. You see the western shore. You had not imagined such enchanting colors. Clouds, seaweed, and waterfalls suffuse in a soft, bluish light. Dozens of rivulets dash down. Granite chunks lie pink in the water, freckled with bright gold algae. Glorious views glow in changing shades of watercolor.

Past Duirinish, you travel inland through the Drumbuie crofting area. You realize your trip has to end soon when you cross the wild coast colored with orange lichen-daubed rocks, tide pools alive with sea creatures, and magnificent vistas of islands with pig-Latin names: Rassay, Scalpay, Loggay, Pabay, and the Crowlin Islands.

Breathe deeply the salty air when you step off in the Kyle of Lochalsh station. The terminus, whose site was blasted from solid rock, is right on water's edge. Fishing boats, cottages, the old hotel, the ferry, and the incomparable scenery make Kyle one of the best-placed stations in Britain. Photographers immediately scurry up the hill behind the Railway Terrace next to the Tourist Information Centre to capture on film the big, sweeping picture of mountains, islands, and the houses that look like white miniatures ready to tumble into the sea.

Kyle is Gaelic meaning "strait" or "narrows." It was simply "Kyle," population 600, until it took on its elegant new name on that historic day in November 1897 when dignitaries from all over Scotland came to declare the railroad officially open.

It is by no means the end of your travels. Adventurers cross free, on foot, aboard the eight-minute shuttle ferry crossings to Kyleakin on the Isle of Skye. From here, travel by bus across Skye to Armadale for the Caledonian Mac-Brayne ferry back to Mallaig and the return West Highland BritRail connection to Fort William on the Glasgow-London mainline.

Some adventurers plan their Kyle visit to connect with one of the thrice-weekly Caledonian MacBrayne sailings to Mallaig.

The Lochalsh Hotel, the old-fashioned resort hotel opposite the train station at water's edge, offers overnighters magnificent views across the sound of the Isle of Skye, except of course when the famous Skye mist descends.

Kyle Line Summer Service

*		*				*	*	*	
0655	1015	1225	1755	dep.	INVERNESS	arr.	0930	1403	1749	1945
0714	1034	1234	1814	dep.	Muir of Ord	dep.	0913	1346	1732	1911

0722	1046	1252	1822	dep.	Dingwall	dep.	0905	1338	1724	1915
0743	1112	1316	1848	dep.	Garve	dep.	0842	1315	1701	1847
0752	1123	....	1857	dep.	Loch Luichart	dep.	0832	1305	....	1835
0759	1131	....	1903	dep.	Achanalt	dep.	0824	1257	....	1826
0813	1146	....	1917	dep.	Achnasheen	dep.	0814	1247	....	1813
0833	1157	....	2028	dep.	Achnashellach	dep.	0752	1226	....	1753
0843	1220	1409	2044	dep.	Strathcarron	dep.	0743	1219	1610	1742
0849	1228	....	2052	dep.	Attadale	dep.	0737	1213	....	1734
0900	1238	....	2102	dep.	Stromeferry	dep.	0725	1200	....	1724
0908	1246	....	2110	dep.	Duncraig	dep.	0716	1151	....	1715
0912	1250	1436	2114	dep.	Plockton	dep.	0713	1148	1543	1713
0916	1254	....	2118	dep.	Duirinish	dep.	0709	1144	....	1709
0927	1304	1450	2128	arr.	KYLE	dep.	0700	1135	1530	1700

*Daily except Sunday.

Caledonian MacBrayne Summer Ferry Service*

dep.	arr.	dep.	arr.	dep.	arr.	dep.	arr.
Armadale	Mallaig	Mallaig	Armadale	Kyle	Mallaig	Mallaig	Kyle
0910	0940	0815	0845	1615	1815	1200	1400
1130	1200	1020	1050	(Tuesdays, Thursdays, and			
1500	1530	1300	1330	Saturdays only)			
1800	1830	1630	1700				
2000	2030	1900	1930				

(Mondays to Saturdays only)

*Covered by Scottish Highlands & Islands Travelpass, but not BritRail Pass.

Isle of Man
Four-Ring Entertainment

Your coastal car swings out to Laxey Head. A splendid view opens beneath you of Douglas's Victorian promenade, its pink-and-green horse trams, and the Irish Sea breaking on its strand. When your climb toughens and your frail car tilts upward more steeply from one in thirty-eight feet to one in twenty-four, you see the rugged coastline stretching out to far Maughold Head.

Your car labors at its effort. It vibrates, shakes, and rumbles. Wood rubbing on wood sings of excellent maintenance.

Your cautious pace gives you time to appreciate the view as you near Ballaragh, meaning "Place of the Rocks." You could not find a better name. Cliffs rise to more than 600 feet. While you run along the cliffside more than 500 feet above the frothy breaking waves of Bulgham Bay, you are traveling on one of the most spectacular railroad stretches anywhere in the British Isles.

When you near the end of your dramatic climb beside the cliff, you reach

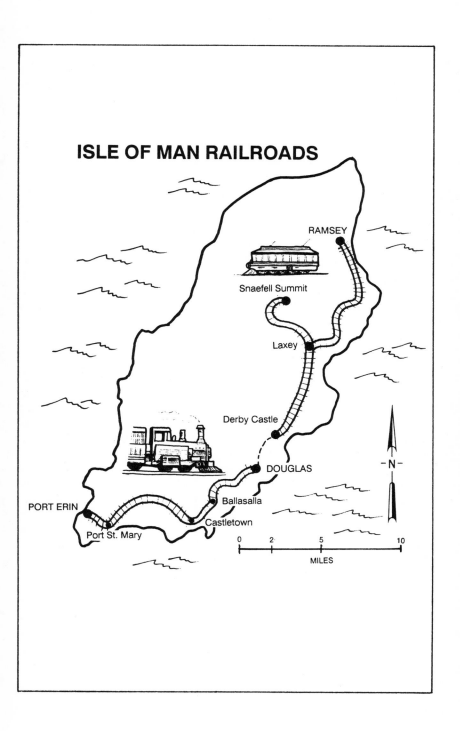

ISLE OF MAN RAILROADS

RAMSEY

Snaefell Summit

Laxey

Derby Castle

DOUGLAS

Ballasalla

PORT ERIN

Castletown

Port St. Mary

- N -

0   2   5   10

MILES

the highest point of Isle of Man's coastline, 588 feet above the crashing surf. Turning inland, your car descends more or less continuously through lush green countryside to Ramsey. The Manx Electric Railroad's (MER) charming electric streetcars trundle through glens and atop cliffs. Aboard its cars you see some of the loveliest and most romantic scenery on the Isle of Man, the thirty-mile-long dot in the Irish Sea midway between the coasts of England, Ireland, Scotland, and Wales.

MER's three-foot-gauge electric fleet is admired by train-lovers the world around. Their pleasing cars have waged a continual battle against modernization and closure since their delivery and first use in 1893-1906. Now that they earn their keep by attracting visitors, they receive funding adequate to ensure their safe running and meticulous maintenance.

The Isle of Man has been heavily hit by changes in vacation patterns. The railroads and the unspoiled environment used to attract workers from the industrial north of England (Birmi ham, Manchester, and Liverpool). Brightly polished steam locomotives, cole ul additions to the countryside, took them to deep Manx glens, patchwork uilts of fields, the breathtaking sea—places their friends in smoke-filled cities could hardly contemplate. Now, "sun holidays" on the Mediterranean lure away its visitors with cheap airfares and mass air transportation.

From 500,000 annual visitors after World War II, Isle of Man now welcomes only 200,000. The result is that you can take advantage of tremendous overcapacity and remarkable, well-maintained electric and mountain railroads and steam trains. With the drying-up of Man's traditional tourist market, a new breed of visitor has discovered this anachronism. The Isle of Man is known the world over as a train-lover's paradise. (For information visit or write the Isle of Man Tourist Board, 13 Victoria Street, Douglas, Isle of Man.)

You board the MER within reach of the salt spray at the north end of the Douglas promenade and climb to almost 600 feet along a precipitous ledge before returning almost level with the Irish Sea in Ramsey, 17¾ miles and seventy-five minutes to the north.

Derby Castle station lies at the northern end of Douglas's Victorian promenade. (The unique steam locomotive trip to Port Erin, from the Douglas Bank Hill station, is described later in this section.) Purchase your tickets at the whimsical ticket house designed with lacquered branches to resemble an illustration in a child's fairy-tale book. BritRail Passes are not honored on the Isle of Man.

One glance around the car reveals meticulous attention to preservation and detail. Your lacquered 1899 car shines with such a gloss that you can make out your reflection in the walnut paneling. Seats covered with flowery maroon plush have reversible backs for travel in either direction.

Leaving Douglas's promenade, anchored on the opposite end by the bright Gaiety Playhouse, your car crawls and squeaks up the persistent rise. Squealing wheels rounding the curves excite remarks from many of the younger passengers. Passing the ungated level crossings, your motorman sounds his air whistle or gongs loudly to tell automobile drivers that he is insisting on his right-of-way. Soon after departure comes the spectacular stretch along the cliffs high above Bulgham Bay. When you near the stone-covered Howstrake station, look down at the splendid panorama of Douglas Bay to the east. To the west, the hedge-lined green fields are filled with grazing sturdy Frisian cows standing like plaster statues ignoring the rain. Black-faced sheep cluster together in the fields; none are the curious four-horned Loaghtans native to the island.

Your car levels and the motorman eases back on his brass handle before swinging sharply inland and starting his descent, one foot in twenty-four, along the wooded approach to Groudle, the terminus of the 1893 line. The long descent past Groudle into Laxey opens the lovely panorama of the Laxey bay and beach, the tiny harbor with its neat, white-painted lighthouses, and the headlands beyond.

At Fairy Cottage and South Cape stops you see the signs, "Alight here for the beach." In summer there is a mini-bus return.

MER shares the brown Laxey station house with the Snaefell Mountain Railroad, which runs daily during the summer. Their terminus lies in a romantic wooded glen in the center of the village, decorated by nearby Christ Church.

While in Laxey, walk down the convenient, well-marked path through the green, gorse-clad valley of Agneash to visit Lady Isabella. She's not a member of the British aristocracy but the name given to the celebrated Laxey Wheel, the largest waterwheel in the world at seventy-two feet in diameter. Built in 1854, the red-and-white wheel pumped the Laxey lead and silver mines until the 1920s. Now it is primarily a well-manicured tourist attraction.

Your car scrapes the white paint of the Mines Tavern leaving Laxey. It is a wonderful, old-fashioned British pub with needlepoint chairs, gleaming brass, shining glasses, darts, and an open fire.

You run parallel to the Snaefell Mountain train until it turns up the mountain and begins to climb at a gradient of one in twelve feet on its thirty-minute journey. When you climb Snaefell in that train, sit on the left side so you can see the rail of the Fell brake mounted on its side between the running rails.

The hardest part of your trip is over. Your MER car seems to fly past farms — sheep, cows, and green- and straw-colored meadows ringed with stone walls harboring scores of cats, not the tailless Manx breed, husbanded in Douglas's cattery, but the common alley variety.

About a mile past the green hut beside the Cornea halt, you pass Ballafayle, the residence of Sir Charles Kerruish. He is the Speaker of the House of Keys, the ancient parliament which celebrated its one-thousandth anniversary in 1979. Look for his Manx "Three Legs" flag fluttering in the breeze.

Descending steadily toward Ramsey Bay, you see the Victorian hotels lining the Ramsey waterfront, a smaller echo of Douglas, and you find this symmetry most satisfying. Your car formerly ran out on the 2,000-foot Ramsey Pier but now you complete your electric railroad run not far from the city center.

Port Erin Line

The Port Erin line, the longest narrow-gauge steam railroad line in the British Isles, uses historic carriages pulled by one of the 2-4-0 engines — Loch (1874), Maitland (1905), Hutchinson (1908), or Kissock (1910) — from Douglas Bank Hill station in the Isle's capital city, to the southwestern hamlet of Port Erin. Remember, BritRail Passes are not honored on the Isle of Man.

The 15½-mile stretch opened August 1, 1874. It is built now much as it was then. The train's story is one of evolution, with change sometimes for the better, often for the worse, but with a spirit of continuity for over a century.

The four steam locomotives still used are a fraction of the sixteen original ones. They are lovingly maintained and professionally cared for. Two are red, one is blue, and one is green, and they are named for original directors of the railroad. They look chubby because of the side tanks holding cold water, and they don't need a tender for supplemental fuel.

Buy your ticket for Port Erin at Douglas's red-brick train station at the head of the harbor. Arched ornamental gates sparkle with domes and pinnacles still glittering with the gold leaf applied in the railroad's more optimistic days.

You depart Douglas with a climb of one foot in sixty-five. You can feel your blue No. 12 engine, the Hutchinson (1908), working hard. Sitting in one of the original wooden carriages, you really know you are traveling by steam. Even the Hutchinson's modest climb produces loud puffing, smoke, soot, and flying cinders, leaving you little doubt that there is a steam engine up front.

You cross the Douglas River on the 1979 girder-span Nunnery Bridge. Past the Nunnery on your left, one of the Isle's "Stately Homes," you enter a narrow rock cutting where engines are prone to lose traction in autumn due to fallen leaves.

After a half-mile, you see spectacular cliff views opening out toward Santon Head in the south, and toward Little Ness in the Douglas direction.

Past Port Soderick station (3⅛ miles, fourteen minutes), you run through the wooded Crogga valley — a treat in bluebell time. In season, dazzling displays of rhododendrons open up beside the line. Children reach from windows to catch wild flowers and the leaves brushing gently against your train as it passes.

Beyond Santon (5⅝ miles, twenty-four minutes), the main highway runs below the track on your left but climbs up and passes over the train at the Blackboards. You don't see any black boards now, but when the road traffic was drawn by horse, a wooden screen was erected between the train and the highway to prevent horses from taking flight at smoke-belching monsters. The airport you see on your left is Ronaldsway, site of the celebrated battle in Manx history. From here, Manx Airlines serves London, Liverpool, and Dublin.

Break your trip at Castletown (9 7/8 miles, forty-six minutes), the capital of the Isle until the 1860s, to explore Castle Rushen, one of the finest preserved medieval castles in Europe. Its Elizabethan clock with only the hour hand is still in use. You also see the Nautical Museum, the harbor, the beach, and King Williams College where Bragg, the Nobel-prize-winning physicist, was educated.

When the Hutchinson pulls you past Port St. Mary (15¾ miles, sixty-two minutes), you see Port Erin in the distance, nestling between ground rising to the south toward the Sound, which separates the Island from the Calf of Man, and the high ground of Bradda Head to the north. Crowned by Milners Tower, Bradda Head makes a popular subject for amateur photographers.

When you arrive at the red-brick Port Erin station (15⅝ miles, sixty-five minutes), head for the beach or train museum. You will see there the locomotive that hauled the first train of 1873, a great sampling of historic locomotives, the coaches used by Queen Elizabeth in 1972, and those used by the Duke of Sutherland on opening day, 1873.

After the electric trams, mountain railroads, and steam locomotives, your four-ring entertainment is completed by returning to Douglas and riding its famous horse trams along the promenade. After being pulled by one of the nineteenth-century iron horses, you wonder which is more temperamental, the four-footed white trotters or the red, blue, and green steam locomotives.

Douglas is served by the m.v. *Tynwald* car ferry (3,763 tons) of the Isle of Man Steam Packet Seaways, with four-hour crossings to Heysham, Liverpool, Fleetwood, Dublin, and Belfast.

Summer Manx Electric Railroad Service
between Douglas, Laxey, and Ramsey (not Sundays)

1000	1200	1400	1500	1700	DOUGLAS*	1145	1310	1445	1645	1745
1012	1212	1412	1512	1712	Groudle	1133	1258	1433	1633	1733
1020	1220	1420	1520	1720	Garwick	1125	1250	1425	1625	1725
1030	1230	1430	1530	1730	LAXEY	1115	1240	1415	1615	1715
1045	1245	1445	1545	1745	Dhoon	1100	1230	1400	1600	1700
1055	1255	1455	1555	1755	Ballaglass	1050	1220	1350	1550	1650

1055	1255	1455	1555	1755	Ballaglass	1050	1220	1350	1550	1650
1103	1303	1503	1603	1803	Ballajora	1042	1212	1342	1542	1642
1115	1315	1515	1615	1815	RAMSEY	1030	1200	1330	1530	1630

*Derby Castle station.

Summer Manx Steam Railroad Service
between Douglas and Port Erin (not Saturdays)

	*								*	
1010	1050	1145	1410	1610	DOUGLAS	1120	1310	1520	1635	1720
1024	1108	1159	1423	1624	Port Soderick	1108	1255	1509	1624	1707
1034	1118	1209	1433	1634	Santon (R)	1058	1245	1459	1614	1657
1046	1130	1220	1446	1646	Ballasalla	1046	1235	1446	1602	1646
1056	1139	1228	1455	1656	Castletown	1036	1228	1437	1553	1635
1100	1143	1234	1458	1700	Ballabeg (R)	1029	1220	1430	1546	1629
1106	1149	1240	1505	1705	Colby	1025	1216	1426	1542	1625
1112	1156	1247	1512	1712	Port St. Mary	1018	1209	1419	1535	1619
1115	1200	1250	1515	1715	PORT ERIN	1015	1205	1415	1530	1615

*Sunday through Thursday, July and August only.
(R) Request stop.

Gwynedd
Sea, Steam, and Slate

Hold on to your tongue. You struggle and stutter on the Welsh consonants of Blaenau Ffestiniog, Tan-y-bwlch, Betws-y-coed, and Llyn Ystradau.

Your adventure in Gwynedd, Wales' north county, takes you beside the crashing waves of the Irish Sea, below soaring thirteenth-century castles, and through green valleys on a narrow-gauge, Victorian steam train.

You first follow the Cambrian Coast of Wales on BritRail. A classic steam locomotive of the Ffestiniog slate railroad takes you on a volunteer-restored narrow-gauge line, and BritRail collaborates once more by sweeping you down the Conwy Valley line past Conwy Castle.

Entering Wales at Machynlleth on BritRail's secondary line from Shrewsbury (with mainline connections from London), guards split your train, so be sure you are in the correct segment. Sit on the left. Once past Machynlleth you have a new feeling—less cultivation and more wilderness. The river pours into the bay. You run past vast tidelands. Waterfowl of all feather are stalking the mud flats for food; boats are aground waiting for the return of the sea. Your train runs along an embankment, through cuttings and tunnels on high ground where the sea thunders against cliffs.

Your train is slow and the panorama great—over salt marsh and fine brown

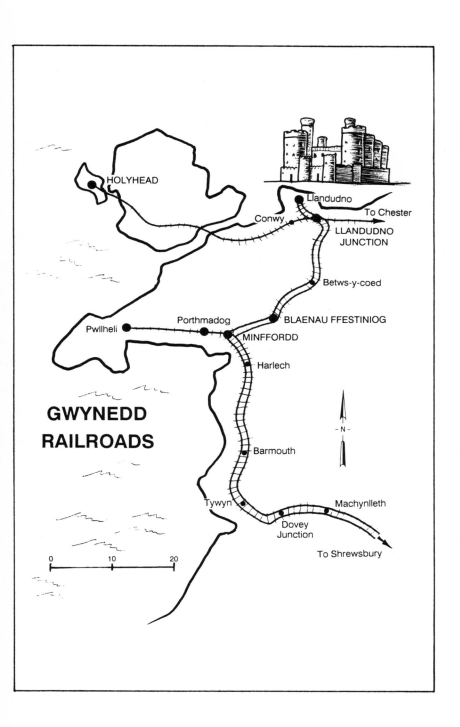

HOLYHEAD

Llandudno

Conwy

To Chester

LLANDUDNO JUNCTION

Betws-y-coed

Porthmadog

BLAENAU FFESTINIOG

Pwllheli

MINFFORDD

Harlech

GWYNEDD RAILROADS

- N -

Barmouth

Tywyn

Machynlleth

Dovey Junction

To Shrewsbury

0   10   20

sand marked only with the footprints of fowl. Fishing boats have found the deepwater channel close to shore. High stone breakwaters show how violent the sea becomes.

Just short of Tywyn station, you pass the Talyllyn Railroad Museum. The sign reads: "Tywyn for the Talyllyn Railway."

Curving high on the cliff, you swing for a memorable vast panorama of the village of Fairbourne (for the railroad of the same name). Steep rocky hills push the track right to the water's edge; you feel the power and beauty of the sea.

Stone walls, and none of them straight, divide the green fields below the mountains into jigsaw pieces filled with sheep of different markings. Rhododendrons bloom profusely.

Soon Harlech Castle comes into view, set on a crag 200 feet above sea level. Look back after passing Harlech for another view of this mighty thirteenth-century fortress.

You debark at the two-level Minffordd station and climb steps up the narrow path to board the private, steam-hauled Ffestiniog Railroad (FR), the greatest of the "Great Little Trains" that steam-train-lovers and adventurers use to explore Wales' normally inaccessible rich, green countryside.

When you have time to spare, board at FR's larger Porthmadog terminus. This gives you a chance to admire Welsh Pony, beautifully painted and lined in the style of the 1920s atop a slate plinth, stroll along Porthmadog's sandy beaches, dine or snack in FR's station restaurant, shop in the large souvenir and model store, and enjoy FR's small museum—but the FR station there is about fifteen minutes across town from the BritRail one.

FR's Minffordd station is unstaffed and lonesome. It has a locked stone station house with green shutters, lonesome green benches, and that's all.

Incorporated in 1832 and operated almost continuously since 1836, the slim-gauge (one foot, 11½ inches) FR stands in the record books as the oldest surviving company in the train transportation business. Now that the volunteers have renewed the operation and restored its antique steam locomotives to their original shine and vigor, FR is a point of pride for everyone of Welsh origin.

BritRail Passes are not accepted on FR, but you can buy a Great Little Trains Wanderer Ticket for eight railroads. Write to the Ffestiniog Railway Company, Harbour Station, Porthmadog, Gwynedd, Wales LL49 9NF.

You sit in first-class observation cars, with high-backed upholstered seats, or third-class two-opposite-one seats. FR won't let you be a second-class adventurer here. (First-class tickets cost about 25 percent more; children under sixteen ride free.)

Your coach is small but your fellow adventurers and the friendly staff give it a happy feeling. The best place to sit to see the rugged scenery is on the east, the same side as the platform at Minffordd. Elbow room is tight, but your interest is fun, not transportation, even while traveling from one end of Wales to the other by using the northern interchange with BritRail.

Your antique locomotive hisses steam and begins its sixty-five-minute trip at Porthmadog's harbor. It runs across the "Cob," an embankment for the toll highway and the railroad across the wide estuary. Its first request stop, Boston Lodge, fenced by original FR ironwork, is the location of the foundry works responsible for maintaining — and in some cases actually building — the rolling stock.

You see the panorama of Snowdonia opening on your left. On the right, you duck your head to see Harlech Castle. Now your rattling carriage begins to tilt upwards for a narrow, tottering, almost continuous climb of one foot in every seventy you pass, sheer above the Vale of Ffestiniog and through the green Snowdonia mountain range with the Dwyryd River meandering below. You look for the pointed summit of Mount Snowdon (3,560 feet), the highest in Wales, barely visible in the distance.

Past Minffordd, your hissing locomotive pauses to take water beside the creeper-covered stationmaster's stone house in Tan-y-bwlch, 7½ miles from Porthmadog. Tracks run around three sides of the parklike bowl in the mountains.

In a few minutes your train puffs through Dduallt and then you begin a spiral — the only one in Britain. A distant nuclear power station appears on your right, on your left, and then on your right again.

Engineers abandoned the original line and built the spiral to gain elevation when the reservoir of the coming Tanygrisiau pumped-storage hydroelectric power station flooded their first tunnel. You pass through a more recent tunnel in a spur of the Moelyn Mountains before you reach the shores of the new manmade lake. Below, you see the former roadbed looking like a grass-topped wall running beside the reservoir (now a gravel highway and perfect for a hiking trail).

From the reservoir, you descend to the Tanygrisiau station, crossing first a road to the parking lot and then Wales' highest road, leading to the top dam of the power station. The automatic traffic lights flash red, the bells clang, and traffic backs up fifteen car lengths, more or less. Some of the motorists take their children from the backseats to have a good view of your classic steam engine hissing past.

In Tanygrisiau look back to a mountain still covered with a shower of chips of slate. It seems more significant to you when you realize this slate is the reason for your train's existence.

It's downhill now. You pass a waterfall and wind between two-story, slate-roof houses built of the same stone as the craggy peaks around you. The calliope-like sound of your train's steam whistle announces your arrival in the FR/BritRail joint terminus in Blaenau Ffestiniog, the slate capital of the world. It was opened virtually on FR's 150th anniversary in 1982.

The Ffestiniog steam operation dates from the grimy times when hand-crafted blue-gray slates were exported around the world for fancy roofing, paving, and fencing. The Welsh slate industry employed 16,000 workers—a quarter of them in the Llechwedd mines in Blaenau Ffestiniog.

Transporting large loads of finished slates became an acute problem by the 1820s. The roads were so rocky that slate had to be first carried in wicker baskets slung over the backs of mules and then transferred to horse-drawn wagons rented from local farmers at rates the slate entrepreneurs considered exorbitant.

After the horses pulled the slates down the Vale of Ffestiniog, the slate was reloaded into small sailing boats, each manned by two men known as Philistines and dressed in tall felt hats like the gamekeepers of the day.

In 1836, management began a simple rail operation. Tracks were laid and gravity-drawn trams loaded with slate were rolled down from the quarries to a new port facility. Horses hauled the empty cars back up (and then returned by riding down in so-called "dandy cars"). Passenger transportation began in 1865, two years after the horses had been replaced by steam locomotives.

On the FR's celebration of 150 years service in 1986, a gravity slate train was run for the first time in nearly fifty years—and stole the show.

To save the railroad, in severe disrepair in 1954, most of its shares were transferred to a charitable trust. More than 6,500 dedicated volunteers and an accomplished salaried staff turned it from near ruin into a top pleasure railroad. Any profit is returned for expansion and improvement.

There are six steam locomotives (the "Merddin Emrys" was returned in 1988 to Victorian-style service), including strange-looking "double" engines known as Fairlie Articulated. These pieces of machinery are polished, buffed, and lubricated to peak efficiency and luster. "Prince," one of the original six locomotives, restored again to a vivid recreation of an early FR livery, is again in regular passenger service. Prince's twin locomotive is the highlight of FR's museum in Porthmadog.

Today FR carries only passengers on its 13½-mile route, giving you an excellent way to see the wooded Welsh countryside once ripped apart by the Industrial Revolution.

At Blaenau Ffestiniog interchange, cross a crooked concrete footbridge above the FR and BritRail lines rather than simply changing platforms. A bus from the train station takes you to the Llechwedd slate caverns, Wales' largest working slate mine.

The Conwy Valley line takes you on your final segment through industrial history because of the stone quarries. You travel from the mountainous heart of the country, following the Conwy River to its estuary. Leaving Blaenau Ffestiniog you travel through a long tunnel through the mountains. Then you follow the twisting route of the River Lledr, winding downward through rocky cuttings and under rough stone bridges.

Be sure to sit up front, behind BritRail's driver, for the excellent view down the Conwy Valley. You meet the North Wales scenic line at Llandudno Junction (where you see a splendid view of the magnificent thirteenth-century Conwy Castle). Here, diesel InterCity high-speed mainline trains will whisk you along the beautiful North Wales coast west to Holyhead (for ferries to Ireland) or east to Chester (for London).

Summer Service of the Ffestiniog Railway

Dep. Harbor PORTHMADOG	Dep. MINFFORDD	Dep. Penrhyn	Dep. Tan-y-bwlch	Arr. BLAENAU FFESTINIOG
Mondays to Thursdays				
0845	0854	0900	0920	0950
0945	0954	1000	1020	1050
1045	1054	1100	1120	1150
1145	1154	1200	1220	1250
1245	1254	1300	1320	1350
1345	1354	1400	1420	1450
1445	1454	1500	1520	1550
1545	1554	1600	1620	1650
1645	1654	1700	1720	1750
1845	1854	1900	1920	1950
Fridays, Saturdays, and Sundays				
0945	0954	1000	1020	1050
1100	1109	1115	1135	1205
1215	1224	1230	1250	1320
1330	1339	1345	1405	1435
1445	1454	1500	1520	1550
1600	1609	1615	1635	1705

Dep. BLAENAU FFESTINIOG	Dep. Tan-y-bwlch	Dep. Penrhyn	Dep. MINFFORDD	Arr. Harbor PORTHMADOG
Mondays to Thursdays				
1000	1025	1045	1050	1105
1100	1125	1145	1150	1205

1200	1225	1245	1250	1305
1300	1325	1345	1350	1405
1400	1425	1445	1450	1505
1500	1525	1545	1550	1605
1600	1625	1645	1650	1705
1700	1725	1745	1750	1805
1800	1825	1845	1850	1905
2000	2025	2045	2050	2105

Fridays, Saturdays, and Sundays

1100	1133	1150	1155	1210
1215	1248	1305	1310	1325
1330	1403	1420	1425	1440
1445	1518	1535	1540	1555
1600	1633	1650	1655	1710
1725	1753	1809	1814	1825

All trains call on request at Boston Lodge, Plas, Dduallt, and Tanygrisiau.

Weekday Summer Service
Machynlleth—Minffordd—Pwllheli

0827	1039	1237	1400	1618	dep.	MACHYNLLETH	arr.	1337	1515	1716	1856	2035
....	1046	....	....	....	dep.	Dovey Jct.	dep.	1316	....	....	....	2026
0848	1101	1258	1421	1639	dep.	Aberdovey	dep.	1310	1453	1654	1834	2011
0855	1112	1308	1448	1649	dep.	Tywyn	dep.	1249	1447	1648	1828	2005
0914	1129	1325	1506	1708	dep.	Fairbourne	dep.	1241	1428	1631	1811	1947
0923	1139	1335	1515	1717	arr.	Barmouth	dep.	1204	1357	1540	1740	1918
1003	1140	1336	1516	1718	dep.	Barmouth	arr.	1202	1355	1538	1738	1916
1025	1204	1357	1540	1740	dep.	Harlech	dep.	1148	1341	1522	1724	1903
1039	1218	1411	1554	1754	dep.	MINFFORDD	dep.	1144	1337	1518	1720	1859
1045	1233	1417	1600	1800	dep.	Porthmadog	dep.	1135	1328	1509	1711	1850
1107	1245	1439	1622	1822	arr.	PWLLHELI	dep.	1120	1313	1454	1658	1835

Conwy Valley Line Weekday Summer Service
Llandudno—Blaenau Ffestiniog

0824	1100	1308	1530	1753	dep.	Llandudno	arr.	1042	1323	1526	1748	2019
0833	1109	1317	1539	1810	dep.	LLANDUDNO JUNCTION	arr.	1033	1313	1517	1739	2010
0901	1137	1345	1607	1838	dep.	Betws-y-Coed	dep.	1004	1243	1448	1710	1941
0931	1207	1415	1637	1908	arr.	BLAENAU FFESTINIOG	dep.	0936	1215	1420	1642	1913

Dublin's Electric Odyssey
A Nice Bit of an Outin'

The Irish know that Howth is a seaside place for fishermen, Dun Laoghaire for gentry, Dalkey for artists, Killiney for lovers, and Bray for all of the above.

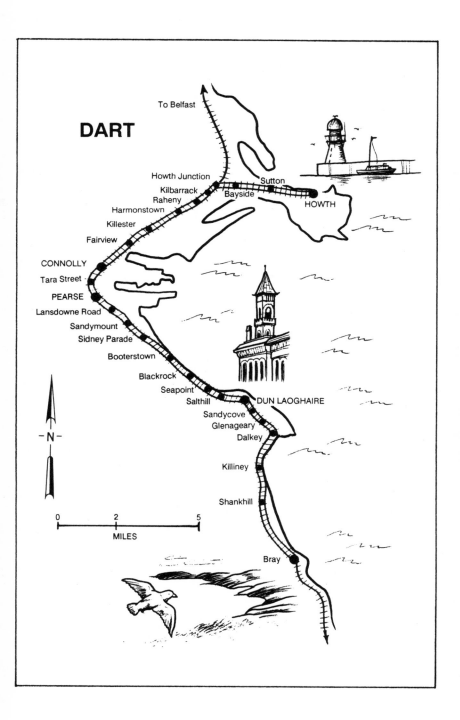

DART

To Belfast

Howth Junction
Kilbarrack
Raheny
Harmonstown
Killester
Fairview

CONNOLLY
Tara Street
PEARSE
Lansdowne Road
Sandymount
Sidney Parade
Booterstown
Blackrock
Seapoint
Salthill
Sandycove
Glenageary
Dalkey
Killiney
Shankhill
Bray

Sutton
Bayside
HOWTH

DUN LAOGHAIRE

– N –

0   2   5
MILES

Visiting adventurers may not be familiar with these distinctions, but the Dublin Area Regional Transit (DART) trains make it convenient for you to explore the area around Dublin for yourself, free on an Emerald Isle or Eurailpass. DART runs north to the picturesque fishing village of Howth and south along one of the most scenic stretches of coastline to Bray. You hop on and off to visit pretty coastal towns and yacht harbors, museums, and restaurants.

Dubliners, among the most critical of people, criticized DART when it was proposed. Now that it is running flawlessly, they have taken it to their hearts. They discovered that it is much more than a boon to commuters or a vast technological improvement; it has taken on the character of a leisure pursuit, giving to Dubliners and adventurers "a nice bit of an outin'."

At the northern terminus of DART, Howth (say "Hooth"; the name comes from the Scandinavian "hoved," meaning "head," as hovedbanegard for "head train station") is a mixture historic village, busy fishing port, and Dublin suburb. The sea gulls in Howth are the fattest in the northern hemisphere. One step out from Howth station and you smell the aroma of fresh salmon selling extremely reasonably.

From the summit of the Hill of Howth, 567 feet above the station at sea level, you can see Bay of Dublin, the Wicklow Mountains, and, on a clear day, the top of Mount Snowdon in Wales.

Stone buildings line the pier facing the station. Dry-docked green-and-white, blue-and-brown fishing vessels are propped above the pier, workers scraping and repairing their hulls.

Your DART electric railcar, appropriately green, leaves Howth past heather-covered islands to the west, across mud flats busy with sea gulls, and past shacks and fishing craft in dry dock. After you glide smoothly south past the rear of Parson's steel-fabrication works, you see across the main road to the east, on the high ground, the spire of St. Mary's Church of Ireland emerging above the trees, and below, almost in the shadow of the spire, the entrance gate to Howth Castle.

You pass the first of at least three golf courses—just as green as all Ireland in spring. Just south of Howth, Sutton station lies at the narrowest part of the isthmus connecting Howth with the mainland. Your next stop, Howth Junction, is the joining of mainline trains from Belfast to the DART corridor south to Dublin's Connolly Station.

At Killester, you reach the famous "Skew Bridge." Built in 1843, the bridge was regarded as a triumph of engineering at the time. From here you run on the original embankment, which was entirely surrounded by water a century ago but now is all but lost amidst the ever-expanding land reclamation.

From Killester you glide south past row houses and parks. You see redsweatered men struggling with bad weather on the golf course to the west, and shipping cranes and storage facilities in the distance to the east.

Dublin's Connolly Station, formerly known as Amiens Street Station, is Dublin's major terminus in size but not in number of passengers served. You have access to the Mainline Booking Office, the Information Bureau, the cloakroom, the cafeteria, the central bus station, and taxis.

In 1980–81, IrishRail renovated Connolly in anticipation of DART's introduction. The platforms, roofing, underpasses, and entrances were rebuilt. DART platforms 6 and 7 are adjacent to the mainline trains using platforms 1 to 4. Use these platforms for trains to Belfast, Sligo, and Galway, and for the boat trains to Rosslare Harbor.

When your DART leaves Connolly, you glide almost noiselessly out onto the beginning of the Loop Line over Amiens Street. Take a look at the Italianate tower of the mainline terminal building facing Talbot Street and the fine old grimy and faded red-brick Victorian railroad offices with yellow brick window arches and dull-blue brick band. Inside, workers pilot the entire "space-age" computerized Central Control of today's rail system.

You pass through the rooftops past the new Irish Life Assurance building complex with golden windows. In front you see the Chariot of Life sculpture, "Look Ma, no reins!"

You travel on the elevated railroad to the stop at Tara Street Bridge over the Liffey River, but Tara Street station has no exit or entrance on Tara Street. The station opens onto George's Quay.

The stretch of the Loop Line between the Tara Street station and Pearse Station (formerly Westland Row) is the shortest distance between any two DART stations, yet for so short a stretch you see much: the notable spire of City Quay Parish Church, the more ponderous roofline of St. Mark's, Hawkins House, the darkly tinted glass of the Irish Press newspaper office, and the distinctive 130-foot watchtower of the Tara Street fire station. Finally you pass through Trinity College. Yours may be the only train actually to run through part of a university. The Loop Line viaduct curves gently across the Botany Bay area of the university, giving you a close-up of Trinity's Parade Ground and science buildings.

You arrive on the green ironwork bridge in red-brick Pearse station with antique girders and a glass arch overhead.

From Pearse Station you reach the interesting three-span skew bridge over the Grand Canal. To the west is the tall, gaunt Guinness malt store. Originally, in 1834, planners sketched a single bridge here, but engineering problems necessitated building two, the first almost square on, and the second a genuine "skew" bridge of thirty-three degrees—and both so low that in later years no double-decked streetcar or bus could pass under them.

At Landsdowne Road station, sports fans depart almost beneath a modern two-tier sports stadium straddling the station and the railroad line. This is the mecca of Irish rugby and a regular site for international and European Cup soccer matches.

The annual fair in Donnybrook nearby gave a new word to the English language. Established by King John in 1204, the fair was finally abolished in 1855 because more fistfights broke out outside the bareknuckle prizefighters' rings than within.

The new DART station in the pleasant seaside village of Sandymount, one of the line's most attractive stops, stands on the site of stations dating back to 1835.

Just after Sandymount, and before you stop at Sydney Parade, you see a fine view of Gothic St. John's Church across the green grass of Monkstown Rugby Club. On a late summer evening the church's warm sand-colored stones and its ornamental windows catch the last glow of the setting sun.

Past Sydney Parade, the setting for James Joyce's short story "A Painful Case," you plunge suddenly into a panoramic scene of the bay. Your railcar, like a child dashing eagerly to water's edge, runs along the sands and as close to the seabirds fishing in the waves as prudent.

Past Blackrock, you watch clammers shoveling through the mud flats, filling their red plastic buckets to the limit. The coastline is alive with windsurfers steering their colorful craft and assembling their bright-as-buttons equipment in parking lots from Blackrock to Dun Laoghaire. Yachts dance in the harbor and seawalls protect oceangoing ferries.

Passengers on the overnight Irish Mail train/boat route from London get their first taste of the DART system at Dun Laoghaire (say "Dunleary"). Buses to and from Dublin's Heuston station are also available.

Dun Laoghaire, which was first called "Dunleary" and then "Kingstown" in honor of the visit of King George IV, is primarily a sea town, the only Irish port directly administered by the government and not by locally elected officials. Between the harbor and the DART station, look for the tiny brick office marked by the green i which combines the tourist information office, the "Bureau de Change," and the Sealink office.

DARTing south from Dun Laoghaire to Sandycove takes you beneath seven overpasses including three major road crossings. To complete DART, these either had to be lifted, rebuilt, and the highway approaches altered, or your train's roadbed had to be lowered by about twenty inches. As a result, you now pass over a one-mile stretch of continuously paved concrete railbed, the first in Ireland.

From your stop at Sandycove you see teams of windsurfers, canoeists, and water-skiers in Scotsman's Bay immediately outside Dun Laoghaire's east pier. Walk fifteen minutes from the station to Sandycove's premiere attraction, the

Martello Tower, built in 1804 to withstand the Napoleonic invasion that never came.

From Dalkey's green cement station house, you, like George Bernard Shaw, see beautiful seascapes. Dogs play in waves. Anglers cast into the surf. The great playwright spent the happiest days of his youth here on Torca Hill, overlooking the splendid sweep of Bay of Dublin.

South of Dalkey, you travel on cliffs overhanging the sea. Mountains rise in the distance. At Killiney you have a chance to walk parallel to the DART line for breathtaking views, or to climb the steep lane opposite the station and in ten minutes reach a charming district distinguished by early Irish Christian architecture. Past Killiney and Shankhill you journey inland; white row houses separate you from the ocean. You pass through the middle of a golf course. All Ireland looks like a golf course in springtime, but this is probably the only golf course with a commuter hazard.

You now approach Bray, one of Ireland's premiere seaside resorts. The welcoming promontory of Bray Head stands high above the sea and Bray crowns the southern shore of Bay of Dublin.

At Bray station you see the original iron pillars bearing the logo, "Irish Engineering Co., Seville Works, 1853." "David's Diner and Market" sells fresh fruit and soft ice cream.

Bray, in County Wicklow, the only city outside County Dublin to be served by DART, is a fishing harbor, a holiday resort, a town of handsome urban architecture, an important shopping area, . . . and the honeymoon capital of Ireland.

First and Last Dublin DART Services

Mondays to Saturdays

	Morning	Night					Morning		Night	
	0655	2255	2345	dep.	HOWTH	arr.	0750	0703	2345	
	0658	2258	2348	dep.	Sutton	arr.	0744	0657	2339	
	0700	2300	2350	dep.	Bayside	arr.	0742	0655	2337	
	0702	2302	2352	dep.	Howth Junction	arr.	0740	0653	2335	
	0704	2304	2354	dep.	Kilbarrack	dep.	0738	0651	2333	
	0706	2306	2356	dep.	Raheny	dep.	0735	0648	2330	
	0708	2308	2358	dep.	Harmonstown	dep.	0733	0646	2328	
	0709	2309	2359	dep.	Killester	dep.	0731	0644	2326	
	0715	2315	0005	arr.	CONNOLLY STN.	dep.	0727	0640	2322	
0700	0716	2316		dep.	CONNOLLY STN.	arr.	0726	0639	2321	2351
0703	0719	2319		dep.	Tara St.	dep.	0724	0637	2319	2349

0704	0720	2320	arr.	PEARSE STN.	dep.	0722	0635	2317	2347
0705	0721	2321	dep.	PEARSE STN.	arr.	0721		2316	2346
0708	0724	2324	dep.	Landsdowne Rd.	dep.	0719		2314	2344
0709	0725	2325	dep.	Sandymount	dep.	0717		2312	2342
0711	0727	2327	dep.	Sydney Parade	dep.	0715		2310	2340
0714	0730	2330	dep.	Booterstown	dep.	0713		2308	2338
0716	0732	2332	dep.	Blackrock	dep.	0711		2306	2336
0717	0733	2333	dep.	Monkstown	dep.	0710		2305	2335
0719	0735	2335	dep.	Salthill	dep.	0708		2303	2333
0721	0737	2337	arr.	DUN LAOGHAIRE	dep.	0706		2301	2331
0723	0739	2339	arr.	Sandycove	dep.	0704		2359	2329
0725	0741	2341	arr.	Glenageary	dep.	0703		2258	2328
0727	0743	2343	arr.	Dalkey	dep.	0701		2256	2326
0731	0747	2347	arr.	Killiney	dep.	0656		2251	2321
0733	0749	2349	arr.	Shankhill	dep.	0654		2249	2319
0739	0755	2355	arr.	BRAY	dep.	0650		2245	2315

Benelux

Vital Tips for the Trains
of the Netherlands,
Belgium, and Luxembourg

*Dutch trains—Belgian trains—Luxembourgois trains—Benelux
high-speed lines—Airport trains—Getting around Amsterdam—
Netherlands Railroad Museum—Crossing the Channel—Benelux
Tourrail—National rail passes*

The well-developed national railroads of the three Benelux countries make it easy for you to travel from city to city. The "Nederlandse Spoorwegen" (NS) network, 1,760 miles, carries more than 600,000 travelers daily from 386 stations on 4,200 passenger trains. The "Societe Nationale des Chemins de Fer belge" (SNCB) (called "Belgische Spoorwegen" in Flemish) and the "Societe Nationale des Chemins de Fer luxembourgois" (CFL) are nearly as busy.

Nowhere do the trains run so often and so efficiently. When GermanRail officials visited the Netherlands, they said, "It is impossible to run a train system this way." The Dutch turn the trick by running primarily short, busy railcars which combine and split frequently. Their platforms are long to serve two or even three trains one after another on one track.

The Belgian railroads are less well finished. Luxembourg, because of its size, requires only a nominal railroad infrastructure supplemented with buses.

Flat countrysides, dense train networks, frequent services, and short distances make it easy for you to see the Benelux nations by train. You can see any of these countries easily from wherever you make your base. You don't have to pack or unpack here.

Dutch Trains

The Dutch railroads' network operates like one efficient rapid-transit area with international services superimposed upon it. The only trains with separate locomotives you ride are those destined for abroad, the Benelux train (see the section describing it below), and the German and French trains traveling to and from their homes. The rest are sets of electric railcars connected together in twos and threes to provide high capacity, frequent service, and great flexibility.

NS runs some 2,288 coaches (including multiple units) providing more than 135,000 seats. About 1,300 of these units consist of electric railcar units (or EMUs) made up of two, three, or four carriages.

The workhorse of the NS fleet is the blue-and-yellow railcar called "Dog's Head." Its distinctive profile says it all.

Your domestic transportation is carried out by "Stoptreins" (locals), "Sneltreins" (fast trains), and "InterCities." You can travel anywhere in the Netherlands speedily by combining them. The yellow departure timetables posted in the train stations are your key to finding your way about easily and quickly. There are usually four domestic sheets and one international one. Find the sheet showing your destination. The simple schematic route diagrams showing you the order of stations on your route make your planning easy.

Figure out what combination of InterCities and locals to take. The departure time and platform number followed by an *a* or *b* are printed beside every train's destination. Pay special attention to these letters, which refer to segments on the platform where your train boards. NS platforms are extraordinarily long in order to accommodate two or more trains at the same time. The train you want will be in the sector indicated on the timetable.

NS's IC-3 "Koploper" railcar was introduced in 1977. You recognize it miles away by its raised driver's cabin which allows the driver a better view and ingeniously permits passengers to cross from one independent unit to another when IC-3s are coupled together. It is the 747 of the train world. You ride this 100 mph train between the Randstad (the high-population-density area stretching from Rotterdam to Amsterdam to Utrecht) and the east and north of the country.

You can tell the Sprinter train by its beveled profile. This electric railcar set was introduced in 1975 for fast acceleration and braking so it could decrease the travel time between nearby stations.

NS's latest acquisitions are the double-deckers. You ride these, in trains made up of multiple units of six or seven, during rush hours on the busiest commuter lines.

The Benelux Train (see the section on this adventure below) takes you between Amsterdam and Brussels. Ride German EuroCity trains to Germany and the French EC Etoile du Nord to Brussels and Paris (Nord). The Etoile du Nord requires supplements payable by those not traveling on a Eurailpass.

NS trains run from about 5 A.M. to 1 A.M. (on Sundays and holidays from about 7 A.M.), but trains on the Schiphol Airport line run all night, so count on hourly overnight service for Rotterdam-The Hague-Leiden-Schiphol-Amsterdam-Hilversum-Utrecht.

Round-trip tickets ("Retour") are less than twice the single fare ("Enkele reis"), but valid on the day of issue only. Children under three travel free; those four to eleven pay one guilder (about fifty cents) when accompanied by an adult over eighteen—limit three children per adult.

With a train ticket or pass, you receive a discount of almost 50 percent on bicycle rentals at train stations. Use this well in the Netherlands, where there are more bicyclists than voters, bike lanes are common, and the land is flat.

Belgian Trains

Brussels' North and South terminals were converted to through stations at the time of the 1958 World's Fair and a new, mainline station, Central, was built underground, allowing you to tunnel through Brussels' central district on all the mainline, crack trains such as the EC Etoile du Nord. EuroCity and international trains do not stop at Brussels Central but you reach it easily by one of the local trains passing through the North and South stations. The North and South stations are used for international connections.

When you arrive in Belgium, get a free copy of the pocket-sized brochure "IC/IR—1001 Fixed Interval Connections." SNCB's timetable is arranged for departures at fixed intervals, i.e., the same minute after the hour, every hour.

You ride four categories of SNCB domestic trains. InterCity trains give you fast connections between major centers of Belgium and foreign terminuses. InterRegio (IR) trains take you to more intermediate stops. Local (L) trains stop everywhere except stations where only peak trains (P-trains) stop. Peak trains are often double-deckers running at busy travel hours.

When you buy an ordinary single or round-trip domestic ticket (including those to the airport), remember your first segment must be used the day you buy your ticket. When you are buying your ticket in advance, be sure to say on what date you plan to travel. A round-trip ticket is valid for three calendar days.

Luxembourgois Trains

Luxembourg City, the Grand Duchy of Luxembourg's enchanting capital, is so well connected to the rest of Europe by international and EuroCity trains that the tourist board is tempted to call it the "Heart of Europe." Once there you easily explore Luxembourg's green mountains and valleys by CFL's extensive bus network.

Luxembourg City's train station is one of the few with leaded glass windows and a striking, green patina steeple. A fourth, functional platform, completed in 1990, has bright, friendly colors and a modern plexiglas cover.

The modern leaded-glass windows picturing the profile of Luxembourg Castle dominate the interior and cast colored southern lights on the central hall. A pleasant cafeteria adjoins the central hall. Use the coin-operated lockers in the main hall. When they are filled, check your luggage with the "Consigne des Bagages" down the hall. You orient yourself with city and regional maps protected in a glass case in front of the station.

CFL's international-standard trains have liveries of military green or green and white. Diesel railcars are purple. Locomotives are purple and yellow. Stripes indicating first class are orange.

The Place de la Gare is surrounded by hotels and banks for changing your money. Turn to your right as you exit for the bus stands where you board both the Luxair airport bus and the city buses to the airport. Past the bus stands, the Luxair terminus accommodates Luxembourg's tourist information office. Make hotel reservations and change money here. Everything closes tightly at noon for lunch.

Make Luxembourg City your base. Like a star, five lines with two electrical systems converge here. Luxembourg lies on the mainline of the orange-livery EuroCity Iris, the EC Vauban, and the Edelweiss running along the Brussels-Namur-Luxembourg-Metz-Strasbourg-Basel route. You travel by EC Robert Schuman, EC Victor Hugo, and EC Goethe to Paris's Est station, Le Grand-Ducal to Brussels' South station, and L'Ardennais to Antwerp.

CFL's northern mainline takes you between Luxembourg City and Brussels via Liege.

Electrification made it possible for you to ride French-made modern railcars north to Diekirch. As electrification proceeds, you will be able to ride farther to Wiltz and then to the Belgian border.

CFL's most scenic line, through "Luxembourgois Switzerland," takes you through the beautiful town of Esch-sur-Sure to Rodange and into France at Longuyon. Use CFL's other secondary line across the Moselle River to Trier, in Germany.

Although the Eurailpass brochure doesn't say so, CFL's national bus system is included completely in your Eurailpass. Simply show your pass to the driver of the tan buses striped with Burgundy red. You can make a number of excursions through the delightful countryside into quaint villages, and because you use your Eurailpass, you visit the same sights as the tour buses without cost. Your bus calls at all small villages, enabling you to see the detail of the landscape and get on and off as you wish to explore.

Benelux High-Speed Lines

Starting in 1993, you will be able to travel in high-speed trains via Lille, France, between Brussels and Paris and between Brussels and London. The line connecting Tournal, Belgium, and Lille is being electrified to provide service at 100 mph in time for the beginning of TGV-Nord services to the Eurotunnel.

The new 186-mph line being built to link the French border at Wanneheim with a junction on the main Mons-Brussels line at Lembeek, twelve miles south of Brussels, will open in 1995.

Also in 1995-96, you will be riding high-speed trains between Brussels and Cologne, Germany, and (via Antwerp) to Amsterdam's Central Station, where platforms 15/16 are earmarked for this service.

Airport Trains

When you arrive by air in Benelux, you have it easy.

Schiphol is one of the best train airports in Europe because of its mainline connections completed in 1986. InterCity trains take you to Amsterdam's airport from as far as Groningen and Leeuwarden in northern Netherlands, Hanover in Germany, or Brussels in Belgium, thus giving you a way to reach your plane from all over northern Europe without changing trains.

A second stretch of rapid-transit line takes you from the station at Amsterdam's RAI (the convention hall), on Amsterdam's outskirts, to Amsterdam's Zuid station, to Schiphol, to Leiden, and to The Hague's CS station (do not confuse with The Hague's NS station, which are on different lines).

The "Airport City Express" rail shuttle service (not covered by Eurailpass) takes you between Belgium's National Airport at Zaventem and Brussels. Hourly trains connect the airport with Brussel's North, Central (tracks "A" and "3"), and South stations and continue to Mons and Quevy during rush hours.

The new stop at South station allows you to make rapid train connections for Ghent, Bruges, Ostend, and Paris. Sabena buses run hourly from National Airport to Antwerp (Crest Hotel and Centrum) and Ghent (Kouter and St. Pieters station).

You can buy tickets to major Belgian cities, as well as Paris, from the rail information desk in the arrivals hall at Zaventem airport.

You have two choices for travel between Luxembourg's Findel Airport and the train station. Most take the blue-and-white Luxair bus leaving every thirty minutes from the front of the airport terminal. Others walk across the airport's small parking lot to the yellow sign marking the bus stop for Luxembourg city bus line 9, which departs every fifteen to twenty minutes and costs about one-fifth that of the airport bus. The city bus takes about ten minutes longer to the train station but stops near many hotels and the youth hostel.

From Luxembourg's train station, Icelandair provides its passengers with discounted train transportation to Switzerland and France, and free long-distance bus service to more than a dozen destinations in Germany, Belgium, and the Netherlands. Telephone Icelandair at 1-800-223-5500.

Getting around Amsterdam

You are fortunate that Amsterdam has an excellent public transportation system. There are sixteen streetcar lines (five originate in front of Central station), thirty bus lines, and two Metro lines plus eight night bus lines.

You will find that buying a strip-ticket is the cheapest and most convenient way to ride streetcars and buses, rather than day or multiday passes, because you can use strip-tickets over a period of days whenever you need to. You are permitted to travel on one validation throughout the entire central city—the large zone that includes everywhere you are likely to go—for an hour and to transfer between streetcar lines, buses, and the Metro. Thus you can make a short trip and return all within an hour using only one validation.

The most economical and convenient strip-ticket is the fifteen-box ticket sold at the white "GVB" transport office opposite Amsterdam's Central Station (or at Prins Hendrikkade, 108, or at Amstel train station). When you buy a strip-ticket on a streetcar it will cost you the same but you receive only ten validation boxes (two boxes equal one trip in one zone). The forty-five-box ticket is only cents cheaper than three fifteen-box tickets, it is cumbersome to carry, and you will doubtless have leftover boxes when you leave Amsterdam.

You can buy day tickets for one, two, three, or more days, but unless you plan to spend a day riding public transportation or traveling to and from Amsterdam's suburbs, strip-tickets are cheaper and more flexible.

Consider these strip-tickets as national currency. Use them for transportation not only on Amsterdam's public transportation, but for transportation in all of the Netherlands' major cities and even on NS trains for local transportation.

For one trip in Amsterdam's large "Centrum," enter the back of the tram and validate your ticket in a validating machine aboard the tram by folding and canceling two boxes. For more complicated journeys—because you are a tourist—enter the front and ask the tram or bus driver to do it.

Netherlands Railroad Museum

The Netherlands Railroad Museum in Utrecht was remodeled for the 150th anniversary celebrations of NS in 1989. The train Expo has gone, but the museum remains, much the richer for the anniversary. It inherited some of the specially refurbished equipment and one of the most entertaining train films you will see, called *Cadans,* for "cadence," the rhythmic clickety-clack that trains make.

You can reach it by a short walk to the south from the exit of Utrecht's huge, new, innovative Central Station.

Crossing the Channel

Crossing the English Channel by steamship is certainly one of the most pleasant, or miserable, events of your European vacation. You avoid airport terminuses but face possible boredom or foul weather. It can be an overwhelming pleasure or a bloodcurdling horror.

Both Belgium and the Netherlands have important sea links to Britain. When you hold a Eurailpass, a Eurail Flexipass, or a BritRail Pass, taking the steamer is the most logical way although the ship fare itself (or cabin, when you travel overnight) is covered by none of them.

To reach London from Amsterdam, ride the Admiraal de Ruyter or Benjamin Britten to Hook of Holland for a day or night boat to Harwich (Parkeston Quai), where you take the boat train to London's Liverpool Street station. Border formalities are fast and the transfer at Hook of Holland is easy because moving walkways and luggage carts help you from train to boat.

The modern, 31,189-ton, Dutch *Konigin Beatrix* and Sealink's *St. Nicholas* (17,043 tons) offer duty-free shopping, three categories of restaurants, movie theaters showing recent American films, first- and second-class lounges, a disco, and space to waste. Tip: guilders are used on the Dutch vessel, pounds sterling on the British. Exchange banks are open aboard ship, but plan ahead to have the correct currency.

Look for special, all-inclusive, bargain offers at the train and tourism offices when you visit Amsterdam, Brussels, or London, and also consult the free "Go BritRail" brochure available from BritRail offices (see Appendix A).

You travel between Belgium and England either aboard air-cushion Jetfoils, or aboard the 3¾- to 4-hour crossing between Dover (Western Docks) and Ostende operated by Belgian Marine and P&O European Ferries.

Jetfoils are fast (one hour and forty minutes), but are often rocky and you see nothing. Your steamship's landing in Dover can be one of your fondest memories because of your views of the famous White Cliffs. When you arrive at Ostende at sunset, you'll see Ostende's surprisingly modern waterfront.

Ostende's entire coast, lined with high-rise apartments and offices, is brilliant in the late sunlight.

Boat trains for Belgium take you via Dover from London's Victoria station. Look for their special ticketing and information office earmarked for this service (see the Britain and Ireland chapter).

Benelux Tourrail

The railroads of Benelux cooperate on a regional rail pass called the Benelux Tourrail. This gives you unlimited travel on the trains of SNCB, NS, CFL, and the bus lines in Luxembourg. You also receive more than a 25 percent discount on Panorama-Tours' city tour in Brussels and at the Antwerp Zoo, which is located next to Antwerp's Central station.

Similar to a flexipass, the Benelux Tourrail is valid for travel on any five days of your choosing within seventeen. Why seventeen? So you can arrange travel over three weekends.

Buy it in the U.S. through offices of the Netherlands Board of Tourism (NBT) (see Appendix A) or in Europe at the larger trains stations and many travel agencies in the Benelux countries. Second-class passes are about one-third less expensive than first-class ones. Those aged twelve to twenty-five buy a second-class Benelux Junior Tourrail for another 28 percent off. Children four to eleven pay half.

National Rail Passes

You save a lot of green with passes on the yellow NS trains. Both the NBT offices in North America and train stations in the Netherlands sell Holland Rail Passes, Seven-day Rail Rovers, and Seven-day Public Transport Link Rovers. When you buy them before you leave you save up to 50 percent (depending on the rate of exchange) and avoid the nuisance of paying in guilders.

The flexible Holland Rail Pass is valid for three travel days within fifteen, either first or second class. With this pass children aged four through eleven (maximum three per adult) can travel with an adult for $2 each.

NBT calls their seven-day consecutive pass a "Rail Rover." In conjunction with this pass adventurers do well buying a Seven-day Public Transport Link Rover to give them unlimited travel on all the public streetcars, city and regional buses throughout the Netherlands and on the Amsterdam subway—a convenient and economical advantage.

Available only in the Netherlands, individuals buy one-day Rail Rovers. During the summer two to six travelers buy Multi Rovers for unlimited travel for one day on weekdays after 9 A.M. The Teenage Rover Rail Pass for adventurers under eighteen is available during the summer and Dutch school holidays for four travel days of choice within ten. NS Railrunner cards allow up to three children, aged four to eleven, to travel with an adult, nineteen or older, for one guilder. Finally, adventuring families buy a Family Rover (Gezinstoer) for unlimited travel on four days of choice out of ten summer days. Children must be under eighteen.

NBT also sells the Holland Leisure Card, which includes free first-class train transfers from Schiphol Airport to Amsterdam or The Hague; a 40 percent discount on a day pass for unlimited train travel in the Netherlands; discounts on sightseeing, car rentals, and domestic flights; plus discounts on hotels belonging to the Golden Tulip, Novotel, and Cok groups. It's an offer you can't refuse. When you also buy a Eurailpass, you won't have to validate it until after you have exhausted the Holland Leisure Card's benefits.

SNCB offers a Belgium Tourrail similar to a Benelux Tourrail, but valid for travel in Belgium only. You buy these at Belgian train stations. SNCB also sells season, or "Runabout," tickets which are valid over the entire SNCB network or particular routes. These are sold for sixteen day- and longer periods for either first- or second-class travel.

The Luxembourg Billet Reseau provides a day's unlimited second-class travel on CFL's trains and buses. Senior travelers receive a 50 percent discount.

Adventure through the Benelux countries by boat across the Netherlands' Zuider Zee, the Benelux Train between Amsterdam and Brussels, aboard Europe's lowest train, and Dutch day trips.

Around the Zuider Zee
Tamed Sea and Steam

Have you ever wanted to sail across the Netherlands' Zuider Zee (now known as the Ijsselmeer)? Crossing this inland sea is smooth as peanut butter. When your train arrives in Stavoren, the *Bep Glasius* is unloading passengers and a line of bicyclists is forming to wheel their "feetsers" onto its deck.

When the ticket collector comes checking, just flash your Eurailpass. Even without a Eurailpass, the fare is modest.

The *Bep Glasius* is primarily a pleasure boat. Those without bicycles have backpacks.

The Netherlands has no rugged Alps or ragged fjords. Its charm lies in its tamed sea and in the fertile, flat farmlands crisscrossed with canals.

A one-day round trip through the north of the Netherlands, across the Ijsselmeer, and south through West Friesland samples the pleasing scenery of

AROUND THE ZUIDER ZEE

NORTH SEA

Leeuwarden

Sneek   Akkrum

STAVOREN

MEDEMBLIK

HOORN   ENKHUIZEN

IJSSELMEER

Zwolle

- N -

AMSTERDAM   Nunspeet

Ermelo

Hilversum

Amersfoort

0   10   20

MILES

Ijsselmeer, and south through West Friesland samples the pleasing scenery of this low country. It is worth a day away from Amsterdam, especially when you are riding it free on a Eurailpass, taking advantage of Benelux's only advertised Eurailpass bonus—the free crossing of the Ijsselmeer during the summer. Plan your departure from Amsterdam for an early hour so you have time to cross the Ijsselmeer, browse leisurely through the Zuider Zee Museum in Enkhuizen, and then travel on the "Bello" steam train. Be sure you board the right segment of your yellow-and-blue InterCity train at Amsterdam's Central station. It divides in Zwolle. One half goes to Groningen. You want to be in the half marked "Leeuwarden."

On its run to Leeuwarden this train makes very few stops. Your first is in Hilversum, the headquarters for Dutch radio. Your second is in Amersfoort, the junction for trains coming from Hook of Holland and Rotterdam. By the time you stop in Zwolle, where your train splits, you are entering Friesland, the land of cows, cheese, and tall, blond people.

Your train proceeds as a local. By the time you approach Akkrum, the land is appealing. Broad fields are peppered with black-and-white cows. You pass ribbonlike, calm canals busy with pleasure motor yachts, sailboats, and barges.

After waiting almost a half-hour in the white-brick Leeuwarden station (you can lunch in the station restaurant or hire a bicycle), you board a second-class-only, "Wadloper," diesel train for a ¾-hour run to Stavoren. The driver revs its motor like an old Ford, and—clickety-clack—off you go past sheep, cows, and horses.

Some farms have black, glazed-tile roofs. This is a region of intensive farming. Of course, one of the dangers of traveling by train through farm country is that the windows will be lowered and farmers will be fertilizing.

Herons stand sentry in stagnant, water-filled ditches. Most passengers get off at Sneek. The farm houses have acre-size red-tile roofs enveloping everything down to the first floor.

The canal running adjacent to your train is packed with small pleasure boats when you reach Workum. You often see curious sights along the tracks. Here you see a stack of bundled thatches for thatching roofs.

From the end of the line at Stavoren, where you find no station house, just a shelter and bicycle parking, follow the signs: "Naar de Boot" to Rederij NACO. The 12 mph *Bep Glasius*, a 300-passenger ship built by Peters' Scheepsbouw in 1966, crosses the Ijsselmeer only in summer. Aboard, you buy sandwiches and fabulous Dutch fast food such as french-fried potatoes and split pea soup in the luncheon area below deck.

From the deck you see a crazy, kaleidoscopic world of sails and ships: sailboats, cabin cruisers, schooners, very daring windsurfers, huge barges, and oddly masted fishing vessels that look like they might be manned by pirates. About halfway, you are met by a fleet of kayaks.

The afterdeck becomes one huge parking place for fully ladened bicycles. After an hour, you finally view the profile of Enkhuizen—the city hall and church.

When you land at one of Rederij NACO's three slips (the others take you to Urk and Medemblik) after your one hour and twenty-two minute crossing, you are greeted with the rare contrasting scene of the train station with a train and boat unloading passengers at the same time.

This area of West Friesland is interesting for its seafaring tradition. West Frisian ships sailed the world's oceans from Enkhuizen, Medemblik, and Hoorn to trade with faraway countries.

Enkhuizen is lined with the old seawall which used to protect the city from storms on the former Zuider Zee, ending at the Old Harbor where you see traditional sailing vessels, the fishing fleet, and numerous yachts. Beyond the seawall is the "living" Zuider Zee Museum, Europe's newest open-air museum, which gives you an interesting picture of the life and work of the people of the region who depended on this inland sea until 1932 when the Barrier Dam sealed the Zuider Zee from the North Sea.

From your landing near the train station, walk five minutes to the boat quay for your boat ride to the Zuider Zee showcase.

Leave the open-air museum on foot, pass through the town proper, and walk back to the train station in order to see the West Church and the South Church and to photograph the old fortified tower named "Drommedaris."

At the brick Enkhuizen station house you rejoin the electrified lines of NS. It takes you slightly less than an hour to reach Amsterdam Central station by Dog's Head Stoptrein, and twenty minutes to reach Hoorn (the namesake for Africa's Cape Horn)—but there's a better way.

Steam-enthusiast volunteers come from all over the Netherlands to donate their time freely so you can travel on the twelve-mile narrow-gauge line from Medemblik to Hoorn pulled by the restored steam locomotive "Bello," built in 1914. (You reach Medemblik by connecting boat from Enkhuizen—or you can travel in the return direction.)

In Enkhuizen, you begin your circle trip by boat at the quay; in Hoorn, you board the green steam train at the station across the overpass from the NS station. This is the same event as an NS day tour (see the "Dutch Treat" section below), but with a Eurailpass you save money because you don't pay for the NS transportation from Amsterdam.

At the midpoint, in Medemblik, you can visit the Dutch Steam Engine Museum. Many engines work regularly.

Most of your train trip back to Amsterdam from Hoorn takes you through lovely farmland: lovely because it is flat and fertile; lovely because colorful flowers are grown for sale. Shortly after Zaandam's bright, new station you see the shipping and shipbuilding on Amsterdam Harbor. Your final stop before Amsterdam's Central Station, at Amsterdam's Sloterdijk station, is interesting not only because of its ultramodern construction, but because it serves cross traffic in two directions from two levels.

Rederij NACO Service

Early July to Mid-August

0844	1144	1444	1744	dep.	Enkhuizen	arr.	1136	1436	1736	2036
1006	1306	1606	1906	arr.	Stavoren	dep.	1014	1314	1614	1914

Middle May to Early July and
Middle August to Middle September

0944	1244	1644	dep.	Enkhuizen	arr.	1236	1536	1936
1106	1406	1806	arr.	Stavoren	dep.	1114	1414	1814

Volunteer Steam Train and Boat Services

(1)	(2)	(2)				(1)	(2)	(2)
1100	1100	1500	dep.	Enkhuizen (Boat)	arr.	1415	1415	1745
1215	1215	1615	arr.	Medemblik	dep.	1300	1300	1630
1315	1315	1645	dep.	Medemblik (Steam)	arr.	1215	1215	1545
1415	1415	1745	arr.	Hoorn	dep.	1115	1115	1445

(1) May, June, and September: Tuesday to Saturday.
(2) July and August: Daily.

Connecting Train/Boat Timings
InterCity trains from Amsterdam to Leeuwarden run hourly.
Diesel trains from Leeuwarden to Stavoren run hourly.
Stoptreins from Enkhuizen and Hoorn to Amsterdam run half-hourly.

Benelux Train
Dutch Yellow and Belgian Bordeaux Red

From Amsterdam's Central station you depart, not pulled by a locomotive in front, but pushed, by the locomotive in back. The driver controls from a special compartment in the front of the train.

Between Amsterdam's Central station, Schiphol Airport, Rotterdam, The

BENELUX TRAIN

AMSTERDAM

Schiphol

Leiden

The Hague

NETHERLANDS

Rotterdam

Rosendaal

Antwerp

BELGIUM

BRUSSELS

-N-

0   10   20   50

To Paris

Hague, Antwerp, and Brussels, you ride the Benelux Train—the crack train and namesake of the Benelux countries. The Belgian locomotives and Dutch carriages are painted in a shared, single livery—a combination of the NS yellow and the Bordeaux red of the Belgian railroads. It is an impressive train: no-nonsense, comfortable, and most convenient for you to ride. It departs hourly, free to Eurailpass holders. The irony is that the proud Benelux Train is imported. The Belgian locomotive was manufactured in France; the Dutch carriages were made in Germany.

SNCB, the Belgian national railroad, procures its locomotives from France because the locomotives there share the same electrical characteristics, but the 100-mph Benelux Train locomotives, built in 1985, are convertible for running in the Netherlands as well as in Belgium.

The carriages were manufactured in 1986 by Waggonfabrik Talbot, in Aachen, Germany, because the Netherlands is too small to support a national train-carriage industry. The Benelux Train's carriages evolved from the design of NS's IC-3 coaches, which Talbot also built. You sit in orange-plush two-opposite-one first-class seats that recline a few inches when you press the orange armrest release; they have sturdy, fold-down tables in their backs. You look through panoramic windows that partially roll down. A clouded-glass partition separates smoking and nonsmoking sections. The interior doors open with a press of the lever. One first-class car is half compartments, half salon style; one contains a telephone booth; and one has a special compartment for bicycles. Linoleum floors and jet-type blowers for ventilation are used throughout.

Take a good look at the doors on this train. They are of a special Dutch design that quickly fly open into two halves to make it easier for you to get on and off faster—and are a boon for anyone bringing a bicycle with them.

Leaving Amsterdam's Central station (CS), you travel first over old track, then over new—past the futuristic elevated stop at Amsterdam-Sloterdijk. After a quick stop at the new Amsterdam-Lelylaan station (accessible by city streetcar line No. 1), you hear the announcement booming over the loud speaker: "Next station: Schiphol." Then you zoom underground, with lights zipping by you like lasers in a special-effects space movie.

At Schiphol, your train's doors open automatically. Schiphol train station has modern digital signs, marble flooring, an electric walkway going up, and abundant, conventional pushcarts (because walkways are used instead of escalators, there is no need for special pushcarts).

Out of Schiphol, refreshment trolleys are pushed down your train's aisle. Vendors wear Bordeaux-red jackets to match their train's livery. Catering is by Wagons-Lits.

About half an hour south of Amsterdam you pull to a stop beside Leiden's brick station house. In 1989 President Bush visited this university city and cited

Leiden as a special city, a place where Americans trace their origins—where the pilgrims came to escape persecution and Rembrandt lived and worked. You stop briefly in the Netherlands' seat of government. The Hague's HS station (do not confuse with The Hague's Central Station; HS was built by the Hollandsche Yzeren Spoorweg railroad), damaged by fire in 1989, has new fittings installed, arches replaced, and the whole refined to achieve a well-functioning new station, but the original red-brick Romanesque facades have been braced and preserved.

Rotterdam Central is a bright, airy station. Buses to North Sea ferries depart from the side door. City information (VVV) and train information share a yellow kiosk in the main hall. Cut flowers usually sold in Dutch stations brightly overflow an entire corner of the main hall.

Passengers disembarking here scurry down the stairs to Rotterdam's Metro station. The streetcar and bus circle is on the plaza in front. (Your national strip-tickets are valid.) The bank and information office ("NS Inlichtingen Bureau") can be found in the entrance hall.

Then you cross the steel-girder Moerdijk bridge, the longest rail (and road) bridge in the Netherlands, to Dordrecht, a charming town on the Meuse river where adventurers enjoy visiting the interesting church. At the red-brick Roosendaal station house, the border crossing, you see a whole carnival of NS equipment, including double-deckers—some blue-painted—on different tracks.

Antwerp's grand Centraal Station (Antwerpians call it the "Railway Cathedral") is chaos with renovation underway to permit through running of high-speed trains between Paris and Amsterdam. It's a large, ornate, and beautifully classic station with direct access to the Zoo next door. Adjacent to Centraal is an access to Antwerp's efficient streetcar network, "Station Diamant," named for the gem quarter nearby. Centraal should be whole before 1993, when Antwerp will be European Cultural City and the amazing new excavation below the present floor of the cathedral is completed.

Your next stop, Berchem, seems abandoned in Antwerp's suburbs. Try to avoid using this station.

When you enter the Belgian capital city's environs, before reaching Brussels' North station, you see to the west the giant aluminum Atomium representing a molecule of iron magnified 200 million times, symbol of the 1958 Brussels' World's Fair. In the same glimpse you see the first of Brussels' many Gothic churches.

Brussels' North station is a newly remodeled and expanded CCN ("Communication Center North") combining train, metro, and airport connections. (Brussels has two metro systems. A twenty-four-hour tourist ticket takes you over the entire city.) It's Brussels' brightest, and includes the Belgian Railroad's Train Museum as well.

The North station's information office is located in the departures hall; make your hotel reservations here. Nearby is a change bank and the "InterCity" pub where beer flows freely. There is also a waiting room in the underground passage between tracks 9 and 10, but adventurers traveling to Luxembourg have no time to waste, for they have only ten minutes before their InterCity leaves. You also board railcars to Brussels' Zavendam Airport here (not covered by Eurailpass) from various platforms shown on the yellow departure signs.

When the Benelux Train leaves the North station, it tunnels underground to Brussels' Central station, an underground station built on the side of a hill so that its entrance is at street level. It is quite like a busy subway stop. Use Central station as your gateway to Brussels because of its location. From Brussels' Central station's platforms, you descend a gracious ramp; an escalator takes you up. The metro is on the highest level. Walk five minutes downhill toward the town hall's spire to the Grande Place. Brussels' tourist information office, for hotel bookings and abundant information, is one block north, at 61, rue du Marche aux Herbes.

Riders to Brussels' airport need to look for the signs "Bruxelles National-Aeroport/Brussel Nationaal-Luchthaven" and an airplane pictograph pointing to Track A, across the subterranean station from all the rest. It is poorly designed, unconscionably marked, and poorly lit.

Continuing south from Brussels' Central station, your Benelux Train emerges into the sunlight at Brussels' Chapelle station, bypassed by express trains, and you see Brussels' Royal Palace to the east.

Brussels' South station also has airport and Metro connections, a bank, a full-course "Pullman" restaurant (open weekdays), and a pleasant "Iris" cafeteria. The post office is next door.

Benelux Train Service

0622	0724	0826	2026	dep.	AMSTERDAM (CS)	arr.	0910	1008	2308	0011
0633	0733	0835	2035	dep.	A'dam Lelylaan	dep.	0900	0958	2258	2359
0642	0742	0844	2044	dep.	Schiphol Airp.	dep.	0851	0949	2249	2350
0658	0758	0900	2100	dep.	Leiden	dep.	0835	0933	2233	2334
0712	0810	0912	2112	dep.	The Hague (HS)	dep.	0823	0921	2222	2323
0731	0831	0931	2131	dep.	Rotterdam (CS)	dep.	0805	0902	2204	2305
0748	0848	0948	2148	dep.	Dordrecht	dep.	0745	0846	2148	2249
0811	0911	1011	2211	arr.	Roosendaal*	dep.	0723	0825	2127	2228
0814	0914	1014	2214	dep.	Roosendaal**	arr.	0721	0822	2125	2226

0843	0943	1043	2243	dep.	Antwerp (C)	dep.	0654	0754	2057	2149
0852	0952	1052	2252	dep.	Berchem	dep.	0646	0746	2049	2146
0907	1007	1107	2307	arr.	Mechelen	dep.	0634	0734	2037	2134
0921	1021	1121	2321	arr.	BRUSSELS (N)	dep.	0619	0719	2022	2119
0926	1026	1126	2326	arr.	BRUSSELS (C)	dep.	0614	0714	2017	2114
0930	1030	1130	2330	arr.	BRUSSELS (S)	dep.	0610	0710	2013	2110

*Netherlands
**Belgium
... and then every hour until:

Flevoline
Europe's Lowest Train

Weesp is your last chance to admire a traditional Dutch village. You leave Weesp's needle-like church spires and traditional drawbridge and head into the Netherlands' new land. You have no feeling you are traveling twenty feet below sea level on Europe's lowest train line.

You would be thrilled to look up and see an oceangoing ship passing on the way up the Rhine River, but everything you see is perfectly natural. Fish swim in canals. Rabbits scamper in fields. Cows amble with full udders. And new cities grow larger brick by brick as you travel through the Flevoland, the reclaimed plot of land which once lay below the Zuider Zee.

This is an interesting adventure from Amsterdam not because of the scenery, but because it shows you the magnitude of Dutch determination—and success—in reclaiming fertile land from the sea.

Of the thirty-mile Flevoline, you travel over twenty-five miles of land newly reclaimed from the sea and descend from a high point of fifty feet above sea level to twenty feet below. Between Amsterdam and Almere, your first stop in the Flevoland, you cross more than one hundred bridges.

The Dutch have been doing battle with the sea for centuries. It is a part of their history and an essential element in their country's security and prosperity. Their story's crowning glory is the Zuider Zee project—the draining of over 616,730 acres of sea; the creation of land in five polders. Three of these—the North East Polder (the oldest, dry for forty-five years), East Flevoland, and South Flevoland (the newest, dry for twenty years)—now make up the new province of Flevoland, northeast of Amsterdam. The provincial capital, Lelystad, is only some thirty miles from Amsterdam.

You have a great deal of luxury choosing your train through the Flevoland. Take a streetcar to Amsterdam's Central Station, look on the yellow departure billboards for "Lelylstad C," and ride an escalator to your correct platform. Stoptreins leave twice an hour at five minutes and thirty-five minutes past the hour and, in addition, six Sneltreins leave at nineteen and forty-nine minutes past the hour during the morning and afternoon rush hours.

The difference between local and fast trains is small. The Sneltreins are likely to be connected "Dog's head" railcars which bypass Almere Muziekwijk and Almere Buiten. The Stoptreins are probably joined-together "Sprinter" railcars which accelerate faster and make all seven stops. The Sneltreins take thirty-six minutes to travel the thirty miles at 50 mph. The Stoptreins take seven minutes longer, and only average 43 mph.

Your train enters Flevoland when water opens on your left and then your right and you cross a causeway parallel to the main highway. This is part of the ring of water left circling the Flevoland, connected to the Markermeer, the remaining southern body of water from the pre-existing Zuider Zee ("Meer" means "lake," "Zee" means "sea").

Your train's first stop is Amsterdam's Muiderpoort station, one of the many satellite stations still in Amsterdam city, which in fact you also can reach easily by streetcar.

From Muiderpoort, you pass a small part of Amsterdam's harbor sheltering many small Dutch naval vessels, industry, and then a private marina.

Before your train slows for your next stop, you see cows of all colors: brown, black-and-white, fawn. The fields are broad and green and the superhighways you pass have eight or more lanes and are black-topped.

You cross over a canal with heavy shipping. Below, a red Belgian fishing vessel cuts under the bridge.

Soon you see the black needle-like church spire of Weesp and modern apartment blocks of brown brick (so common in the Netherlands). You stop at Weesp's open-air station. On departure you pass on your right the only windmills you will see. They aren't large and they aren't rotating, but they are adjoined by several thatched-roof houses.

In Weesp, you also leave the main rail line leading on toward Amersfoort and then to Germany. Traveling on the diverging rails you see IC-3 railcars and a GermanRail train connecting Amsterdam's Schiphol Airport with Hanover.

Flevoland is very grassy and flat, with farmers furrowing their fields with tractors. Past Almere Muziekwijk station you can read "1987" embedded in the concrete.

While your conductor is announcing Almere Centrum station you see an ultramodern steeple to your right, apartment blocks everywhere, and canals. This is the new land.

At Almere Centrum, covered with red tinker-toy struts to support the plastic and plaster covering, you realize the extent to which this is a planned city. Everything you see is modern, blocky, and space-saving, but not crowded. It is obviously a comfortable place to live.

You pass Almere Buiten station, where a city is still abuilding. The station is already in place. Your train skims above the flat furrowed fields and rows of trees acting as windbreaks. You see no windmills. In fact, you travel a long way with no distinctive feature except for green acres and fields brown with the leavings of the last wheat harvest.

Lelystad at last appears in the distance, not so much as a soaring Oz at the end of a yellow brick road, but as a low accumulation of efficient three- and four-story apartment buildings mixed with industrial buildings of so many Dutch and international companies that it appears there has been a financial incentive to build here.

Lelystad Centrum's surprisingly spacious, spick-and-span and uncluttered train station has a "Het Station Petit Restaurant." Inside is a brass plaque marking its opening in 1988 by the queen, GWK bank for changing money, ticketing, bookstore, and bright flower shop—all the amenities that the Dutch consider necessary for a full-service station.

End-of-the-line Lelystad Centrum is like all the new NS stations circling Amsterdam and the one at Schiphol Airport. They feature bright blues, reds, greens, and yellows. These flamboyant colors make the architecturally exciting stations fresh.

Weekday Flevoline Service

Miles	A	B				C	D	E
0	0605	0619	dep.	AMSTERDAM (CS)	arr.	0629	0614	1614
2.5	0610	0624	dep.	Amsterdam (MP)	dep.	0624	0609	1609
4.3	....	....	dep.	Diemen	dep.	....	....	....
8.7	0618	0631	arr.	Weesp	dep.	0616	0601	1601
8.7	0618	0632	dep.	Weesp	arr.	0616	0600	1600
16	0627	....	dep.	Almere Muziekwijk	dep.	0607	0552	....
16	0630	0642	arr.	Almere (CS)	dep.	0604	0549	1550
16	0632	0642	dep.	Almere (CS)	arr.	0602	0548	1549
19	0636	....	dep.	Almere Buiten	dep.	0557	0543	....
30	0648	0655	arr.	LELYSTAD CENTRUM	dep.	0545	0532	1535

A Begins at time shown and runs half-hourly until 12:37 A.M.
B Begins at time shown and runs half-hourly until 8:49 A.M.; then 15:19 to 18:49.
C Begins at time shown and runs half-hourly to 12:45 A.M.
D Begins at time shown and runs half-hourly to 9:02 A.M.
E Begins at time shown and runs half-hourly to 18:05.

Dutch Treat
Netherlands by Day

Netherlands by day. Amsterdam by night. NS has a program for you to maximize your pleasure and minimize your cost.

Take advantage of NS's well-conceived, economical program to see all of the Netherlands by train, learn about the complex customs and history of this small exciting country, and come to understand the Dutch way of life. NS sells all-inclusive tickets to the best things to see in the Netherlands.

Buy individual day-trip tickets (these are not the same as the day cards described earlier) at any train station ticket office. These include the round-trip train journey (originating from any station), the price of the attraction, connecting bus or streetcar fare, and sometimes coffee and cake. You receive a substantial discount, you know the total cost in advance, and you determine your departure times yourself.

If you already have a special train ticket such as a Holland Rail Pass or a Eurailpass, use it for the train journey and buy an "Attraction Ticket" at your departure or arrival station. An Attraction Ticket gives you the benefit of NS's planning and lets you see the same day trip you select but without paying for the train. The money you save on day-trip tickets won't in itself justify buying a Eurailpass, however. To spend as little as possible, plan your itinerary to take these day trips before you validate your Eurailpass or after it expires.

The total program is set out in the booklet, "Er op uit (1001 Ideas for a day out)," which is available in Dutch from ticket offices at stations and from NS's information offices.

To gain a thorough impression of the Dutch way of life, modern and past, take day trips to Rotterdam, Arnhem, Enkhuizen, the Hague, Volendam and Marken, Zaandam, and Maastricht. Railfans enjoy Utrecht's Railroad Museum and enthralling music box and barrel organ museum (as who wouldn't?) and the volunteer steam train between Hoorn and Medemblik.

In Rotterdam, you sail in a motor launch from Willemsplein Quay for a round trip through the city's large, modern port complex. You climb the "Space Tower" in a glass-enclosed lift winding slowly up and around Euromast's steel extension to the very top of the television tower. Your ticket includes the train ride to Rotterdam, the round trip of the harbor, admission to the Euromast and Space Tower, and a day Rail Ranger ticket for the subway, bus, and tram.

In Enkhuizen, visit the preserved Zuider Zee houses and travel by ferry from Enkhuizen's train station to the Zuider Zee Museum and return. Your ticket includes the train, the ferry, and admission to the museum.

At Monnickendam, board the "Marken Express" boat to the Island of

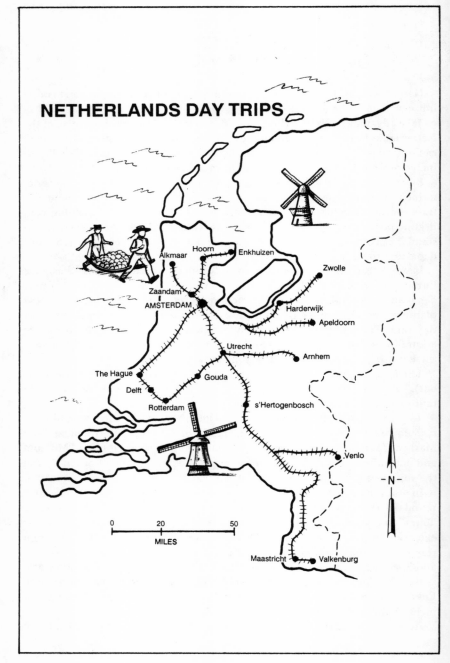

NETHERLANDS DAY TRIPS

Alkmaar
Hoorn
Enkhuizen
Zwolle
Zaandam
AMSTERDAM
Harderwijk
Apeldoorn
Utrecht
Arnhem
The Hague
Gouda
Delft
Rotterdam
s'Hertogenbosch
Venlo
Maastricht
Valkenburg

0   20   50
MILES

N

Marken, see the cottages built on piles in the IJssel lake, dams, dikes, and fishing boats with colored sails, and then continue by boat to Volendam. Your ticket includes the train, bus, and Marken Express boat.

The scale-model town of Madurodam in the Hague shows you how classic Dutch architecture looks to birds with broad wings. Then you visit Scheveningen, one of the Dutch people's favorite seaside resorts with a new pier and sea pool. Your ticket includes the train, admissions to Madurodam and Scheveningen Pier, and a day Rail Ranger ticket.

Curators of Arnhem's Open-Air Museum carefully gathered, rebuilt, furnished, and preserved a magnificent collection of complete farms, houses, cottages, and windmills so you can appreciate how the Dutch used to live. Your ticket includes the train, the museum bus, admission, and a Dutch pancake with coffee.

In Zaandam you see the 1948 village called Zaanse Schans, an open-air museum of seventeenth-century houses and windmills. You visit the Windmill Museum to see how windmills work and cruise on the river Zaan. Your ticket includes the train, a brochure, admission to the Windmill Museum, the river cruise, and a Dutch pancake with coffee.

Another day trip is a walking tour of Maastricht to magnificent churches, historic public buildings, city walls, period houses, and Roman ruins. You cruise on the river Meuse (Maas). Your ticket includes the train, the river cruise, a grotto tour, admission to St. Servaas Church, and coffee with a Limburg open fruit pie.

When you have determined what dates you are going to be in the Netherlands, take out your pencil and note some of the following attractions. Seasonal events are some of the most interesting.

• Keukenhof Lisse — Between the end of March and the end of May tulips are in full bloom.

• Kaasmarkt Alkmaar — On Fridays only from the middle of April until the middle of September, board the "Kaasmarkt Express" from Amsterdam to Alkmaar for the colorful cheese market.

• Westfriese Markten — On Thursdays only from the end of June until the end of August, in Schagen's market you can enjoy a folkloric color pageant with dancing and music.

• Hoornsemarkt — On Wednesdays only from the beginning of July until the end of August, ride to Hoorn to see the 600-year-old town present the famous old-time Dutch market and bring the medieval guilds of trade and artisans back to life. Don't miss visiting also the Friesian Museum in front of the market.

• Kaasmarkt Gouda — On Thursday mornings only from the end of June to the end of August, take the train to the Gouda cheese market in the interesting city that gave the cheese its name.

Write the NBT (see Appendix A). Ask for their free color brochure "Touring Holland by Rail" and their free pocket timetable "Main Train Connections."

Selected Schedule of NS Day Trips

- The Hague, Madurodam and Scheveningen Pier or sea pool
- The Hague, Mauritshuis
- Delft
- Volendam and Marken
- Paleis Het Loo, House of Orange royal palace
- Kroller-Muller Museum, De Hoge Veluwe nature reserve
- Enkhuizen, Zuider Zee Museum
- Flevohof polder
- De Haar Castle near Utrecht
- Zaanse Schans settlement near Zaandam
- Historic triangle by steam train and boat
- Stormvloed barrier, Delta plan, Oosterschelde
- Rotterdam, Europort or Seven Rivers tour
- Rotterdam, Botlek and Euromast
- Utrecht Railroad Museum and Music Box Museum
- Arnhem Open-Air Museum
- Efteling recreation park
- Castle gardens, Arcen
- Maastricht
- Valkenburg
- Giethoorn, the Venice of Holland
- Burgers Zoo and Safari Park
- Anne Frank House, Amsterdam
- Amsterdam Museums
- North Sea cruise, Hook of Holland/Harwich
- Enkhuizen-Urk boat trip

France

Vital Tips for the Trains of France

Getting around Paris—Airport trains—Overnight trains—TER trains—TGV North—Using Eurailpass bonuses—France Railpass—BritFrance passes—France Rail'N Drive

Base your travel in Paris. Paris is the heart of the network of the French National Railroads ("Societe Nationale des Chemins de Fer Francais," or SNCF). Because trains radiate from Paris, you will have difficulty traveling long distances without returning to Paris for connections until the new TGV Interconnect is put into place in 1994. Trains traveling circumferentially are so rare that they have a special name: "transversales."

You seldom travel through Paris without having to change train stations. There are six mainline train stations, serving five separately administered "Reseaux" or networks, each of which is subdivided into "Regions."

France is known for comfortable, convenient, and the world's fastest trains. SNCF's TGV ("Train a Grande Vitesse") is the world's record holder at 320 mph, but all French long-distance trains are a joy to ride. Two TGV networks take you at the fastest operating speeds in the world and station modifications make them easy to use.

TGV Southeast stretches from Paris's Gare de Lyon to thirty-seven towns in southeast France and provides two through routes, one from the north and the other from Normandy. They take you to Switzerland, French ski country, and the Riviera. New stretches will be opened in 1992, 1993, and 1994.

TGV Atlantique takes you to Brittany; TGV Atlantique-Aquitaine takes you through Bordeaux to the Spanish border. Taking the 3:55 P.M. Atlantique-Aquitaine from Paris's Montparnasse station to Irun permits you to reach Portugal faster than by the Sud Express. You change at Irun onto the new overnight train named for the Portuguese writer Eca de Queiroz, which carries sleepers, couchettes, and first-class seats and arrives in Lisbon at 10:56 A.M. Return service leaves Lisbon at 5:55 P.M., reaching Paris at 3:05 P.M.

EuroCity trains from Paris take you into all neighboring countries. Choose between the EC Moliere, EC Parsifal, and EC Maurice Ravel for Germany; the EC Goethe, EC Robert Schuman, and EC Victor Hugo for Luxembourg; the EC Le Corbusier, EC L'Arbalete, and the EuroCity TGVs for Switzerland; the EC Etoile du Nord, EC Brabant, and the first-class-only EC Ile de France and EC Rubens (plus the ECs Vauban and Iris through Alsace) for Belgium and the Netherlands; and the EC Catalan Talgo from SNCF's Geneva station to Barcelona.

Be sure to double-check from which train station your train departs. Gare de Lyon, Paris's origin of the TGV Southeast network, takes you to Lyon, Marseille, Grenoble, the Riviera, Italy, and French-speaking Switzerland. The Gare Montparnasse is headquarters for your TGV Atlantique service to Brittany, Bordeaux, Lourdes, and Spain via Hendaye. The Gare d'Austerlitz will be closed when Montparnasse is fully operational. The Gare de l'Est serves Strasbourg, Luxembourg, southern Germany, and German-speaking Switzerland via Basel. Trains from the Gare du Nord take you to Belgium, the Netherlands, northern Germany, Scandinavia, and the Channel ports for England. The Gare St. Lazare serves Normandy, Le Havre, and Cherbourg for ferry crossings to the Republic of Ireland.

The TGV Atlantique timetables are the most complicated in Europe. You find different schedules for Fridays, Saturdays, Sundays, Mondays, and Tuesdays-Thursdays. Fares and supplements which vary with times of day in addition to days of the week make it difficult to plan in advance.

Fortunately, rail passes save you from this torture. Get a timetable and just tell the reservation agent approximately what time and on what day you want to leave. The reservations/ticketing machines ("Resa 300") you see in the stations almost demand a knowledge of French, but accept coins totaling up to 100 francs and credit cards for sums more than 30 francs.

Finally, validate the tickets you buy in France in the orange, automatic ticket punchers ("Composteur") at the entrances to platforms. When you travel on a rail pass and require only reservations, punch your reservations coupon.

Getting around Paris

Paris has perhaps the most convenient, efficient, and surely the least expensive public transportation system of any capital. There are two independent underground train systems with separate ticketing systems. Plan to use both. You already know about the famous Paris Metro. Its lines are connected with SNCF's RER (Regional Electric Network) full-size (some are double-decked) rapid-transit trains. You ride RER trains between Paris's airports and the city center. Another takes you to Versailles.

Stop at the Paris Tourist Office (127, avenue des Champs-Elysees) for details on public transportation, system maps, and purchase of tourist tickets. Neither Metro nor RER trains are covered by Eurailpass but a France Railpass gives you limited privileges on both (see France Railpass section below).

To transfer between Paris's train stations, the Metro is usually the easiest and cheapest way. Ride the second-class cars (although many French riders don't observe the distinction) unless you hold a first-class "Paris Sesame" ticket issued in connection with a France Railpass. Between Gare du Nord and Gare d'Austerlitz, you will save time by taking the RER and changing at St. Michel/Notre Dame (this takes less than thirty minutes).

You save substantially by purchasing tickets valid for ten single rides, but you save even more with unlimited ride schemes. A "Formule Une" is a one-day Metro pass. Paris Sesame tickets provide you with unlimited transportation for two, four, or seven days on buses and the Metro. Show it to bus drivers; use the magnetic ticket in Metro turnstiles. A "Carte Orange" allows you to use the system for one week but requires a passport-type photograph.

Airport Trains

Use the convenient train connections from Paris's airports on SNCF's high-speed RER system (not covered by Eurailpass). Prices vary with distance, but when you purchase a single ticket at either Charles de Gaulle or Orly Airport you have access to more than a hundred RER stations in the Paris area.

At Charles de Gaulle there are two airline terminals ("Aerogare") with free, yellow-striped, "ADP" shuttle buses serving each. Terminal 2 serves only Air France and a few small carriers. Terminal 1 serves most other airlines, including Pan Am and TWA. (The other American carriers fly into Paris Orly.)

Board the shuttle bus between CDG's two terminals to the SNCF Roissy-Rail station. An RER train departs every fifteen minutes for interchanges at Gare du Nord, Chatelet-les Halles, Luxembourg, and St. Michel/Notre-Dame stations.

From Orly, board the shuttle from Orly Sud to the SNCF Orly-Rail station, then an RER train running every fifteen minutes to the Austerlitz train station, St. Michel/Notre Dame, Musee d'Orsay, Invalides, and Boulevard Victor.

On departure, reach Charles de Gaulle Airport from the Gare du Nord, using the "Banlieue" terminus in a separate structure to the right as you enter the station. Be sure your departure video monitor states "Roissy Rail" at the bottom, for this is just one of the two branches of the northbound RER, and you want to be on the correct train.

Figure thirty minutes at a minimum for the train from Gare du Nord and ten minutes from the CDG train terminus to your airline terminal—if all goes well. The Air France bus (costing about the same as first-class rail) takes about an hour from the Porte Maillot bus terminus near the Arc de Triomphe barring gridlock on the motorway.

There are nine Air France bus departures daily to and from Gare Montparnasse timed to connect with the TGV Atlantique to Brittany. Add another fifteen minutes travel time between the airport and the glassed-in pickup beside the Gare Montparnasse marked "Air France."

Overnight Trains

SNCF's overnight equipment is so good it is exported. You can hardly resist riding overnight on the long routes from Paris because with a Eurailpass you pay no more to sleep in a four-bunk compartment than second-class passengers pay for six-bunk couchettes.

EuroCity Night trains from Paris include EC Stendhal to Milan, EC Palatino to Rome, EC Galilei to Florence, EC Rialto to Venice, and upscale Barcelona and Paris-Madrid Talgo trains.

Budget adventurers may also investigate the Cabines-8 found only on SNCF. These specially configured sleeping carriages are designed for young people who prefer not to pay for sleeping accommodations. Each carriage contains twelve compartments with eight semireclining contoured bunks, four per side.

The bunks are treated as seats for reservations purposes so you pay no supplement. If the threat of claustrophobia does not faze you, these second-class bunks carry the right price. You pay only for a simple space reservation, as you would for a seat on any long-distance train. Cabines-8 travel nightly on the following routes: Paris-Hamburg, Paris-Amsterdam, Paris-Strasbourg, Reims-Nice, Paris-Brest, Paris-Quimper, Paris-Ventimiglia, Paris-Briancon, and Metz-Nice.

TER Trains

Look for modern diesel or electrified railcars, usually consisting of two power cars (on each end) and one passive carriage, to provide you with local connections in most of the regions of France. These TER trains ("Trains Express Regionaux") are lighter than the mainline trains and designed with commuter seating. You won't find them in the timetables available in the United States but their frequent departures will take you from city to city in the provinces, providing you access to cities off the tourist paths.

Metralsace, red with stainless steel sides and the red-and-yellow Alsatian coat of arms on entry doors, takes you through Alsace, white cars striped in green with blue piping—"TER Pays-de-la-Loire"—take you through that department, and red-and-white "TER Limousin" and "TER Aquitaine" trains serve those areas.

TGV North

The construction you see in Paris's Gare du Nord is to accept the new TGV North. Platforms are being lengthened and the suburban trains which formerly used the center platforms are being diverted. A new subterranean parking structure, facilities to provide meal service to the TGVs, and track modifications between St. Denis and Paris are under construction. In Lille, a new underground station is being linked to the present station by a people mover system.

The TGV North will be the third high-speed link of France. By May 1993, it will carry you from Paris via Lille to Frethun for the Eurotunnel terminus for Britain (three hours to London), and to Brussels (one and a half hours).

In 1994, FrenchRail will interconnect all three TGV lines with a new sixty-four-mile high-speed line circling Paris and add two new train stations: one at Charles de Gaulle Airport and one at Marne-La-Vallee to serve EuroDisneyland.

Using Eurailpass Bonuses

In France, take advantage of two of Eurailpass's best bonuses: the Chemins de Fer de la Provence and the Irish Continental Line crossings to the Republic of Ireland.

The Chemins de Fer de la Provence (CP) is a private, narrow-gauge line running between Digne and Nice. Read below about this way of entering the Riviera on its diesel railcars.

The Irish Continental Line takes you to Rosslare or Cork from Le Havre or Cherbourg. See the section about Ireland.

France Railpass

As flexible as a Parisian tart's affections and as thrifty as a Gascon goatherd, the France Railpass makes seeing France by train cheaper, easier, and more fun.

With a four-day France Railpass, you can travel anywhere you choose on SNCF for fifteen days for only slightly more than the round-trip fare on TGV between Paris and Lyon. The nine-day pass is good for travel anytime within a month. All passes must be validated at any French train station (which may be done up to six months after issuance in the U.S.). Fast-train surcharges are covered but you must pay for the required reservations.

First-class prices cost about two-thirds of a Eurail Flexipass; buying second-class travel gives you an additional one-third savings. Children four to eleven pay about 60 percent of the France Railpass price. Those under four ride free.

Structured like the Eurail Flexipass, your France Railpass lets you save your days when you decide to stay in one place. Similarly, it is a do-it-yourself pass. You validate your pass yourself. When you start your trip after 7 P.M., enter the next day's date and travel overnight using up only one validation day.

France Railpass has a format different than a Eurailpass's. It is made up of pasteboard folded into sixths. The front is the blue, green, and violet rail pass good for unlimited train travel.

Write your name and passport number on the front and have it validated at an SNCF station (at an "Orientation" kiosk or ticket window) where the agent will enter the first and last day of validity and stamp the back.

You exchange the first of your perforated coupons at either of Paris's airports for a yellow, magnetically encloded ticket for RER travel to midtown Paris. There is a single yellow-stripe-marked first-class carriage in the middle of the RER train—and yes they do check for first-class tickets during the ride.

You exchange the second coupon ("Formule 1") at either airport, Paris's Gare d'Est, Gare de Lyon, Gare d'Austerlitz, Gare du Nord, Gare St. Lazare, or commuter Quai d'Orsay for a free magnetically encoded Paris Sesame transportation card valid for travel on Paris Metro, RER, and bus lines.

When you buy a four-day France Railpass, the Paris Sesame card you receive is valid for a day's travel anywhere in Paris. When you buy a nine-day France Railpass, your Paris Sesame card is encoded for two days on the RAPD's entire regional Metro and bus transit system to the environs.

The back flap contains the heart of your pass: the specified number of day-boxes that you personally date in ink in numerical sequence on the days you travel.

Finally, use your pass to collect your free gift at Printemps department store near the Gare Montparnasse and visit, free, the Georges Pompidou National Art and Culture Center. Pay less when you visit the SNCF Railroad Museum at Mulhouse. Travel at half-fare on the scenic Chemins de Fer de la Provence (see below) and the Bateaux Parisiens sightseeing cruises on the Seine in Paris. Pay half to visit more than a hundred state monuments at sites throughout France, such as the Arc de Triomphe, the tower of Notre Dame, and Mont St. Michel.

You pay 30 percent less for the guided Paris-Vision City Bus Tour, and receive discounts on admission to the Grevin Wax Works in Paris, Mont St. Michel, and elsewhere. The Pullman/Altea and Ibis/Urbis hotels and "Train + Auto" auto rental agencies in 200 stations offer reduced rates.

BritFrance Passes

When you use these passes as described in the Britain/Ireland section, you need not pay the high-speed surcharges required in France.

France Rail'N Drive

The France Rail'N Drive program allows you to combine the France Railpass with an Avis car rental. Avis has 500 locations throughout France including more than 200 in train stations. SNCF/Avis's fifteen-day package gives you four days of unlimited train travel in France plus three days of Avis car rental with unlimited mileage, VAT (value-added tax), and basic insurance included. (Gasoline is extra.) Their one-month package allows you nine days of unlimited SNCF travel and six days of Avis car rental.

Through travel agents/FrenchRail you can also buy France Fly, Rail & Drive Passes for eight travel days in fifteen or seventeen in one month. These allow travel on a France Railpass, Avis car rental, and either one or two full days (depending on duration of your pass) air travel on domestic flights of Air Inter on either blue or white (nonrush) flights. You make flight reservations for Air Inter through Air France's toll-free number in the U.S. or through Air Inter while in France.

To sample France's rail speed and adventure to offbeat corners, travel on the 186 mph TGV Atlantique to Brittany, the TGV Genevois from Paris to Geneva, the Chemins de Fer de la Provence from Nice to Digne, and Metro Basque from Bayonne to St. Jean-Pied-de-Port described here.

TGV Atlantique
Into Brittany by 186 mph Supertrain

Blasting through Brittany at 186 mph, adventurers use the white-striped, hinged vinyl tables separating their seats to write postcards as smoothly as if they were writing from their nearest library.

You accept the well-known fact that TGV-A ("A" for "Atlantique") is fast. It comes as a surprise that TGV-A's new concept in pneumatic suspension makes its ride as calm as a Breton cow.

Atlantique is a victim of its own success. It moves so effortlessly, without shimmy or shake, that passengers can't appreciate that it holds the world's speed record of 320 mph set on May 18, 1990. Ten-carriage-long return trains

TGV ATLANTIQUE

PARIS-MONTPARNASSE

HIGH-SPEED LINE

Brest

Quimper

Rennes

Le Mans

Vendome

Tours

St. Nazaire

Nantes

Poitiers

La Rochelle

-N-

Bordeaux

0   20   100
MILES

Bayonne

Hendaye

Lourdes

take 2.9 seconds to flick past your window. Atlantique pulverizes rain into nuclei so microscopic that the 186 mph wind wipes them from the windows even before they wet it.

TGV-A impresses you with its substance and power. Its busily finished interiors provide minicompartments for four down one side of the aisle of two first-class "club" carriages. Opposite, pairs along the window chat intimately.

Climb TGV-A's shiny aluminum steps at Paris's bright glass, metal, and red granite Montparnasse station, your high-rise "Ocean Gateway" to the Atlantic network. Your TGV-A takes you to Brittany along a dedicated high-speed track which then branches into two routes, the 386-mile North Brittany line to Rennes, St.-Brieuc and Brest, and the 304-mile South Brittany line to Nantes, St. Nazaire and Le Croisic.

The southern fork of the high-speed stretch to St. Pierre des Corps opened in September 1990. It takes adventurers via the new TGV station in Vendome from Paris to Bordeaux in less than three hours, reaching the Spanish Border in five hours, eight minutes. TGV-A will serve La Rochelle in 1993.

Your blue and silver Atlantic supertrain's livery reflects the sun, sea, and sand of Brittany and the Atlantic coast. Instead of yellow roof-line striping to mark first-class sections, TGV-A's doors are color coded (ocean blue-green for second class, cherry red for first, and yellow for the bar), but you may not even notice this. It is easier for you to rely on the easy-to-see numerals indicating class of carriage.

Check your seat reservation coupon in the vestibule before making your way to your seat. Above the compartments' entrances, LCD signs blink destination, train number, and carriage number.

A horn sounds and TGV-A's doors slide shut. In an instant, you leave Paris so quickly that when you enter tunnels you feel depressurization of your carriage. Above, environmentalists have created playgrounds, open spaces, and a cycle path. In open space, you are already passing the outskirts of Paris along land lucky enough to have been already reserved for a railroad line. This land included a roadbed which had been nearly completed before work was abandoned in 1934 — a highly prized right of way which came close to accommodating a motorway thirty years after the railroad was abandoned. On return, when your ears pop, you know they are signaling your approach to Paris.

It doesn't take long for your TGV-A to run quickly up to speed: 186 mph like a stopwatch. Your speed is programmed by computer.

In first class, passengers read newspapers and fashion magazines and sort memoranda from their briefcases on the tabletops.

Outside, the land is flat, spotted with woods along the high-speed track, but: think frogs. You see some of the ponds where environmentalists spent years relocating endangered species away from the train route and having to protect them from hungry herons.

When you leave the high-speed railbed, past Le Mans, your train takes on a new feel. You hear the familiar clickety-clack of standard rails and slow enough to appreciate the Gothic spires marking every village. You see why Brittany is famous for its characteristic, small black and white prolific milk producers, "Pie Noire" cows, which sometimes mingle with brown "Salers" from Auvergne, in the mountains of France's Central Massif.

When you leave Angers' St. Laud train station (made attractive by tufa stone quarried in the Loire Valley), you see greenhouses, artichokes in the fields, and parasitic mistletoe richly infesting many of the trees. Brittany is the only region in France in which mistletoe grows.

Soon you are running along the right bank of the Loire River, wide and quiet. Magnolia trees and camellia bushes were brought from the French settlements in Louisiana before its sale to the United States in 1803.

You recognize Nantes from a distance by its tall buildings. Nantes train station has two accesses. The South access, added in 1989 with the introduction of TGVs, is modern, and has all amenities, ramps instead of stairs, a small restaurant, and an elevator to the passageways below the tracks. The North access echoes from the sixties, but is well marked and easily accessible.

The new waiting room is called "Salon Jules Verne," named after local boy made good.

The rafters of Nantes's St. Peter and Paul Cathedral, destroyed by a devastating fire in the 1970s, have been rebuilt. Beige tufa pillars soar higher than Westminster Abbey's to make this the brightest and warmest large cathedral in Europe.

In Nantes, take time to visit Passage Pommeraye, an original three-level stepped galeria, the predecessor of today's malls. Completed in 1843, the ancient faces, mice, and snails carved in stair risers and cheerful sculptures scattered throughout lend a feeling of fun.

Nearby, adventurers are lucky when they come across the delightfully decorated La Cigale (meaning "cicada") tearoom. Try a pastry and a cup of coffee (or dinner) just to enjoy the atmosphere. It first opened at 4, place Greslin (facing the Opera) in April 1895.

After your train's three-minute halt in Nantes, new passengers board to join your entrance to traditional Brittany, a rough and tumble land of Celts, bagpipes, and the Breton tongue. In Brittany's center you find evocative regions where followers of King Arthur come to see "The Land of the Round Table" and the enchanted Broceliande forest charred by fire in 1990 where the wizard Merlin met the fairy Viviane and love inflamed them both. (To make sure of keeping Merlin, Viviane enclosed him in a magic circle. It would have been easy for him to escape, but he joyfully accepted his romantic captivity forever.)

You see Merlin's seat and Viviane's bed. From here Sir Lancelot of the Lake set out for England and his seduction of Gweniviere, King Arthur's wife.

Past Nantes you run through fertile farming country where farmers harvest melons, cabbage, and onions. To the south tower the major harbor and industrial zone facilities of St. Nazaire on the Loire estuary.

St. Nazaire grew to a great shipbuilding center, when in 1856, large ships found it difficult to reach Nantes. During the Second World War St. Nazaire was a major German submarine base and the center of strategic fighting, blockades, bombardment and, ultimately, massive destruction.

St. Nazaire train station is the final destination for many passengers. They carry their baggage up the apple-green stairwell.

Past St. Nazaire you enter the well-named Cote d'Amour. Even the sun gets brighter as you approach what many French vacationers to La Baule consider the finest beach in Europe — and they frolic here in July and August.

You stop at La Baule's Escourlac Breton-style station house on the northern tip of the diving, soling (the Olympic sport), and wind-surfing resort, and then you cross the canal to Le Croisic peninsula, traveling close above the salt marshes which identify this region. Women scrape crystals off the surface of the salt flats to obtain the finest quality white sea salt in Europe.

Sea birds watch your train riding bumpily onto a siding at Le Croisic's small station, the end of the line. Its continuation is blocked by Mont-Espirit, the curious ninety-eight foot double-corkscrew mound, built from ships' ballast. From the summit you see the salt marshes to the east, the landmark belfry of Batz-sur-mer to the west, and the Atlantic Ocean in the distance.

Even while you are stepping down TGV-A's aluminum stairs a cleaner is plugging in a vacuum cleaner to make your Atlantique spotless for its return trip.

Your TGV-A has a whole array of features for you to use throughout its ten carriages, including telephone booths and a special diaper room in second class for parents with distressed babies. Probably your biggest surprise is that the mechanism adjusting seats in first class makes them rise or sink at the touch of a button just as in a luxury automobile.

Each first-class table has an individual light. Reading lights are behind the passengers and they control a fluorescent overhead lamp by button.

Walking through the carpeted first-class sections you start behind a power car with the elevated nine-passenger, horseshoe-shaped "Le Salon" with video monitors, and then cross the standard "La Coach," half with two-opposite-one seats facing forward; half backward.

FrenchRail calls the next two cars "Club Cars." "Le Club Duo" pairs gray-and-white striped plush seats facing one another beside the aisle across from

"Le Club Quatre," four seats upholstered with black-and-white striped plush within partially closed, tinted-glass minisalons.

Atlantique's social whole-carriage bar car provides adventurers with staggered rows of vinyl-topped snack counters. Across its stainless steel sales counter, service personnel wearing SNCF badges heat microwave sandwiches and sell magazines, candy, coffee, wine, and minibottles of liquor. Low vinyl counters at the windows are equipped with small swivel stools to give you a fine place to eat, drink, and watch the scenery flashing past. Be sure to drop in. It's a great place to hang out and socialize.

Second-class carriages are divided two opposite two, some smoking, some nonsmoking. The equivalent of club in second class provides facing seats with partial tinted-glass partitions above the seats. Regular salons where half the seats face forward, half backward, have no need for these sound barriers.

Second class features rubber-mat flooring, fold-down footrests, rough-wearing fabric upholstery, and tables that fold down from seat backs. Only in the center, where passengers face one another, are there tables similar to those in first class.

The crowd in second class is definitely younger. They are sleeping and listening to earphones.

Up a few steps at the end brings you to "Le Kiosque," the second-class lounge arranged with two tables and second-class seats designated for single children.

TGV-As on the North Brittany line race from Paris's Montparnasse to Rennes, where its multilevel station is part of the district development plan which provided a shopping street above the tracks, a sweeping access hall to the platforms, elevators, and escalators.

North of Rennes, visit one of the world's foremost pilgrim's shrines, Mont St. Michel. Rennes is your changing point for the local train to Pontorson, the closest railhead to Mont St. Michel. Six miles by bus, taxi, or bicycle rented at Pontorson, STN buses leave six times daily for the abbey. Follow the crowds.

From Rennes, the North Brittany line continues to Brest, allowing you to make the 386-mile trip from Paris in about four hours (including stops). When electrification is completed in the summer of 1992, you will be able to travel also by TGV-A through Rennes to Quimper on the southern Brittany coast.

Reservations costing about $2.50 are required on all TGV Atlantique runs. In first class, you can reserve seats "Club Quatre" in the minisalons or beside the window "solo" for intimate conversations. A "couloir" is an aisle seat, and "compartiment" is compartment.

Supplements are payable when you aren't traveling on a Eurail or France Railpass. These cost about $20–22, first class; $12–15, second class, depending on the time of day you travel.

TGV Atlantique to Brittany

Weekday Service Paris—Rennes—Brest

							*	*	*
PARIS (Mont.)	dep.	0720	0820	1120	1420	1520	1720	1810	1920
Le Mans	arr.	....	0914	....	1514	....	....	....	2014
Le Mans	dep.	....	0916	....	1516	....	....	....	2016
Laval	dep.	....	0959	....	....	....	....	....	....
RENNES	arr.	0924	1035	1324	1631	1724	1924	2012	2130
RENNES	dep.	0927		1327	1634		1927	2014	
Lamballe	dep.	....		....	....		....	....	
St.-Brieuc	arr.	1011		1411	1718		2011	2057	
St.-Brieuc	dep.	1013		1413	1720		2013	2059	
Guingamp	dep.	1031		....	1737		2031	....	
Morfaix	arr.	1059		....	1805		2059	....	
Morfaix	dep.	1101		....	1807		2101	....	
BREST	arr.	1133		1522	1839		2133	2209	

Weekday Service Brest—Rennes—Paris

		**						
BREST	dep.			0702	0918		1303	1757
Morfaix	arr.			0733	....		1334	1828
Morfaix	dep.			0735	....		1336	1830
Guingamp	dep.			0804	....		1406	1859
St.-Brieuc	arr.			0820	1026		1421	1915
St.-Brieuc	dep.	0617		0822	1028		1423	1917
Lamballe	dep.	....		....	....		....	....
RENNES	arr.	0704		0909	1112		1509	2002
RENNES	dep.	0708	0816	0913	1114	1302	1513	2006
Laval	dep.	....	0853	....	....	1340	....	....
Le Mans	arr.	0822	0932	....	....	1422	....	2122
Le Mans	dep.	0824	0934	....	....	1424	....	2124
PARIS (Mont.)	arr.	0920	1030	1120	1320	1520	1720	2220

*Not Fridays.
**Not Mondays.

Weekday Service Paris—Nantes—Le Croisic

PARIS (Mont.)	Le Mans		Angers (St. Laud)		NANTES		St. Nazaire	La Baule	LE CROISIC
dep.	arr.	dep.	arr.	dep.	arr.	dep.	arr.	arr.	arr.
0750	....	....	0919	0921	0956				
0850	....	....	1019	1021	1056	1059	1134	1149	1156

0950	1044	1046	1122	1124	1159				
1125	1219	1221	1258	1300	1336				
*1350	1444	1446	1524	1526	1601	1604	1639	1654	1703
*1650	1744	1746	1824	1826	1901				
*1730	....	....	....	....	1929	1932	2006		
1750	1844	1846	1923	1925	2001				
*1840	....	....	....	....	2041	2044	2119	2134	2142
*1845	1938	1940	2017						
*1950	....	....	....	....	2149				
2050	2144	2146	2224	2226	2301				

Weekday Service Le Croisic — Nantes — Paris

LE CROISIC dep.	La Baule dep.	St. Nazaire dep.	NANTES arr.	NANTES dep.	Angers (St. Laud) arr.	Angers (St. Laud) dep.	Le Mans arr.	Le Mans dep.	PARIS (Mont.) arr.
						0620	0702	0704	0800**
				0636	0712	0714	0751	0753	0850
				0736	0811	0813	....	....	0945
				0836	0911	0913	....	....	1045
0819	0829	0843	0917	0921	0957	0959	1036	1038	1135
				1130	1206	1208	....	....	1340
				1336	1412	1414	1451	1453	1550
1328	1338	1352	1426	1430	1506	1508	....	....	1640
				1732	1807	1809	1846	1848	1945
				1937	2012	2014	2052	2054	2150

*Not Fridays.
**Not Mondays.

TGV Genevois
Computer-Age Anachronism

The inquisitive video monitor inside the Gare de Lyon quizzes you with electronic questions. "Where are you going? First or second class? How many people? Do you accept the supplement?"

You answer, "No supplement," when you are traveling by Eurailpass or France Railpass. The surcharge for the high-tech train to Geneva, the EuroCity TGV Genevois, is covered by your pass.

Still, you must reserve a seat. You may not stand in the aisle. So you feed the stainless-steel slot a ten-franc coin and then one-franc coins. In about two or three seconds it drops down a reservation ticket, but it seems reluctant to accept "No supplement" for an answer.

Rhone River

LYON

Bellegarde

Bourg-
en-Bresse

GENEVA

Macon

LAKE GENEVA

Le Creusot

TGV PARIS-GENEVA

- N -

| 0 | 20 | 50 |

MILES

PARIS

The Genevois is one of the select group of trains comprising the EuroCity network. It carries you on one of EC's most fascinating routes, linking Paris with Switzerland's cosmopolitan city through mountainous regions and past villages still anchored in the nineteenth century.

Until the TGV Atlantique's new railbed opened in fall 1989, your TGV Southeast train was the fastest in the world—but even if it were merely a speedy way of getting from one place to another, you would still find it fun, smooth, and exciting to ride. As it is, you get a scenic eyeful as well.

By using the Paris Metro's Gare de Lyon stop and climbing the escalator to ground level, you reach the the station's TGV platform without ever seeing the light of morning. When you arrive at the platform, you step into the future. Purring, shark-snouted, gray, white, and orange Trains a Grande Vitesse surround you as far as you can see.

The TGVs are screamers. They sound like they are growling as their engines warm for fast getaways. Speeding at 167 mph much of the way, your TGV Genevois cuts your travel time to Geneva by more than 2 hours, to 3½ hours. TGVs conquered air travel and provided excitement for your trip.

TGVs on the Southeast network are single, articulated units of eight air-conditioned cars with engines at both ends. At peak travel times, SNCF couples two units together to double the seating to 772 (222 in first class, 550 in second).

You purchase coffee, Parisian croissants, and reading materials in the bar car. In some carriages, you can order a continental breakfast served on the tray in front of you.

The EC TGV Genevois, followed later in the day by the EC Voltaire, the EC Versailles, the EC Henry Dunant, and the EC Jean-Jacques Rousseau, whisks you away promptly at 7:35 A.M. It doesn't immediately leap forward. While toiling through the suburbs of Paris, it vibrates with restrained energy. If you feel some disappointment, it is because you don't feel a jolt when your Genevois enters the high-speed corridor and accelerates to 167 mph. There is no speedometer to fascinate you.

Past the suburbs of the capital, your high-speed trip to Macon is pastoral. You study spotted cows grazing in the fields and ponder the speed of the train. There are no highways paralleling the tracks so you can't accurately gauge your speed, but the buttercups beside the tracks become a mustard-colored blur and you hear no clickety-clack from segmented rails. You know you must be at maximum speed.

You branch from the high-speed line at the new Macon Loche TGV stop, built outdoors in the midst of farmlands. The clickety-clack reminds you that you have returned to old-fashioned—and slower—railbeds.

Past the Bourg-en-Bresse station, two hours from Paris, you enter the Jura region of France. Green woods roll up the impressive heights above the train line. Old villages of monochrome stone houses center around churches that seem to belong on old sepia-tone postcards.

Your attention focuses on the mountains taking shape in the distance. The French word "grandeur" says it all.

You can't escape the anachronism: speeding through ageless Jura mountains and time-forgotten villages in a computer-age bullet.

The passing scenery becomes so eye-catching that French travelers around you fold up the magazines that had interested them before and put away their attache cases still crammed with unfinished business.

Individual farmers tend little fields. Tiny vineyards spot the hillsides. You notice little details that date from quieter times: a river with lily pads, a fisherman in a leaky rowboat, old towns pressed defensively against high mountains, churches of stone, an outcropping with a statue of an unknown hero on its summit.

Finally your Genevois passes the first of many tunnels. You aren't in the tunnel long, but it breaks the scenery. You continue at a brisk pace — no longer at 167 mph, but still very fast.

You finally slow when a broad river, the Rhone, appears on your right. Battlements of once-powerful castles dot the mountainsides overlooking the Rhone. A modern bridge spans the chasm.

At Bellegarde-sur-Valserine, an industrial city at the meeting of the Valserine and Rhone rivers, the only thing level is the huge rail yard. The city trails down the hillside toward the Rhone.

The connecting railcar for the French Lake Geneva resort of Evian-les-Bains stands across the platform below the patina eaves of the weathered train station. "Evian" mineral water is served aboard the TGV Genevois.

From Bellegarde, a long tunnel brings you to a route that twists miraculously through mountain valleys on embankments braced by stone. Mountains tower around the train. You follow the Rhone River below.

Finally your train levels off. TGV chimes sound. Passengers take Swiss bank notes from envelopes and you approach Geneva's Cornavin station along a level route surrounded by endless vineyards.

You arrive at the French/International TGV terminal at Geneva's Cornavin station. Tracks ("Voie") 7 and 8 are separated from Swiss national train traffic by glass doors kept closed except at arrival and departure times.

Swiss trains provide excellent connections for Milan and Venice, or you can travel by the EuroCity Catalan Talgo to Barcelona. Geneva's Tourist Office occupies a gleaming suite in the train station.

When you leave Geneva through the SNCF terminal for France or Spain, don't arrive more than a half-hour before departure time. You must linger in the modest waiting room until guards open the doors pneumatically. You show your passport here when you file past passport control and customs.

EuroCity TGV Service
between Paris and Geneva

		EC921	EC923	EC925	EC927 Henry Dunant	EC929 J-Jacques Rousseau
		Genevois	Voltaire	Versailles		
dep.	PARIS (Lyon)	0735	1036	1432	1740	1913
dep.	Macon (TGV)	0917	....	1615	....	....
dep.	Bourg-en-Bresse	....	....	1634	....	2111
dep.	Culoz	....	....	1725	....	....
arr.	Bellegarde	1037	1334	1746	2041	2216
arr.	GENEVA	1108	1405	1816	2111	2245

		EC920 J-Jacques Rousseau	EC922 Henry Dunant	EC924 Voltaire	EC926 Versailles	EC928 Genevois
dep.	GENEVA	0709	1002	1301	1650	1929
dep.	Bellegarde	0735	1028	1327	1718	1955
dep.	Culoz	....	....	....	....	2022
dep.	Bourg-en-Bresse	....	....	....	1826	....
dep.	Macon (TGV)	....	....	1454	1847	....
arr.	PARIS (Lyon)	1039	1334	1638	2031	2309

Chemins de Fer de la Provence
Scenic Gateway to the Riviera

You climb to your second summit at St. Andre-les-Alpes station overlooking the stone houses of the village and prominent stone church. A fine, long view of snow-covered Alps opens before you to the south. Climbing higher, you see the weirdly scalloped shores of Le Verdon Lake below to the west, with water so calm ducks scarcely bob on the surface.

Riding "Ligne Digne," CP's blue-and-white railcar with self-contained diesel power, is so intimate and open that you look over the engineer's shoulder at the rails ahead while your train skirts the edges of deep precipices and climbs steeply over the last range of Alps between the French interior and the Mediterranean.

More rock canyons than you will find in any other part of France, and some as deep as 700 or 900 feet, mark your path. Your railcar teeters precariously

CHEMINS de FER
de la PROVENCE

Bleone

DIGNE

Mezel-Chateauredon

L'Asse

Barreme

St. Andre

Thorame-Haute

Le Verdon

Le Fugeret

Annot

Le Coulomp

La Vaire

Le Var

Entrevaux

Puget-Theniers

Le Cians

Touet sur Var

Villars-Var

La Tinee

La Vesubie

La Vesubie

Colomars

Le Var

MEDITERRANEAN SEA

NICE

0   10   20

MILES

on mountain rims and rocks from side to side along a roadbed that chatters your teeth.

You travel down again, past level fields of wheat and mountainsides covered with pine to the Asse River, where you cross into Barreme (pop. 435).

Between Barreme and Digne, the capital of the high country in Provence, you roughly trace the route of former mule paths Napoleon and his handful of supporters took returning from Elba in 1815. "The eagle will fly from steeple to steeple until he reaches the towers of Notre Dame." Villages boast commemorative plaques and monuments bear the flying eagle symbol inspired by Napoleon's remark. A house near Barreme's town square carries the inscription that Napoleon slept there on March 3, 1815.

Nice, in the Riviera, attracts visitors like a sunny magnet. Adventurers enjoy frolicking along the beaches and feeling the charm of the Riviera while sipping coffee on the busy, four-mile-long Promenade des Anglais bordering the Mediterranean through the capital and delightful Queen of the Riviera. Monte Carlo, a destination adventurers enjoy visiting for its casino and princely flavor, is twenty-four minutes away by train.

The little-known Chemins de Fer de la Provence (CP) narrow-gauge private railroad brings you here from Digne through Cote d'Azur's 103-mile-long back door, a bright, crisp ride through sunshine and mountain air, gorges, pre-Alps, and river valleys. It is a little trip, an off-the-beaten-track secret, and CP accepts your Eurailpass.

By comparison with SNCF's bright and efficient Gare de Ville terminal in Nice, CP's Gare du Sud is a shock. Sud is a four-track station, the oldest in Nice, built in 1892, but the Place de Gaulle outside can be an enchantment. You pass the sidewalk fruit-and-fish market and at the kiosk buy snack items ranging from excellent pizza to extraordinary, odd pastries.

The Gare du Sud at the Place de Gaulle is about a fifteen-minute stroll from SNCF's main station. In the Gare du Sud, ask for a map of your route to Digne at the "Voyageurs" ticket counter.

The driver shifts your railcar's large diesel engine into low gear and accelerates sharply through Nice's city streets. You not only cross traffic intersections, but you have to stop for red lights when you meet them. You pass stop signals and cross boulevards bumper-to-bumper with automobiles before entering a black tunnel that takes you out of the city center.

The conductor takes your Eurailpass to record the number. He returns it with a pink "Billet Gratuit" for your 103-mile journey.

You watch the surroundings through panoramic windows. The driver maneuvers jerkily. The orange seats and maroon leatherette headrests do not recline but are comfortably padded. It is a very wide carriage for a narrow-gauge railcar. The rubber-mat floor still shows mop marks.

Running rockily along the river Le Var, you begin to notice strange secluded hilltop chateaux. At St. Martin-du-Var station house, you see tulips and other flowers blooming under the trees in back.

You are traveling parallel to highway N202 on the east and the river on the west. Orient yourself by the names shown on road signs.

After stopping at La Vesubie, you cross La Vesubie River on a gray steel-girder bridge to run counter to the racing river while the highway continues high on the mountainside. The Vesubie, a tributary of the Var, is fed by Alpine snows. Its valley reachs up to your right through gorges cut into vertical walls, a popular area for French tourists. You are entering the mountains and it becomes more fun. A tunnel takes you to the left bank of the cottonwood-lined Var. As you pass, you see a woman cranking up the red-and-white highway barrier to let road traffic resume.

Past Touet sur Var station house and the Cians Bridge, a small road breaks away to your right for the Cians gorges, some of the finest in the Alps.

Puget-Theniers, the largest village along this route (pop. 2,000), is a southern town at the meeting of the Roudoule and Var rivers. You leave the Maritime Alps district and enter Alps de Haute Provence — at one and the same time the High Mountains and Provence.

You see high chateaux on the hillside before entering Entrevaux, a surprising fortified town (pop. 1,040) surmounted by its citadel. It lies on the west bank of the Var at the foot of a curious rocky spur.

When you leave Entrevaux, rocks take on strange, worn shapes. You first see distant snow at the time you enter your first snow tunnel. Streams in the Var Valley become wilder. Horses — grown mares and brownish-gray yearlings — romp in the fields.

You leave the Var to the east, flowing from the Daluis gorges, and continue up the Coulomp valley below landslide-scarred slopes to the Var's tributary, the Vaire, and then follow the Vaire Valley.

Rising above Annot's church steeple and red-tile roofs surmounting high facades, you gain your first true Alpine sensation. The mountainside is terraced in rock. Above Le Fugeret, your train wanders freely, through tunnels and loops, to gain altitude. Snow remains on the ground until April.

Passengers peer from the windows and take an interest in the jagged rocks to the east and the curious birds flapping as you pass through a jagged gorge. Everything looks greener.

You cross the Vaire River and pass through a black tunnel onto a second bridge across the Verdon River, a tributary of the Durance, which forms magnificent gorges in the limestone of the Haute-Provence. The fresh pine-scented air has a mountainous feeling to it.

You reach the first summit of your mountain railroad. Thorame-Haute's newly built mountain stone church looks handsome beside the flower-decorated station house.

Now you travel downhill through the upper valley of the Verdon in the same direction as the rushing river to the east. The hills are covered with trees of many different shades of green. You receive a hint of the Alps by forests of beech, pine, and larch. The crisp air and bright sky make this a summer tourist destination for the people of Provence.

Geologists recognize the name Barreme for the name "Barremian," given to part of the lower cretaceous layer.

Past Barreme, your train seems to be speeding downhill, but it can't be going too fast, because new Renaults on highway N85 outdistance you with little trouble. Children in the backseats fan the air with their waving at you.

Past the stone Chaudon-Norante station house, you enter the pre-Alps of Digne, climbing through tunnels and along a creek to that capital of the Lavender Alps—a mountain city looking onto Alps nearby.

Lavender is characteristic of Haute-Provence. In the 1930s, farmers began cultivating plantations of this wild-growing mountain flower on higher slopes. Breathe deeply in July, when mauve flowers scent the air.

In Digne, a pleasant spa town, the CP and SNCF stations share the same building and use side-by-side rails. You might expect it would be easy to transfer from one to the other for through connections, but Digne is on a secondary line sadly underserved by SNCF. Connections to and from Paris are terrible. Because it is outside the city, the Digne train station offers no hotels, facilities, restaurants, or snack bars nearby. Walking into the city takes fifteen to twenty minutes, but usually a bus waits for your train so you may hurry aboard after your arrival (not covered by pass).

Chemins de Fer de la Provence
Summer Service between Nice and Digne

0620	0835	1230	1700	dep.	NICE (Sud)	arr.	1003	1400	1655	2035
0643	0855	1258	1708	dep.	Colomars	dep.	0944	1340	1634	2013
0652	0904	1308	1738	dep.	St.-Martin-Var	dep.	0937	1332	1627	2007
0700	0910	1315	1745	dep.	La Vesubie	dep.	0929	1324	1619	2000
0705	0915	1322	1752	dep.	La Tinee	dep.	0922	1317	1614	1953
0718	0929	1337	1807	dep.	Villars-Var	dep.	0903	1258	1554	1937
0725	0937	1345	1815	dep.	Touet sur Var	dep.	0854	1248	1545	1929
0745	0958	1352	1823	dep.	Puget-Theniers	dep.	0841	1234	1531	1916
0749	1003	1358	1831	dep.	Entrevaux	dep.	0835	1229	1526	1911
0814	1027	1419	1854	dep.	Annot	dep.	0815	1210	1507	1851
0821	1032	1424	1858	dep.	Le Fugeret	dep.	0808	1204	1458	1838

0828	1038	1429	1902	dep.	Meailles	dep.	0758	1157	1453	1830
0842	1050	1443	1915	dep.	Thorame-Haute	dep.	0750	1149	1444	1818
0855	1106	1454	1926	dep.	St. Andre-les-Alpes	dep.	0737	1137	1430	1802
0913	1116	1511	1943	dep.	Barreme	dep.	0722	1122	1415	1749
0930	1137	1528	2000	dep.	Mezel-Chateauredon	dep.	0703	1103	1357	1729
0942	1154	1541	2012	arr.	DIGNE	dep.	0645	1045	1340	1715

Summer Connections between Digne and Paris

1404	dep.	DIGNE	arr.	1556
1516	dep.	St. Auban*	arr.	1448
1607	arr.	Veynes	dep.	1358
1613	dep.	Veynes*	arr.	1354
1816	arr.	GRENOBLE	dep.	1201
1829	dep.	GRENOBLE*	arr.	0955
1948	arr.	Lyon (Part-Dieu)	dep.	0848
2149	dep.	Lyon (Part-Dieu)*	arr.	0845
2215	dep.	Macon (TGV)	dep.	....
2359	arr.	PARIS (Lyon)	dep.	0645

*Change trains.

Metro Basque
Heart and Soul of Basque Country

Local Basque leaders call the railcar that takes you to the heart and soul of French Basque country, "Metro Basque." It runs between Bayonne, the northern limit of the Basque coast in France, and St. Jean-Pied-de-Port, a different world thirty-one miles, one hour, and 515 feet above it. St. Jean-Pied-de-Port, as its name suggests, sits at the foot of the pass of Roncevalles in the Atlantic Pyrenees, the gateway to Spain only five miles above.

Breaking your journey here on a trip between Madrid and Paris is an adventure, a diversion, and a prerequisite when you are interested in Basque culture.

Many Americans of Basque descent return every two or three years to visit their relatives. St. Jean's busy season is July and August, when French, German, English, and American visitors (not counted are Spanish Basques, who are not considered tourists) swell the population of St. Jean's 3,000 permanent inhabitants to 12,000 to 15,000. You enjoy the many summer festivities such as jai alai (which is as important to the Basque as the church), folkloric dancing, and serenades of choral groups.

Many young Basques came to the New World because at home only the oldest sons inherit their parents' farms and properties. Without property, the

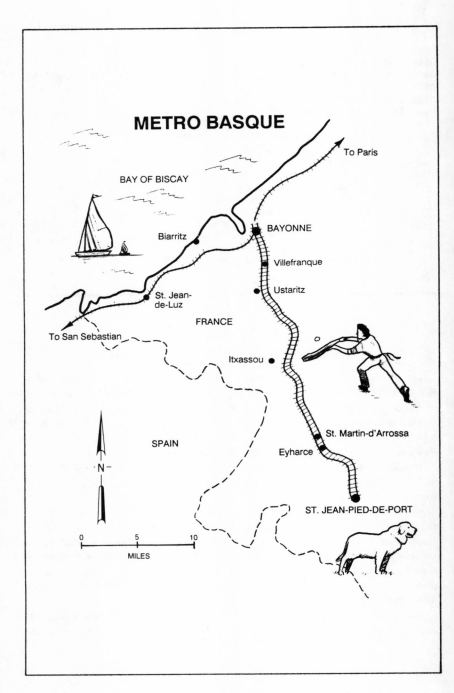

METRO BASQUE

BAY OF BISCAY

To Paris

Biarritz

BAYONNE

Villefranque

St. Jean-
de-Luz

Ustaritz

FRANCE

To San Sebastian

Itxassou

St. Martin-d'Arrossa

SPAIN

Eyharce

-N-

ST. JEAN-PIED-DE-PORT

0   5   10

MILES

younger sons tended to immigrate to the New World to make their fame and fortune. Many did become prosperous. Because Paul Laxhault is of Basque origin, many Basques have a keen interest in American politics and a fondness for American visitors.

Even now the population is not increasing.

Bayonne's station, where you begin your climb, is remodeled to accommodate TGVs from Paris, grand, distinguished by the preserved clock tower on the outside, and efficient inside. You snack in the modern buffet adjacent. Look for the departure times posted prominently above the information office and ticketing windows.

You see waiting on track No. 1 a pair of modern red-and-white railcars built by Francorail in 1981 which are part of the TER Aquitaine regional train system. The first-class section in the rear contains sixteen seats for nonsmokers and eight, through an automatically opening glass door, for "fumeurs."

It's a comfortable, modern, pleasing train, no doubt completed by the same interior designers who won awards for the Corail trains.

Both cars have seats arranged like salons. First class has two-opposite-two maroon bucket-type seats facing each other. Second class, through another glass door that you open with a push on a lever (like Corail), is configured similarly with slightly less distance between brown leatherette seats. There is almost no difference between first and second class except for the blue carpeting in first and nonskid rubber flooring in second. Both are modern, spotless, and decorated with tidy, plaited curtains.

A few minutes late for departure, and concluding his chatting with the driver, the white-capped dispatcher waves his white-and-green paddle. The driver scampers aboard, closes the doors, and starts your electrified railcar on its single track away through a tunnel.

While your conductor checks the tickets and nods at your Eurailpass or France Railpass, you cross the Nive, a broad, brown river, and enter a second, long tunnel. Woods and fruit trees surround your line. Thorny berry thickets flourish on the slopes of the elevated railbed while you pass through flat farm country, with cornstalks thriving in the fields.

Your conductor announces your first stop, Ustaritz, on the speaker system. Ustaritz's station house is brown stucco with brown trim. All stations on this line are clearly marked even when the signs are covered with climbing, green vines.

You still travel on the level, running parallel to the slow-flowing Nive, to your second stop, Cambo-les-Bains, where white postwar homes are roofed with tiles.

Your next stop, Itxassou, is interesting because villagers here still don curious costumes and perform their annual, elaborate Corpus Christi procession.

Now you are beginning to climb modestly past whitewashed farmhouses with sagging tile roofs. Many Basques drive up the parallel two-lane blacktop highway, but still prefer the train occasionally to relish the scenery.

You feel the temperature cool when you slow for the station house serving St. Martin-d'Arrossa and the nearby villages of Eyharce and Osses. This is the junction of two rivers which form the now-raging Nive. You see large white Basque houses with cornerstones and brown or green shutters and trim. A few passengers change here for buses to Saint Etienne de Baigorny.

Finally you see black-faced sheep for the first time, happily munching the long green grass on the slopes. Some sheepherders own them; some rent. You see merinos with long, fine, silky wool, and the Basque sheep, manech, which are black and white with curved horns. But if you visit during the summer, you must go to the peaks of the Pyrenees to find them. The sheep are kept in the cities for six months until May 1, and then they spend six months in the high mountains.

On every side of the wide valley, trim Basque villages nestle amid manicured pasture lands. Each is centered on a church with a clock tower — the local custom is to toll the hour twice. Everything is green, casual, pastoral, the epitome of quiet.

High above the ridges, hawks cry and immense golden vultures soar on the breeze, eyeing the flocks of long-wooled sheep below. Herds of sleek, blonde Basque cattle graze beside shaggy dark ponies called "pottoks," which are horses unchanged in appearance since they were portrayed on the walls of the Paleolithic limestone caves not far away.

At last you see St. Jean-Pied-de-Port, the former capital of Lower Navarre, built by Garcia Ximenes in 716. It became a French town as a result of the Treaty of the Pyrenees in 1659. Louis XIV had it fortified by Vauban and you can still see its ramparts, its walls, and its citadel dominating the town and the Pyrenees. When Wellington crossed the Pyrenees in 1813, he entered France via St. Jean-de-Port.

You are on the pilgrim's route through northern Spain to Santiago de Compostela. (Read this book's section on the Talgo Pendular to Santiago de Compostela.)

Bracken fern, green in spring, reddish brown in the fall, cover the steep slopes of the surrounding mountains which dwarf the wooded hill above the town. Farmers scythe fern into tall, conical stacks for fodder, or simply burn it, turning the air blue with pleasant-smelling smoke.

Disembark at St. Jean-Pied-de-Port and walk from the train station to the city center along steets clearly posted with signs. The Syndicat d'Initiative in the center (on the left as you approach) is located in a modern building.

Inspecting the seven Gothic gates in the wall that used to surround the whole town (which were formerly locked at night) gives you an excellent grasp of the complex angles and divisions of this curiously exciting village.

St. Jean consists of shops and stone houses, each with two or three apartments, scattered along cobblestone streets fronted with steps instead of sidewalks. The crosspieces over the doors proudly proclaim who built them and when. Like all Basque houses, town and country, these are sturdy, half-timbered with stone and whitewashed stucco facades. Green or red-brown shutters are obligatory, for they are the Basque colors, but "Basque red" comes in many shades these days, depending on where the owner buys his or her paint.

The citadel you see brooding over the rooftops is used as a high school in winter and a museum in summer. Sheep graze in its moat.

The church's clock tower set into the city wall contains a small room that served as the city hall in medieval times. From the gate in the base of the tower, you cross a graceful stone bridge arching over the Nive.

Monday is market day all year long, all day long, in St. Jean, as it has been for centuries. You can buy berets (black only) from traveling peddlers, rope-soled canvas Basque slippers, Citroen tractors, Michael Jackson cassettes, fresh-killed wild doves and ripe cheeses. Two thousand lambs are bought here every Monday.

Summer Metro Basque Service

BAYONNE	dep.	0939	1206	1602	1809	2030
Behereharta	dep.	....	....	....	1817	....
Villefranque	dep.	....	....	....	1822	....
Ustaritz	dep.	0954	1222	1617	1827	2045
Jatxou	dep.	....	....	....	1830	....
Halsou-Larressore	dep.	....	....	....	1834	....
Cambo-les-Bains	dep.	1003	1232	1626	1842	2055
Itxassou	dep.	1011	1240	1634	1850	2103
Louhossoa	dep.	1018	1247	....	1857	....
Pont-Noblia	dep.	1025	1254	1647	1904	2116
Osses-St. Mart.-d'Arrossa	arr.	1035	1304	1657	1914	2126
Osses-St. Mart.-d'Arrossa	dep.	1036	1305	1658	1915	2126
ST. JEAN-PIED-DE-PORT	arr.	1050	1319	1712	1929	2140
ST. JEAN-PIED-DE-PORT	dep.	0554	0755	1342	1536	1752
Osses-St. Mart.-d'Arrossa	arr.	0608	0809	1356	1550	1806
Osses-St. Mart.-d'Arrossa	dep.	0609	0809	1356	1550	1807
Pont-Noblia	dep.	0619	0819	1406	1600	1817
Louhossoa	dep.	0626	....	....	1608	....

Itxassou	dep.	0633	0833	1420	1616	1831
Cambo-les-Bains	dep.	0641	0842	1428	1626	1841
Halsou-Larressore	dep.	0646	....	....	....	....
Jatxou	dep.	0649	....	....	....	....
Ustaritz	dep.	0652	0851	1437	1635	1850
Villefranque	dep.	0657	....	....	....	....
Behereharta	dep.	0702	....	....	....	....
BAYONNE	arr.	0710	0907	1453	1651	1906

Iberia

*Spanish   trains—Riding   RENFE's   overnight   trains—Using
Madrid's and Barcelona's train stations—Airport connections—
Rail clubs—Portuguese railroads—National rail passes*

Spanish Trains

Look for Spain's least conspicuous trains. The low-to-the-ground, gray-and-cream tilting Talgo Pendular units are some of the most comfortable you ride in Europe.

Forget old news. The trains of Spain have changed direction. Now you will agree they are innovative, fun to ride, and charged with excitement of 1992's Summer Olympic games in Barcelona and World's Fair in Seville, which organizers guarantee to be the largest event of the twentieth century.

You use sparkling new stations like Madrid's Atocha and the one in Vigo; you ride brilliant trains such as the Talgo Pendular and the TAV (for "Tren de Alta Velocidad," or "high-speed train") to run in 1992; you transit well-managed hubs such as Madrid's Chamartin station; and you relax in first-class lounges open free to Eurailpass travelers. You agree that Spain is a great nation to visit by train.

RENFE, the acronym for the Spanish Railroads, "Red Nacional de los Ferrocarriles Espanoles," requires reservations on most of its long-distance trains, but RENFE's computerized system makes them easy for you to obtain at any RENFE office or train station or even up to two months in advance from the U.S., although Madrid's downtown RENFE office at Alcala, 44 (use the Banco de Espana Metro stop) is often more convenient. RENFE accepts bank credit cards for payment, but be sure to flash them in advance to alert the booking agent. Reservations on Talgo Pendulars cost about $2.50.

RENFE's better trains have supplements also payable by point-to-point ticket purchasers, but you are exempt if you hold a Eurailpass or Spain Railpass (see "National Rail Passes" below).

RENFE's flagship train is the EC Catalan Talgo between Barcelona and Geneva, the only one to use spacious "Internacional" carriages. You also ride articulated Talgo IIIs (which are excellent), InterCity trains, ELTs ("Electrotrens"), and TERs ("Trens Espanol Rapido"), which are fast diesel railcars for short and medium distances. These higher-class trains are all air-conditioned. Choose Talgos whenever you can, but new TERs give you a nice ride on their runs.

RENFE, which now runs trains exclusively on wide-gauge (5 feet, 6 inches) rails, is taking its first steps to convert its network to new European standard-gauge (4 feet, 8½ inches).

Until RENFE constructs European gauge to the French frontier, you must change trains when you cross or your train must be accommodated to the change of gauge. RENFE changes gauge by either adjusting the wheelsets or physically jacking up the carriage shells and switching undercarriages so delicately that sleeping travelers seldom notice it. On night crossing of the Puerta del Sol and Sud Express trains the couchettes are raised and new bogies substituted while passengers riding in first- and second-class carriages get off the train, file through passport inspection, and carry their belongings to their new train. Talgo trains are designed so mechanics in a work pit at the border widen or narrow their wheelsets while everyone remains aboard (e.g., the Paris-Madrid, Pablo Casals, and Catalan Talgo trains).

RENFE's new European-gauge tracks will carry 186 mph TAVs first between Madrid and Seville. Then, before the end of the century, when RENFE's new European-gauge tracks run to the French frontier, adventurers will enter Spain with no delay for change of gauge and probably no customs or passport-inspection formalities and race to major Spanish cities as far south as Seville.

RENFE's first priority is to carry adventurers aboard twenty-four new, 186-mph, TGV Atlantique trains between Madrid and a special stop for these trains right on the site of the enormous 1992 World Exposition. The permanent terminus called Santa Justa is being constructed in Seville on Avenida Kansas City (named for Seville's sister city).

At the same time, Seville's magnificent, Eiffel-designed, neo-Mudejar Plaza de Armas station has been converted to a major art exhibition center and Seville's San Bernardo station has been decommissioned.

Work on new TAV track is proceeding in three segments: 1) Madrid to Brazatortes (a village in the Sierra Morenas mountains), 2) Brazatortes to Cordova, and 3) Cordova to Seville. Building the northern segment broke all construction speed records. In one year the infrastructure was completed. The second segment is being built through difficult mountainous terrain. It is requiring construction of fourteen tunnels and fourteen long bridges.

TAV's maximum speed will be controlled by terrain, but on some stretches you will race up to 186 mph. In 1992, you will reach Cordova from Madrid in 2 hours; Seville in 3 (possibly 2½). Presently you require about 6½ hours to reach Seville from Madrid partially because the roundabout route followed by the old rails skirts the mountains.

The TAVs have cosmetically changed nose profiles midway between FrenchRail's Atlantique and GermanRail's ICE, and their livery is being modified to present a distinctive RENFE appearance. Interiors will feature videos, like RENFE's present Talgo trains.

When you wish to travel to Portugal circumventing Madrid, the classic way from France is aboard the legendary Sud Express, which is one of the famous nostalgic trains. Sud Express carries French couchettes between Paris and Lisbon via San Sebastian and Medina del Campo, Spain, and crosses the famous Eiffel Bridge en route. For faster travel, take the new overnight train named for the Portuguese writer Eca de Queiroz and change at the French border for speedy service aboard the connecting TGV-A train.

Adventurers curious about visiting Andorra should use French overnight train No. 4415 (carrying first- and second-class French couchettes and through carriages) from Paris at La Tour-de-Carol, France, your bus gateway to the tiny principality. From there it connects with a fast Spanish train for Barcelona.

To transit Spain for Morocco, your best bet is the French second-class couchette departing Paris-Austerlitz at 10:30 P.M. on train No. 307, which is coupled to the Media Luna night train, arriving in Algeciras at 7:30 A.M. on the second morning for your ferry crossing. Riding this couchette obviates your need to change trains at the border or in Madrid. Be sure to reserve in advance.

Many adventurers are surprised to learn about the well-running secondary train network across the north of Spain because they don't see it on the Eurailpass train map—for the reason that FEVE does not accept Eurailpasses. FEVE, "Ferrocarriles de Via Estrecha," claims to be the longest continuous narrow-gauge network in Europe—a claim that is echoed by Switzerland's Rhaetian Railroads.

Riding RENFE's Overnight Trains

RENFE's standard domestic overnight trains are called "Estrella," and provide you with accommodations in second-class brown-and-white couchette carriages (French Corail equipment), through cars with nonreclining seats, and well-worn first- and second-class sleeping cars.

As different from the Estrella as the sun from stars, RENFE's overnight Talgo trains on trunk lines from Madrid and Barcelona are a force in overnight European travel. They carry only sleeping accommodations and white-linen restaurants—no couchettes or sitting coaches. Very pricey, the EuroCity Barcelona-Paris Talgo, the Barcelona-Madrid Talgo, the Seville-Madrid Talgo, and the EuroCity Madrid-Paris Talgo give you the most comfortable overnight travel in Europe.

RENFE's top of the line is the EuroCity Pablo Casals "Gran Clase" overnight Talgo train between Barcelona and Zurich, Switzerland (with a branch to Milan, Italy). Swiss bankers and financiers boarding in Zurich, Bern, and Geneva fill it during the summer. The segment which separates during the night for Milan's Centrale terminus makes Pablo Casals your best train connection between Spain and Italy.

Gran Clase compartments are equipped with showers. First-class passengers reserve single compartments, with the top price tags in Europe, including shower and breakfast. Two-bedded ones include optional shower and breakfast. Passengers with second-class tickets may reserve beds in four-bedded compartments. Eurailpass holders don't pay for tickets, but they pay hefty supplements to cover sleeping accommodations and meals. International Talgo trains may be ticketed and reserved from North America by telephoning 1-800-GO-TALGO, but this service does not extend to pass holders.

The EC Madrid-Paris Talgo is the fastest night train in the world, taking 12 hours, 50 minutes, to travel 905 miles at an average speed of 71 mph.

At the other extreme, you can ride (three times a week) a Soviet Railroads (SZD) through sleeping car from Madrid to Moscow that takes four days and negotiates three breaks of gauge.

Using Madrid's and Barcelona's Train Stations

Madrid is the hub of Iberia. You will probably arrive or depart from Chamartin station, one of Europe's brightest, in the northern outskirts of the city. In the west of Madrid, the smaller "Principe Pio" station (also called "Norte") dispatches trains to Galicia, Salamanca and for regional transit.

Madrid's 1989, glass-and-cement Atocha train station replaced the old Eiffel-designed terminal you see directly adjacent. Architects relied extensively upon unpretentious red brick, concrete, and matte-texture cast iron. Atocha is sure to confuse many adventurers by its many levels of activity.

Reach Chamartin, Norte, and Atocha stations by underground Metro. (Ask for a Metro map—"Plano"—upon entering the system.) To reach Atocha station use the Metro stop called "Atocha RENFE" (do not confuse with "Atocha" stop). A ten-ride magnetically encoded ticket for the Metro costs about $3.50. It gives you a substantial per-ride savings and eliminates the bother of buying separate, fifty-five-cent tickets for each Metro trip. Some Metro cars are old and creaky, like boxcars; others are modern with upholstered seating. "Sol" Metro stop below the Puerta del Sol, the center of Spain, is the hub of Madrid's Metro.

Along the underground train tunnel between Chamartin and Atocha stations, look for "Nuevos Ministerios" and "Recoletos," RENFE's two small stations resembling subway stops. Frequent regional trains pass through these stops taking you to Leon, Segovia, Burgos, Valladolid, El Escorial, and Avila (among others). Depending on where you stay in Madrid, you board here more conveniently than going all the way to Chamartin or Atocha (check RENFE's timetable and posters on the walls).

You may find also that RENFE's frequent rapid-transit train service ("Cercanias") between Nuevos Ministerios/Recoletos and the big stations gives you more convenient access to long-distance trains originating at Chamartin and/or Atocha than by a long Metro ride or surface transportation—and these Cercanias are covered by rail pass.

Reach Nuevos Ministerios RENFE station by Metro lines 6 and 8. Follow the signs: "Accesos RENFE."

In Barcelona, a complex of three major train terminuses and rambling subway lines confuses you. The mainline platforms at Barcelona's Termino station are closed temporarily for reconstruction to serve the Olympic games. Trains that normally would call at Termino are being diverted to Barcelona's Sants station (also called "Central"). Most trains also stop at the smaller, underground Passeig de Gracia station, with a large reception hall, which is very likely the most convenient place for you to debark because its central location places you adjacent to Barcelona's subway line 3 and only four blocks north of the Placa de Catalunya.

Airport Connections

Discussions are taking shape over connecting Baranjas, Madrid's airport, with Madrid's city center. Arrivals presently travel by airport bus to Colon Square or take a relatively inexpensive taxi. Engineers are studying the advantages and disadvantages of building a monorail train, a Maglev-propelled vehicle, or a European-gauge train which would call at Baranjas as a stop on a new Madrid-Valladolid/Barcelona Y-shaped high-speed line.

In Barcelona, board trains for the airport at Barcelona's Sants ("Central") station, which you reach by Metro lines 3 and 5.

Rail Clubs

RENFE's first-class lounges ("Rail Clubs")—like first-class airline lounges—are oases of quiet and gentility featuring overstuffed furniture, magazines, and television, with free coffee and soft drinks brought by enthusiastic staff. For admission, the receptionist checks for a first-class reservation coupon ("Billette Plazas Sentadas y Literas") on one of the Spanish EuroCity trains (the Paris-Madrid Talgo, the Barcelona Talgo, the Pablo Casals, or the Catalan Talgo), in a sleeping compartment, or on a domestic Spanish Talgo, InterCity, or Electrotren. You must reserve these trains anyway, so all first-class passengers including Eurailpass holders are entitled to use these havens.

For quiet before boarding, look for "Rail Clubs" at Madrid-Chamartin station (between the entrances to tracks 13 and 14), Madrid's Atocha station, at Barcelona's Sants station (opposite the cafeteria), in the Vigo terminal (brightly marked in the center), in Cordova, Valencia's Termino, and Zaragoza.

Portuguese Railroads

The Portuguese Railroads ("Companha dos Caminhos de Ferro Portugueses," or "CP") suffered for years from Portuguese economic difficulties and political uncertainties. Things are looking brighter. Except for occasional red-and-cream carriages, all CP carriages and railcars have stainless-steel exteriors built in Portugal by Sorefame to Budd Company designs, except for the new Alfa Service equipment built by Sorefame to French Corail specifications. The first-class cars are clearly marked with broad yellow stripes.

CP's trains run on wide-gauge rails, the same as Spanish trains, so you won't be delayed by changing trains at the border, but brusque customs inspections make some border crossings unpleasant.

RENFE's trains between Madrid and Lisbon (which in the past have been very shabby) have been updated. During the day you travel on a red Talgo III train called the Luis Camoens ("Camoes," in Portuguese). Overnight the Estrella Lusitania takes you in brown-livery first- and second-class sitting and second-class couchette (half a carriage is a food section) French Corail carriages that RENFE purchased from SNCF as well as two sleeping cars with yellow-highlighted blue livery which were formerly Wagon-Lits, but are now owned by RENFE. You need reservations for these trains.

Adventurers use two other less-traveled routes for crossing the border between Spain and Portugal on secondary lines. In the north, railcars, with first- and second-class seating, take you between Vigo's 1988 station and Porto's Sao Bento station.

In the far south, a ferry crosses the Guadiana River at Vila Real de Santo Antonio. Take the Algarve train through Vila Real de Santo Antonio (see below) to the "Guadiana" stop. This connects CP's local service through Portugal's Algarve region to the Damas bus company's eight-times-daily service between Ayamonte and Huelva/Seville (not covered by Eurailpass). Talgo Pendulars and Estrella trains run once daily between Huelva and Madrid. Presumably when the new 2,000-foot suspension bridge across the Guadiana at Ayamonte is completed, bus service will replace the ferry.

Adventurers seeking a shortcut between Portugal and Africa may prefer the Monday, Thursday, and Saturday crossings of the ferry, *Lusitania Expreso* (not covered by rail pass) between Faro (served by the Algarve train; see below) and Tangier, Morocco.

National Rail Passes

Spain Railpasses and Spain Flexipasses for unlimited travel on RENFE are among the least expensive rail passes you can buy in North America (from travel agents through FrenchRail, RENFE's official representative in North America). Supplements for your use of all trains, including those normally requiring "A" supplements, are included, but not sleeping or eating surcharges. Buy first- and second-class consecutive passes for eight or fifteen days or the Spain Flexipass for four travel days in fifteen. FEVE does not honor these passes.

Ask in Spain and Portugal about buying Spain-Portugal rail passes valid for travel on the networks of both countries.

CP grants adventurers over sixty-five years of age a 50 percent reduction from their usual prices. For all adventurers, CP has first-class (only) national rail passes available for seven, fourteen, and twenty-one days, but there is little reason to buy them. Portugal's small size limits your train traveling potential. Ask about them at the train information office in Lisbon's Santa Apolonia station.

The four train adventures described in this chapter take you aboard the Talgo Pendular from Madrid to Santiago de Compostela, the unusual ride along Spain's Costa del Sol, the terrifying trams through Lisbon's Alfama district, and stretches letting you visit almost the whole length of Portugal.

Tilting Train Pilgrimage
Lazy Way to Santiago de Compostela

While you are lounging lazily on Spain's sparkling Talgo Pendular train, waiting for the television to blink on and wondering whether this posh new entry for Europe's greatest-train honors really tilts around curves as designed,

SANTIAGO de COMPOSTELA TALGO

Atlantic Ocean

La Coruna

SANTIAGO de COMPOSTELA

Vigo

Bay of Biscay

Orense

To Porto

PORTUGAL

Puebla de Sanabria

SPAIN

Zamora

Medina del Campo

Avila

```
0    20        50              100
|----|---------|---------------|
            MILES
```

MADRID

you might consider reading Chapter XIII, "Santiago de Compostela," of Michener's *Iberia*.

You are entering the Galicia region from Madrid and are still three hours from Santiago, your destination.

When one traveler made this trip, he came alive with Michener's sentence: "I was fortunate in reaching Compostela at the precise point in the year when I could best witness the significance of the town and its cathedral in Spanish life, for El dia de Santiago (the day of St. James) occurs each year on July 25, and is the occasion for a religious celebration of great dimension." The traveler looked at his watch. It was indeed July 24.

A pilgrimage to Santiago de Compostela is still important not only for the devoted, but for casual students of world history. In 812 A.D., a hermit saw in the heavens a bright star hovering over a vacant field where the body of St. James (Sant Iago), uncorrupted by the passage of time, was unearthed. The apostle, who became known as St. James Matamore, the Slayer of the Moors, was later seen riding a white horse and instilled the spirit for the reconquest of Spain from the infidels. Today Santiago de Compostela's cathedral stands where that vacant field presumably lay.

The pilgrimage aboard the Talgo Pendular, free on a Eurailpass, is the convenient, but lazy, way to visit Europe's number two (after Rome) holy city and the site of one of Christendom's most venerated cathedrals.

During the eight-hour, 420-mile run, you are treated to the scenic contrasts of desiccated Old Castile and the twisting adventure of a mountain railroad into green Galicia.

The train leaves from Madrid's third station, Principe Pio (also known as "Norte" station). It has the advantage of subway service to and from the platform (use the "Norte" Metro stop). Principe Pio is a boring terminus. The day's major excitement occurs when the slate blue and white Talgo begins boarding. A comely stewardess sporting a chic brown derby, brown skirt, and yellow blouse, struts along the platform. She greets passengers with free copies of Madrid's *El Pais* newspaper.

Talgo Pendulars are among the most comfortable-riding and innovative in Europe. Talgo stands for "Tren Articulado Ligero Goicoechea y Oriol." The last two names are those of the inventors of the system and the first three words mean "lightweight articulated train." Because they are articulated units, the string of shorter, connected, low-profile parlors bends around curves like a rubber snake. The latest generation, called the Pendular, additionally tilts according to ingenious design. Suspension from above the center of gravity causes the bodies to swing centrifugally and round curves so smoothly you'll see scarcely a ripple in your coffee.

You stretch out in oversize, two-opposite-one, deep bucket seats. They have folding tables in their backs, but when you recline, your seat's cushions slide forward so you don't disturb the person behind you. The twenty-one-inch wide seats have a thirty-nine-inch pitch in first class. Each first-class parlor holds twenty-six seats; the second-class parlors, four across, hold thirty-six.

The bar located between the first- and second-class sections is magnificent, circled with an elaborate golden frieze. All is stainless steel behind the serpentine glass counter fitted with thirteen cantilevered stools (three more at a back bar). The adjacent kitchen is equipped with a gas griddle and two rings.

The Virgen del Pilar diesel locomotive pulls away from Madrid at 1:30 P.M., exactly on time, with a rumble like thunder. You see a long, panoramic, industry-free view open back on the city through a forest of encina, or live oak, trees. Spanish children delight in eating these trees' nuts, which are similar to chestnuts and almonds.

Almost instantly the conductor comes through to check your reservation card and ticket or pass. About halfway to Avila (pop. 40,000), your Talgo enters the summer-parched high plateau known as Old Castile. Outside, the ground is rocky and not very rich, so you are hardly surprised when you come eye-to-eye with a black bull snorting angrily and pawing the yellow leavings of a wheat harvest.

Entering Avila, watch for Europe's most vivid enduring example of medieval fortification. When the station no longer blocks your view, your eyes rivet to the sight and you can trace out the cathedral and the crenulated walls and battlements not far to the south.

Past Avila, the rocks become more hostile and the live oaks juiceless. Your Talgo climbs relentlessly. It is uncompromising country.

Lunch, catered by the Wagons-Lits company, is served aboard the Talgo Pendular between Madrid and Santiago. The four-course menu, served at your seat, costs about $15 and consists of 1) fish, 2) beefsteak or chicken, vegetables, and potatoes, 3) cake, cheese, or yogurt, and 4) choice of fruit. Wine and mineral water cost extra. Dinner is not served, but the bar car is available for snacks.

When your Talgo reaches Medina del Campo (3:27 P.M.), busy agricultural market and major railroad junction, and pulls to a stop next to the Eiffel-designed canopy of the brick train station, you can't but remark how green things are becoming. Sunflowers are tall, pines begin dotting the hills, and farmers are harvesting leafy vegetables.

Your Talgo makes a "V" turn when the Virgen del Pilar shuffles by on an adjacent track and the new Virgen de la Macarena diesel locomotive takes charge of your train and pulls away with passengers facing backwards. You rotate your seat to look forward once more.

At 4:10 P.M., your Talgo passes Toro, the fine-looking village with picture-book profiles of the Romanesque Collegiate and San Lorenzo churches. The Duero below, one of Spain's five major rivers, flows slowly but still looks fresh and blue. Wheat flourishes north of the river, grapes to the south. The light blossoms of almond trees dot the landscape in spring.

Irrigation takes hold outside. There is heavy cultivation. Stalks of corn line the fields, peach and pear trees droop with fruit, tractors ready the slopes for vegetables and, in the distance, sheepherders prod their flocks with crooked staves.

When the Virgen de la Macarena locomotive begins its serious climb into the Leon Mountains, it passes hay deposited in peaked piles. Burros and horses mill about. The land is now dry and soon changes into mountains.

Except for the handsome Romanesque facade of the train station, modern-ized to look very efficient, historic Zamora (4:26 P.M.) now seems to be composed entirely of tall red-brick and white-brick apartment structures. The return Talgo arrives on the adjacent track. It left from Vigo/La Coruna thirty minutes earlier than you started.

With hardly a warning, the video lights up on four television sets suspended from the ceiling so that every passenger can see them easily without craning their necks. The train manager passes down the aisle renting out blue-and-yellow earphones that plug into the outlet in your armrest (about $2). If you don't appear to speak Spanish he will pass you by. The audio is all in Spanish. *Jaws* and *The Mouse that Roared* are evergreens with RENFE.

At about 5:30 P.M., you first glimpse the mountain lake of Sanabria (3,280 feet), spotted with vacationers kayaking and windsurfers maneuvering their bright sails.

The mountain village of Puebla de Sanabria is a postcard-perfect picture of houses with granite roofs and white walls. It lies at the foot of the Sanabria valley, which is alive with streams rushing through its undergrowth. The black slate-covered station house with white lawn chairs overlooking the lake could be a model for a miniature railroad display.

You see the train is entering different countryside, wet and green and chock-full of granite. This is the isolated, rainy region at the northwestern corner of the Iberian peninsula called Galicia. There are no seductive Carmens or fla-menco dancers here. Myrtles and camellias bloom. Beaches are empty and churches full. General Franco came from here.

Galicia is one of Spain's least affluent regions and also one of its most inde-pendent. Its language is half-Portuguese. Its wealth of granite sets it apart from the rest of Spain just as its culture and Celtic heritage. Bagpipes are the native instrument.

Builders have turned their abundance of the gray-and-white stone into barns, corncribs, garages, homes, terraces, and fences that range across the countryside in elaborate mazes only goats understand.

By the time your Talgo reaches La Gudina (6:18 P.M.), thoughts of dried Old Castile are replaced by the view to the north beckoning with charisma. An occasional flock of sheep meanders to the train line.

The Virgen de la Macarena curves in and out of tunnels. This is the true mark of a mountain railroad. Fields look like patchworks. Ferns flourish on embankments beside the windows. Pastoral fields of corn and vineyards spread below. The majestic Cantabrian Cordillera Mountains rise before you, almost blue in the distance, crisscrossed with brown firebreaks.

This corner of Spain is on the western fringe of the Middle European Time Zone. In summer, the sun is high even at 7:15 P.M.

At Orense (pop. 87,000), your carriage for Santiago dawdles while workers split the train. Passengers lug their suitcases up and down the aisle to get into the correct half. Some continue to the spanking new terminal at Vigo (pop. 265,000) overlooking its busy, beautiful, natural harbor on the Atlantic coast north of Portugal. The segment taking you to Santiago continues farther to La Coruna (pop. 250,000), Galicia's principal port and city.

It is getting late. You are restless to arrive, but the vistas are some of the most idyllic in Spain. You see tiny, cone-shaped haystacks and grapevines trained on wooden trellises. The hills roll as far as the horizon.

The Virgen pulls steadily on a long, steady climb until finally, a few minutes late, it snakes through the crisscrossing pattern of rails to arrive at track No. 1 in Santiago de Compostela (pop. 100,000).

The station is across town from the cathedral, but still it is the popular destination for throngs of modern-day pilgrims and students. The guardrails are lined with silver-painted, cast-iron cockleshells. This symbol honors those who came, beginning in the eleventh century, not by tilting train, but by wearing out countless pairs of stout sandals.

Across from the cathedral try to inspect Santiago's five-star Hostal de los Reyes Catolicos, which is part of Spain's National System of Paradors. This national monument, an inn for pilgrims dating from the sixteenth century, is the most desirable hotel in Galicia.

Talgo Pendular Service
Madrid to Santiago de Compostela

1330	dep.	MADRID (P. Pio)	arr.	2200
1448	arr.	Avila	dep.	2036
1449	dep.	Avila	arr.	2035

1527	arr.	Medina del Campo	dep.	1954
1539	dep.	Medina del Campo	arr.	1942
1626	arr.	Zamora	dep.	1851
1629	dep.	Zamora	arr.	1848
1740	dep.	Puebla de Sanabria	dep.	1740
1818	arr.	La Gudina	dep.	1702
1916	arr.	Orense-Empalme	dep.	1600
1921	dep.	Orense-Empalme	arr.	1538
1947	arr.	Carballino	dep.	1515
2058	arr.	SANTIAGO DE COMPOSTELA	dep.	1353
2100	dep.	Santiago de Compostela	arr.	1351
2200	arr.	La Coruna-San Cristobal	dep.	1300

The Welcome Train
Secret of the Costa del Sol

Jet lag is merciless. When the glass doors of Malaga's "Gateway to the Costa del Sol" airport snap shut behind you, you are newly arrived, glazed with jet lag, and too groggy to glance up to the tiny overhead sign pointing to the train: "Ferrocarril."

Lined-up taxis and standing buses offer you transportation to your beach apartment, condo, or hotel, but your best ride is the Costa del Sol train.

At first you may be chagrined at the tackiness and disrepair of the Costa del Sol, but after you get to know the convenience of the Costa del Sol train and the Portillo bus system you move around easily and discover a fascinating and very enjoyable experience.

The train runs twenty miles along the most popular stretch of Spain's sunny strand, from Malaga (pop. 505,000) to Fuengirola. The arrow at the airport points out a paved path (perfect for luggage with wheels) that leads for two minutes through the parking lot to the elevated train stop.

RENFE's Costa del Sol train is kept the best secret in the south of Spain because it loses money. The national railroad makes no pesetas on this cheap service with a view that gives you a clever budget way to orient yourself to the fascinating jumble grown up along the warm water beaches.

An excursion on this cunning train shows off the many sights of the coast stretching west from Malaga. From the windows you get marvelous views of the quaint village of Mijas snuggled in the mountains, the blue Mediterranean lapping at the sand, rows of olive trees and eucalyptus groves, snow-covered Sierra Nevada mountains in the distance, artichokes, horses, and truck farming. Of course, you also see the endless houses, condos, and hotels embracing starkly modern, traditional Spanish, and elaborate Moorish styles, all distinguished by the identical color: blinding white.

Mijas •

FUENGIROLA

Benalmedena

COSTA DEL SOL
RAILROAD

TORREMOLINOS

Mediterranean Sea

To Cordoba

MALAGA

0   2   5
MILES

Designers have modified the no-frills, yellow-striped, blue train carriage for airport service. They created floor space for suitcases at the entry doors and built special overhead racks broad enough to support piles of luggage. The two-opposite-two maroon leatherette seats are in good condition despite heavy use, but the linoleum floor is scuffed from the dragging of countless suitcases.

The efficient, self-propelled, electric train set, a "Unidad Electrica" railcar with attached carriage, is the workhorse of local and regional transportation throughout Spain. Each unit seats 260 (700 standing) at a maximum speed of 87 mph. They have run reliably since 1974, so RENFE is continuously adding new units.

Carriages pass half-hourly between Malaga-Guadalmedina and Fuengirola. Show your Eurailpass or your RENFE Tourist Card or buy a ticket on board. Only at the bigger, fully staffed stations do personnel in ticket booths at the entrance sell tickets.

A ticket from the airport to Torremolinos (trains are second class only) costs 50 pesetas (about forty-five cents). Riding the entire stretch, twenty miles, costs 150 pesetas (about $1.35). Round-trip fares are less.

Most of the line is above ground, but in Malaga, Torremolinos, and Fuengirola the stations are subterranean. The entrances to the underground Torremolinos and Fuengirola stations are difficult to see — even when you are standing next to them. Escalators take you to street level, but descend by stairs. There are nineteen stops between Malaga and Fuengirola. Making the complete run takes fifty-one minutes.

This line gives you easy access to a series of communities, none far from the line, but most passengers board at Malaga-RENFE, Malaga airports (National and International), and Torremolinos. Note that there are two airport stops. The one closer to Torremolinos, which used to be called "Vuelos Charter," is for the International terminal. The one closer to Malaga, "Aeropuerto," is for the National terminal. This is probably the one you will use, but be sure to check in advance.

The underground Torremolinos station entering on the square between Avenida Santos Rein and Calle de Emilio Estaban is the most complete of the line. Decorated with blue, green, red, and yellow tiles and blue benches, there is a magazine stand, a few lockers, a ticket kiosk, and a public telephone.

A tunnel connects the Malaga-RENFE stop to the separate mainline Malaga train terminus, where rays of red and yellow gleam through Moorish colored-glass windows. Luggage lockers are on the far side (125 pesetas). A second exit leads directly to the parking lot and taxi stand, the post office in back, and the bright snack bar/cafeteria and bank across the street.

A Talgo Pendular leaves from the mainline station in the afternoon for Madrid by way of Cordova. Four overnight trains run the same route: the Talgo

"Costa del Sol" sleeper to Madrid, an express to Madrid only with first- and second-class coaches, a first-class sleeper, and a second-class couchette train. The Estrella Picasso continues through Madrid to Bilbao three times a week and the Estrella Gibralfaro goes via Cordova to Barcelona. Branch lines lead to Seville, Granada, and Algeciras.

Spaced along the Costa del Sol's main arterial highway, parallel to the railroad, you will see Portillo bus stops. After you have stored your luggage, the Portillo bus company is an easy way to get around. Riding their relay system of long-distance, middle-distance, and local buses stretching from Malaga to Algeciras (for an excursion to Gibraltar) is actually more convenient than renting a car and finding a place to park it.

The Costa del Sol is now a string of "urbanizations" (real estate developments) rambling end-to-end along blue Mediterranean shores like suburbia overflowing — not entirely admirable, but agreeable and comfortable for everyone. After the initial surprise of the clutter, it becomes fascinating to discover its hidden pleasures.

You will soon find that this area is not typically Spanish. It is a unique international settlement that takes on a flavor of its own when all the Norwegian restaurants, Danish bakeries, Swedish smorgasbords, Irish pubs, and Finnish coffeehouses merge with German Bierstuben, English teahouses, Canadian beer bars and American hamburger cafes, shopping malls, golf courses, yacht harbors, and beaches.

The marvelous result of this conglomeration is that it works. The English tongue is the common denominator. Nationals of all ages from everywhere in Europe, America, and the British Commonwealth coexist in harmony and shared enthusiasm.

It is said that the Costa del Sol is not for everybody, but when it's a good place for gray-haired folks (tearooms, short distances, warm weather), swinging singles (bars close at 6 A.M.), and families with children (activities, beach), you wonder exactly who wouldn't enjoy an inexpensive, warm-weather visit here.

Welcome Train Timetable

Distance in Miles	Station	Time in Minutes
0	Malaga-Guadalmedina	0
1	Malaga-RENFE	3
2	San Andres	6
3	Los Prados	8
5	Vuelos Nacionales (Aeropuerto)	11
6	Vuelos Internacionales (Charter)	15

7	San Julian	18
8	Campo del Golf-Campamento	20*
9	Los Alamos	21
9	La Colina	23
11	Torremolinos	29
11	Montemar-Alto	32
12	El Pinello	33
13	Arroyo de la Miel	36
16	Torremuelle-Benalmedena	40
17	Carvajal	45
18	Torreblanca	46
19	Los Boliches	48
20	Fuengirola	51

*Service three times daily.

Terror Trams of Alfama
Adventure Cheap and Easy

You swoop and rise through hills and drops that measure a good 500 feet. You clutch, white-knuckled, at the grips of the advertisement-pasted cars while rows of pastel houses whiz beside you and glimpses of churches flash at you from cobblestone alleyways.

You look up and see stairways leading toward blue skies. Automobile horns honk on streets above your head. On your train's grinding struggle to the summit, your trolley wheezes, jerks, creaks, and chatters so loudly that many passengers standing elbow-to-elbow wonder, "Can this wreck take it one more time or is its axle going to snap and take me with it?"

Circling through Alfama, Lisbon's Moorish neighborhood that survived the murderous earthquake of 1755, you ride the most infamous stretch of rail adventure in Europe. Portugal's capital city of 812,000 can easily claim to have the most thrilling streetcar network built. Their tram system is widely held to be the most terrifying in the world.

Riding through Alfama on one of the rickety, two-axle trolley cars is an adventure that ages you prematurely, like a ride on a killer roller coaster. Part of the excitement comes from riding on cars that groan from neglect and seem to go back to shortly after Ulysses founded Lisbon. They climb the hills with the reckless drive of San Francisco's cable cars—but vehicles in Lisbon advertising blue jeans, beer, and vacations in Paris have no strong cables to save them from breaking away and skidding into the Tagus River below.

Most of the little trams (not covered by Eurailpass) are only large enough for fourteen sitting on the green leatherette seats and twenty hanging on the cracking leather straps or clutching at the chromium-plated poles. The floors are made of brown, abused wooden slats with dust accumulated in their crevices.

Riding downwards, fascinating side scenes plunge past you and the rows of houses you glimpsed ahead seem to twirl around and fly past you on the opposite side.

Lisboans on the electricos (the name began in the early twentieth century when electric-powered trams replaced horse-drawn vehicles) gaze calmly at the passing sights. Mothers cradle their babies and hum lullabies while young boys stretch and rap the church windows alongside and smudge fingertips against the stuccoed walls sweeping past. Some alleys are so narrow that the streetcars fill the few feet separating houses. Pedestrians dodge nimbly into doorways to avoid the pushy, onrushing trams. Stop-and-go signals are essential on the narrowest curves to regulate traffic and reduce the number of head-on collisions.

Instead of the automatic, electric signal lights you expect to see, you are amazed to find casually dressed guards still assigned to blind corners, directing traffic by hand with a signal baton and rickety box to sit on, coping with streetcars plummeting down the wrong direction of one-way streets and mad auto drivers sneaking behind them.

The most daring of the lines climbing the Alfama hills is renegade line No. 28. It is your ultimate test. It runs the wrong way—against auto traffic. Visiting Lisbon and not riding a No. 28 streetcar is like visiting San Francisco and not riding a cable car or visiting a theme park and not riding a roller coaster.

So that the trams could maneuver through the claustrophobic maze of streets, engineers laid the tracks narrow-gauge (only 23.6 inches) with only one pair of thin rails. Luckily, just when an approaching tram seems ready to crash into another and panicky tourists realize the emergency brakes might not be working, the tracks part at the last instant and the cars veer sideways as if testing the riders' nerves and sanity.

Double trolley carriages are out of the question. It would be an indictable murder offense to try to pull passive passenger trailers around the curves.

In such a hodgepodge, the safe use of vehicles secured by tracks embedded in cobblestones is essential. Their limited freedom prevents reckless or annoyed tram drivers from nicking or scraping the already peeling whitewash on the house walls (or the advertising on the trams, for that matter).

The Lisbon streetcar system is one of the largest and one of the creakiest in the world. It has thirty struggling lines. The youngest is older than most of today's straphangers. Although the network was consolidated in 1974 with the opening of the Lisbon subway, the last extension of the tram system was in 1958.

In all fairness, in a city offering magnificent surprises to walkers, the trams are convenient, if unnerving, and inexpensive. Considering the hilly terrain and capricious nature of the streets, it is surprising the trams do as well as they do.

You find your way by use of a free map from the tourist office. Schedules pinpointing the zigzagging routes of trams and buses throughout the city are posted on the walls of glassed-in bus stops in the business district. A thorough guide to the public transportation system of Lisbon and its environs (including an official map of bus and tram lines) is sold in the booth at the foot of the Santa Justa elevator ("Eiffel elevator").

To sample the dashing of the remarkable trams through Alfama, take Nos. 10, 11, or 28 to the Graca terminal, which is more of a four by eight-foot orange-and-white kiosk than a terminal. Riders leap onto the trams whenever they can—anytime one slows enough to make leaping reasonably safe. They enter the back and pay on board to the conductor—not the driver.

The conductor will be dressed in civvies but you will spot him easily by his shoulder strap, his leather pouch, his paper punch, and especially his interest in collecting the fare from you. Don't worry if you don't find him at first. He'll find you. Fares vary depending on your destination. To exit, divide the glass doors to the front behind the driver and climb off through the driver's compartment.

Along your route you will find the excellent Miradouro (meaning "belvedere") Santa Luzia, where you will see a splendid panorama of Lisbon and shipping on the Tagus River. The Belvedere of Santa Luzia is an oasis of trellises, benches, and blue-and-white-tiled murals. Under the vines' shade, local men play cards and checkers. There are bathrooms and a tourist office here, too. This is the perfect place to begin a walking tour of Alfama. Bus line No. 37 loops right at the portals of the Castelo da Sao Jorge.

Happy to be back to steady terra firma, you nod to your fellow passengers to say, "Well, we made it—this time at least."

Convenient and reasonably priced special tourist transportation tickets allowing travel on all of Lisbon's subways, trams, and funiculars cost about $6.25 for four days, or $8.60 for a week. They are sold Mondays through Fridays from 8 A.M. to 8 P.M. at Carris kiosks throughout Lisbon. You will find them outside the Santa Apolonia station, in the so-called "Eiffel elevator," and at the foot of the Park Eduardo VII near the Praca Marques Pombal.

Subways and Double-Decker Buses

Lisbon has a limited but inexpensive subway system. The main station, "RS" for Rossio, is at the apex of the V-shaped system in the downtown area. The subway entrances on the Avenida da Liberdade are indicated by large red *M* (for "Metropolitano") signs on the street. The metro stations are impressive and are elegantly adorned with azulejos (glazed colored tiles).

To use the metro, obtain a pocket map at a tourist office or check in any subway station the maps of the system at the foot of stairs leading from the street. Save money by buying your tickets from the orange-colored ticketing machines (directions are printed in three languages, including English) for 35$ (about twenty-five cents). Tickets sold by agents (in some stations only) cost 40$ (about thirty cents), but books of ten cost 320$ ($2.35). You board the train in the direction of the last station shown on the branch you wish to use.

To complete Lisbon's public transportation system, Carris purchased venerable, green, double-decker buses directly from London. Sitting in the front seats on the top level of these jolly green giants is a treat, but standing on the platform in the back of a jammed bus at rush hour is a giant green terror. You will need both hands to hang on and a foot to hold your packages.

Portugal Up Close
Algarve, Alfa, and Choice of Commuters

"Under no circumstances should you take the train from the Algarve to Lisbon." Algarvian Senhor Jaoa Lima, graduate of the University of Wisconsin, was very adamant. He waved his arms like a sea gull. "If you must, take a bus. They have videos."

"We didn't come all the way from California to the Algarve to watch a video in Portuguese. We want to see Portugal up close, the people, and how you live."

Lima looked discouraged. "The videos merely have Portuguese subtitles."

"We complain continuously to the government for better train service to our region," he confided. "If you want to ride an excellent train, take the train from Lisbon to Porto."

Contrary to Lima's expectations, the Rapido train taking you from Portugal's Algarve region is spacious and clean, often arrives in Lisbon seven minutes early, and is as quiet as a dormitory—except for the raucous noises you hear resounding from the bar two carriages away.

Many Portuguese are critical of their country's facilities, but even their secondary trains are decent, their food is never bad even in the bistros, and Lisbon's subway is convenient. On the other hand, when you say the facade of their magnificent neo-Manuelino Rossio train station is dirty, they say it is "discolored."

Because of the network structure in Portugal, you are virtually locked into using Lisbon as your base for train travel. There are no through trains passing through Lisbon. Lisbon has five stations and five lines.

Santa Apolonia Station

Conveniently near the foot of Alfama is the dark-rose-colored Santa Apolonia train station, your gateway to the trains of Europe and where you may have your Eurailpass first validated at window No. 11.

PORTO
Gaia
Aveiro
Coimbra-B
Alfarelos
Entroncamento
LISBON
Barreiro
Ermidas-Sado
LAGOS
Portimao
Tunes
Faro
Vila Real de Santo Antonio

ATLANTIC OCEAN

PORTUGAL'S ALFA
AND ALGARVE

SPAIN

-N-

0   50   100
MILES

Santa Apolonia faces out on a taxi loop and a modern sculpture honoring immigrants to Portugal. Buses and trams pass by on the main roads. You reach Santa Apolonia easily by walking from the city center or by streetcar Nos. 3, 16, or 24. It is a tidy station, but small. Santa Apolonia is literally the end of the line for international traffic.

When you enter, you find the ticket windows 1 to 11 straight ahead. On your right, the agent at window 11 sells international tickets and reservations. Although usually a formality, because except for the Lisboa Express TER train to Madrid the trains are rarely totally filled, CP requires you to make seat reservations for all CP's Rapidos and name trains to Spain even if only shortly before departure—and then only at your departure station. Computerized reservations have yet to come to Portugal.

On the right hand wall is a booth where you can change money (open 9 A.M. to noon and 2 to 6:30 P.M.). On the left is a kiosk with magazines, cigarettes, etc. The train information office on the far left (look for the sign) functions as a tourist office after international train arrivals. English-speaking ladies give train information and will book hotels for you without charge. Along the left corridor, train schedules are posted on the walls and you find a post office and a baggage checking counter.

Through the middle is the train gallery. You must show your ticket or Eurailpass to pass through the gate. Track No. 3, where the "Sud Express" leaves for Paris, is on the left and on the right is track No. 5. You must walk farther down the gallery to find track No. 1, Alfa Service to Porto.

Alfa Service

Alfa Service is the name CP gives its proud seven-times-a-day fleet of 1985 Corail carriages between Portugal's two major cities, Lisbon and Porto.

Because the trains are Rapidos you need reservations. Book in advance at Santa Apolonia station (about $2) or—when the train is not filled—buy them at the special day counter beside track No. 1.

The exteriors have been fabricated in Portugal of stainless steel but the interiors duplicate snappy French Corail materials and design. The only difference is the language of the newspapers the passengers read.

The bar car features "Corail Servico Alfa" with sandwiches, cakes, coffee, and bottles of liquor. Hostesses wearing red bandannas and chic, striped aprons take orders from your seat.

The highlight of your trip to Porto comes after your train stops for clearance in Vila Nova da Gaia and you inch across the Douro River on the bridge designed entirely of metal in 1877 by the French engineer Eiffel. The best general panorama of the old stone city of Porto (pop. 330,000) spreads on the right bank before you. You see the old town, topped by the towers of the cathedral and the Clerigos belfry, rising in tiers from the Douro. Overlapping series of hillside alleys are lined with architecturally dazzling houses decorated with corbels and (occasionally) tiled facades.

Sadly, you leave this view when your train enters the tunnel and comes to a stop in Campanha station, but this gives you a chance to board one of the many connecting trains and continue to the downtown Sao Bento station to see the great display of artistic tiles covering the walls of the reception hall, the pride of CP. Although in need of a good cleaning, they're a feast for the eyes. Painted in 1930 by Jorge Colaco, these tile pictures include a full-color frieze of everyday life in Portugal and feature historic panoramas in blue: Joao's entry into Porto (top right) and his capture of Cueta (bottom right).

Algarve Service

The best train to the Algarve, the "Portuguese Riviera" stretching along Portugal's sunny southern shores, is the crack InterCity Rapido Sotovento ("South Wind"). Like its sister evening InterCity Rapido, it runs daily, whisking you in 4 hours from Lisbon's waterfront Terreiro do Paco station to Faro. Less expensive InterRegional trains take you along the same route in about 5½ hours.

Terreiro do Paco station, decorated with tiles depicting Algarvian city crests, lies adjacent to the finest square in Lisbon, the Praca do Comercio, known to all as Terreiro do Paco, the "Palace Terrace." Here you board, through separate first- and second-class entrances, CP's half-hourly blue-and-white ferries across the Tagus River to the Barreiro station. Eurailpasses are accepted aboard.

Allow time at Terreiro do Paco to obtain reservations for the Rapidos (about fifty cents). You can only make them in this station. Similarly, you can only make your return reservation at your Algarvian destination.

After your ferry crossing to Barreiro, follow the crowd down a ramp past kiosks, shops, and a waiting room through a ticket-checking station onto your waiting, stainless-steel train.

Running 155 miles in three and a half hours to Tunes, the junction for connecting trains to the western Algarve, your Rapido is not fast, but comfortable, and gives you just the right pace to distinguish the harvest years painted on the cork trees. You see sights you never see from the colorless, commercial highway. You absorb the feeling of the region as you observe casual cowherds with staff and cap and brown bulls with wicked-looking horns drinking from streams. You see olive trees, orange groves, pine and eucalyptus forests, and many small farms.

You cross what seems like an invisible line across Portugal. South of the line the villages consist of boxy, flat-roofed houses. North of it, they are all peaked with tile roofs.

The Sintra Train

Your trip to Sintra to see its palace begins at Lisbon's Rossio station. Rossio station is the busy commuter station located in the heart of Lisbon across from the Teatro National (National Theater) on Rossio Square. You enter the station through one of the most astonishing facades of the European railroads. It is in the neo-Manuelino style of the nineteenth century (connected to the adjacent hotel so royalty could proceed directly), but terribly dirty/discolored by the traffic exhaust from Rossio Square in front.

On the ground floor there is an information counter (English spoken), but follow the stairs and several flights of escalators all the way past various shops to "Gare," where adventurers without Eurailpasses buy tickets. Enter the side door on the top level (with taxi access) when you follow the steps ("calcada") leading down from the crest of the hill above.

Electric signboards display coming train departures and their track numbers. At the head of each track (5, for Sintra), another electric sign shows the next departure time and the current time. Schedules are posted in an alcove beyond track 10.

The two-class stainless-steel electric trains depart through a long tunnel into Campolide station. Lisbon appears to be a hodgepodge of suburbs along the railroad line to Sintra. Finally, you see to the left the Royal Palace atop the moutainside above the Portela de Sintra station.

On fast trains your trip takes forty-five minutes; nearly one hundred trains run on weekdays. Outside the end-of-the-line peeling-paint Sintra station, taxis stand offering to take you to the palace.

Estoril Railroad

Take the frequent electric trains from Lisbon to Estoril departing from Cais do Sodre station terminating at Cascais. Your trip along the coast is an excursion along the Tagus River, also covered by Eurailpass. You easily reach (and find) the Cais do Sodre station because it is the end of the line for many streetcar and bus lines (buses No. 45 and 35 from Santa Apolonia station), which therefore carry "Cais do Sodre" on their signboards.

With a Eurailpass you walk through Cais do Sodre station's gates to the boarding area, where videos will inform you of your track number (according to destination) and departure time. Departures of the simple, one-class stainless-steel trains are shown on videos between track Nos. 2 and 3.

After the Alcantara station, your Estoril Railroad passes under the Ponte 25 de Abril suspension bridge—Portugal's "Golden Gate." You run a block from the Tagus until you reach the Henry the Navigator Memorial, where you begin to travel alongside the sailboats and Tagus promenade. Your best view of the bridge is looking back immediately before you reach the Belem station — a superb view.

The Belem station is a convenient place to debark to view the Belem Tower, the great Jeronimos Monastery across the highway, and the Henry the Navigator Memorial.

Past the Alges stop, your train travels closer to the Tagus and you have a better view of the shipping, the breakwaters, and then the beaches. All along the stretch from Alges to Cruz Quebrada to Caxias, looking back toward Lisbon gives you a fine long view of the graceful suspension bridge.

You don't appreciate the splendor of the coast — the blue water and frothy waves breaking on the white sand — until just before your stop at S. Pedro do Estoril station, where you see a nice panorama of things to come.

Estoril is your glamour stop, in front of the Casino. The tourist office is across the street. Past Estoril to Cascais, you pass beaches and luxury hotels. The beach for which Cascais is famous begins just before its unsheltered end-of-the-line train station.

There are departures for Estoril and Cascais about every half-hour until 2:30 A.M. Departures for Belem leave Lisbon about every fifteen minutes. On weekdays more than one hundred trains run daily in both directions. Your trip to Estoril takes about twenty-five minutes. The faster trains make nine stops along the way.

Alfa Service, Lisbon to Porto

LISBON (Apolonia) dep.	Coimbra-B dep.	Aveiro dep.	Villa Nova de Gaia dep.	PORTO (Campanha) arr.
0715	....	....	1007	1015
0840	1040	1113	1150	1200
1105	1305	1338	1415	1425
1440	1640	1713	1750	1800
1700	1900	1933	2010	2020
2020	....	....	2312	2320

Alfa Service, Porto to Lisbon

PORTO (Campanha) dep.	Vila Nova de Gaia dep.	Aveiro dep.	Coimbra-B dep.	LISBON (Apolonia) arr.
0715	0722	....	....	1015
0830	0839	0915	0949	1150
1110	1119	1155	1229	1430
1445	1454	1530	1604	1805
1710	1719	1755	1829	2030
2025	2034	2110	2144	2345

Through Service between Lisbon and the Algarve

Exp871	IC581	IC583				IC580	IC582	Exp872
0740	1410	1800	dep.	LISBON (T.P)	arr.	1145	1830	2255
0810	1440	1830	arr.	Barreiro	dep.	1115	1800	2225
0825	1455	1845	dep.	Barreiro	arr.	1100	1748	2212
0842	....	....	dep.	Pinhal Novo	dep.	....	....	2154
0900	....	....	dep.	Setubal	dep.	....	....	2140
1101	....	....	dep.	Fucheira	dep.	....	....	1940
1112	1754	2139	arr.	Tunes	dep.	0801	1453	1826
1222		2205*	dep.	Tunes	arr.	0744		1805
1225		2219	arr.	Alcantariha	dep.	0731		1751
1307		2255	arr.	Portimao	dep.	0657		1716
1333		2321	arr.	LAGOS	dep.	0622		1645
1217	1759	2144	dep.	Tunes	arr.	0757	1433	1811
1226	1807	2152	dep.	Albufeira	dep.	0751	1432	1805
1300	1834*	2157*	dep.	FARO	dep.	0720*	1402*	1732
1338	1927	2348	dep.	Tavira	dep.	0534	1258	1648
1410	2005	0030	arr.	Vila Real de Santo Antonio	dep.	0450	1210	1615

*Change trains.

Scandinavia
and Finland

Vital Tips for the Trains
of Scandinavia and Finland

Riding Swedish trains—Riding Norwegian trains—Riding Danish trains—Riding Finnish trains—Stations and subways—Midnight sun travel—Your gateway to Russia—Using Eurailpass bonuses—ScanRail Pass—National rail passes—Capital-city travel cards

Hans Christian Andersen traveled by mail coach and sailing ship on his first trip from his home, Odense, on the island of Funen, to the Danish royal capital of Copenhagen in September 1819. You can make that trip now in less than three hours by Danish "Lightning" train.

The great Scandinavian writer was the consummate adventurer: "To travel is to live." He realized travel meant meeting new people, visiting new surroundings, absorbing new impressions, discovering new joys in nature, and feeling vibrantly alive.

Traveling by train through Scandinavia is easy using the 1,250-mile network of the Danish State Railroads (DSB), the 2,650 miles of the Norwegian State Railroads (NSB), and the 7,000 miles of the Swedish State Railroads (SJ). The 3,650 miles of the Finnish State Railroads (VR) complete your Nordic adventuring. Ride them from where the storks nest in the chimneys of Denmark to the blue fjords and stark glaciers of Norway to where the Midnight Sun beats down on the land of the Lapps above the Arctic Circle in Sweden and Finland. Your most likely gateway to Scandinavia is the mainline named for the migratory flight path of birds from Germany via train aboard alternating half-hourly DSB and GermanRail ferries from Puttgarden to Rodby and on to Copenhagen. From here, you travel up Sweden's West Coast to Gothenburg and Oslo and across Sweden to Stockholm.

Remain in your carriage while it is being shunted aboard the ferry to Rodby, then dine, shop, and return to your compartment when it docks. Don't miss your chance to enjoy an open-faced sandwich, Danish pastry (better on a DSB ferry than a German one), and Danish beer in the cafeteria. You buy cigarettes and liquor in the twenty-four-hour duty-free shops aboard the ferries. Even at prices higher than at home, they are bargains here — something obvious by the long lines of Swedish shoppers struggling with bulging red plastic shopping baskets. Be sure to do enough duty-free shopping to last throughout your entire stay in Scandinavia.

GermanRail EuroCity trains Merkur, Hansa, and Skandinavien (which don't require reservations) between Copenhagen and Germany are adventurers' most popular way to reach Copenhagen for their jumping-off to Norway and Sweden/Finland. EC Alfred Nobel, the GermanRail night train originating in Hamburg with only first- and second-class couchettes, bypasses Copenhagen during the night and thus saves you time to Oslo, Gothenburg, and Stockholm directly. Some ride the Alfred Nobel going one way and stop over in Copenhagen going the other.

Inclusion in the Eurailpass system of the ferries connecting Warnemunde, Germany, with Gedser (Denmark) and Sassnitz with Trelleborg (Sweden) provides holders with interesting, alternate routes to Denmark and Sweden directly from Berlin.

In addition to mainline train to Oslo, you can also reach Norway by several ferries from Denmark or by train via Storlien, Sweden, to Trondheim. Reach Finland by Silja Line ship from Stockholm or by bus (covered by rail passes) north of the Gulf of Bothnia between Sweden and Finland. VR closed the rail line from Kemi to the Swedish border in 1988.

Riding Swedish Trains

The tilting blue-and-stainless-steel, four-headlight (required by law in Sweden) trains you see between Stockholm and Gothenburg are Scandinavia's fastest (125 mph), sleekest, and most innovative trains.

Lacking a large population base to support massive investment in megaspeed trains, yet threatened by loss of business to domestic air travel, SJ put into production the train it calls the X-2, a train to comfort adventurers' rides around curves by tilting like the Italian Pendolino (see the chapter on Italy) except that the power car remains upright in order to simplify transmission of electricity.

SJ leapfrogged building a prototype X-2 because of the success of the extensive research and development of their X-15 test train dating from 1975. SJ is cautiously introducing passenger units and checking to incorporate possible modifications in further production units.

Traffic analysts determined that hourly departures for X-2s were essential to attract business travelers. Because of their frequent runnings, X-2s are short trains consisting of single power cars, three intermediate passenger coaches (either first or second class), a restaurant car, and a driving trailer incorporating second-class seating.

The new train has three design innovations, but you will probably notice only the tilting feature making it possible to travel faster rounding curves. It's not easy to appreciate wheelset design and electrical plant innovations.

Building separate dedicated high-speed railbeds was not within SJ's financial means, so SJ took a cost-effective approach to upgrading existing lines. Travel times continuously decrease as newly upgraded stretches are put into service segment by segment.

X-2's premier running on September 3, 1990, carried paying passengers from Gothenburg to Stockholm. SJ's publicists spent that day arranging television coverage and political welcomings while engineers combed the train with check-out gauges. When X-2 returned to Gothenburg, it carried passengers in three hours, thirty minutes, instead of the four hours needed on the former timetable. Air passengers need two and three-quarter hours from city center to city center. Motorists take about five hours to drive.

SJ's second X-2 trainset came into service in December 1990. SJ plans to present one unit every second month until the full first series is running smoothly in March 1994.

Simultaneously with delivery of the X-2s, line upgrading is permitting their travel times to be reduced to less than three hours in 1992, and to two hours, fifty-five minutes, when SJ completes a separate line through Stockholm's suburbs in 1994.

Eventually, X-2 will serve the Stockholm-Malmo-Gothenburg triangle where 80 percent of Sweden's population lives. When the high-speed triangle is completed, half of Sweden's 8.5 million inhabitants will have access to it.

SJ's shiny business-class "City" and tourist-class "InterCity" services share the same equipment on the populated southern triangle. Their seats are widest in Europe and recline more than those in other European trains. Seat backs are high and tables are high — to fit the tall Swedes.

First- and second-class carriages are divided into segments with differing seating innovations and pleasant arrangements. The trains carry restaurant cars divided by sales kiosks. Half is set for first-class service with white linen; half provides second-class cafeteria service.

You need reservations on all City and InterCity trains. City trains are timed for business travelers, first- and second-class. Their obligatory first-class reservations cost nearly $20 (which rail pass holders must pay) and allow travelers a breakfast in the morning or a snack on afternoon trains. Second-class reservations cost over $6, with no food.

These high prices discourage adventurers from traveling first class on prime-time City trains. They prefer InterCity trains using the same comfortable carriages but costing just over $3 for reservations, which is about standard throughout Europe.

Riding Norwegian Trains

NSB trains run on three mainline routes from Oslo: south to Stavanger, west to Bergen, and north to Trondheim. From Trondheim adventurers continue north to Bodo or transverse into Sweden by diesel-hauled train.

NSB requires reservations on their Express Special ("ET") trains—the fastest trains on these routes. You pay NSB's mandatory fee even when you board your train at the last minute and find an empty seat.

NSB's fresh-smelling "B7" carriages, maroon with black detailing, sparkle with good space, high-quality materials, and unexcelled ambience. These "Tomorrow Trains" take you on Express Special routes from Oslo north to Trondheim and south to Stavanger. You enjoy their appealing shapes, colors, and textures; drinking fresh water from stainless-steel water fountains; and rinsing your hands with spraying heated water.

B7 carriages have smooth aerodynamic profiles, making them look different from other European trains. Longitudinal aluminum sections make them five to six tons lighter than steel cars, dynamic undercarriages send them around curves 10 percent faster, and air-filled rubber cushions dampen track noises and vibration.

Their panoramic windows, almost twice as wide as high, are safer and give you even broader views ahead. The interior decor is in earth tones—not your conventional train appearance.

Riding Danish Trains

DSB and a few private railroads make traveling easy in Denmark by covering the country with a dense network of modern services supplemented with buses on quieter sections.

The white slivers with recessed drivers' cabins that you see on DSB's mainlines are modular IC-3 diesel trains still being introduced. They are the world's most computerized — they sniff the temperature outside and decide how early to turn themselves on in the morning.

Adapted to the Danish countryside, where there is less than fourteen miles on average between cities, they accelerate and brake rapidly. On June 2, when the summer timetable is introduced in 1991, they will travel up to 112 mph, cutting twenty minutes off the earlier InterCity schedule.

Combined with DSB's older cardinal-red Intercity trains, these "Lyntogen," meaning "lightning trains," take adventurers along the great crescent mainline from Copenhagen to the northern tip of Denmark. West from Copenhagen InterCities and Lyntogen take you across the Great Belt waterway (reservations obligatory), and need only three hours to reach Odense; then forty minutes more to Fredericia, the junction for international trains from Hamburg.

At Fredericia, adventurers continue on the mainline trains north on the Jutland peninsula to Aarhus (one hour, twenty minutes), Aarhus to Aalborg in one and a half hours, and finally take thirty-seven to thirty-nine minutes to Hjorring. There, adventurers take the connecting second-class-only private train for the twelve-mile trip to Hirtshals (twenty to twenty-five minutes), for the Fred Olsen Lines crossing to Kristiansand, Norway, or continue a half-hour more to Frederikshavn for the Stena Line crossing to Gothenburg, Sweden, or Oslo, Norway, the Larvik Line crossing to Larvik, Norway, or the DA-NO Linjen crossing to Oslo.

Riding Finnish Trains

In Finland you travel aboard new, 87-mph red-and-white InterCity trains with flashing LED displays on the outside showing their destinations and times of arrival; "PS" Special Express trains consisting of blue-gray 1980s carriages of older fashion, running with slightly less velocity; blue-gray "P" ("Person") trains, which are often second-class-only, diesel-hauled trains; and reddish "Lokal" trains, which provide frequent commuter service to and from Helsinki's outlying suburbs.

VR times InterCity trains primarily to suit business travelers who want to reach Helsinki in the morning and depart in the afternoon. When you ride an InterCity train, a staff member offers you a Finnish newspaper, and when you decline in English, she replies, "We have cold meal service and I come by here — with a trolley." First-class IC reservations costing about $16 include a light meal. The expense-account open-face sandwich on black bread is fine. It would cost $4–5 in the train station because of the high costs in Finland. You also must reserve second-class seats on IC trains, but even paying about $6.50 for the reservation doesn't merit you the snack.

InterCity trains' expensive reservations lead adventurers to prefer VR's three Special Express trains, which run slightly less fast (because they are longer) on

Finland's electrified mainlines and require reservations costing about $3. EP Lapponia travels between Helsinki, Tampere, and Oulu; EP Savonia between Helsinki, Kuopio, and Kontiomaki; EP Karelia between Helsinki, Lappeenranta, and Joensuu. Their first-class carriages consist of compartments with fixed seats and an end salon with fixed seats at the ends and swivel chairs around red plastic tables.

Diesel-hauled P trains usually consist of older EP carriages, sometimes outfitted with video monitors showing American movies with Finnish subtitles. They require no reservations. You usually will ride them on secondary lines.

VR uses the same wide gauge (five feet) as in the Soviet Union because the lines were laid before Finland became independent of Russia. VR's wide-gauge electric locomotives were manufactured in the Soviet Union; the diesels and carriages in Finland.

Helsinki's red granite, 1919 train station is a wonder. On both sides of the main entrance you see granite figures holding lanterns in their hands. Its 156-foot tall clock tower is still one of the highest in Helsinki. The preserved wooden station houses you come upon in the countryside are often quite picturesque. Count on them being painted either ocher or rust red and trimmed with white. And almost always, you see an ancient black steam locomotive standing nearby on a pedestal.

Stations and Subways

Plan to use the centrally located train stations in all of Scandinavia's capital cities as your bases. Frequently running suburban rapid transit systems are a convenience for everyone. When you book a hotel room at a hotel reservations counter in or near a station, ask whether your chosen hotel is near a rapid-transit station. Using these trains saves you time, struggling with luggage, and is free with a rail pass.

Copenhagen H. (for "Hovedbanegard," or "head train station") has been refurbished with a new post office and shops. An "InterRail Club" (open during the summer only) is a young adventurers center open to holders of Eurail Youthpasses. Oslo Sentral is sparkling—christened by King Olav V in February 1987. Stockholm Central is an expanded multilevel complex with all services. The 1989, gleaming Cityterminalen annex contains change bank, cafeteria, and buses anywhere you want to go. Take the escalator down from Helsinki's station and you find a busy shopping center and subway station connected underground.

In Oslo, twice-an-hour local train service tunnels through the heart of the city. Use stops such as "National Theater" to get around. Subways ("T-Bane") take you throughout the Oslo area. Similarly, Stockholm's Central station and Helsinki's station are well connected to their regions with subways. Look for a

T ("Tunnelbana") in Stockholm and an *M* for "Metroon/Metron" in Helsinki. S-Bahn stations in Copenhagen and Helsinki's city train stations provide fast and frequent transit to the limited number of terminuses.

Midnight Sun Travel

The long distances you travel, especially in Norway and Sweden, and the long summer daylight hours make you want to seriously consider traveling around the clock.

All the Nordic railroads own their domestic couchettes and sleeping cars. Prices for three-bedded sleeping cars compare favorably with those of six-bunk couchettes in the south. Reserve them as early as possible when you are in Scandinavia. Incompatible computer interfaces don't allow you to book them outside the area except by mail.

DSB's "Project Night Train," using BritRail Mark III carriages with superior Danish interiors and painted blue with golden moon and stars, produced a renaissance in overnight travel between Copenhagen and Frederikshavn, Arhus, Esbjerg, and Fredericia. First-class compartments have one bed and second-class ones have two. Couchettes sleep five per compartment.

You ride NSB's 1987 red-and-black (to match NSB's "Tomorrow Train" carriages) pairs of WLAB-2 sleeping cars between Oslo and Bergen, Trondheim, or Stavanger. One car is made up for first-class travel, one for second. They are the longest and quietest in Norway and the widest in Western Europe (which means the corridor accommodates jump seats and tables, and still has room for refreshment trolleys to pass).

Don't overlook riding overnight in NSB's sleeping cars between Oslo and Flam or Andalsnes where your carriages are coupled in the dark of night and you avoid having to change trains. These are older but excellent for sleeping.

SJ's couchettes and sleeping cars carry you on their routes between Narvik, Stockholm, Malmo, Helsingborg, Copenhagen, Gothenburg, and Oslo. VR has no couchettes, but large, very inexpensive sleeping cars—single and double-bedded in first class; double and three-bedded in second. They run north all the way to Rovaniemi from Helsinki; four sleeping cars depart from Turku. Especially consider the no-change sleeper between Helsinki and Savonlinna to avoid changing trains at Parikkala. Second-class prices are lower when you depart Mondays through Thursdays.

Your Gateway to Russia

Two Russian trains a day depart from Helsinki. Your Eurail or FinnRail Pass is valid to the Russian border so you save nearly half between Helsinki and Leningrad when you time your trip to coincide with the beginning or expiry of your pass. Eurailpass holders entering Finland from Russia may have their passes validated by the Finnish train conductor on board. You need a Russian visa, of course, to enter Russia so you should arrange this in advance.

The "Repin" departs Helsinki at 1:12 P.M. for Leningrad. It stops at Vyborg on the Soviet side of the border, where you can change your money. "Tolstoy" night express train departs at 5:10 P.M. for Moscow.

Using Eurailpass Bonuses

Eurailpasses (and ScanRail Passes) give you a direct route between Berlin and Scandinavia via the free ferry services between Gedser (Denmark) and Warnemunde (Germany) and between Trelleborg (Sweden) and Sassnitz (Germany). In addition, TT Saga line gives Eurailpass holders a 50 percent reduction on normal fares for the ferry crossings between Trelleborg and Lubeck-Travemunde (Germany).

Until the new tunnel/bridge is completed, Eurailpasses, ScanRail Passes, and regular DSB train tickets include passage aboard the MF *Kronprins Frederik* or her six sister super ships which take you—in your train—across Denmark's Great Belt waterway separating Copenhagen's island of Funen from the Jutland peninsula. When your train reaches one of the embarkation ports, Nyborg or Korsor, your conductor locks its doors. After your train is shuttled onto the ferry, its doors are unlocked and you are free to roam the ship. Color-coded sections guide you. Both the red and the blue sections have their own restaurant, cafeteria, and fast-food kiosk.

You cross the fifteen-mile Great Belt in an hour, the better part of your travel time to Odense. The train ferries are streamlined: your train comes off the same end it was onloaded, meaning your seat will be facing the opposite direction when you continue your trip.

Your Eurailpass-covered steamer crossing between Frederikshavn (Denmark) and Gothenburg, Sweden's second city, is operated by Stena Lines (a private steamship company) and is a good way to reach Gothenburg, but not if you plan to continue onward. The steamer landing is far from the train station and to get there you must carry your luggage through crowded public transportation or take a taxi.

The Fred Olsen Lines gives Eurailpass holders a 30 percent reduction on the trip between Hirtshals near the northern tip of the Jutland peninsula and Kristiansand in Norway. To reach Hirtshals, change at Hjorring from DSB's Frederikshavn mainline to a twelve-mile-long private railroad. In Kristiansand, board the Sorlands mainline between Oslo and Stavanger.

The Danish navigation company, Oresund, gives you a 50 percent reduction for travel on the hydrofoil between Copenhagen and Malmo, Sweden. This is the only fare you pay for a "Round the Sound" trip—one of the most interesting one-day excursions from Copenhagen. Board the hydrofoil at Havngade in

Copenhagen for the half-hour trip across the Oresund to Malmo. In the brick station house adjacent to the landing in Malmo, change to SJ's local train for the forty-mile run through Skane, Sweden's chateau country. Break your trip to enjoy historical sights and the pastoral scenery. On return, board a DSB or SJ ferry from Helsingborg to Helsingor and then continue by DSB train to Copenhagen H.

Also use your Eurailpass to make several other excellent one-day excursions. Make a round trip via the Great Belt to Odense to see the house where Hans Christian Andersen grew up (historians agree that no one knows the house where he was born) and the 1988-remodeled Railroad Museum, to Roskilde to see the Viking Ship Museum, to Hillerod to see Frederiksborg Castle, and to Humlebaek to visit the Louisiana Art Museum.

You receive free transportation from Stockholm to Finland (Helsinki or Turku) on Silja Line's great blue-and-white ferries, but must pay full fare for cabin space (see the "Crossing the Bothnia" adventure).

Finally, you may ride free the ferries crossing the Samso Belt via Kalundborg between Copenhagen and Aarhus, and train ferries between Kundshoved and Halskov or Bojden and Fynshav (for Sonderborg Castle on the island of Als). You receive a 20 percent reduction on the normal fares of the Scandinavian Seaways Co. between Copenhagen and Oslo, Esbjerg (there are inexpensive couchettes connecting here from Copenhagen) and Harwich or Newcastle, England, or the Faroe Islands.

ScanRail Pass

The railroads of Denmark, Norway, Sweden, and Finland together offer first- and second-class flexible ScanRail Passes sold by travel agents in North America through FrenchRail, Inc., and Danish National Railroads agents in Florida (see Appendix A). They are valid for unlimited travel on a flexipass basis on their four networks. Buy them for four travel days in fifteen, nine in twenty-one, or fourteen in one month. The nine-day ScanRail Pass is your best value because it saves nearly one-quarter over the price of the nine-day Eurail Flexipass. On a per day basis the four-day ScanRail Pass costs about the same as a five-day Eurail Flexipass. Adventurers not planning to ride any of the Swedish or Finnish first-class trains with high supplements payable buy ScanRail Passes for second-class travel to save themselves an additional one-quarter.

At any train station in Scandinavia or Finland you buy similar twenty-one consecutive-day passes called "Nordturist Med Tog" which offer similar benefits (plus half off when riding the Nord-Norge bus lines). Nordturist cards bought in Denmark cost approximately the same as the fourteen-day flexible ScanRail passes valid for one month. First-class Nordturist cards cost about 15 percent less than twenty-one-day Eurailpasses. A second-class pass (not offered by Eurailpass) saves an additional one-quarter.

Passes issued in North America consist of a computer-printed master ticket for your name, passport number, signature, and validity limits that the agent enters when you present it for validation and stamping in Scandinavia or Finland. The second coupon consists of day boxes for you to complete sequentially when you travel.

With a ScanRail Pass, you receive most of the bonuses listed for Eurailpass, above, including the free ride on the Silja Line crossing between Stockholm and Turku, but with a ScanRail Pass you must pay half-fare between Stockholm and Helsinki. You also lose the reductions on the Fred Olsen Lines steamship between Hirtshals and Kristiansand and on the steamships between Copenhagen and Oslo and from Esbjerg, but you receive half off round-trip ferry transportation from Copenhagen and Sweden to the island of Bornholm.

National Rail Passes

Denmark is so small that with the transportation bargains available, getting around is a steal. It will make you feel like you are robbing a bank when you buy a Danish Rail Pass for a month's first-class unlimited travel for about two-thirds of the cost of a Eurailpass, or for a month's travel, second-class, for about two-thirds of the cost of a Eurail Youthpass (but open to all ages). They are valid on Denmark's domestic ferries as well. Children four to twelve pay half; under four ride free.

Danish Rail Passes are available at any train station in Denmark, as are half-price tickets for travelers over sixty-five and groups of three or more traveling together.

A Norwegian Bargain Rail Pass is a one-way, second-class ticket valid for travel on Mondays through Thursdays for seven days. You are not limited in mileage and you can stop over as you wish within the seven day period. The price is about $55. NSB automatically gives 50 percent off to travelers over sixty-seven for travel on any train. Buy passes and tickets at any train station in Norway.

Unlimited-travel FinnRail Passes are available for first- or second-class travel for eight, fifteen, or twenty-two days at about 70 percent of the cost of Eurailpasses (less than the cost of one round trip between Helsinki and Rovaniemi). Second-class passes are recommended here because of the hair-raising surcharge assessed adventurers on first-class IC business trains and because many trains are second class only. They cost one-third less. Further, groups of three receive 20 percent off these passes.

Adventurers aged sixty-five and over buy Senior Passes in Finland costing about $12.50 for half off travel on all working days.

Buy FinnRail and Senior passes at VR's major stations or when you step off the Silja Line ferries in the Silja Line terminals or through Holiday Tours of America, Suite 1602, 40 E. 49th Street, New York, NY 10017 (Tel. 212-832-9072 or 800-223-0567) or Scantours, 1535 Sixth Street, Suite 205, Santa Monica, CA 90401 [Tel. 213-451-0911, 800-223-SCAN (nationwide), or 800-233-SCAN (California)].

Capital-City Travel Cards

Also look for four capital-city travel cards to save you money on local trains, buses, subways, and sometimes ferries. Buy them valid for one, two, or three days at train stations, tourist offices, and kiosks in their areas.

These cards are especially economical for local train transportation when you are traveling with a Eurail or ScanRail Flexipass because they allow you to save your day-box validations for longer trips.

The Copenhagen Card is priced for both adults and children aged four to eleven. You receive free transportation on the S-train network and buses in the entire metropolitan region including all of North Zealand, Roskilde, and Koge; discounts to Sweden; and free admission to fifty surprisingly varied museums and castles, such as the HT Museum for streetcars and buses in Rodovre and the Classic Automobile Museum.

Oslo Cards provide you free travel, free car parking, and more. The seventy-two-hour ticket gives you half off one round-trip train journey to Oslo from points in Norway.

Stockholm Cards also provide free travel on the "Tourist Line" city tour, free car parking, boat sightseeing at half-fare, and admission to sixty-two museums, palaces, and other attractions. When you need only a subway travel card, buy at subway station entrances for one-third to one-fifth the price "SL Tourist Cards" valid for a day (either for the inner city only or the whole network) or three days on the networks of suburban trains, subways, and buses in the county of Stockholm (except the SAS airport bus) and on Djurgarden ferries. When you stay longer, a monthly (or yearly) card is your most cost-efficient way to get around. A fifteen-trip strip card saves you 30 percent. Buy all tickets at kiosks called "Pressbyran" and at the central station, "T-Centralen."

Helsinki Cards include free local travel, a city sightseeing bus tour, boat trips, and admission to more than fifty sights and museums. For one-third off, you can buy a "Tourist Ticket," a one-day pass limited to subway trains, trams, and buses or a ten-trip ticket giving one-sixth off the single fare price. A similar card is available in Tampere, Finland's second city.

Gothenburg, the capital of Sweden's West Coast, promotes the Goteborg Card covering free travel on buses, trams, archipelago boats, and free entry to dozens of places of interest, museums, sports and recreation facilities. It includes a free round trip on the Stena Line to Frederikshavn in Denmark that alone would cost more than the card. The Goteborg Card is included free in the "Goteborg Package" for hotels during the summer—a good value.

Ready yourself for fresh clean air and sparkling fjords as you travel through Lapland and the land of the Midnight Sun on the following adventures: Norway's Bergen and Flam line, a trip into the Arctic Circle, Norway's Rauma Train, a crossing by deluxe ferry from Stockholm to Finland, and a circle trip through Finland's natural lakelands.

Bergen and Flam Trains
Travel with the Trolls

The plateau is a vast stretch of mountaintop, uninhabited, treeless, flat. You see no spiked Matterhorns here, just featureless mountains with tops swept away by glaciers—a frozen, crystalline surface, polished by howling wind. It is Arctic, remote, lonely, and it is only your brick-red train that keeps you from feeling stranded on the top of the world.

You have passed Taugevatn, the highest point of this Norwegian line (4,267 feet), well above the timber line so far north. Now you run along the stark, clear-aired, snow-pocked edge of the Hardanger Plateau.

It is so white that any speck of color seems to be out of place. Just before you stop at Myrdal, you look to your right and see the browns and greens of the mountain walls of a grand canyon of a rift. Peering through openings in the north wall of the snow tunnel, you gasp at the sight so many hundred feet down of the temperate Flam valley.

The Oslo-Bergen route—free on a Eurail or ScanRailpass—is NSB's important flagship route. Without it, Norway's second city would be isolated by land from the rest of the country. Behind Bergen, the wall of the Hardanger Plateau forms a dead end.

When you look at a topographic map of Norway, you can appreciate that this route is an engineering triumph. Engineers successfully designed the line to climb and descend safely from sea level to 4,267 feet in inaccessible, hostile Arctic country.

Your Pernille Express Special train hurried out of Oslo Sentral station punctually at 7:21 A.M. through built-up Oslo and past the suburbs. Climbing alongside a broad river, your long, brick-red, electric train first passes flowery meadows and placid lakes. Then you hear the whine of sawmills at work and see tractors idling beside red farmhouses in patchwork fields close by the rails.

You cross through meager and noticeably thinning farmland, past natural, untouched emerald valleys, and finally out of pine groves and woods of ringed

BERGEN

BERGEN and FLAM LINES

Voss

Flam

Myrdal

Finse

Ustaoset

Geilo

Aal

Gol

Nesbyen

Honefoss

OSLO

0   20   50

MILES

silver birch trees, away from the temperate environment of the Oslo fjord and up into the mountains. You see the waters run faster. The trees thin. Patches of snow appear. The country is mantled in white by the time you arrive in Geilo. At 2,650 feet, you are only miles short of the timberline.

Skiers clunk off down the platform, even in midsummer. They tilt their skis proudly over their shoulders, eager for a good afternoon's sport. Geilo is the St. Moritz of Norway.

As you continue to climb, the scenery changes from ski resort to glacier. You leave the last of the trees at Ustaoset.

At Finse, thirty minutes later, the landscape glares whitely. It is dominated by the frigid Hardanger glacier looming in the south higher by 2,000 feet than Finse (4,010 feet). George Lucas filmed here the bitterly cold opening sequences of *The Empire Strikes Back.*

Finse is the highest station on the line — the entire NSB network, in fact. If you are riding a local train, you might have time to tramp into the snowbanks to take spectacular photos of the glacier, or peek at the old steam-powered snowplow. It is the lonely headquarters for the Bergen line's thirty- to forty-worker crew against nature. They clear snow from the tracks during nine snowy months and repair snowsheds splintered by the power of the snow during what should be their vacation.

Now at Myrdal station, dominated by a mountain with icy whiskers of frozen waterfalls, you don your parka and bundle onto the waiting coaches of the Flåm train, each seating thirty-nine on maroon, leatherette-covered benches for two and three, accented with brass studs and hand fixtures. The scuffed brown linoleum floor has seen much service and the heavy-duty overhead racks have carried many backpacks.

You leave behind a high, bleak, and contrary glacial plateau for the green and serene beauty of one of Norway's most pleasant fjords. Your trip doesn't take long — less than an hour — but minute for minute, as your train inches down Europe's steepest route and turns surprising corners, you are rewarded by one of the most breathtaking of Norway's adventurous trains. The conductors also make it Norway's friendliest.

The Flåm valley you see is an immense opening through the mountains, similar to the Grand Canyon in the sheer inclination of its mountain walls. You board the Flåm line — free on a Eurailpass — at its upper railhead, Myrdal, 2,845 feet above sea level. The lower terminus, Flåm, near the ferry landing on the Aurlandsfjord, is fifty minutes (forty-one, going up) and twelve miles down the valley. This section is the steepest of any NSB line. In one stretch you drop one foot for every eighteen you travel, quite brave for an adhesion train without cogwheels. The five braking systems give your cautious engineer more sureness than a Norwegian mountain goat. Any one system is enough to halt the train safely.

This line was not built for passenger traffic. Perhaps that is why it is so unspoiled. It was built in the wilds, connecting fjord and glacier, to carry construction materials and heavy machinery for completing the central section of the Oslo-Bergen line. They were ferried up the fjord to Flam and then carted by horses up to Myrdal. You see the surviving horse trail of 1895-96 still paralleling the line.

You follow a tortuous path of twenty-one hairpin curves, in and out of tunnels. On the most scenic sections, your engineer thoughtfully slows or stops, so you can linger and absorb the impact of views more dazzling than you have imagined. You see sturdy wild mountain goats peering curiously at the train from granite boulders only a few feet from your window.

At first descent, your Flam train moves roughly parallel to the Bergen line, between snow fences, but after your halt in Vatnahalsen, a stop with a fine hotel and superb view over the steep slopes below, splendid panoramas quickly begin to unfold. You soon reach the highlight of your trip. Your train trudges across a sturdy embankment and the engineer stops politely.

Beside the line, so close you can feel the pressure of the roaring action filling cameras' viewfinders, a fury of foam plunges over a cliff, raging down at you in a smoking torrent. It is not so much a waterfall as rapids out of nowhere. Just before you it vanishes safely into a natural tunnel beneath the trestle supporting your train. This is Kjosfoss, "foss" meaning "waterfall."

You appreciate the announcements, in English, over the loudspeaker by the conductor. These men take a sincere interest in the well-being and pleasure of adventurers who come to visit their proud little valley.

If they feel a certain affinity for Americans, it is because more than a third of the population left this valley during the hard years of 1845-65 to settle in the New World, mostly in the Midwest. More than 1,000 emigrated. More than a century later, 2,000 live here, mostly making their living from farming, and English is widely spoken.

The conductors actually encourage passengers to scatter off the train onto the wooden-plank platform and soggy turf at Kjosfoss, to gawk and admire and pose for photographs before the powerful, raging waterfall/rapids less than a stone's toss away. Its fury easily drowns out the accumulated sounds of shutters clicking.

Farther down, you cross lesser wild rivers without benefit of bridges. (There are no bridges on this line.) Here again, the viaducts were blasted out of the mountains just as the construction engineers blasted the looping tunnels. When you enter the longest tunnel, Nali (1,476 yards), you look back and see the extraordinary sight of the railbed cutting four ledges of the mountainside, one almost above the other.

When you leave the tunnel, you have a brief glimpse of the highest Flam valley farm, where 3,000 goats are kept to produce orange-colored Norwegian goat cheese. Another waterfall, Fjoandfoss, drops 400 feet down the mountainside in the afternoon shade.

At Hareina (158 feet), a timid little village beside the prospering Flam River where anglers make their catches at the break of day, your views from between tunnels and cuttings disappear, the valley widens, and you see the panorama of the highest toylike farms below. The fields here seem more vividly green than possible because your eyes are still adjusting from the white glare above. Looking ahead, you see the 300-year-old Flam Church, flowering fruit orchards, the blue of the fjord coming near, and the brown of the mountains behind.

The wooden Flam train station is the center of activity for the village. The black-topped platform extends to the landing of the ferries for Balestrand and Gudvangen and the hydrofoils for Bergen. The tourist information office stands nearby. Local buses depart from the kiosk in the parking lot behind the station to the shore of the fjord.

With an adjoining cafeteria open until 8 P.M., the Hotel Fretheim Touristhotell is white with wooden lace and seems more like a romantic summer cottage or guesthouse than a dignified vacation hotel with mostly British visitors. You know before you enter that everything will be spotless, the waitresses will wear dirndls, and all guests will be snoring by 10:30 P.M. but will be up at the crow of the cock and the glimmer of dawn—except that in summer, day breaks at 2 A.M. and roosters crow all night.

Returning to Myrdal and continuing west toward Bergen, leaden-looking, chilling, and forbidding lakes surround you. Reindeer race between boulders and leap over patches of snow. Afternoon sun on granite boulders seems to shiver against icy, rushing rivers. Tattered tunnels burrow like snow snakes. You catch glimpses of brown, purple, and flaky yellow mosses through gapes in the drifts.

Then you suddenly realize the snow is melting and the water is running west instead of east, and you know your train is descending to Bergen and the North Sea's warm Gulf Stream.

You pass giant waterfalls, leaving bleak and wind-scoured snowland and entering valleys with dazzling, purple rhododendrons blooming all around you. No sooner do you clear your ears from the increasing air pressure than you are rolling along the shores of Sorfjorden and then through the five-mile Ulriken tunnel into Bergen's end-of-the-line train terminal.

You still see evidence of Bergen's former isolation. Hansa merchants came to Bergen in the Middle Ages, making it their trade center for dried fish. Even now new buildings are patterned after Hanseatic architecture. Houses have a red- and black-brick look similar to northern Germany's Hansa cities. But this architecture is deceiving, because the Bergenese soon reveal the city is fiercely Norwegian. You have plenty of time to seek out a hotel and orient yourself to Norway's second city before nightfall. The tourist office is a healthy walk down Kaigatan past the lake for Torgalmenningen, if you neglected to book a hotel in advance. The Bergenese are particularly friendly to Americans, sophisticated, and many speak English. Bergen is a vital city, a major gateway opening on the West, a devoted cultural city, the former home of Edvard Grieg, the center of an international music festival, and has reputedly the finest youth hostel in the North.

For a fine overview and orientation of Bergen and its harbor setting, make your first project the five-minute funicular ride to the top of Mount Floien.

Bergen Line Service

Per-nille	Bergen Express				Henrik	Bergen Express
0721	1530	dep.	OSLO (Sentral)	arr.	1405	2211
0754	1603	arr.	Drammen	dep.	1332	2138
0757	1607	dep.	Drammen	arr.	1330	2134
0849	1703	arr.	Honefoss	dep.	1241	2042
1014	1828	dep.	Gol	dep.	1114	1912
1035	1849	dep.	Aal	dep.	1055	1852
1055	1909	dep.	Geilo	dep.	1033	1828
1106	1920	dep.	Ustaoset	dep.	1022	1815
....	1930	dep.	Huagastol	dep.	....	1804
1138	1953	dep.	Finse	dep.	0951	1740
1209	....	arr.	MYRDAL	dep.	....	1708
1210	....	dep.	MYRDAL	arr.	....	1706
1250	2105	arr.	Voss	dep.	0839	1625
1251	2107	dep.	Voss	arr.	0838	1623
....	2137	dep.	Dale	arr.	....	....
1350	2208	dep.	Arna	dep.	0738	1523
1358	2215	arr.	BERGEN	dep.	0730	1515

Connecting Flam Line Service

1215	1630	1710	dep.	MYRDAL	arr.	1141	1541	1615
1219	1634	1714	dep.	Vatnahalsen	dep.	1138	1538	1602
1308	1708	1800	arr.	FLAM	dep.	1100	1500	1520

Overnight Sleeping Car Service between Oslo and Flam

2250	dep.	OSLO (Sentral)		arr.	0700

0445	arr.	Myrdal	dep.	0110
0500	dep.	Myrdal	arr.	0046
0504	arr.	Vatnahalsen	dep.	0043
0545	arr.	FLAM	dep.	0005

Lapland Excursion
Midnight Sun to Narvik

Your steep descent into Narvik on the northernmost train in Western Europe is heady stuff. Each bend of your Ofot train opens up the quintessence of Norwegian adventure. You see new vistas of unspoiled mountain, sea, and sky. While your Iron-Ore Railroad train passes through stands of spruce, wild reindeer leap between snowbanks. You lean forward to better watch — on your right — your climactic, precipitous descent down to the Ofot fjord.

The direct descent from the summit is twenty-seven miles, but your zigzagging descent on this stretch of the Lapland train takes nearly a full hour.

First you see pleasing, long views of the waves of the Norwegian Sea breaking on the shores. Then you begin to make out Narvik's wooden houses. Brick shops form a patchwork pattern of color against black conveyer belts and iron-ore loading facilities.

When you adventure by train beyond the Arctic Circle, there is only you, your chugging, solitary locomotive, moonlit freshwater lakes, wild moose, reindeer, cackling birds, and the rich, sweet smells of pine forest and mossy brook.

It's a long thirty-hour trip north from Denmark through Sweden to Norway — an experience for the intrepid, romantic adventurer who admires the green and blue (and white) outdoors. Sweden has the most lakes of all nations.

Setting off in Copenhagen, you travel through the heart of the Scandinavian peninsula to Narvik, Norway's end-of-the-line train station on the Ofot fjord. You see it all while it is light in the domain of the Midnight Sun.

Copenhagen's red-brick train station is a comfortable, busy antique dating from 1911. Metal beams arch over the cheery island of shops and stalls populating the central hall. You validate your Eurailpass or buy a ScanRail Pass in the train information office through the international ticketing ("Billetter udland") room. Young adventurers visit the Inter Rail Center, a haven for those holding Eurail Youthpasses or their equivalent.

One of your highlights comes early in your trip. Your ferry crossing from Helsingor, Denmark, to Helsingborg, Sweden, takes you so close to Kronberg Castle that you can study its emplaced cannons pointing toward Sweden. Shakespeare set *Hamlet* here. No one drawn to this place by the Bard's tragedy has a more photographic view than you from your deck on the train ferry.

Svolvaer

NARVIK

Kiruna

Arctic Circle

Bodo • Fauske

Boden

Vannas

SWEDEN

Trondheim

Ange

LAPLAND ARROW

NORWAY

OSLO

Orebro

STOCKHOLM

NORTH SEA

Nassjo

- N -

Hassle-
holm

Helsing-
borg

DENMARK

Malmo

COPENHAGEN

0   100   200

MILES

You are crossing the most heavily traveled international ferry route in the world. Twenty-two million passengers cross from Denmark to Sweden every year. There is a ferry crossing every seven minutes, 4 train ferries an hour, 400 train carriages a day. Each crossing takes twenty-five minutes. There are 8 train ferries, 7 car ferries, and 3 passenger ferries. Every ferry makes a round trip in an hour.

Duty-free shopping is limited by customs inspections to a pack of cigarettes, but you have time aboard for a quick snack. After landing in Helsingborg's Ferry train station, a polite, English-speaking SJ conductor inspects your ticket or pass. He wants to make sure you are in the correct carriage for your destination because your Lapland train is the epitome of an omnibus train. It takes carriages to and from dozens of destinations in Sweden.

Even if you stocked up with provisions before you left, you will probably use the one-class cafeteria car (open 6 A.M. to 10 P.M.) during your long journey. Coffee refills are free on SJ.

Your Lapland train bypasses Stockholm while traveling north to Narvik, through fir forests and lakes mirroring the serene beauty of the sturdy, rounded mountains. The lonesome clickety-clack of your train tattoos over and over because of spaces between the northern rails.

In the eerie midnight glow, you inhale the sweet scent of pine in the air and gaze at foggy mists in the rocky terrain and in the birches leafless until early summer. Clouds in the silvery sky reflect in the remote, silent lakes. And then a shimmering orange globe rises in the northeast. It seems like it should be on the eastern horizon, but it is the wee hours and your train is entering the domain of the Midnight Sun. Birds chirp at this unlikely hour. Then the red of sunrise spreads across the peaceful lakes and creates a fragile, glassy pink, beginning your second day north.

In Boden you find a pretty frontier city set along a blue lake. While carriages from Lulea on the Gulf of Bothnia are attached to the head of your train and a new locomotive is added, you have twenty minutes to get off and buy provisions at the kiosk beside the train station.

About 1¼ hours out of Boden, your train slows for photographs. Have your camera cocked for the large, neat sign on your left: "Arctic Circle."

From here you pass through barren and remote tundra, climb past scraggly trees and then scrubby bushes, until you reach Kiruna (pop. 27,000), pre-eminent iron-ore mining city and most northerly town in Sweden. You see on the hill the colorful wooden houses painted rust-red, green, brown, and yellow with copper and tile roofs, but you can only imagine the huge, labyrinthine tunnels of the world's largest underground mine.

You thread your way northwest from the mines of Kiruna through green spruce and clean earth damp with melting snow. White stripes of birch trunks pattern the blanket of deep, green grass. Lovers of the outdoors and mountaineers leave your train at primitive outposts. This is one big national park north of the Arctic Circle.

You are traveling along the route of the Iron-Ore Railroad built specifically to carry ore from Kiruna in Sweden to Narvik, Norway, the all-year port kept free of ice by the Gulf Stream. Swedish politicians would have preferred to use a port in Sweden for export of their ore, but the freezing up of the Gulf of Bothnia in winter left them no choice.

Although your line actually crosses Norway, Swedish train experts insist this line carrying twenty million tons of ore annually is the most exciting piece of track in the SJ system. When conditions allow, you can see the complete disk of the sun at midnight from May 26 to July 19.

Thirty hours from Copenhagen you approach Narvik, following that thrilling plunge described at the beginning of this adventure. Narvik (pop. 20,000) is a pup among cities. In 1880, there were but one or two isolated farms and a few not-so-contented cows grazing here. Narvik was dedicated on May 29, 1901.

The low but constant angle of the sun on the horizon causes very little temperature change between day and night. It is already warm when you awake and still pleasant late into the evening.

The cableway ten minutes from the city center, at the head of Kongensgate ("King's Street"), lifts you 2,000 feet to the very top of Mount Fagernesfjell in only thirteen minutes. When you rise in the gondola above the city, your perspective adjusts. First you see the iron-ore loading facilities open up and then the fjords systematically surround and then dwarf the village while snow-covered mountains appear to rise in the distance.

From the top of the lift, the sun warms the terrace of the restaurant and you see the "Sleeping Queen," a panorama resembling Queen Victoria reposed, 5,191-feet high. The official name of Narvik at the turn of the century was "Victoriahamn," meaning "Victoria's Harbor."

Across from the prizewinning city hall, a small, thought-provoking museum records Narvik's place in history. In May 1940, the British sank ten Nazi destroyers in Narvik fjord and temporarily recaptured the city, the first Allied victory of World War II.

You can return by train directly to Stockholm, take the Nord-Norge buses north to Kirkenes near the Russian border, or take the long and tedious Nord-Norge bus trip south across fjords to Fauske Station for connections with NSB's mainline trains. (Tickets are sold aboard the buses, but Eurailpasses are not honored.)

A more adventurous way south from Narvik, and worth the additional cost, is to take the steamers operated by the Ofotens S. S. Co. to connect with coastal steamers north and south. You can sit snugly in the cafeteria of the thirty-knot m.v. *Skogoy*, built in 1985, or go on deck to watch the landings and deliveries of cargo at the tiny hamlets along the way. You reach the codfish city of Svolvaer for a change to the much larger cruise ships of the Coastal Express Service. This gives you a few hours in Svolvaer to explore the interesting codfishing harbor.

Summer Service
Copenhagen to Narvik and Return

*	**				*	***
1245	1225	dep.	COPENHAGEN H.	arr.	1524	1624
1330	1330	dep.	Helsingor (ship)	arr.	1435	1535
1355	1355	arr.	Helsingborg F.	dep.	1329	1457
1427	1437	dep.	Helsingborg F.	arr.	1329	1457
1520	1540	arr.	Hassleholm	dep.	1233	1400
1523	1600	dep.	Hassleholm	arr.	1230	1343
1817	1917	arr.	Linkoping	dep.	0947	1050
	1930	dep.	Linkoping	arr.	0932	
	0319	arr.	Ange	dep.	0137	
	0856	arr.	Vannas	dep.	1953	
	1256	arr.	Boden	dep.	1548	
	1315	dep.	Boden	arr.	1530	
	1717	arr.	Kiruna	dep.	1140	
	1740	dep.	Kiruna	arr.	1125	
	1911	arr.	Abisko	dep.	1005	
	2043	arr.	NARVIK	arr.	0830	

  *End of May until middle of August.
  **Middle of August until end of September (second class only).
***Year around.

Nord-Norge Bus Service
between Narvik and Fauske Station

0730	1715	dep.	Bodo	arr.	1120	2235
0845	1835	arr.	FAUSKE station	dep.	1010	2125
0920	1900	dep.	FAUSKE station	arr.	1000	2105
1445	0010	arr.	NARVIK	dep.	0500	1540

The Rauma Train
Marvels per Minute

You look down the valley and see three railroad lines. You are twisting along one, there's another farther on, on the edge of a cliff, and still farther, below

ANDALSNES

Lesjaskog

Lesja

Dombas

TRONDHEIM

**NORWAY'S RAUMA
AND DOVRE LINES**

Lillehammer

NORWAY

Hamar

Eidsvoll

Lillestrom

OSLO

SWEDEN

-N-

Oslo Fjord

0   20   50   100

MILES

a cascading waterfall on the other side of the valley, you see a third. All three belong to the Rauma Line, carrying you in a huge double spiral to reach the valley floor through two circular tunnels in the Norwegian mountainsides.

Halfway down the seventy-one-mile Rauma Line to Andalsnes, you are still nearly 1,700-feet above sea level, the best scenery is yet to come, and you have to get down somehow. Your train must circle to lose altitude. You pass wild mountains, soaring peaks, and crashing waterfalls and then you enter mountains cored by internal twists and spirals.

The first tunnel you enter, the Stavem, is 4,650 feet long. In the heart of the mountain, you retrace your path. When you return to daylight, you are running on the second segment, opposite to your direction a few minutes ago. You are several levels farther down the valley and see the Vermafoss falls straight ahead plummeting in misty cascades about 1,250 feet down the mountain ridge opposite.

The Rauma River below you dashes with all the gusto of a Norwegian hare, tumbling down over steep precipices and slabs of rock.

Entering the Kylling tunnel, you sweep through the mountain and under the highway in a long shallow curve, 1,500 feet long and so gentle you don't feel it. Back into daylight, you cross Kylling Bridge over a narrow gorge and see again the Rauma River, now frothing and foaming untamed only 200 feet below. As though to make itself most beautiful, the river snakes around pebbly white islets and sandbars of white granite powder and jumps across rapids, trailing glorious white bubbly wakes.

You have reached the third and lowest track and finally you can look back on this ingeniously engineered line from below. The complex double curve made the Rauma Line about five miles longer, but allowed you to descend 330 feet safely.

While the Rauma River gradually tires and meanders more calmly through wide gentle bends, the mountain scenery by contrast turns starker and more rugged and you are entering a new episode in the adventure of the Rauma Line. You are now traveling at the foot of towering rocky precipices and looking up at triple-divided, monstrous waterfalls crashing down at you.

This is what makes train travel exciting. You have passed from one spectacular phase into one differently wondrous. Passengers run from side to side on the train, putting their heads through pulled-down windows, pointing and shouting to each other with delight. One rider, her hair blowing wildly, shouts above the wind, "This is the most beautiful ride in the world."

This 1½-hour jaunt, unfolding rich detail and color, justifies you making a single memorable trip to Norway, and is, happily, completely covered by Eurail and ScanRail Passes, like all NSB travel.

Dovre Arrow and Dovre Express Special trains halt in Dombas, your mountain railhead for the Rauma Line, but their connections take you by bus on an ordinary descent by highway (not covered by rail pass). Prefer to arrive by Dovre Arrow in Dombas, lunch in the cafeteria in Dombas's brick station house, and board the continuation of the fast second-class-only train from Oslo. Returning to Oslo you can make a connection with the Dovre Arrow. Adventurers traveling second class do even better by riding on the two fast (meaning slower than Express Special) trains from Oslo that carry you directly to Andalsnes, leaving Dombas through the Gudbrandsdal and Romsdal ("dal" means "valley").

Your four- to five-hour trip north from Oslo takes you through rich farmlands and then up the eastern shore of Lake Mjosa, Norway's largest, deeper than the North Sea. On the lake you see the one-funnel steamship, the P. S. Skibladner (say "Shebladner"), the world's oldest paddle steamer still in regular service, built in 1854, in Sweden. You pass red-and-brown wooden summer cottages, and wild flowers dancing like yellow fire—dandelions, buttercups, mustard, and rapeseed (for monounsaturated oil).

Your first stop on Lake Mjosa is in the important hub of Hamar, at the widest point. Inhale deeply here. The air is fresh and pure, reputedly the most healthful in Scandinavia at Hamar and at your second stop on the lake, the vacation center of Lillehammer, where the Norwegian government is spending about $370 million to prepare for the 1994 Winter Olympic Games.

Past Lillehammer, you enter Gudbrandsdal, the "Valley of Valleys." Farmers here still maintain the old building styles. You pass lined-up farmhouses climbing the mountainsides like soldiers.

In Dombas you change to the Rauma Line. Now, looking forward as you wind down toward Andalsnes on the Ice fjord, the sheer face of unscalable Trollveggen, meaning Troll Wall, stands in front of you. You must crane your neck to see the summits of the huge mountains soaring heavenwards on either side, one after another. From a terrible height, famous waterfalls drop from the mountainside like countless silver fingers.

When you approach Marstein, where the mountains stand so high the stationmaster only sees the sun seven months of the year, your ride has settled down to merely splendid (although you will eventually reach the Trollveggen). You watch capricious mists of cloud dancing midway up sturdy cliffs nearly barren of trees.

You wind around the wedge-shaped, 4,250-foot high Mongegjura Mountain and the weird range of peaks resembling a row of trolls squatting menacingly over the valley. Its gray walls, scarred and stained, rise sheer from the valley floor to 6,000 feet.

An encampment of trolls reputedly established themselves here to gain an advantage over their enemies, gnomes on the valley floor. In one battle, they hid until the gnomes appeared at the foot of the mountains and then hurled down a terrible avalanche to bury them in rock and stone. But the gnomes triumphed in the end, for they had tricked the trolls, who are permitted to roam only at night. For their foolish midday attack, the trolls fossilized into these jagged blue-gray mountain massifs, so steep the snow will not lie on their slopes nor will any vegetation grow.

The valley is almost entirely surrounded by the peaks above you. You cannot see the top of the Romsdalshorn. Finally, you look up at the 6,300-foot Trollveggen, the highest vertical rock face in northern Europe.

Now you descend. You have always been dropping, of course, but now you sense it by the multiplication of the flowering wild plants and the passing of the terrible, high mountains.

You see the river joining the fjord and rows of pleasant homes along ordered streets. This is the tidy township of Andalsnes, where you come to a halt.

Andalsnes (pop. 2,500) is one of the loveliest settings along the coast of Norway. Situated on the Ice fjord, the head of the Romsdalsfjord, at the foot of the Romsdal, it is framed by the Setnefjell mountain on the west and Mount Nesaksla on the east.

You won't find much in Andalsnes but scenery, but that is more than enough. Molde, the stopping place for the coastal steamers, is a superb 2½-hour mail boat trip across the fjord.

Express Special trains from Oslo continue from Dombas to Trondheim, Norway's third city. About twenty-five minutes north of Dombas, you pass the highest point of the line, about 3,360 feet, and see the snow-capped, highest mountain in Norway (7,500 feet) to the west. The Dovre Arrow brings you in good time to orient yourself. Trondheim (pop. 135,000) is a busy, colorful port, one of the most beautiful in Scandinavia. Norway's kings are crowned here in Nidaros Cathedral, a national shrine.

Dovre Line Service

Dovre Arrow ET41	351*	353*	Dovre Exp. ET43				Dovre Exp. ET42	352*	Dovre Arrow ET44
0755	0855	1455	1523	dep.	OSLO (Sent.)	arr.	1507	1639	2217
0813	0918	1518	1543	dep.	Lillestrom	arr.	1446	1618	2158
0844	0957	1616	1616	dep.	Eidsvoll	dep.	1417	1533	2126
0921	1041	1642	1700	arr.	Hamar	dep.	1339	1449	2049
0923	1045	1644	1702	dep.	Hamar	arr.	1337	1446	2047
1004	1134	1731	1745	arr.	Lillehammer	dep.	1254	1359	2004
1006	1138	1733	1747	dep.	Lillehammer	arr.	1252	1357	2002
1048	1228	1818	1829	dep.	Ringebu	dep.	1210	1312	1923
1105	1254	1847	1847	dep.	Vinstra	dep.	1152	1254	1906

1125	1318	1901	1914	arr.	Otta	dep.	1130	1232	1846
1128	1321	1903	1916	dep.	Otta	arr.	1128	1230	1844
1158	1355	1935	1946	arr.	DOMBAS	dep.	1100	1158	1816
1200	1355	1935	1948	dep.	DOMBAS	arr.	1058	1151	1814
....	1530	2115	....	arr.	ANDALSNES	dep.	....	1020	1640x
1256			2046	arr.	Oppdal	dep.	1001		1718
1258			2048	dep.	Oppdal	arr.	0959		1716
1348			2138	arr.	Storen	dep.	0908		1625
1430			2220	arr.	TRONDHEIM	dep.	0825		1545

*Second-class-only fast train.
xChange trains in Dombas.

Crossing the Bothnia
Free Deck to Finland

"Tervetuloa. Welcome aboard the Silja Line." The veteran captain speaks from the bridge of your ship crossing from Stockholm to Finland—Turku or Helsinki—a vantage point some one hundred feet and twelve stories above the water.

You watch fir trees gliding by your deck chair. Your entry to Finland across the Gulf of Bothnia is not absent of scenery as you might expect. You sail through an endless archipelago of 80,000 islands, rocks, and skerries. Some are tree-covered. All are remnants of the glacier era and the geologic rising of the earth's crust under the gulf.

Almost everything is fresh aboard ship—and well kept up. Passengers are doing whatever pleases them. Their natural mobility aboard ship allows them to gather into compatible groups. Everyone seems friendly. You hear that Finnish is the predominate language on board, but everyone speaks English to you. All announcements are in Swedish, Finnish, and English.

Most of the travelers seem to be in their twenties, although active elders are gathering on the deck chairs. You can also hear a few infants, and dogs trot down the decks on midnight walks led by their masters and mistresses.

Nordic children seem to be having the best of it. Northern countries know how to look after their offspring. Children frolic in a glassed playroom filled with colored plastic bubbles. You can see that they are returning from a family excursion to the "big city" of Stockholm.

Several cruise lines, including the beautiful red-and-white ships of the Viking Line, carry passengers across the Gulf of Bothnia from Stockholm to Turku or Helsinki, but Eurailpass holders are particularly interested in the Silja Line. They can board free and the deck-passage price is deducted from the normal cabin cost if they prefer.

CROSSING
THE BOTHNIA

Umea

Langsele

-N-

GULF OF BOTHNIA

FINLAND

Tampere

Gavle

TURKU

HELSINKI

Aland
Islands

MARIEHAMN

Tallinn

SWEDEN

STOCKHOLM

SOVIET UNION

0   50   100

You depart from Silja Line's Stockholm pier in the port of Vartan—in the northeastern part of town. Silja Line's information and ticketing offices are located there and you can also make use of a self-service cafe, children's playroom, souvenir kiosk, tourist information (for arrivals), waiting room, telephones, rest rooms, lockers, and check-in counter which opens two hours before sailing. A mailbox is outside.

Pickup is free by a white Silja Line bus from City Terminalen, the new bus terminal on the bottom floor of the 1990 World Trade Center attached to Stockholm's Central train station. You can also take a Tunnelbana (subway) train to Ropsten, the end-of-the-line station, or Gardet, next to the end of the line. From Gardet you walk—a relatively easy, ten-minute hike. Signs to Vartahamnen, Silja Line's port, are posted in the subway.

The attraction of free passage is irresistible on ships offering a tropical Sunflower Oasis with water slides, swimming pools, steam bath and bars; a play area for children; a promenade atrium covered in teak, lined with reasonably priced restaurants and shops and overlooked by cabins above; a casino with Las Vegas-style slot machines; a popular dance floor; a mandatory duty-free market; gourmet restaurants sprinkled throughout the ship . . . and moonlight walks in fresh salty air.

Silja Line's twenty-three-knot luxury liner sailing nonstop to Helsinki, 1990's m.s. *Silja Serenade,* which incorporates cruise vessel luxuries never before seen in the industry, is joined by the 1981, twenty-two-knot m.s. *Silvia Regina.* The *Serenade* carries up to 2,500 passengers, the *Silvia Regina* up to 2,000 on their daily voyages year-round (except for Christmas eve).

Two 33,800-ton sister ships, the m.s. *Svea* and m.s. *Wellamo,* put into service in 1985 and 1986 respectively, carry you on the shorter passage to Turku with afternoon berthings at Mariehamn in the Aland Islands.

Silja Line's ships were designed for service between Finland and Sweden, but they also comply with rules of construction for long international voyages and meet the requirements for ice-navigation without the help of icebreakers. Due to dense traffic and narrow routes in the archipelagoes, the bottoms of the hulls are designed for minimal wave generation and minimal response to heavy seas.

You board free with a Eurailpass or (free to Turku only) a ScanRail Pass. How you sleep is up to you. The ferries carry nineteen categories of cabins, "Sleep-in" couchette bunk beds, and reclining Pullman chairs free to deck passengers. The bunk beds in the "Sleep-in" compartments are allocated for passengers purchasing basic transportation on a first-come, first-served basis. When some are left over, Eurailpass travelers may use them without charge. Free Pullman chairs ("Sittsalong") are surprisingly comfortable with spacious washrooms nearby. You stow your small bags in nearby lockers. Leave your large luggage in the luggage room.

The cabins are a good value when you are not paying for a ticket. Because of the Eurailpass discount a bunk in a four-person cabin costs about the same price as a second-class couchette on a train. The ships' cabins give you many comforts: shower, bunk beds, mirror, toilet, wash basin, and open closet. (Advance reservations: Silja Line, 505 Fifth Avenue, New York, NY 10017. Tel. 212-986-2711.)

Choose between two daily departures from Stockholm to Turku (morning and evening) and one only at 6 P.M. to Helsinki. Note that the time in Finland is an hour earlier than in Sweden. Steamers departing from Turku and Stockholm in the morning call at Mariehamn in the Aland Islands—an interesting stop for postage stamp collectors.

When the captain announces your ship will be docking in Helsinki in half an hour, look to your left entering Helsinki's harbor. Your ship's only possible navigable channel takes you through Suomenlinna, Finland's Seafortress, a complex of six islands fortified in 1748. Once the greatest fortress of the Swedish empire, it was surrendered to the Russians in 1808 and then bombarded by the British fleet in 1855 during the Crimean War. It finally became Finnish in 1917 when it was renamed "Finland's Seafortress."

The first building you spot in Helsinki will probably be the white capitol-like dome of Uspensky Lutheran Cathedral. On debarking, pass through the customs hall and you will see an office to change money and a tourist office where you can buy Helsinki Cards for transportation or book a hotel room in the city for a small service charge. Tram 3T goes to Market Square a few blocks away and Tram 3B (which runs the opposite direction of Tram 3T) takes you to the train station.

Sailing into Turku, you see an unmatched view of high Turku Castle, a medieval bastion (but now a museum) guarding the harbor. Turku's Harbor train station is separate from the main Turku station. Slate-gray and cream-colored coaches with bright apricot-colored plush upholstery wait at the Harbor station to take you onto the VR network with diesel trains to Helsinki, Tampere, and Joensuu. These carry cafeteria cars with snacks and coffee. You can buy train tickets in the Silja Line terminal.

Service between Stockholm and Turku or Helsinki
by Silja Line, Train, and Bus

0815	1800	2115	dep.	STOCKHOLM (Vartahamn.)	arr.	2015	0900	0700
1445	....	....	dep.	Mariehamn (Vastrahmn.)	dep.	1545	....	....
2015	....	0800	arr.	TURKU (Harbor)	dep.	1000	....	2130
2030t	....	0825t	dep.	Turku (Harbor)	arr.	0927t	....	2054t
2300t	0900	1100t	arr.	Helsinki (Etelasatama)	dep.	0702t	1800	1830t

t—Train connection to/from Helsinki train station. There are also arrivals and departures at Turku Harbor for Tampere.

Round Finland by Train
Lakeland and Nature

You suddenly come within inches of a granite sculpture. The powerful figure sitting on the ground cradles its head with one arm and peers steadily down upon you at the window of your train. Then you enter a black tunnel and when you emerge, the medieval towers and ramparts of Olavinlinna castle, the best-preserved in the Nordic countries, unravel a double vision dancing in the calm waters of Kyronsalmi Straits on your left.

Nature becomes redefined: quiet waters, firs towering, birds singing, pine needles on forest floor filtered by magical light. About 180 endangered Saimaa fresh-water seals frolic in the lake, their last refuge. It is said that trout fight among themselves to be the first to take anglers' lures in Kyronsalmi straits.

The lakeside village of Savonlinna is your heart of Finland's Saimaa Lakeland. The community grew around Olavinlinna castle, and together with the captivating countryside has become Finland's most magnetic place. The branch line from Parikkala brings adventurers to the Savonlinna Opera Festival every year throughout July which is held on the stage magnificently located within the walls of Olavinlinna. The sculpture that greeted you marked the entrance to the Retretti Art Center at Punkaharju, the largest art center in the Nordic countries. Curators fill its subterranean grottoes with outstanding exhibits of modern and traditional international art.

Finland does not end with Helsinki. The beauty and serenity of Finland lies in the lake districts. Luckily for adventurers, the geography of Finland dictates that rail lines originally built for lumber transport must link lakeside villages and reveal Finland's secrets to train travelers.

Like the limbs of a pear tree, with Helsinki at its root, VR's Ostrobothnian line shoots to the north beside the Gulf of Bothnia, VR's Karelian line branches north beside the Soviet Union's border, and the Savo line shoots straight north between lakes. At Joensuu the Karelian line bends and attaches itself to the Ostrobothnian line at Oulu and thus completes a raindrop-shaped ring around Finland's two magnificent lakelands and makes a circle trip not only feasible, but essential to absorb the grandness, greatness, and captivation of the Finnish enchanting lakeland.

Ten percent of Europe's fifth-largest country is water — lakes and rapids. The rivers flow garnet in Finland, tinted with soluble iron ores. The Saimaa Lakeland runs from Lappeenranta in the south to Nurmes in the north. The

Western Lakeland is bounded by Tampere on the west and Hameenlinna on the south.

Varieties of trees commingle on the flat Finnish countryside as happily and thickly as birds on their limbs. Pines prefer dryer land and make up more than half of Finland's forests. Spruce make up about one-third; birch about one-tenth. In the south occasional oak, lime, ash, and maple join the forests.

The diesel-hauled train that brought you to Savonlinna's Olavinlinna castle connected with the electric train from Helsinki at Parikkala. This thirty-seven-mile spur is the jewel of the Finnish State Railroads.

Starting your trip from Helsinki's startling red-granite Central train station, where you ask for the free pocket timetable, "Taskuaikataulu" (English is the first foreign language in Finland), you leave from a central train yard with all departures marked by electronic signs.

When your train branches onto the Karelian line north toward Lappeenranta, away from the route leading into the Soviet Union, the land by the tracks looks marshy but the trees look sturdy. Looking north, you see your first lake. Now your adventure begins.

Reaching Parikkala, your train for Savonlinna waits across the platform, only two miles from the present border of the Soviet Union.

Parikkala is a lure for birders. Siberian birds nest and fly over the Siikalahti Conservation Area, as far west as they venture.

You continue north to Joensuu, the provincial capital meaning "river mouth," where the branches of Finnish State Railroads thin. Trains arriving here send north only second-class coaches pulled by an ordinary red 75-mph diesel locomotive driven by a Viking. You have reached the top branch of the tree of electrified lines.

Out of Joensuu, you pass through rolling hills with stands primarily of spruce. You see lakes everywhere, but no one using the waters. Occasionally you see an abandoned canoe pulled up onto turf or a quiet outboard motorboat with its motor lying beside it.

At Lieksa station the black steam locomotive that usually stands on display outside every Finnish train station is not present. Instead you see a tiny railroad cart loaded with a single, cut commemorative segment of tree trunk, honoring the origins of this railroad as a lumber-hauling operation.

For contrast, look opposite your train. Flat car after flat car are loaded with timber, stretching out of sight beyond the curve in the rails.

You travel up the east shore of sixty-mile-long Lake Pielinen, the biggest lake in Karelia, until you halt on the northern tip of the lake at Nurmes, center of ski and hiking trails. Nearby is the touristic Karelian settlement of Bomba. You recognize Karelian architecture by its log houses with wide balconies, pillars, balustrades, overhanging eaves, and ornate "pretty" window frames giving them a cutesy charm.

Your trip north from Nurmes is the least traveled of any VR route. One 35-mph diesel-pulled train a day (which originates in Helsinki as an overnight sleeper) runs sixty-eight miles to Kontiomaki, where you can choose to return south to Helsinki via the Savo line on the EP Savonia. Adventurers making the great loop north continue to Oulu on the Gulf of Bothnia after using their twenty-two minute break in Kontiomaki to dash to the snack counter.

Better maintained tracks to Oulu allow faster speeds, and you travel your last 101 miles, Kontiomaki to Oulu (Uleaborg in Swedish), at 50 mph.

After your passing through solitude, Oulu surprises you. Dynamic and progressive, happy and prosperous, 100,000-population Oulu claims to be the Silicon Valley of northern Scandinavia. You find astonishingly modern hotels such as the Rivoli and the Eden at half the price of Helsinki hotels on weekends and in June and July, a university town, a marvelous Science Museum, a magnificent Lutheran cathedral, and preserved neo-Renaissance architecture. Oulu is your natural jumping-off point to see Lapland or travel by bus north of the Gulf of Bothnia to Sweden and Norway.

South from Oulu, you join the fully electrified Ostrobothnian line. Trains run faster. The EP Lapponia is the fastest way to return to Helsinki. As your EP Lapponia approaches Tampere, you see that you are entering the Western Lakeland — and welcome it is to see — as Lake Nasijarvi opens to your east. Crossing the long bridge across Tampere's Tammerkoski Rapids, you stop in the city center.

One glance at Tampere's bricks stacks and you see that Tampere is industrialized — in fact it is the most heavily industrialized city in Finland, but here industry does not look like the dirty word that travelers fear. Tampere charms you as you walk wide boulevards past quiet green parks and see the plentiful hotels, art nouveau architecture that Finland adopted its national Romantic style, rolling hills, and blissful lakes. Those quiet stacks give vertical thrusts to Tampere's beautiful setting like exclamation points.

Situated as Tampere is, the hub of the electrified Ostrobothnian line and the east-west spoke from Puri to Pieksamaki and Joensuu, Tampere is your natural home for the Western Lakeland. To reach Tampere's tourist office, head four blocks straight down Hameenkatu from in front of the station and then turn left at Verkatehtaankatu, 2.

As your EP Lapponia approaches Hameenlinna, look for one of the most impressive sights you can see from a mainline train. While you feel your train braking for the station house, look across the narrow lake to the brick Hameenlinna ("linna" means "castle"), dating from the 1260s. It was built by the

Swedes to link the Hame region with the mother country and—you guessed it—to collect taxes from the relatively wealthy area.

Hameenlinna was the northern terminus of Finland's first railroad line from Helsinki in 1862, when goods were transloaded between railroad and lake steamer for further shipment along the lake system to and from the north. Rapid progress soon connected Hameenlinna station to St. Petersburg (now Leningrad). The present station building was erected in 1920 following the old one's demolition during the Finnish revolution when Germans, who were supporting "White" Finns in their battles with the "Red" Finns, exploded a railroad carriage filled with gunpowder.

Returning to Helsinki, the buildings become higher and contemporary. When you arrive seeking a hotel, go not into the arrival hall. Cut through the passageway to your right to the bungalow marked "Hotelcentralen," where agents upstairs make reservations for you and give you all information about Helsinki as well as other Finnish towns which you may want to visit.

Helsinki—Oulu via Karelian Line EP 7/8 Karelia

1701	dep.	HELSINKI	arr.	1230
1750	dep.	Riihimaki	arr.	1142
1822	dep.	Lahti	arr.	1108
1856	dep.	Kouvola	dep.	1036
1942	dep.	Lappeenranta	dep.	0949
2006	dep.	Imatra	dep.	0925
2043	arr.	Parikkala	dep.	0846
2136	arr.	SAVONLINNA*	dep.	0750
2156	arr.	JOENSUU	dep.	0735

*Arrive Savonlinna via connecting train from Parikkala; depart via connecting bus to Parikkala.

0720	dep.	JOENSUU	arr.	2214
0837	dep.	Lieksa	dep.	2054
0930	dep.	Nurmes	dep.	2004
1147	dep.	Kontiomaki	dep.	1815
1348	arr.	OULU	dep.	1547

Helsinki—Oulu via Ostrobothnian Line EP 57/58 Lapponia

1600	dep.	HELSINKI	arr.	1400
....	dep.	Riihimaki	arr.	1310
....	dep.	Hameenlinna	dep.	....
1750	arr.	TAMPERE	dep.	1200
1753	dep.	TAMPERE	arr.	1156
1919	dep.	Seinajoki	dep.	1034
2034	dep.	Kokkola	dep.	0917
2230	arr.	OULU	dep.	0720

Germany

Vital Tips for the Trains of Germany

Riding intermediate distances—Riding the German "Pendolino"—
Using secondary lines—S-Bahn trains—Airport trains—Holiday
trains—Using Eurailpass bonuses—German Railpass

Traveling in politically integrated Germany is an exciting concept; German-Rail's trains take you everywhere you want to go. The train network in the west is more intensive, where fast, efficient trains take you to the Alps, North Sea beaches, the Rhine River, and the Black Forest. They cover 15,000 miles of train tracks and call at 6,000 train stations in an area the size of Oregon. Many conductors and staff speak English. The eastern German network has been unified with astonishing speed. Good through trains take you to Berlin, Leipzig, Dresden, the Harz Mountains, and the Thuringen Forest.

GermanRail's combined western and eastern timetable is complicated to understand. ICE ("InterCity Express"), IC, IR ("InterRegio"), EC, and FD ("Holiday Express") trains crisscross western Germany one after another, with fast, on-time connections. Only a few IC and IR trains travel east. Older D ("fast") and E ("semifast") trains run along secondary routes and to the east. You find Ex (express diesel) trains in the east. S-Bahn trains give you extensive urban transportation. In addition you ride local and overnight trains.

GermanRail's primary claim to greatness comes from its unmatched network of 150 InterCity trains serving all of western Germany's big cities and Leipzig, too. In addition, GermanRail's EuroCity trains take you by day into neighboring western countries. By night, GermanRail's best sleeping train, the EC Alfred Noble, takes you to Oslo and Stockholm while other GermanRail sleepers and couchettes whisk you within Germany and across its frontiers.

You receive an on-board timetable called "Ihr Zug-Begleiter" ("Your Train Companion") on every high-speed IC, EC, and even D train showing not only your time of arrival and departure at every stop along your way, but—more useful—telling you where to change for your ultimate destination.

It is possible for you to board at any of the sixty IC-network cities and, by following the on-board timetable, arrive with all speed in any other station you might choose by making only one split-second across-the-platform change or two at most. GermanRail's platforms are designed to simplify connections. Find your carriage by consulting the "Wagenstandanzeiger" train-composition boards on the platforms or the digital signs overhead which in addition to the usual departure information also show you where the first- and second-class sections come to rest. When you change from one IC train to another, it is likely that a corresponding car, first- or second-class, will be waiting for you just twenty feet across the platform. The June 1991 running of ICE trains, with decreased travel times between connecting cities, causes a dislocation of timings, but GermanRail still provides for easy connections.

GermanRail's newest IC carriages stand out with fire-red liveries, lavender stripes down the sides, and swivel-opening push-button doors. Don't look for a yellow stripe denoting first class. Rely instead on the bold "1" and "2" numerals on the shiny exteriors. New restaurant carriages are lettered "Bord-Restaurant" on the red exteriors.

Some IC, EC, and even D trains use older carriages of standard GermanRail livery. Red-and-cream carriages are first class; blue-green-and-cream ones are second. Don't look for yellow stripes to indicate first class on these carriages. Look to the color of the body.

Most of GermanRail's IC and EC trains carry one or two salon carriages while the rest of the train consists of compartment carriages. Dining cars are located between the first- and second-class sections.

GermanRail's reservations fees for their fast trains are included in their surcharge, which Eurailpass holders don't pay or need. However, if you insist on a reservation, pay the surcharge.

Larger GermanRail stations have escalators to the platforms (Dusseldorf, Hamburg, Hanover, Heidelberg, Mannheim, etc.) and forty-three smaller ones have automatic conveyer belts for your luggage (eighty-seven more are being so equipped). Most of them provide luggage carts free, although a few, like Munich's Hauptbahnhof, require a coin for release.

GermanRail does not accept credit cards, but train conductors accept traveler's checks—in U.S. dollars, German Marks, and English pounds sterling only.

Riding Intermediate Distances

For pleasant, medium-range travel you ride GermanRail's new, "friendly" InterRegio (IR) trains. GermanRail conceived IRs as distinctive attractions with twenty-first century arrangements of plush and plastic products, brightly colored interiors, large tables, exact air-conditioning, extensive use of glass, and new bistro cafes with stand-up counters and stools around tables offering snacks, freshly baked goods, hot and cold drinks and—no surprise in Germany—beer on tap.

You find infinitely variable minisalons and haphazard rows of light-green seats mixed in every carriage, jump seats for children, and high chairs that convert to tables. Parents with children find special compartments; one per train is for handicapped in wheelchairs.

GermanRail timed its IRs to arrive and depart at regular two-hour intervals, so you know in advance at what minute to expect IRs. They average at least 56 mph, but reach 125 mph (compare this with the D trains they replace, which averaged 40, and peaked at 87 mph).

The IR network, when completed, will consist of 1,200 carriages (200 first class, 850 second class, and 150 dining cars). Of these, 250 have been made pressure tight so you can ride them on GermanRail's new high-speed lines.

Look for IR's new livery carriages (sky blue, sea blue, and white for second; white, lavender, and red for first class), for example, on lines running in two-hour intervals connecting Hamburg-Hanover-Gottingen-Kassel/Fulda; Kassel-Giessen-Frankfurt-Darmstadt-Offenburg (over the Black Forest Route, see below)-Konstanz; Duisburg-Hamm-Paderborn-Kassel-Bebra; Cologne-Hanover-Braunschweig-Berlin; Saarbrucken-Stuttgart-Ulm; and Karlsruhe-Stuttgart-Munich.

Riding the German "Pendolino"

In Germany, you ride new VT 610 trains based on the Italian Pendolino concept (see Pendolino/Italy chapter), but you don't recognize it until your train starts to tilt.

GermanRail's units look conventional when you see their standard profiles and GermanRail's white-and-green liveries. Inside you find all modern amenities and newly developed seating. But underneath, Italian-developed Pendolino mechanisms allow them to tilt on curves and increase speed on winding stretches of track in order to decrease your travel time and increase your comfort.

Look for GermanRail's ten new prototype diesel units on a pilot program with the state of Bavaria called the Regional Fast Train (RSB) between Nuremberg and Bayreuth/Hof. With hourly departures at an average speed of 68 mph, RSBs cut your travel time between Nuremberg and Bayreuth by 35 percent and between Nuremberg and Hof by 40 percent.

Using Secondary Lines

GermanRail's sea-green, smooth-riding regional railcar, VT 628, is the cornerstone of its cost-cutting secondary-line concept. You won't be asked for a ticket on these railcars. They run without a conductor. They are pleasing to ride, comfortable but Spartan, with two tablelike forms in first class which give you space below for suitcases.

The second-class section behind the driver has jump seats providing room for baby buggies and bicycles. Riders in front watch over the driver's shoulder as he accelerates to a maximum speed of 75 mph.

S-Bahn Trains

Use GermanRail's rapid-transit, frequent-service "S-Bahn" trains in seven independent regions of intense train travel in and around Frankfurt, Hamburg, Munich, Nuremberg, the Ruhr, Cologne, and Stuttgart. Hamburg's system is the oldest; Nuremberg's the newest. You will especially appreciate them in Munich, where S-Bahn trains parallel Munich's subways and use the same underground station entrances along the Hauptbahnhof-Marienplatz-Ostbahnhof corridor. Look for the green-and-white S signs marking station entrances, and remember that a Eurailpass is valid on the S-Bahn trains, but not on the U-Bahn trains.

Airport Trains

The Frankfurt Airport is Europe's model for excellent train/plane connections. S-Bahn trains leave five or six times an hour eastward to Frankfurt, stopping at Frankfurt's main train station and three other city stops, or take you westward to Mainz and Wiesbaden.

Frankfurt's airport stop is so useful because GermanRail's big trains, Inter-Cities and EuroCities, take you directly between the airport and Vienna, Copenhagen, Munich, Paris, Amsterdam, Milan, Geneva, Hamburg, Basel, Hanover, and Berchtesgaden. All of these trains are covered by Eurailpass and German Railpass.

Frankfurt Airport is intimidating with its size and complexity. The agent at the GermanRail counter on the arrivals level of Terminal C (transatlantic arrivals) reserves trains for you throughout Europe, but you must tell him the train numbers because his office's facilities are limited. You also validate your Eurailpass, buy (and validate) German Railpasses, and make InterCity hotel reservations here. Don't go to the DER travel agency counter next door.

To board your train, simply follow the blue-and-white signs illustrating a GermanRail locomotive. Push your luggage on the airport's escalator-friendly carts right to the doors of your train at the train station below.

Dusseldorf's airport is connected to Dusseldorf's main train station by S-

Bahn trains that you reach by escalator right from the airport's main hall. Passengers using LTU, the charter airline, can use buses of the Rhine-Ruhr Transport Association (also covered by passes) and the S-Bahn without charge.

In Hamburg, S-Bahn train line 1 takes you to the airport. Munich-Erding Airport will be served by six three-section S-Bahn trains in 1992 that will take you to the city center and throughout the area's S-Bahn network. Linking Munich's airport into GermanRail's IC network is in the discussion stage.

Berlin's eastern Schonefeld Airport lies on the mainline south from Berlin. Many through trains call there with connections to and from Leipzig, Dresden, and Erfurt — even Prague and Frankfurt/Main. Reach it by S-Bahn from Friedrichstrasse, Marx Engels Platz, or Alexanderplatz stations. Trains run every twenty minutes from 4 A.M. to 1 A.M. A shuttle bus takes you the 550 yards to the air terminal when you don't want to walk. Buses run from Schonefeld every half-hour to western Berlin's television tower and Central Bus Station. Reach western Berlin's Tegel Airport by city bus No. 9 from Zoo train station or by No. 8 from Kurt Schumacher Platz station on U-Bahn line 6.

The Lufthansa Airport Express is a system of fast electric GermanRail Series 403 railcar units integrated into GermanRail's IC network. The four-car trains are leased from GermanRail, but carry Lufthansa's livery and Lufthansa staff. They are ticketed separately from the railroads, by flight coupons issued by travel agents. Although they are primarily used by Lufthansa passengers, people flying on any airline into Frankfurt can use them as connecting "flights" to Dortmund, Dusseldorf, Cologne's Deutz station (across from Lufthansa's headquarters), Cologne's Hauptbahnhof, and Bonn.

The one-class Lufthansa Airport Express trains offer first-class airline service, including flight attendants serving breakfasts or lunches and drinks, while you are running along the Rhine River admiring the magnificent scenery.

Lufthansa Airport Express service to Stuttgart's Hauptbahnhof uses a conventional train with three newly fitted InterCity carriages seating 120 passengers.

Lufthansa staffs check-in counters in Munich's Hauptbahnhof, Dusseldorf, Mannheim, Hanover, Cologne and Bonn train stations.

Holiday Trains

In summer you have the option of riding special holiday trains without change to small holiday villages in Bavaria, Austria, and the Harz Mountains. These trains, identified as "FD" trains in GermanRail's timetable and on the digital platform signboards, are GermanRail's way of weaning vacationers away from their automobiles. FD trains leave early in the morning, use modern carriages, carry a cafeteria or Quick-Pick self-service cafeteria, make few stops, and deposit adventurers in small holiday destinations while it is still light.

Using Eurailpass Bonuses

Eurailpasses take you over the entire network of GermanRail, both eastern and western Germany. They also give you free two of the most popular excursions in Europe: Romantic Highway and Castle Road Europabus (Lines 189 and 190) trips, and the famous Rhine Cruise.

In addition, you receive free Moselle River cruises and free use of a broad range of regional bus transportation giving you train and bus access to practically every hamlet in the west. Buses in the east are not covered.

Your free Moselle River cruise is provided by the KD German Rhine Line between Koblenz and Cochem. Regional transportation is provided by the following bus companies: AutoKraft GmbH, Kiel; Kraftverkehr GmbH—KVG Stade and KVG Luneburg; Regionalverkehr Hanover, Cologne, Oberbayern, and Schwaben-Allgau.

Eurail Youthpass holders ride the express steamers on the Rhine by paying a surcharge, while all Eurailpass holders must pay extra to travel by hydrofoil ("Tragflugelboot"). Specifically not included are the tourist cruise ships making multiple stops between Basel and Rotterdam and between Trier and Koblenz.

Adventurers to Scandinavia from Berlin use the free Warnemunde-Gedser (Denmark) and Sassnitz-Trelleborg (Sweden) ferries. They also receive half off the normal fares for the TT Line's ferry crossing between Lubeck-Travemunde and Trelleborg.

Fringe benefits include half off the fares on the regular steamer services on Lake Constance; half off the Freiburg (Breisgau)/Schauinsland Railroad; and 20 percent off some half- and full-day Oberbayern GmbH excursions out of Munich. Students with a valid student ID get 25 percent off the bus fare between Berlin and Braunschweig operated by Bayern Express and P. Kuhn Berlin.

German Railpass

While the western German Bundesbahnen and the eastern German Reichsbahnen remain separate, German consecutive-day Railpasses are valid for unlimited travel only in western Germany and GermanRail Flexipasses (like Eurailpasses) are valid throughout all Germany.

Buy GermanRail Flexipasses from travel agents through GermanRail, DER, and FrenchRail offices (see Appendix A) for five, ten, or fifteen days of travel valid within one month, either first or second class. Adventurers under twenty-six buy second-class ten- and fifteen-day GermanRail Flexipasses for about 40 percent off the adult price, but are not offered a discount on five-day passes, thus making a ten-day Junior Flexipass cheaper than a five-day adult Flexipass.

For those adventuring only in western Germany, first-class German consecutive-day Railpasses are available for shorter time periods than Eurailpasses. Adventurers buy them for four, nine, or sixteen days, either first or second class. Buying second-class ones saves them one-third. The Junior German Railpasses (not available for four days) are so cheap that adventurers under twenty-six devise various combinations with other passes to save money by using them end-to-end.

German consecutive-day Railpasses and GermanRail Flexipasses give you all Eurailpass's national travel bonuses (see above), but not the ferry connections to Scandinavia. In addition you travel free on the segment of the Rhine River between Dusseldorf and Cologne (although this is not as interesting as the segment south of Koblenz which is included in both passes) and receive free admission to the German Transportation Museum in Nuremberg. Movenpick hotels offer a 20 percent discount off the best room category in Germany, Austria, and Switzerland with any rail pass purchased through GermanRail (Tel. 800-333-3333).

Anyone under twenty-three and students under twenty-seven can buy in Germany a one-month "Tramper" ticket for only slightly more than the sixteen-day Junior German Railpass.

One-year "Junior" passes allowing travel at half-fare are sold to young adventurers. All between eighteen and twenty-two, and students under twenty-seven, are eligible for the "Tramper" ticket valid for one month. All between twelve and seventeen may buy the "Pocket-Money-Pass" for even less.

When you limit your travel to only one region or district, choose one of the many regional "Netzkarten" or local "Bezirkskarten."

Adventurers planning to combine train travel and automobile driving may buy, before departure, a German "Rail and Drive" package combining three days of car rental with the GermanRail Flexipass of your choice.

Adventurers in Germany ride Europe's largest and most expensive supertrain, cruise up the Rhine, ride through the Black Forest, travel by Europabus through well-preserved medieval towns, and venture into Germany's eastern states.

GermanRail's ICE Age Arrives Wide, White, and Whizzing at 155 mph

A funny thing happens in your InterCity train north from Wurzburg. Your train pauses and the rear vestibule fills up with German travelers peering out the exposed rear window, chattering all together and repeating things they have just read in GermanRail's on-board magazine.

For over twenty years GermanRail has been planning new construction of high-speed track and reconstruction of existing segments to support a record-breaking domestic high-speed network. For the first time on June 2, 1991, adventurers will be riding trains at 155 mph (capable of 174 mph) on new track between Munich — popular adventurers' destination, home of Fasching and the Oktoberfest, the "World City with Heart," capital of Bavaria in the south — and the Hanseatic city of Hamburg in the north.

GermanRail's completion of two long, entirely new stretches between Hanover-Wurzburg and Mannheim-Stuttgart, six re-engineered line segments, and punctual delivery of sophisticated new ICE (for "InterCity Express") trains, allow inauguration of new ICE Line 6 between Hamburg and Munich via Frankfurt and Stuttgart on June 2 and Line 4 via Hanover and Wurzburg on the last Sunday of May 1992.

Your IC from Wurzburg pulls up the ramp built especially for two parallel pairs of strong rails and concrete sleepers onto an overpass and into the Rossberg tunnel. You are flying over the southern segment of the Hanover-Wurzburg high-speed stretch.

New fences and flourishing seedlings border your route. It doesn't seem like you are traveling so fast — there are no roads or houses and very few cows to stare at you — until you pass another train flying in the opposite direction. It disappears into a speck before a cow can swish its tail.

The opening of the 60-mile segment between Wurzburg and Fulda cut a half-hour off the normal travel time between Munich and Hamburg and set the tone for GermanRail's 1,200-mile ICE network.

The twenty-six ICE trains with first service over new ICE Line 6 carry adventurers over the Mannheim-Stuttgart high-speed railbed. The second fifteen ICE units set to begin service for summer 1992, over new ICE Line 4, use the new high-speed Hanover-Wurzburg construction.

When both new lines are operational, adventurers will speed across 265 miles of new high-speed track, through 77 new tunnels with a total length of 97 miles, and over 384 new bridges with a total length of 22 miles.

GermanRail's goal is to operate sixty ICE trains on three ICE lines over 1,200 miles of high-speed track. The first of 41 power cars were delivered by Krauss-Maffei in Munich in September 1989; the first of 492 passenger carriages in April 1990.

While their high-speed lines were being financed and laboriously constructed, GermanRail engineers approached the design of their first-generation high-speed trains with admirable scientific method. First, engineers built a full-size "InterCity Experimental" train, a research and demonstration tool; loaded it with sensors and recorders; tested it under various conditions of speed, track condition, weather, loading, and evaluated every significant variable.

These tests led to two important developments in train design technology and provided a firm basis for ICE's final design and cosmetic appearance.

• Depressurization caused by high speeds in tunnels had to be considered unacceptable.

Depressurization of the InterCity Experimental train while racing through tunnels caused riders to complain. (Engineers recognize the Bernoulli effect at work.) GermanRail's new trains had to be made pressure tight. It was a blow, especially because the Landrucken tunnel lies on the line chosen for ICE's inaugural run. It meant not only sealing ICE's windows, doors, and ventilation, but redesigning its closed toilet systems.

• A wider train would ride more efficiently.

Serendipitously, engineers found they could increase ICE's width. By making the ICE slightly wider than conventional trains, GermanRail could allow adventurers to ride more comfortably. Instead of 111.2 inches, the width of GermanRail's present InterCity carriages, GermanRail made the ICE 118.9 inches wide. Passengers riding second class are profiting most from their wider seats. Also, dining cars, toilets, and compartments are larger and more comfortable.

Ironically, this widening subjected GermanRail to great criticism within Germany when the German public realized that their expensive ($30 million each) new domestic trains were just that: domestic. Because of the increased width and differing electrical power supplies in neighboring countries, ICE could not travel internationally except on a few routes.

• Cosmetic changes would increase the marketing appeal of the train.

The rounding of the nose of the power car was given a sharper radius to reduce its drag coefficient and improve its appearance. A grill introduced between the headlights ventilates the driver's compartment.

The drivers' cabin is celebrated as a haven for railfans and government ministers making publicity trips. It was redesigned to make it more photogenic and functional.

The carriages have a distinctive exterior appearance because of the continuous window band. They conform to the color codes of the GermanRail: GermanRail-red and pink with a gray-white background. Horizontal striping was wrapped below the nose of the power car to make it appear more streamlined. Prominent gray "ICE" letters were painted on each side of the power car.

Sensationalism fell from the ICE when FrenchRail's TGV Atlantique began setting new world speed records one after another (the last was 317 mph on May 9, 1990), surpassing the earlier ICE speed record of 253 mph. It became apparent that first running of 155-mph ICE in Germany two years after implementation of 186-mph TGV Atlantique service in France would no longer be considered by the world as a breakthrough, but rather the heart of Europe catching up.

It is an epochal event nevertheless. ICE does not merely provide point-to-point service as in France, Italy or Spain, but is an integrated network fitting the entire transportation structure throughout western Germany, and thus is a much larger, more complex, and more expensive enterprise. ICE surpasses everything running in travel comfort and service; it is environmentally friendly, fast, and safe.

When the Eurotunnel is opened, two prototypes of ICE-M ("M" for multi-system) will be ready for operation on the electrical lines of France, Belgium, and the Netherlands. It won't be until 1998, at the earliest, that adventurers will ride high-speed trains across the European diameter of London-Paris-Brussels-Cologne-Frankfurt-Stuttgart-Munich-Vienna.

The high-speed section north of Wurzburg, where GermanRail set the former world rail travel speed record with important ministers aboard, shoots you from tunnel to tunnel—from the Rossberg to the Muhlberg to the new Landrucken, now GermanRail's longest (6.7 miles). Above the tunnels the gracious thick forests do not appear to mind the velocity beneath. In the tunnels, you just see lights flying through the blackness.

Construction of these tunnels and placing rails between gently sloping embankments helped GermanRail solve troubling environmental issues, particularly noise pollution, one of the concerns of German environmentalists.

German landscape architects also planted grasses and trees alongside the new tracks, not only to protect the earth from erosion, but also to provide habitats for birds and small wildlife. Native hazelnut, rowanberry, and fragrant wild roses require little care and complement the existing ecological system.

ICE's twelve aluminum-body middle carriages include four first- and seven second-class cars, a specially fitted carriage, and a dual-service dining car called a "BordRestaurant"; on-board portable telephones, designed to work without interruption even in the many tunnels punctuating the lines; separate toilets in each carriage for men and women (and one per train for the handicapped); thirty seats featuring mini-TV screens; individual passenger controls for electronic entertainment and information; and LED readouts announcing the coming stop.

Interior earth tones alternate from carriage to carriage. In first class, you see two color combinations; in second class, three. In each carriage you find modules of three different interiors. The first module is arranged in rows with seats reclining forty degrees for napping and a central aisle. The second module consists of classic compartments off a side aisle with five seats in first class and six in second class. Finally, you find an open salon with tables. Sculptured ceilings with alternating bright and dark areas eliminate the stiffness often found in trains.

In the BordRestaurant, a central kitchen serves a sit-down, white-tablecloth dining room on one side and a casual, self-service bistro-style cafe on the other. Bright modern pink, blue and white interiors with beechwood fittings have large showcase windows, recessed lighting and raised ceilings which recall the panorama of the former TEE Rheingold observation cars, and provide an airy, spacious feeling. Smoking is not permitted in the dining room, but allowed in the bistro cafe.

Seating modules in both carriages adjacent to the BordRestaurant are positioned so that meal service can overflow to these cars during periods of heavy demand.

The specially fitted carriage includes a conference room, the handicapped WC, facilities for snack trolleys, personnel offices, and a second-class salon.

Itineraries for ICE Trains

Line 6 Effective June 2, 1991 (26 trains)	Line 4 Effective May 1992 (15 trains)	Line 3 Effective Spring 1993 (19 trains)
HAMBURG	HAMBURG	HAMBURG
Kassel	Hanover	Kassel
FRANKFURT/M	Fulda	FRANKFURT/M
Mannheim	Wurzburg	Mannheim
Stuttgart	Nuremberg	BASEL
Augsburg	Augsburg	
MUNICH	MUNICH	

Rollin' on the Rhine
Lured by a Siren's Song

The Rhine River is squeezed down to one-third its width. The Lorelei towers 430 feet above you. You feel the rock's magnetism and almost hear the beautiful Lorelei's singing attracting fishermen and causing their deaths on those rocks and cliffs close to the prow of your white steamer.

The quiet of your waterway's west bank is constantly pierced by shrieks of ICs, ECs, and other fast trains racing along GermanRail's mainline below

RHINE CRUISE

To Cologne

KOBLENZ

Ehrenbreitstein

Moselle

Schloss Stolzenfels

Burg Lahneck

Lahn

Marksburg

Boppard

Feindliche Brude
Burg Maus
Burg Katz
Burg Rheinfels
St. Goar

Lorelei

Schonburg
Oberwesel   Kaub

Pfalz

Stahleck
Bacharach

Assmannshausen

Burg Ehrenfels
Niederwalddenkmal
Mauseturm   RUDESHEIM

Bingen

To Mainz

Nahe

N

0   5   10
MILES

castles and above barges. On the east bank freight trains and passenger trains rumble between the wine villages dotting that shore.

Traveling by train along the Rhine in one of GermanRail's comfortable ICs or ECs, studying the scenery from above the river, epitomizes relaxing train travel at its finest. Every once in a while a hilltop jewel sparkles into your eye. Your cruise from Koblenz to Mainz gives you time to savor the beauty of this river. Vater Rhein, Europe's busiest waterway, carries a constant stream of barges and passenger ships, including the KD German Rhine Line steamer you are riding without charge courtesy of Eurailpass.

You are participating in Eurailpass's most beloved bonus.

Eurailpass holders ride free on the KD German Rhine Line (Koln-Dusseldorfer Deutsche Rheinschiffahrt) making regular runs between Cologne and Frankfurt/M, but Eurail Youthpass holders must pay an extra charge for riding express steamers.

Dusseldorf and Mainz are the end stations, but your best compromise is a 5½-hour trip upstream (or 3½ hours downstream) from Koblenz to Rudesheim. You sail past the Lorelei, the Rhine gorge, dozens of world-famous castles, and through the Rhine's most scenic region.

You have little trouble making train connections on either end.

It is best to make the cruise on a sunny day. In the morning the west bank presents portraits for your camera and in the afternoon the east bank puts its historic castles in the right light.

When you commence this stretch filled with castles, it is useful to remember that the English word "castle" has two equivalents in the German language. You pass both "Burg," a fortified castle built for defensive purposes, and "Schloss," a palace which may or may not have been fortified and was usually the seat of royalty.

Should you begin your trip in Koblenz, where the Moselle (Mosel) River flows into the Rhine, check first in the office of the KD German Rhine Line in the Koblenz Hauptbahnhof. Either take bus line No. 1, marked "Rhein," which runs to the landing every twenty minutes from across the street in front of the station (the round Tourist Office side) to the Deutsches Eck monument (the ferry dock is at the river below). Only when you are sailing upstream ("Rheinaufwarts") — walk ten to fifteen minutes directly east down the Markenbildchenweg to the "Rheinanlagen," KD's second landing on the Rhine. Ships sailing upstream call here five minutes after casting off from KD's main Koblenz landing.

Seamen release the ropes and your ship bound upstream steams against the current of the Rhine. Passengers scramble for chairs.

Huge Festung Ehrenbreitstein, atop the hill overlooking your vessel, is one of the strongest fortresses in Europe. The French captured it in 1799 only by starving out its defenders. The neoclassical architecture that you see today was added between 1817 and 1828.

Below the railroad bridge, you see orange-brown Schloss Stolzenfels with crenelated turrets and walls high on the west bank. Once a customs point for the city of Trier, Friedrich Wilhelm IV of Prussia had it reconstructed in 1825–45 for a summer residence.

At the confluence of the Lahn and the Rhine, you dock in Oberlahnstein, formerly a rich and important center because of its toll station and local silver mining. Burg Lahneck was built to protect it. Over the centuries this castle has collapsed into ruin, thus becoming an inspiration for Rhine Romanticists.

The best-kept castle on the Rhine, high above Oberlahnstein, is the Marksburg on a steep slate cliff 490 feet over the Rhine. It contains cannons, weapons, chastity belts, and a good castle inn. Nowhere else on the Rhine are the Middle Ages so well preserved as in the Marksburg. Now it is the seat of the German Castles Association and houses the largest collection of castle-related literature in Europe.

All high castles have one aspect in common: a lovely view. Long sight lines on the river were necessary to supervise the collection of tolls from passing ships and an overview of the surrounding lands and forests was necessary for protection from enemies.

A big curve in the Rhine takes you past Osterspay which is famous due to Schloss Liebeneck, high above on the east bank, erected around 1700 as a hunting and summer castle. You still see the original baroque forms despite the numerous subsequent alterations.

The barren hills are interrupted by lovely Boppard, a popular stop-off.

The yellow-and-gray Lufthansa Express streaks down the western shore. This airport train is the only one with a flight number.

On top of the hills sit the castles of the Feindliche Brude. Legend has it that two arguing brothers erected ramparts between their castles. Since then the castles have been referred to as "The Hostile Brothers."

Passing Bad Salzig on the west bank in springtime is unforgettable because of its flowering cherry orchards. You sail back to the west bank below Burg Maus ("Mouse Castle"), one of the technically outstanding structures of its time. It was built in 1356 by the Archbishop of Trier. In 1806, it was partially destroyed and rebuilt between 1900 and 1909.

St. Goarshausen, with partly intact city walls, on the east bank, is hemmed tightly below Burg Katz on a jutting cliff. The castle was built in 1393, by the Counts of Katzeneinbogen, one of the richest families in medieval Germany.

St. Goar back on the west bank is a pilgrim's center for the grave of St. Goar, who died in 611, below the Rheinfels ruins.

Burg Rheinfels is so close it seems you could reach up and rub the dust off the walls of its rambling terraces. This mighty ruin used to be the greatest castle on the Rhine. It was destroyed by the French in 1797.

Now you are below the Lorelei rock. When you pass the cliff, your captain plays a tape of Heinrich Heine's poem about the Lorelei virgin combing her golden hair and singing to lure sailors to the rocks. Now the song of the beautiful Lorelei is the best-known folk song of the Rhine. This is the narrowest spot of the river. In the water you see the rocks of the "Sieben Jungfrauen" (Seven Virgins) turned to stone.

In Oberwesel, on the west bank, you pass the homes of fishermen and Rhine sailors. It is a tiny and romantic place dominated by its fourteenth-century, red-brick Gothic Liebfrauenkirche (church), narrow and steep like a ship.

Schonburg castle is situated above Oberwesel. It was built in the twelfth century. At one time it served as an imperial castle. Today parts of it are used as an international youth hostel.

The five-sided customs fortress in the center of the Rhine upstream from Kaub, the "Pfalz," was completed in its current form in the seventeenth and eighteenth centuries. Its many pinnacles and little towers contain a naval museum. From water level it looks like a stone barge on the swirling Rhine. Following its restoration it was repainted in the old Gothic colors.

Above Kaub on the east bank, a friendly city profiting from slate quarrying, you see Burg Gutenfels (1200), one of the most important examples of defensive and living structures in the period of the Hohenstaufer. It is now used as a hotel.

Crossing again to the west bank you arrive in Bacharach, a village with sixteen watchtowers and black-slate-roofed Burg Stahleck above. Burg Stahleck, built in 1134, was destroyed in 1689. Beautifully rebuilt between 1925 and 1967, it serves as a youth hostel.

Eleventh-century Burg Nollig was erected upstream of Lorch as part of Lorchhausen's main fortifications. Ships which had to avoid the Bingerloch, the whirlpool on the Rhine, docked here for reloading of their cargoes onto smaller ships or for transportation overland.

You sail past the Mauseturm ("Mice Tower") on an island near the west bank. Since the rise of Rhine Romanticism, Mice Tower on a rock in the Rhine has become Bingen's emblem although it actually once was a customs house belonging to Burg Ehrenfels, the magnificent tower on the opposite bank. Later Mice Tower served as a signal tower for this once perilous stretch of the Rhine. Now that the danger of the Bingerloch, the whirlpool, has been alleviated, the tower merely serves to remind you of the story that Bishop Hatto, who fled here after burning starving farmers' barns, was eaten alive by thousands of rats who swam the Rhine and scaled the tower's walls to reach him. Since its renovation in 1972, you again see the Mauseturm in its medieval hues.

Where the Nahe River flows from the west into the Rhine, you stop in the wine village of Bingen, below Burg Klopp. Bingen's train station is on the mainline west of the Rhine, but is not large enough for InterCity or EuroCity trains to stop, so you must take a local train to Mainz or Koblenz for connections. Famous Rudesheim is an excellent village to stop over or to conclude your trip on the Rhine with a glass of wine on the famous Drosselgasse, a street only about 10 feet wide and 200 yards long, but resounding with the constant percussion of bands playing traditional oompah to modern music. Enjoy a free wine-tasting session at a celebrated winery. You will feel the Rhineland's "Frohsinn," gaiety, everywhere.

Be sure to top off your trip with a gondola ride up over Rudesheim's vineyards to the colossal Niederwalddenkmal, the neoclassical memorial on an outlook plateau 980 feet above the city, commemorating the unification of the German Empire after the 1870 defeat of the French. Born of national enthusiasm in an era fond of monuments, the proportions of the lady are equally optimistic. She is about 125 feet tall and weighs some 700 pounds. From her feet you see one of the top ten panoramas in Germany.

Rudesheim's train station is well situated below the village near the east bank of the Rhine. From here you make connections on the secondary line running along the east bank of the Rhine and into Mainz.

Mainz is an excellent place to stay overnight. It is only eighteen minutes to the Frankfurt airport, it lies on mainlines served by InterCity and EuroCity trains, and you push your luggage carts to the hotels across the Bahnhofplatz from the station with no stairs to climb.

KD German Rhine Line sails frequently during July and August, less often in the spring and fall, and not at all between late October and late March.

KD German Rhine Line Summer Service

Upstream, Cologne to Mainz

COLOGNE	dep.	....	....	....	....	....	0930	1100
Bonn	dep.	....	....	....	....	0845	1200	1345
Bad Godesberg	dep.	....	....	....	....	0915	1230	1415
Konigswinter	dep.	....	....	....	....	0930	1255	1430
Bad Honnef	dep.	....	....	....	....	0950	1315	1450
Remagen	dep.	....	....	....	....	1025	1350	1525
Linz	dep.	....	....	....	....	1045	1410	1545
Bad Breisig	dep.	....	....	0815	....	1115	1435	1615
Andernach	dep.	....	....	0905	....	1205	1525	....
Neuwied	dep.	....	....	0925	....	1225	1545	....
KOBLENZ	arr.	....	....	1045	....	1350	1700	....

KOBLENZ	dep.	....	0900	1100	1230	1400	....	1800
Niederlahnstein	dep.	....	0925	1125	1255	....	....	1825
Braubach	dep.	....	0955	1155	1325	1455	....	1855
Boppard	dep.	0900	1040	1240	1410	1540	....	1935
St. Goarshausen	dep.	1010	1150	1350	1520	1650	....	....
St. Goar	dep.	1015	1155	1355	1525	1655	....	....
Bacharach	dep.	1120	1255	1455	1625	1755	....	....
Assmannshausen	dep.	1225	1350	1550	1720	1850	....	....
Bingen	dep.	1255	1420	1620	1750	1920	....	....
RUDESHEIM	arr.	1310	1430	1630	1800	1930	....	....
Eltville	dep.	....	....	1740	1910	....	....	....
Wiesbaden-Biebrich	arr.	....	....	1825	1955	....	....	....
MAINZ	arr.	....	....	1845	2015	....	....	....

Downstream, Mainz to Cologne

MAINZ	dep.	....	0845	....	1015	1200	....	....
Wiesbaden-Biebrich	dep.	....	0905	....	1035	1220	....	....
Eltville	dep.	....	0925	....	1055	1240	....	....
RUDESHEIM	dep.	0900	1015	....	1145	1330	1400	1620
Bingen	dep.	0910	1030	....	1200	....	1415	1635
Assmannshausen	dep.	0925	1045	....	1215	....	1430	1650
Bacharach	dep.	0955	1115	....	1245	....	1505	1720
St. Goar	dep.	1035	1200	....	1335	....	1550	1800
St. Goarshausen	dep.	1045	1210	....	1345	....	1600	1810
Boppard	dep.	1125	1255	....	1440	....	1645	1850
Braubach	dep.	1145	1320	....	1510	....	1715	1920
Niederlahnstein	dep.	....	....	....	1535	....	1735	1940
KOBLENZ	arr.	1220	1350	....	1550	....	1755	2000
KOBLENZ	dep.	....	1405	....	1605	....	1805	....
Neuwied	dep.	....	1450	....	1650	....	1850	....
Andernach	dep.	....	1505	....	1705	....	1905	....
Bad Breisig	dep.	....	1535	1635	1735	....	1935	....
Linz	dep.	....	1555	1650	1750	....	....	....
Remagen	dep.	....	1610	1705	1805	....	....	....
Bad Honnef	dep.	....	1635	1730	1830	....	....	....
Konigswinter	dep.	....	1650	1745	1845	....	....	....
Bad Godesberg	dep.	....	1700	1755	1855	....	....	....
Bonn	arr.	....	1720	1820	1915	....	....	....
COLOGNE	arr.	....	1845	1950	....	....	....	....

Through the Valley of Hell
Cuckoo Clocks and Characteristic Houses

Your ride through Hell's Valley ("Hollental") is romantic enough for an arch-duchess on her way to her wedding. Marie Antoinette's advisors planned her

BLACK FOREST RAILROADS

Strasbourg

GERMANY

FRANCE

OFFENBURG

Hausach

Triberg

FREIBURG

Villingen

Hinterzarten

Titisee

DONAUESCHINGEN

Neustadt

To Konstanz

-N-

Basel

SWITZERLAND

0   10   20

MILES

carriage trip through this scenic valley in 1770, on her way from Vienna to Paris to marry the future King Louis XVI. She was 14½ years old at the time. She was beheaded 23 years later.

When you travel on the Black Forest Railroad, you see the famous Black Forest houses, onion-dome churches, and even occasional cuckoo clocks. Its sixty-two miles from Offenburg to Donaueschingen take you over the crest of the Black Forest in an unusual series of loops. In the heart of the Black Forest you change to your connecting Hell's Valley ("Hollental") train, which justifies its name in only a few spots. Both are covered by Eurailpass.

When German railroad construction from Paris reached Freiburg, now the western terminus of the Hell's Valley train, dreamers talked of linking Paris to Vienna by train through Hell's Valley. On May 23, 1887, the Hell's Valley Railroad was opened—the first German State railroad with mixed cogwheel and adhesion traction.

It remained that way until 1933 when the cogwheels were taken out and special locomotives put into service on the steep stretch. The line was electrified in 1936 on a trial basis and patched into GermanRail's grid in 1960. Now you ride in one of GermanRail's Spartan railcars, but the landscape remains more romantic than on most other stretches.

Beginning north from the mainline at Offenburg (522 feet) in one of GermanRail's new IR trains, the first stretch of the Black Forest Railroad takes you past vineyards, fruit trees, wheat, hops, corn, and below a striking Romanesque hilltop castle.

While you pass along a pretty stream with fishermen in green jackets and hats on the right of your train, the hillsides grow steeper and more wooded and the first houses with red geraniums in window boxes appear. This is a sure sign the Black Forest is not far away.

The eye-catching gilded minute and hour hands and numerals on the brown-and-tan clock tower give Gengenbach a Black Forest feeling. The newer houses tend to have long sloping roofs.

When you stop at Hausach (790 feet), the Black Forest store across from the station is decorated with multicolored baskets on a rope. From Hausach, you begin one of the most rugged and picturesque stretches in Germany.

The valley is more romantic with black-and-white cows in the fields and houses with gigantic roofs. They have eaves on four sides and balconies of hand-carved wood, front and back, but not the sides where the tentlike roofs overhang nearly to the ground.

Soon you see thatched, wooden Black Forest houses to your right—just like in the tourist literature—and an onion-shaped church belfry, also on your right. Some houses offer rooms to let: "Zimmer Frei."

The farms get bigger, the trees get bigger, and the climb gets steeper. You are traveling across the pages of a picture book of the Black Forest. It is pleasant to see all these textbook examples from the comfort of a train.

At Hornberg (1,260 feet), you come to a stop at a site overlooking the village and looking up at a castle on a hill, flying a small black, red, and yellow German flag.

Across the valley you see a cuckoo clock factory. Hikers wearing leather shorts and green knee-socks and carrying walking sticks tramp through forests down the mountainsides.

Now it gets wilder suddenly. You pass through tunnel after tunnel—every one punctuated by screeches from the train's whistle. Read their conveniently placed names as you enter. Between tunnels, you have picture-postcard views of farms and forests.

Triberg (2,020 feet), the watch- and clockmaking center, is the highlight of this stretch, in the heart of the Black Forest. This is a good place to break your trip. Walk directly to the Black Forest Museum to enjoy quietly (except for the blasting mechanical organ) old local costumes, watch- and clockmaking exhibits, and a working model of your Black Forest Railroad.

Back on your IR train, you continue to climb. You emerge from a long tunnel into a thick forest.

The Black Forest is more attractive than other woods not because the trees grow close together, but because they are evenly spaced, not wild. They are uniform, almost tailored, so they don't allow much light to fall except for a few spots of sunlight on the flooring of pine needles.

After you cross the summit you pick up speed. Although you aren't rushing, your pace seems breakneck compared to your slow ascent.

Past Sommerau (2,729 feet), the hills below you still have their wild look. Exiting the tunnel before St. Georgen brings a whole new experience. The surroundings are mundane, more developed, and modestly industrialized. The excitement and enchantment is over. By the time you reach the large brown-brick, tile-roofed Villingen station house (2,309 feet), industry has sadly triumphed over the Black Forest.

In Donaueschingen (2,221 feet), change from your Black Forest train, which continues to Lake Constance, for the Hell's Valley train.

GermanRail's sea-green railcar takes you west again. You reenter the Black Forest. The trees grow stronger and stronger and surround your slick railcar as you glide downhill toward Hufingen (2,220 feet) in Hell's Valley. You are making a charming if not spectacular journey through forests, fields, and meadows in a second section of the Black Forest.

Titisee (2,814 feet) is your major stop on the Hell's Valley line. Titisee ("See" means "lake," although it's not visible from here), the premier resort of the Black Forest. It is a hiker's and vacationer's paradise. On your right stand vacation homes; on your left forests trail down to the valley.

The segment between Hollsteig and Hinterzarten takes you up at a gradient of one foot for every eighteen you pass. This is the third steepest segment in Germany using adhesion traction.

Hinterzarten (2,903 feet), a stylish mountain resort, is the highest point of the Hell's Valley Railroad, higher even than the summit of the Black Forest Railroad. You are surrounded by trees of every sort, leaves rustling in the breezes, hiking trails, and timbered houses. The air feels woodsy.

Downhill you travel through the thick of the Black Forest. It must be idyllic if Marie Antoinette passed here. You see trees, mountains, and many autos. Then you see nothing. You are passing through a tunnel. The conductor checks your Eurailpass. You enter two tunnels and pass Posthalde station without stopping. Then you reach another tunnel.

There are supposed to be nine tunnels between Posthalde and Freiburg, but it seems you pass at least a dozen. Many are very short and are possibly counted as underpasses. In GermanRail's list the shortest tunnel is 157 feet long, by Ravennaviadukt. Maybe 150 or 125 feet is too short to be counted as a tunnel.

By the time you reach Himmelreich (1,493 feet), you have left behind most of the heavy forest.

When you stop in Kirchzarten (1,286 feet), across from Gasthaus Alte Post, the kilometer markers show you have 11 km (6.8 miles) left to travel.

You travel through a broad valley, mountains surround you, rye and corn flourish, and you near Freiburg-Littenweller stop (1,040 feet) on the outskirts of Freiburg. Still in the Black Forest, you see red-tile roofs, gardens for pensioners, picnic grounds, and a sports stadium on your right.

Now you have 5.6 km to the main train station. But that didn't used to be true because the train ran through the middle of Freiburg. In 1934, the track was moved and the line rerouted in a loop around the city, thus adding another 1.4 kilometers to your trip. This meant all kilometer markers had to be changed, but the administration skimped. They changed only the markers near their offices in Freiburg. When you reach Freiburg-Wiehre's green station house (918 feet), you come to kilometer marker "0."

When you arrive in Freiburg's Hauptbahnhof you have entered the "Twilight Zone." You have traveled on a line with a negative length. Look for the enameled, black-on-white kilometer marker: "-1.4," with numbers arranged vertically.

Freiburg (pop. 200,000), which is more completely known as "Freiburg im Breisgau" to locate it specifically, is a jewel of southern Germany. It was founded in the twelfth century by the Dukes of Zahringer. Its Gothic cathedral, octagonal tower, and dazzling market square make your visit here unforgettable. It was in Freiburg on May 4-5, 1770, that Archduchess Marie Antoinette said goodbye to Austria and entered France at Strasbourg.

Black Forest Railroad Service

FD	E	IR				IR	E	FD
1514	0741	0834	dep.	OFFENBURG	arr.	0821	0918	1210
....	0748	....	dep.	Gengenbach	dep.	....	0910	....
....	0755	....	dep.	Biberach	dep.	....	0903	....
....	0801	....	dep.	Haslach	dep.	....	0857	....
1536	0807	0854	arr.	HAUSACH	dep.	0801	0851	1147
1537	0808	0855	dep.	HAUSACH	arr.	0800	0849	1146
1546	0816	0903	arr.	HORNBERG	dep.	0752	0842	1137
1547	0817	0904	dep.	HORNBERG	arr.	0751	0841	1136
1602	0830	0917	dep.	TRIBERG	dep.	0739	0828	1122
1618	0841	0932	arr.	ST. GEORGEN	dep.	0723	0813	1105
1619	0845	0933	dep.	ST. GEORGEN	arr.	0722	0812	1104
1633	0855	0944	arr.	VILLINGEN	dep.	0714	0804	1054
1635	0858	0945	dep.	VILLINGEN	arr.	0712	0751	1052
....	....	....	dep.	Klengen	dep.	....	0747	....
1646	0907	0954	arr.	DONAUESCHINGEN	dep.	0703	0741	1040

E trains and IR trains alternate departures every two hours on the minute until 8 P.M.
FD—FD Bodensee Holiday Express train.

Hell's Valley Railroad Service

0822	dep.	DONAUESCHINGEN	arr.	0937
0824	dep.	Doggingen	dep.	0929
0835	dep.	Loffingen	dep.	0914
0840	dep.	Rotenbach	dep.	0910
0857	arr.	NEUSTADT	dep.	0900
0901	dep.	NEUSTADT	arr.	0855
0907	arr.	TITISEE	dep.	0849
0908	dep.	TITISEE	arr.	0848
0915	dep.	Hinterzarten	dep.	0846
0931	dep.	Himmelreich	dep.	0829
0934	dep.	Kirchzarten	dep.	0824
0939	dep.	Freiburg-Littenweller	dep.	0820
0943	dep.	Freiburg-Wiehre	dep.	0817
0947	arr.	FREIBURG (Breisgau)	dep.	0812

Trains depart every two hours on the minute until 7 P.M.; additional trains run hourly between Neustadt and Freiburg.

Medieval Germany by Europabus
Castles, Romance, and Rococo

In the 1890s the city fathers decided never to build a train station. They expected iron horses to corrupt the ambience of their fair city. They wanted Rothenburg ob der Tauber (on the Tauber River) to remain the finest surviving medieval town.

This city, by law, remains as it was in the seventeenth century, after the Thirty Years War. The city council regulates progress so carefully that even house colors are set out in official government rule books. The householder with the prettiest window-box flower display wins a cash prize.

Adventurers with even the slightest curiosity in seeing old gabled houses, Gothic roofs, oriel windows, fortress walls, fairy-tale watchtowers, cobbled streets, and graceful, flowing fountains make visiting here top priority.

Take a local train to a small secondary station outside the city walls, or better, travel to Rothenburg aboard a sea-green Europabus along the Romantic Highway and Castle Road. It is the cheapest way when you hold a Eurailpass. You ride free.

Romantic Highway and Castle Road Europabuses converge on Rothenburg after passing along the most scenic coach routes in Germany. Because they are operated by a subsidiary of GermanRail, you ride them free with a Eurailpass or German Railpass.

Europabus is the network of long-distance motor coaches throughout most of Europe operated in association with the national railroad administrations. Their vehicles are usually luxury coaches with continuous windows and ample luggage space below. Passengers on the scenic routes are assisted by English-speaking guides giving personal directions and showing the highlights along the way.

Sorry, "Romantic" does not necessarily refer to boy meets girl.

Instead, you feel a special Romance—a nostalgic pleaure in half-timbered houses, restored ramparts, town gates, baroque cherubs, palace gardens, arching stone bridges over rivers, and royal castles implanted on steep, rocky slopes.

The Romantic Highway gives you the essence and spirit of picture-book Germany. It seems like the founders of the medieval villages deliberately lined up all the worthwhile sights of the region in order to show you everything without making you detour. They could not have done it better.

Your big, smooth-riding coach takes you through one charming village after another. Discovering Dinkelsbuhl makes the whole trip memorable. Nordlingen and Donauworth are pleasant surprises with their carefully preserved and colorfully painted Romantic structures.

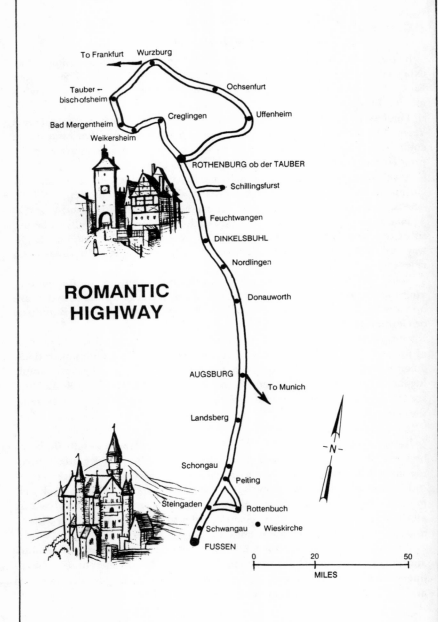

To Frankfurt   Wurzburg

Tauber –
bischofsheim

Ochsenfurt

Bad Mergentheim   Creglingen   Uffenheim

Weikersheim

ROTHENBURG ob der TAUBER

Schillingsfurst

Feuchtwangen

DINKELSBUHL

Nordlingen

Donauworth

**ROMANTIC
HIGHWAY**

AUGSBURG

To Munich

Landsberg

~N~

Schongau

Peiting

Steingaden   Rottenbuch

Schwangau   • Wieskirche

FUSSEN

0   20   50

MILES

The Romantic Highway and the Castle Road crisscross at Rothenburg ob der Tauber, giving you the option there of changing from one to the other and starting or ending at eight worthwhile terminuses on the octopus network. You board southbound Europabuses in Frankfurt, Wurzburg, Mannheim, and Heidelberg, or connect from Nuremberg. Northbound, you travel from Fussen, Munich, or Augsburg.

Depending on your connection, you have about two hours in Rothenburg to climb the Town Hall belfry, dating from the fourteenth century, and to walk along the wide city wall — but first head directly from your stop on the Schrannenplatz straight down the Schmiedgasse to see the Plonlein, the most photographed scene in Germany (and every photo is a gem).

Traveling south from Rothenburg during the summer, you choose either a Europabus to Fussen in the Allgauer Alps or one to Munich, the beer-hall city and bright spot of Bavaria. Both buses pause in Dinkelsbuhl. On a good day you arrive at the Schweinemarkt, but alternate stops are often used. Ask your guide for directions to the Deutsches Haus. You do not want to miss photographing this admired fifteenth-century gabled building which you see on the "Visit Germany" travel posters.

Your Europabus driver to Munich pulls onto the Autobahn at Augsburg, bringing you into Munich's Starnberger station next to Munich's Hauptbahnhof, but if you plan to change to a train, save time by getting off at the Augsburg train station.

The driver of the second Europabus south from Rothenburg continues through Bavaria to Fussen with distant views of King Ludwig's fantasy Neuschwanstein Castle. You bypass the astonishing church in the Wies going south, but stop there northbound. Its breathtaking rococo interior makes it often mentioned as Germany's finest church.

On Sundays only you connect with the EC Schweizerland to Munich. On other days Fussen is the end of your line. Its only welcome is a nearby youth hostel.

The Castle Road between Rothenburg and Heidelberg is so-called because it connects red-sandstone Heidelberg Castle, heart of Romanticism, on one end, with the gray-granite Neuschwanstein Castle on the other, and features castles, large and small, around every curve of the Neckar valley (Heidelberg to Rothenburg). Board either in Mannheim or in the "Student-Prince" university town, spend your lunch hour in Rothenburg, and then join a Romantic Highway bus to Fussen or Munich.

Make reservations at a Europabus office in Germany or by postcard (to arrive at least three days before departure) to Deutsche Touring GmbH, Am Romerhof 17, 6000 Frankfurt/Main 90, Tel. 069-7903240. Indicate date, route, and number of seats you require. Seat reservations are free of charge.

Europabuses from Frankfurt to Munich operate daily the year round, but additional buses run during the summer from Wurzburg to Fussen and from Mannheim/Heidelberg to Fussen beginning early in June until late in September.

You must pay a nominal registration and baggage checking fee for luggage. It includes insurance up to about $1,200.

When you want to tempt the rage of Rothenburg's city fathers, use the small, local railroad that is, in fact, outside of Rothenburg's city walls. Rothenburg's train station is served via Steinach, seven miles away, on the mainline between Wurzburg and Nurnberg. Connections are poor and bus service is sometimes substituted (covered by Eurailpass), especially on weekends. Be sure you check the timetable for the day you will be traveling. Bus connections are usually a few minutes different from train connections.

Romantic Highway Summer Europabus Service

between Frankfurt and Wurzburg and Augsburg, Munich, and Fussen

....	0815	dep.	FRANKFURT/M (Hbf./Sud)	arr.	1955	....
....	....	arr.	Wurzburg (Omnibusbf.)	dep.	1810	....
0900	1015	dep.	WURZBURG (Omnibusbf.)	arr.	....	1920
....	1035	dep.	Ochsenfurt (Mainbrucke)	dep.	1745	....
....	1055	dep.	Uffenheim	dep.	1720	....
0940	....	dep.	Tauberbischofsheim	dep.	....	1840
1005	....	dep.	Bad Mergentheim (Bf.)	dep.	....	1815
1025	....	arr.	Weikersheim (Marktplatz)	dep.	....	1755
1045	....	dep.	Weikersheim (Marktplatz)	arr.	....	....
1055	....	dep.	Rottingen (Marktplatz)	dep.	....	1740
1110	....	dep.	Creglingen (Omnibusbf.)	dep.	....	1730
1115	....	arr.	Creglingen (Kapelle)	dep.	....	....
1130	....	dep.	Creglingen (Kapelle)	arr.	....	....
1200	1135	arr.	ROTHENBURG o.d.T. (Schrannenplatz)	dep.	1700	1700
1330	1345	dep.	ROTHENBURG o.d.T. (Schrannenplatz)	arr.	1515	1535
1335	1350	dep.	Rothenburg o.d.T. (Bf.)	dep.	....	1530
1355	1410	dep.	Schillingsfurst (Post)	dep.	1450	1515
1415	1430	dep.	Feuchtwangen (Omnibusbf.)	dep.	1430	1455
1430	1445	arr.	DINKELSBUHL (Schweine.)	dep.	1415	1440
1500	1530	dep.	DINKELSBUHL (Schweine.)	arr.	1235	1310
1520	1600	dep.	Wallerstein (Sparkasse)	dep.	1200	1235
....	....	arr.	Nordlingen (Rathaus)	dep.	1155	1230
1525	1605	dep.	Nordlingen (Rathaus)	arr.	1140	....

1555	....	dep.	Harburg (Marktplatz)	dep.	....	1215
1610	1635	dep.	Donauworth (Kirche)	dep.	1105	1200
1655	1735	arr.	AUGSBURG (Hbf.)	dep.	1020	1110
1705	1740	dep.	AUGSBURG (Hbf.)	arr.	....	1100
....	1755	dep.	Freidberg (Marienplatz)	dep.	0955	....
....	1855	arr.	MUNICH (Starnberger Bf.)	dep.	0900	....
1755		arr.	Landsberg (Hauptplatz)	dep.		1015
1815		dep.	Landsberg (Hauptplatz)	arr.		....
1830		dep.	Hohenfurch (B 17)	dep.		0955
1835		dep.	Schongau (Bf.)	dep.		0950
1840		dep.	Peiting (Meierstrasse)	dep.		0945
1845		dep.	Rottenbuch (Post)	dep.		0935
1850		dep.	Echelsbacher Brucke	dep.		0930
1855		dep.	Wildsteig	dep.		0925
1857		dep.	Abzw. Ilchberg	dep.		0922
1900		dep.	Kohlhofen (Abzw. Wies)	dep.		0920
....		arr.	WIESKIRCHE	dep.		0915
....		dep.	WIESKIRCHE	arr.		0850
1905		dep.	Steingaden (Postamt)	dep.		0840
1915		dep.	Trauchgau	dep.		0835
1920		dep.	Buching	dep.		0830
1925		dep.	Schwangau (Verkehrsburo)	dep.		0825
1930		dep.	Hohenschwangau	dep.		0820
1935		arr.	FUSSEN (Bf.)	dep.		0815

Castle Road Summer Europabus Service

between Mannheim, Heidelberg, Nuremberg, and Rothenburg

0730	dep.	MANNHEIM (Hbf.)	arr.	2040
0745	arr.	HEIDELBERG (Hbf.)	dep.	....
0800	dep.	HEIDELBERG (Hbf.)	arr.	2015
0814	dep.	Neckargemund (Bf.)	dep.	1950
0820	dep.	Neckarsteinach (Bf.)	dep.	1949
0825	dep.	Neckarhausen (Bf.)	dep.	1945
0830	dep.	Hirschhorn (Schiff)	dep.	1941
0840	dep.	Eberbach (Neckaranlagen)	dep.	1933
0845	dep.	Lindach (Schiff)	dep.	1928
0848	dep.	Zwingenberg (Anker)	dep.	1925
0902	dep.	Neckarelz (Schulzentrum)	dep.	1912
0907	dep.	Neckarzimmern (Rathaus)	dep.	1900
0925	dep.	Bad Friedrichshall-Jagstfeld (Bf.)	dep.	1855
0953	dep.	Ohringen (Stadthall)	dep.	1824
1003	dep.	Neuenstein (Schloss)	dep.	1815
1010	dep.	Hohebuch-Waldenburg	dep.	1809
1014	dep.	Kupferzell (Rathaus)	dep.	1804

	1025	dep.	Braunsbach (Marktplatz)	dep.	1755	
	1040	arr.	Langenburg (Rathaus)	dep.	1730	
	1120	dep.	Langenburg (Rathaus)	arr.	....	
	1135	dep.	Blaufelden (Bf.)	dep.	1715	
	1140	dep.	Schrozberg (Friedhof)	dep.	1710	
0845	....	dep.	NUREMBERG (Hbf./ZOB)	arr.	....	1830
....	1200	dep.	Rothenburg o.d.T. (Bf.)	dep.	1650	....
1045	1205	arr.	ROTHENBURG o.d.T. (Schrannenplatz)	dep.	1645	1630

Adventuring to the East
Times Have Changed

Adventurers entering the Railroad Museum in Dresden can't miss the splendid map showing train connections as they were before the First World War. Berlin was the center of the German Railroad network. Links radiated like spokes across the entire empire as far as Konigsberg, which is now Kaliningrad in the Soviet Union.

After the Second World War, east-west connections withered, crossings were closed, Russians tore down catenaries, weeds overgrew rails, and the western German network was realigned along new north-south routes.

At 8:48 A.M. on May 27, 1980, officials welcomed the "Johann Sebastian Bach" at Bebra and the first unified German InterCity train crossed the border to join both halves together with improved-speed, quality service. The second IC, the "Max Liebermann," connected Berlin and Hamburg in fall 1990 with nostalgic TEE equipment. In addition, three InterRegio trains now take you to Berlin; two to Leipzig. Before the wall fell in 1989, there were eighteen regularly scheduled trains and three seasonal trains between east and west. In 1990, there were about two hundred. Traffic increased 600 percent. Earlier international trains were permitted to cross the border at three places. Now adventurers cross at nine. May 1991 marks the first publishing since the Second World War of a timetable combining both railroads. In 1992, construction begins on the Hanover-Berlin line to add it to the European high-speed train network by 1997.

Adventurers use Hamburg, Lubeck, Kassel, Nuremberg, and Munich as jumping-off places for trips to eastern Germany, but their most popular path for Berlin takes them through Hanover's Hauptbahnhof because of good connections there by InterCity trains from all over Germany and EuroCity (EC Tiziano, EC Mont Blanc, and EC Helvetia) trains from Copenhagen, Switzerland, and Milan.

They also can choose day trains including those between Cologne and

BERLIN
Friedrichstrasse
ZOO
Wannsee
Potsdam

BERLIN TRANSIT

Magdeburg

Marienborn

Helmstedt

Braunschweig

N

0   10   20   50

MILES

HANOVER

Leipzig, Cologne and Magdeburg, Nuremberg and Gorlitz, Nuremberg and Gera, Duisburg and Erfurt, and Hamburg and Rostock. Trains between Dusseldorf and Chemnitz run daily and are supplemented by an overnight service. A Munich-Warsaw train runs daily between Munich and Dresden.

At Hanover, escalators take you up and down to the platforms, luggage carts are plentiful, an InterCity hotel integrated into the station can be reserved in advance from any GermanRail office, and GermanRail ticketing counters are set aside specifically for Berlin ticketing and discounts.

Along the corridor from Hanover via Helmstedt, the most heavily traveled line to Berlin, the scenery is disappointing. The 112 miles of landscape you see from your train's window on your way to Berlin is dull, flat as a breadboard. Occasionally you glimpse a village in the distance.

When your train comes upon Potsdam, your only pleasant view of the trip extends over a lake to a collection of high-rise postwar construction. By themselves, the buildings would not be worth noting, but the lake reflects attractively their yellow-brown striping.

Then you immediately pass the great dome of the Nikolai Church dominating Potsdam, but your view is spoiled by the pedestrian Inter Hotel placed in front of it.

It isn't long before you realize you are suddenly back in civilization. And civilization must mean Berlin. Your train stops at the Berlin Wannsee train station in western Berlin. This is the first of several western Berlin stops. Adventurers gather together their luggage, carry-ons, and parkas for their mass exodus at the Berlin Zoo train station in the center of western Berlin.

Your ticket and destination signboards you see all say "Berlin Stadtbahn," meaning "Berlin city railroad," but there is no station of that name. The Stadtbahn is the 1882 elevated railroad corridor across Berlin's center following the river Spree, with eleven stations, including mainline platforms at Charlottenburg, Zoologisher Garten ("Zoo"), Friedrichstrasse, Alexanderplatz, and Schlesischer Bahnhof (now "Hauptbahnhof"). Tickets marked "Berlin Stadtbahn" are valid for travel to or from any of these stations. Zoo station is your terminus for Kurfurstendamm and the west; Friedrichstrasse station for the east.

A short walk out of the front of Zoo station (remodeled for Berlin's anniversary celebrations in 1987) leads you to the western Berlin tourist office in the Europa-Center complex. Follow the signs. The route is so well marked that managers of other western German city tourist offices must be envious.

The Europa-Center across the Kurfurstendamm from the Zoo station is a city within a city. It is the focus of twenty-four-hour western Berlin. You find beautiful restaurants and an outdoor cafe, countless boutiques, a gambling casino, nightclubs, a quizzical fountain in the shape of a ball representing the planet Earth, and a multistory water clock which attracts passers-by to watch its gurgling changes of hours.

Berlin city tours take you past a succession of high points and historically interesting sights, including a stop at Potsdamer Platz to see the remains of the Berlin Wall. The bus visits the neoclassical Brandenburg Gate, copied from Athens; Checkpoint Charlie, made famous during the Berlin Airlift; and the Reichstag, which Hitler ordered burned.

Tours continue to Charlottenburg Palace with its green patina dome; the 1936 Olympic Games' stadium with its five rings; Schoneburg's town hall, where President Kennedy delivered his "Ich bin ein Berliner" speech; the huge International Congress Center; and on the Kurfurstendamm, where you start, the Kaiser Wilhelm Memorial Church and the Europa-Center.

After you have seen the remodeled Zoo station, visit the delightful jewel-box Wittenbergplatz subway station, Germany's first and finest. It has been brightly restored in Jugendstil as a historical monument.

After Zoo, your train's next stop is Friedrichstrasse station. South on the street of the same name you find two of the big hotels, the Metropol and the Grand, but walk south to Unter den Linden and then west to the historic Brandenburg Gate, site of the Wall and former military watchtowers. East of Friedrichstrasse station, on Museum Island in the Spree, visit one of the world's greatest museums, the Pergamon.

Friedrichstrasse station has five platforms on three different levels. Three platforms are on the Stadtbahn viaduct, one is at basement level, and one is in a deeper sub-basement. Five tracks are used by S-Bahn (Schnellbahn, not Stadtbahn) trains and two by long-distance trains.

Alexanderplatz, the second S-Bahn stop east of Friedrichstrasse, is the spacious showpiece of eastern Berlin, dominated by a soaring television tower with viewing platform. Here you find Stadt Berlin and Palast hotels, and the Rathskeller.

Your other two major rail hubs in eastern Germany are Leipzig and Dresden. Your best train from western Germany is the InterCity Johann Sebastian Bach between Frankfurt (Main) and Leipzig via Bebra, carrying first- and second-class carriages and a restaurant car. Traveling via Bebra takes you along one of the prettiest stretches you see in the east. Your train passes rolling, forested hills, village houses with tiled roofs, and half-timbered farmhouses. Beside the tracks, yellow-flowering bushes and blue larkspur are far brighter than the condition of the villages and farms.

Dresden is a sad city, yet the cultural center of the east. There are two train stations, but you are likely to use only the Hauptbahnhof. Bahnhof Neustadt takes you to Nuremberg and aboard trains to the east.

Your route from Dresden to Leipzig was the first long-distance railroad in Germany, 150 years old in 1989. By contrast to Dresden, Leipzig is a happy city. The Hauptbahnhof here is Europe's largest, a giant. Although it is now very rough, over 90 years old, it is still impressive—consisting of an east hall and a west hall. Even handling more than 450 internal and international trains carrying over 500,000 passengers, usage is way below capacity, making it a relaxing place. The Goethe statue stands in front of the Handelsborse, which seems to define the phrase "jewel box." Across the street, statues of Goethe characters stand at the entrance to Auersbachskeller, which is located in an original arcaded shopping mall.

Overnight service to Berlin is provided by trains carrying second-class couchettes from many major cities in the west. Adventurers also sleep aboard overnight services from Hamburg and Frankfurt/Main to Leipzig and Dresden, and Stuttgart to Leipzig.

Frankfurt (Main) — Leipzig
InterCity Johann Sebastian Bach

IC155			IC154	
0638	dep.	FRANKFURT/MAIN (Hbf.)	arr.	2104
0657	dep.	Hanau	dep.	2045
0748	dep.	Fulda	dep.	1954
0820	arr.	Bebra	dep.	1920
0830	dep.	Bebra	arr.	1910
0916	dep.	Eisenach	dep.	1852
1006	dep.	Erfurt (Hbf.)	dep.	1819
1018	arr.	Erfurt (Hbf.)	dep.	1729
1034	dep.	Weimar	arr.	1709
1151	arr.	LEIPZIG	dep.	1546

Best Trains Cologne — Hanover — Berlin

		D 341	IR 343	D 243	IR 347	D 345	D 247	IR 349
COLOGNE (Hbf.)	dep.	....	0530	0613	0930	....	1340	1530
HANOVER (Hbf.)	dep.	0701	0901	1021	1300	1501	1701	1901
Braunschweig	dep.	0738	0939	1100	1339	1547	1740	1940
Magdeburg (Hbf.)	arr.	0854	1055	1236	1459	1706	1904	2055
Magdeburg (Hbf.)	dep.	0858	1058	1239	1502	1709	1907	2056
Potsdam (Stadt)	dep.	1018	1213	1353	1616	1826	2055	2215
Berlin (Wannsee)	arr.	1038	1223	1404	1627	1836	2033	2226
BERLIN (Zoo)	arr.	1041	1237	1419	1641	1850	2048	2240
Berlin (Friedrichstr.)	arr.	1104	....	1442	1706	1903	2105	2301
Berlin (Hbf.)	arr.	1118	....	1500	1720	1917	2127	2316

Best Trains Berlin — Hanover — Cologne

		IR 348	D 246	IR 346	D 344	IR 342	D 242	D 340
Berlin (Hbf.)	dep.	0544	0721	0943	1135	....	1454	1740
Berlin (Friedrichstr.)	dep.	0558	0740	0957	1149	....	1510	1758
BERLIN (Zoo)	dep.	0613	0811	1014	1205	1414	1531	1816
Berlin (Wannsee)	dep.	0627	0826	1028	1218	1428	1545	1829
Potsdam (Stadt)	dep.	0637	....	1038	1228	1438	1555	1839
Magdeburg (Hbf.)	arr.	0752	0957	1155	1347	1557	1713	1958
Magdeburg (Hbf.)	dep.	0755	1001	1200	1355	1601	1716	2001
Braunschweig	arr.	0918	1122	1321	1513	1724	1838	2119
HANOVER (Hbf.)	arr.	1001	1201	1401	1554	1802	1919	2157
COLOGNE (Hbf.)	arr.	1322	1515	1724	....	2124	2332	....

Best Trains Munich — Nuremberg — Leipzig/Berlin

D 303	D 307	IR 403	IR 401				IR 400	IR 402	D 302	D 306
0600	1120			dep.	Berlin (Hbf.)	arr.			1737	2319
0614	1134			dep.	Berlin (Frdr.)	arr.			1723	2305
0628	1152			dep.	BERLIN (Zoo)	arr.			1704	2251
0642	1206			dep.	Berlin (Wann.)	arr.			1649	2237
....	....			arr.	LEIPZIG	dep.			....	....
....	....	1452	1558	dep.	LEIPZIG	arr.	1052	1346	....	....
....	....	1726	1823	arr.	Saalfeld	dep.	0839	1104	....	....
....	....	1734	1827	dep.	Saalfeld	arr.	0835	1100	....	....
1141	1653	1820	1904	dep.	Probstzella	arr.	0800	1020	1207	1736
1151	1703	....	1913	dep.	Ludwigsstadt	dep.	....	....	1158	1726
1233	1749	....	1951	dep.	Lichtenfels	dep.	0705	....	1112	1639
1251	1808	1932	2010	arr.	Bamberg	dep.	0649	0915	1054	1621
1253	1810	1934	2011	dep.	Bamberg	arr.	0648	0913	1051	1617
1319	1835	1955	2032	dep.	Erlangen	dep.	0628	0854	1025	1551
1329	1845	....	....	dep.	Furth	dep.	....	....	1014	1540
1337	1855	2010	2047	arr.	Nuremberg	dep.	0613	0839	1006	1532
1356	....	2016	....	dep.	Nuremberg	arr.	....	0828	0948	1516
1559	....	2207	....	arr.	MUNICH (Hbf.)	dep.	....	0630	0736	1334

Best Trains Munich — Regensburg/Nuremberg — Dresden

D 464	E 462	D* 1462	D 460				D 461	D 1463	D 465	E 467
0846	1354	1527	2150	dep.	DRESDEN (Hbf.)	arr.	0604	1439	1851	2104
0929	1434	1612	2232	dep.	Freiberg	dep.	0520	1356	1812	2021
1013	1522	1656	2319	dep.	Chemnitz	dep.	0429	1307	1728	1936
1046	1555	1728	2356	dep.	Glauchau	dep.	0340	1229	1649	1858
1106	1615	1747	0018	dep.	Zwickau	dep.	0332	1214	1634	1843
1126	1635	1806	0038	arr.	Reichenbach	dep.	0305	1152	1612	1821
1137	1647	1819	0058	dep.	Reichenbach	arr.	0249	1139	1558	1811
1206	1717	1846	0125	dep.	Plauen	dep.	0221	1114	1534	1747
1300	1800	1930	0214	dep.	Hof	dep.	0132	1013	1448	1638
1328	1820	1933	0217	dep.	Hof	arr.	0058	1010	1425	1627
1550	2045	....	0429	arr.	Regensburg	dep.	2240	....	1216	1419
1557	2100	....	0446	dep.	Regensburg	arr.	2232	....	1204	1405
....	....	2125	....	arr.	Nuremberg	dep.	....	0817	....	....
1722	2228	....	0620	arr.	MUNICH (Hbf.)	dep.	2108	....	1041	1228

*Departs Dresden Neustadt station.

Austria and Hungary

Vital Tips for the Trains of Austria and Hungary

Austrian trains—Hungarian trains—Connecting Vienna and Budapest by EuroCity Lehar—Austria's private lines and steam trains—Vienna's train stations—Getting around Vienna—Vienna's airport train—Budapest's train stations—Using Eurailpass bonuses—Austrian Rabbit Card—Hungarian Railpass— European East Railpass

You reach Austria, one of the world's most beautiful countries, with eighteen EuroCity trains, but that number is misleading because several call only in Innsbruck, not in the heart of the OBB ("Osterreichischen Bundesbahnen," the Austrian Federal Railroads), and three travel between Munich and Switzerland, touching only Bregenz en route.

OBB sends fewer carriages on international routes than the railroads of its neighboring countries, but you can take advantage of several useful connections. OBB's flagship EC Transalpin takes you between Vienna, Salzburg, Zurich, and Basel. OBB's Austria Express takes you in orange-and-white OBB carriages all the way from Graz, Klagenfurt, and Salzburg to Amsterdam via Munich and Cologne.

Most adventurers visit Vienna before Budapest, but you can reach Budapest directly via three through trains which continue from Vienna's West Bahnhof en route. GermanRail's EC Franz Lehar is a fast way to Budapest (Keleti) from Dortmund, Cologne, and Frankfurt. OBB's overnight Wiener Walzer (with dining during the day) brings you from Basel through Zurich and Salzburg. FrenchRail's Orient Express (not the luxury train) connects from Paris, by way of Strasbourg, Stuttgart, and Munich.

Austrian Trains

The OBB provides excellent, punctual service with a full complement of express trains (Ex), fast trains (D), intermediate-speed trains (E), and local trains (no letters).

All of OBB's express trains are name trains (Ex 263 is the "Orient Express" running between Paris, Salzburg, Vienna, Budapest, and Bucharest). Even some of OBB's D trains carry names.

Hungarian Trains

The Hungarian State Railroads ("Magyar Allamvasutak," known as MAV) is a small, but capable, diesel- and electric-train operation of local, fast, express, the EC Lehar and International trains.

MAV's red-livery trains are slow but reliable, and travel is very cheap. Yellow stripes mark first class.

The train stations are all well posted with arrival and departure signs. The Thomas Cook European Timetable gives you the relevant schedules.

Trains to the countryside are pulled by red diesel locomotives. The yellow paint on their front is marked with a red star.

The only difference between fast and express trains (marked with a boxed *R* in the timetable) is that the latter permit seat reservations costing about 25 cents—if you can figure out the system. Reservations give you peace of mind but are unnecessary.

Although train fares are cheap in Hungary, a Eurail, European East, or Hungarian Railpass really pays for itself in the time and hassle you save trying to buy a correct ticket. You thank your lucky stars for a rail pass that allows you to escape the incredible confusion of the complex and unmarked ticketing windows.

Now that MAV is a member of Eurailpass and travel restrictions have eased, more adventurers find interest in traveling by train to Hungary. You must visit Budapest, which is as dazzling a city as you will find in Europe, but sightseeing in the flat Hungarian countryside is disappointing. Hungary is a breadbasket. You imagine Ghengis Khan sweeping across the plain; horsemen with no barriers to hinder them; the run of the country by horseback—yet, from the train you see no horses.

Do not expect the same comfort as you find aboard Western European trains. The Hungarian language barrier is difficult to break, and excursions into the countryside are not as scenic as those in the West.

Each little train station in the countryside is alive with flowers and boasts a showpiece black steam locomotive on a pedestal in front, but you don't see charming villages nor church spires, no thatched roofs nor typical architecture — just the opposite, a monotonous postwar drabness.

Connecting Vienna and Budapest by EuroCity Lehar

The morning EuroCity Lehar is your most comfortable and convenient way to reach Budapest from Vienna. Leaving from Vienna's South station, the Lehar, the first EuroCity train to run into an Eastern country, speeds you between Vienna and Budapest in record-breaking time. This is a quick one-day excursion from Vienna to Budapest and return from Budapest's Deli station at 6:30 P.M.

The Lehar consists of two first-class blue-and-gray MAV "Komfort" salon-type cars (with yellow first-class stripes), one similar-livery restaurant car, and six bright, newly painted, red-and-dark-gray 1981 Siemens OBB cars for passengers with standard compartments in second-class coaches.

MAV's Komfort cars, brown carpeted with matching brown-striped curtains, are simple, but first class all the way. Some of the amenities making these carriages special include the overstuffed seats with oceans of leg room, curtained-off coat closets, and a magazine table with travel literature, Hungarian newspapers, and Austrian-printed Lehar timetables.

The hostess helps you find your seat (reservations are not required, but recommended) and offers snacks en route. The Komfort cars are reversible with a TV monitor at one end.

Your border crossing at Hegyeshalom is shortened to ten minutes by the trick of using two-frequency electrical locomotives compatible with the networks of both OBB and MAV and by performing border passport, visa, and customs inspections aboard the Lehar. For the first time since 1932 (when the legendary Hungarian train "Arpad" raced along this route), you can travel between Budapest and Vienna in less than three hours.

Austria's Private Lines and Steam Trains

Austria, with high Alps and rolling countryside dotted with spectacularly beautiful lakes, offers adventurers a chance to leave mainline trains for local and private lines. These include trains still operating with steam locomotives on a scheduled basis, steam rack railroads climbing up steep inclines to lofty mountain tops, standard- and narrow-gauge short lines with frequent steam excursion trains, and numerous museum trains with fan trips throughout the summer.

One of Austria's provinces is a railroad operator in its own right. Styria runs both standard and 2½-foot gauge lines under the banner of the

Steiermarkische Landesbahnen with headquarters in Graz. Its longest line, the forty-eight-mile narrow-gauge Murtalbahn, runs from Unzmarkt to Mauterndorf. On Tuesdays and Wednesdays during the summer you ride steam along half of this line.

You are welcome to call numerous train enthusiast groups in Austria. For more details, contact the Austrian National Tourist Office (see Appendix A).

Vienna's Train Stations

The heart of Austria—and the OBB—is Vienna. Vienna has five train stations; two are important. You arrive at the West train station, the "Westbahnhof," unless you arrive from Italy. Vienna's West station handles all traffic from Switzerland and Germany. Vienna's South train station, the Sudbahnhof, connects with Italy, Yugoslavia, and the eastern countries.

Adventurers arriving from the west or south must use surface transportation to change from the Westbahnhof to the Sudbahnhof or vice-versa. This inconvenience makes Vienna an obvious place to break your journey, but here's a tip: you can shave at least an hour off your travel time by getting off your train from the west in Vienna-Hutteldorf, where all international trains stop, before it reaches Vienna-Westbahnhof. In Hutteldorf, change to S-Bahn Line 3, where you make direct, hourly connections to the Sudbahnhof.

Vienna's third station is the striking glass-fronted Franz Josefs-Bahnhof, a model for the modern trend toward integrating train facilities with commercial shopping centers. Two trains a day serve Prague, Dresden, and eastern Berlin from FJB, but most of its traffic is the electrified commuter service along the southern bank of the Danube and north of the Danube, including Krems (for Danube River steamers).

Vienna Nord connects the airport, the city, the small area north of the Danube, and Czechoslovakia.

West Train Station

The highly glassed Westbahnhof is a big, well-organized structure rebuilt in 1953 to handle all electrified train traffic in the direction of Western Europe. It was renovated in 1990 to handle ground-level access for the new Line 6 U-Bahn facilities. Information for hotels and trains is available in one office in the middle of the hall. The tourist information office opens early, to accommodate adventurers arriving on the first international trains, and remains open late.

Luggage carts fitted for the escalators are available.

South Train Station

The Sudbahnhof is a graceful station because of the moving walkways leading to two upper levels.

The top floor of this airy terminus is devoted to service to the south, "Sudbahn." There are waiting rooms and kiosks selling travel provisions ("Reiseproviant"), as well as a sit-down coffee shop.

The middle level, the "Ostbahn," serves the east, meaning the Balkan countries. There are rest rooms, a cafe/restaurant, and a buffet.

On the expansive ground floor, you find nearly every service you need, including money changing, tourist information, train information, ticketing, lockers, a barbershop, and showers.

Getting around Vienna

Adventurers first taste Vienna's excellent public transportation network in front of Vienna's West station where Line 6 U-Bahn station was opened in 1990.

Plan to use Vienna's four means of transit: the surface streetcar and bus network, S-Bahn, U-Bahn, and Badner Bahn (Stadtbahn), the art deco elevated/underground tram. They interchange at Karlsplatz on the Ring. A ticket for one is good for unlimited transfers to all.

Buy single tickets on the tram from the conductor in the first car or from an automat in one of the subway or S-Bahn stations. You receive a good discount on sets of five tickets sold at train stations and Vienna Transport Authority ticket offices or from any of the tobacco kiosks around the city. When you use these on unattended ("Schaffnerlos") trams, validate them in the automatic canceling machines aboard the tram.

Take advantage of the twenty-four- and seventy-two-hour Vienna Network passes (effective from the hour you first validate them) or, even cheaper per day, an Environment Card ("8-Tage-Umwelt Streifennetzkarte") valid for eight dates of travel. Environment Cards are stamped individually per person, so that more than one can use them. For example, two adventurers can travel together for four days or eight for one day. Eurailpasses are valid on S-Bahn trains in Vienna, including S-Bahn Line 7 between the city and the airport.

Reach the Sudbahnhof from Vienna's West station by U-Bahn Line 6 to Meidling station, changing to S-Bahn Lines 1, 2 or 3. From Franz Josefs-Bahnhof to the Westbahnhof, it is easiest to walk a block toward the Danube to the Friedensbrucke U-Bahn station where U6 takes you to the Westbahnhof.

Vienna's Airport Train

Ride S-Bahn Line 7 free on a Eurailpass for a direct link to Vienna's Schwechat Airport. It leaves hourly from Vienna's North train station with a stop at the Mitte and several intermediate stations. Reach Vienna's North train station by S-Bahn Lines 1, 2, and 3 and U-Bahn Line 1. Allow thirty minutes transportation time by S-Bahn between Vienna-North and Schwechat. Airport buses travel hourly to and from Vienna's West station—with stops at Vienna's South station—taking thirty-five minutes.

Budapest's Train Stations

Budapest's three train stations are all connected with each other and within the city with two ("blue" and "red") no-graffiti subway lines, the world's second-oldest (after London's). The subways and subway stations are excellent. You can travel directly between Deli Pu and Keleti Pu ("Pu" means "train station") on the "red" line, but to reach Nugati (West) train station you change at Deak subway station. Be sure to go to the correct station for departure.

The most convenient place for you to buy train tickets in Hungary is at Ibusz (the Hungarian Travel Bureau) offices. Someone there usually speaks English. Ibusz has branch offices in all train stations, but agents at Ibusz' main office, Felszabadulas ter 5, not only sell train tickets, but make room arrangements, change money, and distribute free information and pamphlets in English. MAV requires that you reserve express trains (gyorsvonat) a day in advance, but local trains need no booking.

You can buy a subway/streetcar/bus map at a Metro station ticket office, but the Metro stations are so well posted you will not need one when you confine yourself to Metro travel.

The three train stations of Budapest have much in common. They are large, sprawling, and bewildering. All have modern (now standard) digital departure signboards in the departure hall and at the heads of platforms. The escalators all work and all have attached, well-marked Metro ("M") stations. Signing is by international pictographs that you may be hard pressed to find because they are not displayed prominently, and the agents will never speak English. Moreover they all give you a hard time and can be extremely difficult to deal with.

Only Hungarians read Hungarian ("the devil's tongue") so the written signs ring no bells for you. Follow arrows. Search for pictographs. And trust to common sense.

Keleti Pu

Traveling to Hungary from the West, you arrive at Keleti Palyaudvar (East train station), a large, ranging station on the Pest bank of Budapest. Statues of George Stephenson, inventor of the locomotive, and James Watt, creator of the steam engine, grace the front of the eclectic, charming exterior of the tremendous nineteenth-century structure.

Keleti's arrival hall has thirteen tracks, but only 6 through 9 stretch to the front. The Orient Express departs from track 9. On the side next to platform 6 you find a wing containing an Ibusz agency, train information (English not spoken), and a couchette and sleeping car reservations counter. Find ticketing at Window 20, which is not identified in English. Currency change (look for the German "Geld Wechsel" sign) is everywhere although you will also be approached by black market operators.

Keleti is connected by an escalator to a Metro station crowded with shops, more ticketing windows, vending machines, and a hot dog/pizza/pretzel kiosk. You can purchase a cup of espresso coffee on the terrace. Frequent Metro service takes you to the city center and under the Danube to Deli Pu.

Nyugati Pu

The Baltic-Orient Express to Prague, Dresden, Berlin, and Stockholm leaves from Budapest's spic-and-span West station at the head of Lenin Street just before it reaches Marx Square.

Budapest's Nyugati is another sprawling train station. The Victorian-looking red- and brown-brick facade features blue-gray latticework.

You find all the facilities, luggage check, water, barber, traveler's sleeping facilities, Ibusz, money change, etc., beside platform 10 so walk to the back of platform 10 for the escalator exit to this complex.

Every nook and space is filled with push-wagons. Their vendors sell salami sandwiches, soft drinks, newspapers, other snacks, and curios.

Below is a complex subterranean shopping plaza/Metro station on the blue line. The real sales activity takes place here.

Deli Pu

Trains take you to Vienna's South train station and to Lake Balaton from Budapest's new South station (Deli Palyaudvar) in the west (!) of town. Deli is Budapest's most modern station, with an exterior of aluminum, glass, and concrete. Inside you find a post office in addition to money change, souvenirs (hard currency only), shops of every nature, and sweeping staircases. The station is also the farthest from town, lying in the Pest side of the Danube (Duna). There is a cafeteria adjacent to the arrivals hall, but it is not reliable.

Deli's platforms have pushcarts and drinking water from fountains with spigots.

Using Eurailpass Bonuses

When you enter Austria or Hungary via train from a country that doesn't honor Eurailpasses, you need not prevalidate it at a train station; the Austrian or Hungarian conductor assumes the responsibility.

Two of the most delightful Eurailpass bonuses are described in the adventures below: the Puchberg am Schneeberg-Hochschneeberg rack railroad and the steamers operated by the Erste Donau-Dampfschiffahrts-Gesellschaft (DDSG) between Passau and Vienna. In addition, adventurers who want to go south of Salzburg into the beautiful Salzkammergut should take advantage of the free St. Wolfgang-Schafbergspitze rack railroad and the free steamers on Lake Wolfgang leading to it.

Not advertised by Eurailpass, the Steiermarkische Landesbahnen grants a 50 percent reduction to holders of Eurailpasses and OBB's postal coaches honor Eurailpasses.

Use the Austrian port of Bregenz (site of the summer lake festival) to begin journeys on Lake Constance, for which Eurailpass allows you a 50 percent reduction.

Austrian Rabbit Card

OBB's "Rabbit Card" is a flexipass valid for four travel days in ten of first- or second-class unlimited travel on the OBB network (except between the Austrian border and Hegyeshalom, Hungary), the Schneeberg and Schafberg rack railroads, and OBB ships on the Wolfgangsee. Those under twenty-six buy "Junior Rabbit Cards" for more than one-third less than elders pay, for either second or first class (the discount on first-class travel offered to juniors is one of the few in Europe).

Buy Rabbit and Junior Rabbit cards from your travel agent through GermanRail and FrenchRail offices in the United States.

For adventurers spending more time in Austria, there is the one month Austrian Network Pass, first or second class, which includes the bonuses of a Rabbit Card plus a 50 percent reduction on Lake Constance and DDSG Danube ships and on a number of private railroads. Children aged six to fourteen traveling with an adult receive 50 percent off the purchase price of an Austrian Network Pass. (You can even buy one valid for one year.)

You can also buy a card for about $90 allowing you to receive 50 percent off tickets of OBB and private lines for a year.

Anyone under twenty-six is eligible for the "Austria Ticket," for nine or sixteen days of second-class travel (only) on the lines of the OBB, some private railroads, all postal and railroad buses, the Steiermarkische Landesbahnen, the DDSG, and the ships of the OBB on the Wolfgangsee. Countless mountain funiculars give you a 50 percent reduction.

Regional Network Cards allow unlimited travel for between four and ten days on OBB services within any one of eighteen different regions and with 50 percent reduction on a number of private railroads.

Finally, OBB offers a Kilometer Bank scheme whereby up to six adventurers total their travel mileage and receive discounts of up to 35 percent.

Hungarian Railpass

First-class Flexible Railpasses valid for five days in fifteen or ten in one month are available from travel agents through FrenchRail. Because travel in Hungary is covered by Eurailpass and European East Railpass, few adventurers will have occasion to take advantage of their very cheap price, but for those not purchasing either of these, buying a Hungarian Railpass will give them a tremendous convenience skirting the language problem.

Tickets valid for ten, twenty, or thirty days ("Turista Berlet") for unlimited travel on MAV in either first or second class are available at offices of Ibusz/Danube Travel in Budapest, Cologne, Frankfurt, London, Munich, Stockholm, or Vienna. At main train stations you can extend this Hungarian Rail Runabout Ticket to include the GYSEV Railroad.

Public transportation fares are very inexpensive in Budapest and you can buy tickets in your hotel, but day passes give you the convenience of unlimited travel on the trams, electric buses, metro, and HEV Railroad in the Budapest area. For an additional charge, buy one including city bus travel as well.

European East Railpass

The four-country European East Railpass lets you travel as you please over the OBB and MAV networks and through Poland and Czechoslovakia. These passes are your most convenient way to travel about Poland and Czechoslovakia, which like Hungary present language difficulties. Good international train connections take you from Vienna and Budapest to Prague and Warsaw.

European East Railpasses are flexible. You buy them for five days travel in fifteen or ten in a month, for first-class travel only. Their price is based on the one-way Salzburg/Vienna/Budapest/Prague/Warsaw Eurail Tariff price, so when you travel more than this stretch, you save money, especially when you make Vienna your gateway to Eastern Europe.

The two adventures described in this chapter, the DDSG steamers from Passau to Vienna and Austria's Schneeberg Rack Railroad, make your traveling exciting in Austria and are both covered by Eurailpasses, Austria Rabbit Cards, and European East Passes.

Cruising the Mellow Danube Off with Your Shoes

Passengers pull their deck chairs closer to the railings. Their maps, guidebooks, and disc cameras threaten to fall into the Danube. They read their texts aloud, compare notes, chatter excitedly, and click their cameras at the sight in front of them.

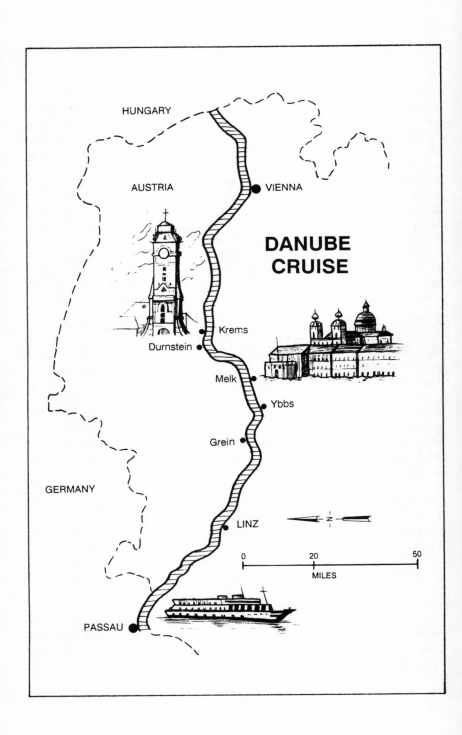

HUNGARY

AUSTRIA

VIENNA

**DANUBE
CRUISE**

Krems

Durnstein

Melk

Ybbs

Grein

GERMANY

LINZ

0   20   50

MILES

PASSAU

You see the castle where Richard the Lionhearted, King of England, was imprisoned by his enemy, Leopold V, Duke of Austria.

The sights of castles, abbeys, and picture-book villages and the warmth of the wine- and fruit-bearing slopes makes the Wachau district in Austria on the deck of a river steamer one of the great river adventures. To show it off, proud Austrian hosts take their foreign visitors on the deck of a river steamer for that "special occasion."

The First Danube Steamship Company, DDSG ("Erste Donau-Dampfschif-fahrts-Gesellschaft"), takes you on cooling, mellow two-day, two-segment cruises along the Danube River through Austria between Passau, West Germany, and Vienna, the capital of Austria. This trip passes through the highlight Wachau district, but shorter excursions through just this stretch take 1 ¾ hours. The trips are free to Eurailers.

The Danube flows through Austria only 224 miles, but it is the most beautiful segment of Europe's second river (after the Volga). Your principal landings are at Linz, Melk, Krems, and of course Vienna. This one-eighth segment of the river is wholly navigable so you see commercial vessels, even Russian ones, all along its length, some traveling all the way from West Germany to the Black Sea.

Commerce pays your freight, so to speak. It keeps the river navigable so you can see the most picturesque sections of the Danube valley right from the surface of the river itself.

You can make this two-day trip in either direction, but there is something more rhythmic and restful about the throbbing of your ship going downstream from Passau to Vienna.

The Danube is a good river. Its color is always changing, depending on the time of day, weather conditions, time of year, whether the sun is rising and lightening it, whether it is overcast and gloomy, and whether it is carrying the spring glacier runoff or sediment. It is lined by castles, sparkles like an emerald in bright sunlight, and remains joyful for you to travel by ship. It is a real bargain when your passage is paid by Eurailpass.

DDSG's ships are all one class and shipshape in every respect. The Austrian government celebrated their 150th anniversary in 1979 by issuing three postage stamps showing ships of the company.

Passau to Linz

Passau, the German port at the very head of the stretch of the Austrian Danube covered by your Eurailpass, occupies a beautiful site on the peninsula formed by the Inn and Danube rivers.

Reach Passau's DDSG landing from Passau train station by bus No. 5 from the steps in front of the station. Disembark the bus before it crosses the long Danube Bridge.

After the junction of the Inn River with the Danube below Passau (the Inn is the larger at this point), the Danube is wide and majestic and bordered with wooded, rocky slopes. Gravel plains along the valley were formed when glaciers receded. You sail past green meadows, marshes, and evergreen forests now covering the hills.

After your ship stops at Engelhartszell, you see the river open out into a magnificent lake. This is the reservoir of the Jochenstein Dam. The rocky island in the river was supposedly the dwelling of a water fairy called Isa, the sister of the more infamous Lorelei of Rhine River notoriety.

Past Wesenufer, a pretty village with flowers on the balconies, you make a wide, sunken loop called the "Schloegener Schlinge," meaning "Sling of Schloegen." At the outermost point of your great U-turn, a Roman castle of the second century has been excavated. It guarded communications between Castra Batava (Passau) and Lentia (Linz).

After stopping at Aschach, where you see the surprising brown, blue, and orange colors used to decorate the villages in this area, you continue to Linz for a stopover in "The Excursion Center on the Danube."

Linz

You embark in Passau or Linz to cruise downstream. Book a cabin from Passau and spend the night on board in Linz, but if this is too much trouble, plan to board directly in Linz, the vital capital of Upper Austria. Train connections are good here because it is a pass-through station.

Before you sail from Linz in the morning, visit Linz's showpiece main square, the Hauptplatz, only a block from the Hauptstrasse Bridge over the Danube from where you see the embarkation station for the cruise ships downstream. It is an easy walk.

You see a striking ensemble of diverse buildings on the Hauptplatz. The fascinating baroque Trinity column dominates the center of the square. Emperor Charles VI directed that it be erected in 1723 to celebrate the escape of the city from the plague, fire, and Turkish invasion. You see baroque columns of this type in many towns of Austria and Bavaria, but this is the best example.

You can use the tourist information booth and money change office right in the Linz train station. Both open at 8 A.M. If you arrive earlier, you find a warm waiting room in the station giving you the comfortable feeling of Austrian gemutlichkeit.

A streetcar in front of the train station takes you to the Hauptplatz and the DDSG pier along the river.

Linz is a convenient port for you to board for the day trip to Vienna.

Downstream is lined with industrial growth, but when you see the hills grow green and wooded and the houses and barns become picturesque and when you find yourself peeping into the lives of dwellers by the river, washing and boating and threshing and piling hay into yellow haystacks, your cruise begins to unroll like a continuous reel of travelogue color adventure. You have well begun the singing, guitar-strumming, cooling swing down the Danube.

Your cruise is a marvelously soothing change from the helter-skelter madness of rush-around sightseeing, cathedrals that all look alike after a while, fortresses perched at the ends of dusty climbs, endless museums, crowded palaces, and bumpy cobblestone streets in the summer sun which finally make you believe your feet will burst into flames any minute. Your Danube cruise is fun.

Off with Your Shoes

Shortly after leaving Linz at 9 A.M., the youthful aboard shed their shirts, shoes, and socks and gather to play guitars. Even more reserved passengers take this opportunity to slip off their shoes and socks and wiggle their toes from the ship's deck in the fresh, cooling breezes above the river.

Passengers scrape their deck chairs to the railings and compare their geography texts with the highlights of the passing countryside. You overhear no English. You are adventuring off the common tourist path, but all the deck personnel cheerfully answer your questions in English.

Downstream, about noon, you are hemmed between rocky, wooded slopes. Your approach to Grein is beautiful. This pleasant little town, guarded by its castle, lies ideally at the foot of a wooded bluff watching over the entrance to the Strudengau gorges.

Below Grein begins the most dramatic section of the Austrian Danube. At one time river passengers feared the infamous rapids of Strudel and Wirbel. Now with the dangerous rocks blasted away, you pass around willow-covered islands, past the ruins of the castles of Struden and Sarmingstein, and soon find yourself on a placid lake nearing the Ybbs-Persenbeug dam, a major power station.

The crew members are excited and rushed. They scurry passengers below and rope off the upper deck while the locks of the power station loom larger and larger. When the Danube is high, the clearance between your steamer and the locks is so slim that anyone poking his head above the ship's railings will be seriously injured.

When you pass Persenbeug, look for the castle where the last Austrian emperor, Charles I, was born.

From Persenbeug, at the head of a well-tilled plain where the river bends to Melk, you pass through the valley you know from episodes in *The Nibelungenlied*. You may hear echos of Brunhild and Kriemhild, Gunther and Siegfried.

Pochlarn, on the right bank, was settled in the tenth century by the Babenbergs, who began the vigorous growth of the Austrian monarchy.

The Wachau

The stretch of the Danube from Melk to Krems, the Wachau, is considered the most interesting stretch of river landscape in Europe. You see charming villages lining the river, the ruins of fortified castles crowning the crests, and onion-shaped belfries adding notes of fantasy to the countryside.

The Wachau is a beautiful sight regardless of whether the trees are in blossom, apricots are bright on trees, or grapes are heavy on vines and every wine village is celebrating the harvest.

You are making one of the premiere excursions from Vienna. Frau Vera Kreisky, wife of the president of Austria at the time, took Rosalynn Carter on this trip on June 16, 1979, while the Austrian and American heads of state were in Vienna attending to business.

In addition to the full-day sailings of the Danube, you may take the shorter trip through the Wachau free on a Eurailpass. Pick up your boarding pass at the "Kassa," meaning cashier.

The Wachau makes a splendid debut at Melk where the buff-and-gold, 1726 Benedictine abbey rises like a vision above fine middle-class houses. You pass below the abbey's south wall, nearly a quarter-mile long, overlooking the Danube from a 150-foot rocky bluff.

Additional ships supplement this most-popular section. The smaller *Prinz Eugen*, for example, takes you on three decks, but primarily you use the rubber-mat and plastic bench vista on the top deck.

Melk's Donauarm landing is directly below the abbey, a fifteen- to twenty-minute walk from the mainline train station served by expresses from Vienna and Linz.

An English-speaking agent sells tickets and a simple leaflet program at the DDSG station house at the Donaustrom dock.

As you cruise out to the main Danube current, the chords of the "Blue Danube" waltz strike a romantic and unforgettable note.

Soon after casting off from Melk you see Schonbuhel Castle, which has guarded entry to the Wachau since the ninth century.

After docking at the yellow-painted village of Aggsbach, your steamer proceeds five minutes to Aggstein, precipitously below the castle, one of the largest and most formidable of the towers high on the mountain. This castle is notorious as a robber baron's haunt where prisoners were forced to jump to their deaths.

Passing Willendorf is especially interesting because the famous "Venus of

Willendorf" prehistoric limestone statuette found here proved that man lived in the hills surrounding you since the dawn of civilization.

Spitz is almost the center of the Wachau, and its largest village. You see houses clustering below a hill, graceless but prosperous. The rows after rows of vines make it famous as "Thousand Pail Hill," known for the staggering amount of wine it produces in a good year.

Past Spitz on the left, fifteenth-century St. Michael appears—the oldest church in the Wachau. Thriving vineyards continue to cover the hillsides with green vines terraced in parallel rows. This region has the mildest climate in Austria.

The next picturesque village, marked by the fortified steep red-tiled roof, is Weissenkirchen, the center of the region known as "Wahowa" that gave its name to the entire Wachau.

Then, after sweeping past a broad bend in the Danube, you see the most famous scene in the Wachau—Durnstein—a historical, fortified town. As you near, you can feel its almost completely preserved medieval and baroque character.

Richard the Lionhearted in disguise was seized on his way back to his native England at the end of the Third Crusade. His faithful troubador/detective, Blondel, discovered his master here in Durnstein by strumming his mandolin and singing Richard's favorite ballad while searching through the castle.

Your next landing marks the end of the Wachau. You pass under a 500-year-old bridge at Krems, the historic wine-growing city (not village) on the left bank. At the foot of loam hills covered with prominent, terraced vineyards, you cross the famous "Iron Route," an ancient trade artery. Now a simple city, Krems was once an imperial fortress, more important than Vienna because of Danube trade.

You have completed the exciting part of your trip. Wachau steamers debark in Krems, where you take OBB's second-class-only diesel train into Vienna's Franz Josefs-Bahnhof. The Krems station is far from your ship's landing. If you are aboard a ship making the two-day trip from Passau to Vienna, you can stay aboard and alight at the DDSG's well-fitted stations in Vienna-Nussdorf wine village or in Vienna's city center.

From Krems, the Danube spreads broadly over a wide plain. It does not narrow until just above Vienna, where you pass solid, stone embankments. It will be darkening as your ship from Passau nears the Vienna Woods at Greifenstein.

Your ship docks first in Vienna at the Nussdorf landing, but you continue to the Schiffahrtszentrum, sailing under the reinforced-concrete Reichsbrucke, meaning "empire bridge" (the former one suddenly collapsed one morning in 1971 and fell into the river), and docking at the modernistic DDSG facility. Its reflecting blue glass and white concrete may remind you of the movie *Star*

Wars. Proceed into the terminal's "Passagierhalle." This futuristic complex has everything including taxi stops outside and access to trams and the subway nearby.

At DDSG's information service office, you can make hotel reservations and pick up maps and directions to Vienna, the capital of Austria and for five centuries the seat of the Hapsburg dynasty.

Breakfast, lunch, and dinner are served in the ships' dining salons. Refreshments are available all through the day at the kiosks on deck.

Cabins accommodating two are available aboard the MS *Stadt Passau* between Passau, Linz, and Vienna. You use them overnight in Linz during your journey, or even if you are boarding or disembarking in Linz. Going downstream, you occupy your cabin at 8:30 in the evening before your next day's sailing from Linz. Arriving from Vienna, you may remain overnight in your cabin at Linz until 6:30 A.M., but you must disembark at that time if you do not want to sail on to Passau.

Overnighting on board after arrival in Vienna or Passau is not permitted. Advance reservations are recommended or you can apply to the steward's office immediately upon boarding. The DDSG office is at Handelskai 265, 1021 Vienna (Tel. 0 22 2/26 65 36).

Daily Summer Steamer Service

through the Wachau

1000	1400	1530	dep.	MELK (Donauarm)	arr.	1330	1505	1905
1025	1425	1555	dep.	Aggsbach Dorf	dep.	1245	1415	1815
1030	1430	1600	dep.	Aggstein H.	dep.	1235	1405	1805
1055	1455	1625	dep.	Spitz	dep.	1200	1330	1730
1110	1510	1640	dep.	Weissenkirchen	dep.	1130	1300	1700
1125	1525	1655	dep.	Durnstein	dep.	1105	1235	1635
1145	1545	1715	arr.	KREMS	dep.	1030	1200	1600

Summer Steamer Service

between Passau, Grein, and Vienna

1530	dep.	PASSAU	arr.	1415
1610	dep.	Obernzell	dep.	1315
1655	dep.	Engelhartszell	dep.	1235
1710	dep.	Niederranna	dep.	1210
1720	dep.	Wesenufer	dep.	1200
1735	dep.	Schlogen	dep.	1140
1800	dep.	Obermuhl	dep.	1110

1825	dep.	Neuhaus-Untermuhl	dep.	1040
1910	dep.	Aschach	dep.	0950
1920	dep.	Brandstatt-Eferding	dep.	0935
2030	arr.	LINZ	dep.	0800*
0900*	dep.	LINZ	arr.	2245
1010	dep.	Mauthausen	dep.	2125
1145	dep.	Grein	dep.	1915
1250	dep.	Ybbs	dep.	1755
1315	dep.	Marbach/M.-Taferl	dep.	1720
1330	dep.	Pochlarn	dep.	1705
1430	dep.	MELK (Donauarm)	dep.	1610
1455	dep.	Aggsbach Dorf	dep.	1525
1500	dep.	Aggstein	dep.	1515
1525	dep.	Spitz	dep.	1440
1540	dep.	Weissenkirchen	dep.	1410
1555	dep.	Durnstein	dep.	1345
1615	dep.	KREMS	dep.	1310
1800	dep.	Tulln	dep.	1030
1940	arr.	VIENNA (Nussdorf)	dep.	0825
2000	arr.	VIENNA (DDSG)	dep.	0800

Passau-Linz and Grein-Vienna, daily; Linz-Grein, twice weekly.
*Next day.

Puffing up the Schneeberg
Wieder Kaputt!

The first thing you feel is the chattering of the cogwheels. While your comic steam train pulls you slowly out of the Austrian village of Puchberg, your glimpse ahead does not promise as much as your creaky train finally delivers. The Schneeberg Rack Railroad may be your slowest, steamiest, jerkiest adventure, but may be the most fun. This diverting day's excursion is a free bonus to Eurailpass holders.

Then you hear the nasty hissing of the tough steam engine and see the black clouds swirling behind you. The Schneeberg Railroad has enough antique and functional features to turn a railfan's heart into Apfel Strudel.

What the Austrians call a "schmalspurige dampfbetriebene Zahnradbahn" is a narrow-gauge, steam-driven, cogwheel railroad. It is fired by coal from Poland and belches fumes as black as a loan manager's heart.

When you leave Puchberg am Schneeberg, south of Vienna, each chug of the steam-driven pistons shoves your little engine inches more across the highway and up onto the mountain. Chagrined, you have no doubt you can walk faster than the train can climb, but as your train tilts upward through wild

HOCHSCHNEEBERG

PUCHBERG am SCHNEEBERG
RACK RAILROAD

Baumgartner
Haus

Ternitzer Hutte

Hengsthutte

Hauslitzsattel

Schneeberg Dorf

PUCHBERG

To Vienna

N

0   0.2   1.0

MILES

ground, the engine seems to leap ahead and virtually races past the perspiring mountaineers struggling up the nearby trails.

To reach Puchberg from Vienna, you use the Sudbahnhof (South train station). Trains to the south — all covered by Eurailpass — run via the city of Wiener Neustadt. Puchberg is a local stop bypassed by express trains, so change in the city of Wiener Neustadt unless you start your trip on a local.

When your OBB train from Vienna reaches Puchberg, you file down the platform a few feet to the carved wooden sign: "Zahnradbahn." The Puchberg terminal of the narrow-gauge Schneeberg (meaning "Snow Mountain") cogwheel railroad lies about fifty miles and 1½ hours southwest of Vienna.

At Puchberg, show your Eurailpass at the counter and take a "Zahlkarte," a number for boarding one of the little wooden cars to the summit of the Schneeberg. Without a Eurailpass buy a "Wanderticket" valid for OBB transportation to Puchberg and the rack railroad's climb to the summit. Attached is a coupon ("Gutschein") for a luncheon meal. Buy these tickets at the "Inland" ticket counters in Vienna's South train station or stops en route.

Try to sit on the left going up. Your car is crammed five abreast with so many passengers the interior seems like Noah's ark. Schneeberg is considered by the Viennese as their home in the mountains. The fascination of your trip is the little, black steam locomotive with tilted fireboxes.

Passengers complain about the hard seats and crowded conditions. They give thanks for small favors: at least the north wind is blowing the steam locomotive's noxious fumes away from them.

Pushing from the rear of your train to prevent possible breakaway, the engines (built by Krauss and Company, Munich and Linz, in 1897) are nose-down into the earth like a Viennese professor peering over his spectacles. They look like their front axles have collapsed and they are grubbing for worms.

While your train scales the steep mountainsides, this odd-looking design keeps the boiler tubes horizontal to maintain heat transfer and holds the firebox level to prevent firebrands from tumbling onto the footplate.

After about twenty-five minutes you reach Hauslitzsattel (2,717 feet); your engine brakes. You see blue cornflowers, red poppies, and a dozen delicate Alpine blooms — and, for the first time, smell forest odors. This is the first of a vast system of mountain huts constructed throughout the Austrian Alps for the benefit of mountaineers.

Twelve minutes later you are high enough to see the majesty of the green valley floor below when you reach Hengsthutte, surrounded by pines. Hikers are stepping downhill with bouquets of wild flowers, sweaters tied around their waists.

You make an unscheduled stop at Ternitzer Hutte. It is considerably cooler here. Your angle of ascent is so steep, and because you perceive the interior of the carriage as being horizontal, the fir trees outside appear to be growing diagonally out of the mountainside. No one takes the stop seriously. Passengers disembark but watch their seats so as not to lose them. They are restless and wonder why the train stopped.

This is an escapist trip. Few carry a camera to burden them. They are ready for the freedom of the hiking trails above.

A ten-minute halt is scheduled at Baumgartner's new station house (4,582 feet). Your locomotive is recoaled while you go inside for refreshment or a snack. Try the prune bread loaf for a pleasant treat.

Now comes your real climb! For a short while, at least, you drive uphill on the cog-tracks through forests, wild valleys, mountain huts, and brooks gurgling down the mountainside. Then you make another unexplained stop. "Wieder kaputt!" ("Broken again!") maintains a stout Bavarian visitor wearing Lederhosen.

Suddenly, the person in front of you sees wild chamois ("Gemse") near your train. As one, fifty passengers stand, point to these small antelope, and shout, "Gemse!" The Gemse are near the first patches of snow and fleeing uphill.

Now you enter a tunnel. Passengers sitting next to the windows hurry to shut them tightly to prevent steam locomotive fumes and soot from flooding the carriage. Smoke billows between carriages.

When you exit the tunnel, condensate has covered the train windows. Passengers lower them immediately.

Shortly you enter a second tunnel. People close the windows once again, but the train stops and sits and they reopen them. "Wieder kaputt!" shouts the Bavarian.

Finally underway, the train's lights come on in the tunnel. Emerging, you are above the timberline. You see swathes of tightly bunched, gold and blue wild flowers blooming through the snow. A pinelike shrub grows in patches. To your right is the green-copper-topped stone chapel, the Elizabeth Kirche. Down the rail line to your left is the OBB-owned Berghaus Hochschneeberg (5,889 feet)—but eager hikers are already well on the winding way up the path in the opposite direction. The summit is Enzian paradise. This tiny, much-admired, blue flower (the gentian) is used for Alpine schnapps. Go immediately into the station house to select your "Zahlkarte" for your choice of return times.

You can cash in the "Wanderticket" coupon for a meal at the Berghaus Hochschneeberg, where they also serve a "Kaisermenu" duplicating that of the the Kaiser when he visited in 1901—or use your coupon at other locations. The mountain hotel contains a sauna and solarium.

In addition to experiencing the novel train, this excursion gives you a choice opportunity to hike high in the northern limestone spur of the Austrian Alps. The Schneeberg retains a covering of snow throughout the summer.

Trails take you around the Waxriegel peak (6,193 feet) to the Dambockhaus, where serious hikers buy inexpensive meals and sleeping accommodations.

Top off your excursion by walking (2½ hours round trip) up to the Kaiserstein peak (6,762 feet) for the Alpine panorama north as far as the Vienna Woods. Or climb to the Klosterwappen summit (6,808 feet) for the view south across the ravine called "Hell's Valley" (Hollental) to the Rex Plateau, the geologic twin of the Schneeberg.

Your ride down is rocking, swaying, and squeaking like a rusty spring. It takes less time going down, about an hour, but it is more subdued because passengers are tired.

Across the street from the Puchberg train station, an idyllic lakefront promenade is perfect for picnicking. The Puchberg station has a buffet serving meals.

Summer Connections to the Schneeberg Rack Railroad

		a			e		
VIENNA (Sudbahnhof)	dep.	0650	0705	0921	1000	1306	1400
Wien Meidling	dep.	0655	0710	0926	....	1311	....
Modling	dep.	0704	0718	0941	....	1328	....
Baden	dep.	0712	0727	0954	....	1338	1417
Wiener Neustadt	arr.	0724	0740*	1021	1029*	1404	1429*
Wiener Neustadt	dep.	0730	0752	1034	1034	1435	1435
Puchberg am Schneeberg	arr.	0810	0846	1126	1126	1524	1524
Puchberg am Schneeberg	dep.	0830	0900	1140	1140	1552	1552
HOCHSCHEEBERG	arr.	0950	1020	1300	1300	1719	1719

Summer Connections
from the Schneeberg Rack Railroad

		b	c	d		a	
HOCHSCHNEEBERG	(departures as required)						
Puchberg am Schneeberg	dep.	1617	1714	1805	....	1815	1916
Wiener Neustadt	arr.	1709*	1804	1854*	....	1854	2007*
Wiener Neustadt	dep.	1720	1811	1908	1928	1903	2010
Baden	arr.	1735	1826	1925	....	1917	2023
Modling	arr.	....	1834	1933	....	1924	2030
Wien Meidling	arr.	1754	1847	1943	1954	1933	2039
VIENNA (Sudbahnhof)	arr.	1800	1854	1949	2000	1940	2045

a "Schneeberg" E train (Saturdays and Sundays only).
b Mondays through Saturdays only.
c Sundays only.
d Mondays through Fridays only.
e "Fischer von Erlach" Ex train.
*Change trains at Wiener Neustadt.

Italy
and Greece

Vital Tips for the Trains
of Italy and Greece

*Italian trains—Crossing between Italy and Greece—Greek trains—
Airport trains—Using overnight trains to Italy—Italian private
railroads—Sardinian connections—Using Eurailpass bonuses—
Italian Railpass—Greek Railpass*

Italy is a flashy and artistic country. Expect no less of the showpiece Italian
State Railroads, "Ferrovie dello Stado" (FS). FS's 10,000-mile network has
touches of a maestro.

Greece is a country of great history. It's curious how trains mirror the nature
of the countries. Don't expect the trains of "Organismos Siderodromon Ellados
(OSE)," the Greek Railroads Organization, to provide you with great comfort,
speed, or convenience. The best travel experience in Greece is on the Aegean
ferries.

Italian Trains

The trains of Italy are as long as a Roman's nose, and just as full of character.
You ride top-notch long-distance trains from the Italian Alps to Palermo on
the tip of Sicily.

FS's EuroCity trains are orange-livery, identical to the trains in Austria. A total of twenty-one EC trains commute to Italy, including the EC Colosseum (Frankfurt/Rome), EC Hermann Hesse (Stuttgart/Milan), EC Raffaelo (Basel/Rome), and both EC Gottardo and EC Manzoni (Zurich/Milan). FS's high-grade InterCity network uses new equipment on some routes, but on the Naples-Rome-Florence-Milan/Venice routes uses 1985 and 1986 maroon-and-gray carriages and the same deluxe gray-and-white, red-striped 1973 and 1974 FS coaches that comprised former Trans Europ Express trains. They retain their superior ambience and convenience with features such as behind-the-seats coat closets. The trains carry white-linen restaurant cars or "Self Service" cafeteria cars staffed by Wagons-Lits.

The food selection and cashier sections of the FS's "Self Service" cafeteria cars are conventional, but the facilities for eating your meal are unusual. Your dining area consists of orange formica saw-tooth spaces with swivel stools placed along the windows and separated with orange dividers. Diners on one side of the train look forward; the other half looks backwards. Perhaps this is to minimize dawdling.

You ride FS's IC trains from Rome to Bari and Reggio di Calabria in green-and-white railcars of several designs. The prestigious IC Peloritano between Rome and Palermo consists of 1988 second-class gray-and-white, blue-striped carriages and the orange-livery first-class cars.

You must make seat reservations on most of FS's IC trains. If you board and find an unreserved seat, the conductor will charge you for the seat, plus a penalty!

The rest of FS's fleet takes you to villages and the seaside in an eclectic set of equipment. You ride Rapidos (R), Espressos (Expr), Direttos (Dir), or Trenos Locale (Locale), in decreasing order of desirability.

FS's trains are clean inside and out. Train and window washing is performed in Rome Termini, Florence S.M.N. (Santa Maria Novella), and Venice Santa Lucia stations by motorized machines that are steered past the trains.

Major FS stations have train information computer consoles to answer your punched-in questions in English—that is, if kids stop playing with them and you are going to an FS destination in Italy.

At most stops in Italy, trackside vendors with fully loaded pushcarts are eager to sell you cold drinks, sandwiches, and candy. Listen for their persistently tinkling bells. Just open your window and make your orders from the train.

Crossing between Italy and Greece

Greece is a magnet to adventurers because of the free Eurailpass ferry transportation and the carefree stopover on Corfu's beaches.

Eurailpass holders reach Greece by the joint ferry service of the Greek Hellenic Mediterranean Lines (HML) and the Italian Adriatica Lines. Remember
those names. Brindisi is alive with frauds advertising Eurailpass crossings on
other lines. These tickets are not valid.

Your European acquaintances traveling on European rail passes take the
train through Yugoslavia, where their passes are valid, and not on the ferries,
where they are not. You all rendezvous on the Aegean. HML and Adriatica
Lines alternate crossings. Adventurers disagree which line is more acceptable.
They usually say the line they didn't take is better.

Hellenic Mediterranean uses the m.v. *Lydia* (1,215 passengers, 105 cars) and
the m.v. *Corinthia* (1,100 passengers, 300 cars). Adriatica uses the m.v.
Espresso Grecia (835 passengers, 210 cars) and the m.v. *Appia* (1,130 passengers, 150 cars).

There are up to three sailings a day during high season from Brindisi to
Patras and vice versa. Some stop in Corfu en route and some take you without
stop. Others take you between Brindisi and Corfu and a second Ionian island,
Igoumenitsa, but don't continue to Patras.

When you plan to visit Corfu, HML offers noon departures in late August
only, or board Adriatica's 10:30 P.M. or HML's 10 P.M. departures which both
depart daily during high season. When you want to sail nonstop to Patras,
board one of HML's and Adriatica's alternating-day departures at 8 P.M. Returning, there are departures for Brindisi at 6 P.M. (Adriatica) and 5 P.M. (HML)
on alternating days.

At Patras's landing you board either a train or bus. Buses park near the ship's
landing. Trains are a short walk away. Buses are not covered by Eurailpasses;
trains are.

When you talk with others about this crossing, you hear horror stories. It is
sensible to approach this journey with careful planning.

Make train reservations to Brindisi and also from Brindisi if you know in
advance when you will return. Allow extra time for possible train delays en
route. Trains run to Brindisi from Rome's Termini station and down Italy's
Adriatic coast from Bologna. New carriages have been placed on the Naples/
Brindisi route. Station timetables indicate these trains are for "Lecce." Brindisi's Centrale station is the stop before Lecce.

Your best train for the ships is the "Parthenon" train, which carries first- and
second-class carriages and second-class couchettes between Paris and Brindisi's
Marittima station. It departs Paris's Lyon station at 8:12 P.M. and calls at
Lausanne and Milan's Lambrate station during the night. You make connections in Bologna at 7:24 A.M. or Rimini at 8:42 A.M., arriving at 5:39 P.M. at
Marittima station next to the pier, but bring food or purchase snacks from
trainside vendors along the way.

Your return Parthenon leaves Brindisi's Marittima station at 12:18 P.M., arriving in Paris at 10:02 A.M. the next day.

• Be sure to take one of the Eurailpass-honoring ships mentioned above. Hucksters lining the street leading to the docks try to mislead you.

• Dress coolly. It is sometimes stiflingly hot waiting for the ferry.

• Take your own food aboard the ships. Food served on the ships is unreliable.

• Take a cabin for the crossing. Although it is not covered by Eurailpass, you will avoid inconveniences. Make your arrangements when you board.

• Allow extra days. When you lay out your overall itinerary, allow several days for unexpected developments.

• Reserve ahead your room in Athens. Especially when you arrive late in Athens, the unfamiliar alphabet and Athens' remote train station can cause difficulties for the unprepared.

• Stop over in Corfu. Anyone who has read about Corfu or is interested in casual beach life will not miss this opportunity.

• Allow extra time in Brindisi before boarding. You pass through customs, passport, port tax payments, ticketing, and boarding bureaucracies. (The pier is about a half-hour's walk down the main street from Brindisi's Centrale station.)

Greek Trains

When you reach Greece, you travel on two train networks. The meter-gauge line circling the Peloponnese Peninsula takes you between Patras and Athens. The northern, standard-gauge network connects Athens to Thessaloniki (Salonika) and the trains of the Balkans and central Europe.

Traveling with a top speed capability of 100 mph (which set speed records in Greece), OSE's newest train on their core route, 318 miles between Athens and Thessaloniki, takes six and a quarter hours averaging 53 mph. This master route's train consists of red-and-white railcars of eastern German origin and carries 180 passengers without standing.

OSE's twelve air-conditioned railcars carry you in four carriages including driver's cars with second-class salons front and back and two middle carriages. The thirty-six-seat first-class middle carriage includes a bar and a kitchen.

OSE's Kalavrita Railroad in the Peloponnesus is usually considered Greece's most scenic train ride. Adventurers leave from Diakofto, near Patras on the line from Athens. The fourteen-mile-long cogwheel railroad line climbs 2,300 feet in one hour, taking you through the spectacular Vouraikos River gorge to Kalavrita. Three-quarters of an hour by foot or on donkey from the Zahlorou stop, the Monastery of Mega Spileo attracts many pilgrims but only men can overnight here.

Because of OSE's two gauges, Athens—which is the hub of both networks—has two major train stations in the city's northwest section connected by an overhead footbridge. There are no through trains. When you take the train from Patras, you arrive in the Peloponnese station. When you arrive via the Balkans or from Thessaloniki, you arrive in Larissa station. For both, take trolley 1 or 5 from Syntagma Square.

Tourist information is unavailable in either train station. The tourist information office at the National Bank of Greece building on Constitution Square has a great supply of useful information for you.

Train reservations on the international trains to the north are required. Make these at the OSE offices at 1-3 Karolou Street or 6 Sina Street.

The port of Athens is Piraeus, just five miles south. This is your gateway for the ferries to Greece's Aegean islands. Take the subway from Athens' Omonia Square.

Airport Trains

Trains between Rome's Fiumicino Airport and Ostiense train station, where you can transfer by subway to Rome's Termini train station and reach destinations throughout the Eternal City, cut substantially your travel time compared with taking the undependable bus connection through grid-locked highway traffic. Trains run at fifteen- or twenty-minute intervals for most of the day; half-hourly during late evening.

Passengers flying domestically can use Pisa's airport train service.

Using Overnight Trains to Italy

Because of the long travel distances between Central Europe and Rome and between Rome and Sicily or Brindisi, adventurers and Central Europeans leaving their homes often travel to Italy in overnight trains.

FS's overnight trains are frequently crowded and stuffy (because of the warm climate). Rather than hoping for space to stretch out in sitting compartments, Eurailpass and first-class Italian Railpass holders are more comfortable booking FS's first-class couchettes. These contain only four bunks instead of the six you find in second class, yet FS's maroon-and-gray "cuccette" cars are madness-on-wheels because of overcrowding until they settle down; too many travelers arrive without reservations and have to be put off. You must have couchette reservations or take your chances.

You won't find FS's "Sleeperettes" mentioned in the Thomas Cook European Timetable, but you can also ride in these first-class-only blue, orange, and white carriages with deeply reclining seats arranged in a salon, so you will avoid paying for a sleeping car. Look for the reclined seat symbol in FS's timetable and departure billboards in the train station.

For upscale comfort (as discussed in "Iberia" chapter above) you ride the EC Pablo Casals between Milan and Barcelona in unprecedented luxury. This is your best connection between Italy and Spain.

Italian Private Railroads

In addition to FS, there are numerous private railroads in Italy, either providing commuter service or serving rural districts and reaching villages not connected to FS. None honor Eurailpasses. Buy not the official FS timetable when you arrive, but the "Orario Generale," listing both FS and private lines, at the bookstores in the stations.

Sardinian Connections

Your fastest crossing from Rome to Golfo Aranci on Sardinia is aboard FS's connecting trains to Civitavecchia, where FS's newest car ferry, the "Logudoro," was put into service in 1990. From Golfo Aranci, connecting trains take you to Olbia and Sassari. Tirrenia Lines also serves this sea route.

Tirrenia Lines has extensive steamship service to Sardinia from the Italian mainland and Sicily. You sail from Genoa to Olbia/Arbatax or Porto Torres, from Leghorn (Livorno) to Porto Torres, or from Palermo to Cagliari. Porto Torres, north of Alghero, is in turn connected to Alghero by diesel railcar service through Sassari.

Using Eurailpass Bonuses

Some of the most-used Eurailpass bonuses are the free ferry crossings on the ships of the Adriatica and Hellenic Mediterranean Lines. From June 10 to September 30, inclusive, you must pay an $8 high-season surcharge. Eurailpass recommends advance reservations ($2) during July and August. You must pay port taxes in local currencies. Sleeping accommodations such as cabins or airline-type seats cost extra. Before boarding, you must check in at the shipping line's office at the pier. If you wish to stop over in Corfu or Igoumenitsa, you must so state when you receive your steamer ticket. When you ticket only to Corfu, you cannot change your mind and continue to Patras. Clearly, there is much bureaucracy involved.

Eurailpass holders do not pay FS fast-train surcharges but must pay for seat reservations where required on FS's InterCity trains. They also must pay meal surcharges on the Pendolino.

The concept of unlimited travel during a limited time frame has expanded to include discounted (30 percent) steamer travel aboard the Adriatica Line from Venice to Piraeus in Greece, Candia (Heraklion) on Crete and Alexandria in Egypt, on the m.s. *Espresso Egitto*. The same 30 percent discount applies to your travel between Italy and the island of Malta.

You also receive free travel on FS buses in Italy and save 10 percent on CIT guided sightseeing tours in Florence, Milan, Naples, Palermo, Taormina, and Venice.

Italian Railpass

The Italian Railpass is valid for unlimited travel on FS's 10,000-mile network, including the train ferries between Reggio di Calabria and Messina.

It is more comfortable traveling first class in Italy. Second-class trains are sometimes crowded and the Italian habit of lining the corridors can make it hard to move around. First-class passengers ride FS's first-class-only trains, the Pendolinos (where they pay meal supplements), and Rapidos, which require no supplement.

The Italian Railpass lets you make all seat reservations free—and these are required on all Pendolino and on most InterCity trains. Like the Eurailpass, the Adriatica Line allows Italian Railpass holders a 30 percent discount on its fares between Venice and Piraeus or Alexandria. You are permitted to make such trips before validating your Italian Railpass and within two months after it expires.

Buy through your travel agent Italian Railpasses valid for eight, fifteen, twenty-one, or thirty days, either in first or second class. Italy Flexi Railcards in both classes are also available for four travel days in nine, eight in twenty-one, or twelve in thirty days of validity.

Greek Railpass

A flexible Greek Railpass is available in North America from your travel agent through FrenchRail, Inc. The Greek Railpass allows you to travel on OSE trains and buses for five days in fifteen or ten in one month, either first or second class.

In Greece adventurers buy Greek Tourist Cards allowing them unlimited second-class travel for ten, twenty, or thirty days on the trains and buses of the Greek Railroads. Its cost depends on the number of people traveling together, up to five, with decreasing per-person cost with each additional adventurer.

Senior cards allowing five single trips free (dates restricted) and 50 percent reduction thereafter are granted to adventurers over sixty.

For information about these tickets, use the OSE offices in Greece (see Appendix B).

Adventuring in Italy takes you aboard the sleek Italian Pendolino network and through Sardinian highlands and beside seashores on private trains. Four great train stations serve as your bases.

FS's Indulgent Pendolino
The Lamborghini of the Rails

Your Pendolino from Milan picks up speed and streaks at 125 mph across the flat Po Valley toward Bologna. Then you negotiate the main ranges of the Apennines over a direttissima track through tunnels one after another built in the 1920s, skirt Florence, and race uninterrupted to a stop in Rome's Termini station.

Check your watch: three hours and fifty minutes. You covered the distance between Italy's two largest cities, 393 miles, in less than four hours at an average speed of nearly 103 mph.

FS's bullet-nosed high-speed train with the FIAT nameplate is long, lean, and all first class. Giving you a taste of speed, service, and extravagance, FS's tilting maroon-and-red Pendolino trains take adventurers between Rome and Milan in less time than it takes you to visit the Vatican Museum.

The captain of your train is pleased when you ask about his Pendolino. "Si, si," he says, nodding to the conductor beside him.

Then he volunteers that indeed you are riding the Italian Railroad's (FS) Pendolino, meaning "Little Pendulum," because its body tilts gently whenever it rounds a curve, thus minimizing the forces of gravity, but he laughs when he calls it "Little Banana" to describe its long and thin profile.

Your aerodynamic train is officially designated ETR 450, for "Elettotreno," or electric train. Adventurers ride it along Italy's core route north from Rome to Florence, Bologna, Milan, Venice, and Turin. Branches take you through Pisa to Genoa and south to Bari.

Pendolino's crew is congenial. They are not direct employees of the Italian State Railroads, but hand-picked employees of FS's subsidiary, "Ristofer," hired to staff these beautiful trains.

In roped-off check-in and departure areas at the heads of platform 20 in Milan Centrale and platform 1 at Rome Termini, blue-uniformed stewardesses and stewards hand you your computer-printed boarding pass and seat number. But when you step aboard the eye-catching maroon-and-red unit at the intermediate stop in Bologna Centrale train station, a staff member wearing a blue blazer opens the door to help you aboard and show you to your seat. The instant you sit, two more attendants, snappily uniformed, hurry to your seat to offer you Italian-language-only newspapers.

It becomes a crowd around you when a fourth suggests (in English) a breakfast at your seat and a fifth offers you refreshments or coffee.

FS began Pendolino service in May 1988, giving you more comfort than flying and more speed than a red Lamborghini racing down the Autostrada. Now

ROUTE OF THE PENDOLINO

MILAN

Bologna

Florence

ROME

N

0 10   50
MILES

connecting a mininetwork on Italy's heavily traveled tourist and business routes, Pendolinos don't compete with the speed of French TGVs, but take you in great luxury and give you more time to see the detail of the Vatican, the Uffizi, and Basilica San Marco.

The secret of Pendolino's speed is FS's modern railbed between Milan and Rome ("MI-RO"). The double-tracked direttissima line cuts an almost straight swath across Latium, Umbria, and Tuscany. Tunnels, including the 8.7-mile Adriana tunnel, eliminate all road-level crossings, and connect FS's older, more wandering route to the new line at various points. In effect, FS created a four-track system between Rome and Florence.

Pendolino trains depart Milan and Rome morning and evening with up to ten carriages and a service carriage, thus seating 442 passengers in first class.

Like French TGVs (although the concept was not original with them) sleek integral power cars front and back pull the Pendolino unit. Power cars seat thirty-eight and contain the driver's cabin. First-class carriages in the middle (one is reserved for smokers) accommodate forty-six and provide the luggage space. The fabrics, materials, and designs remind you so much of airplane interiors that you can't help comparing them to first-class travel on an airplane.

Seven name Pendolinos originate in Rome's Termini station. Four take you through Rifredi station in Florence's outskirts (be sure to note that this is not Florence's downtown main station) and Bologna Centrale. Two continue to Padua, Venice-Mestre and Venice's Santa Lucia station facing the Grand Canal; one continues through Milan to Turin. IC 500 Giotto terminates at Milan Centrale. IC 617 Cristoforo Colombo's route to Genoa takes you through Pisa. IC 517 Borromini serves Bari, Puglia's capital.

Pendolino's luxurious interiors allow you to fold down tables (for your included meals) and stretch out in the twenty-two-inch wide, fresh-smelling aquamarine and slate-green plush seats, which are lined up two-opposite-one, with a thirty-nine-inch pitch. Wall-to-wall carpeting is blue; cooling and heating originates at baseboards.

The windows are streamlined, longer, but not nearly so high as on older trains. You pass through fearless gangways between carriages so you don't feel terrified crossing from car to car while purring along up to 125 mph. Leave your luggage in the luggage racks near the door when you enter.

The environmentally correct closed-cycle toilets in front are also similar to those on airlines, except the Pendolino's are larger and have a rubber mat flooring.

The conductor arrives after meal service because several passengers have neglected to make advance reservations and he had to write the necessary paperwork and collect the penalty for their oversight.

Try giving him only the reservation coupon you obtain at your station. He asks for your Eurailpass (or Italian Railpass) and checks it against the pass number written on your reservation coupon. He looks frustrated and asks something of the train captain, who looks unhappy.

Soon they are scowling — not at you, but at the situation. They are wondering how to explain to you, an obviously important first-class English-speaking adventurer (they assume all Pendolino passengers must be important), that all passengers, including those with Eurailpasses or Italian Railpasses, are required to pay a hefty surcharge in addition to your reservation on this first-class-only VIP train for the overpriced meals that you receive whether you want them or not.

To save further sorrow, now produce the supplement slip you purchased in the station. The conductor is delighted. The train captain dances.

On the straightaway, the green Po Valley's farmland whizzes past you at 125 mph, but you look ahead and see you are approaching a considerable curve. Watch to see how your Pendolino performs. You are seriously startled to observe one side of your carriage physically rising. Pendolino masters the curve magnificently. It tilts positively, holds it through the arc, and returns you comfortably to the horizontal once more.

Your ride is like gliding on olive oil; considerably smoother than the first-class Trans Europ Express trains that Pendolinos replaced.

Buy your reservations at specially marked express windows at stations along the line. When you are traveling without rail pass, a one-way trip in the morning costs about $85, in the evening about $93. The difference reflects the size of the meal served. Children under twelve pay $67, the basic transportation charge.

Holders of Italian Railpasses pay only the meal supplement (about $18 in the morning, about $26 in the evening) to ride the Pendolino. Eurailpass holders pay this supplement and an additional $2 for the required seat reservation. Second-class pass holders must also pay the difference to upgrade from second to first class.

Nonstop Pendolinos take three hours, fifty minutes between Rome and Milan. Hourly InterCity trains, stopping in Florence and Bologna, take five hours and ten minutes. Slower trains take you six to seven hours.

Compare these times to flying between Rome and Milan. You would spend an hour and five minutes in the air, but by the time you add an hour (more from Rome, less from Milan) at each end to get to and from the airports and then allow time to check in before your flight and collect your luggage afterwards, the time you spend traveling from city center to city center is about the same. Yet, you spend it more restfully on the Pendolino and arrive more relaxed and better fed. And, even including the extraordinary surcharge for the meals on the Pendolino, it costs about three-fourths of the air fare. Perhaps you would rather drive the Lamborghini and pay the tolls on the Autostrada, but you will arrive earlier with the Pendolino at a fraction of the cost.

ETR 450 "Pendolino" Service

Nonstop Rome—Milan

IC 510		Botticelli		IC 509
2000	dep.	ROME (Termini)	arr.	2320
2350	arr.	MILAN (Centrale)	dep.	1930

Rome—Milan—Turin

Giotto IC 500	Guido Reni IC 506				Guido Reni IC503	Giotto IC 511
0640	1900	dep.	ROME (Termini)	arr.	1100	2345
0819	2039	arr.	Florence (Rifredi)	dep.	0920	2204
0822	2042	dep.	Florence (Rifredi)	arr.	0917	2201
0911	2134	arr.	Bologna (Centrale)	dep.	0824	2109
0914	2137	dep.	Bologna (Centrale)	arr.	0821	2106
1045	2312*	arr.	MILAN (Centrale)	dep.	0655	1937*
	2315*	dep.	MILAN (Centrale)	arr.	0640	1934*
	0027	arr.	Turin (Porta Susa)	dep.	0527	1822
	0035	arr.	TURIN (P. Nuova)	dep.	0520	1815

*Milan P. Garibaldi station.

Rome—Florence—Venice

Carracci IC 508	Veronese IC 504				Veronese IC 501	Carracci IC 507
1945	0855	dep.	ROME (Termini)	arr.	1015	1900
2124	1034	arr.	Florence (Rifredi)	dep.	0835	1720
2127	1037	dep.	Florence (Rifredi)	arr.	0832	1717
2217	1128	arr.	Bologna (Centrale)	dep.	0740	1626
2220	1131	dep.	Bologna (Centrale)	arr.	0737	1623
2328	1238	arr.	Padua	dep.	0633	1519
2340	1240	dep.	Padua	arr.	0631	1517
2352	1304	arr.	Venice (Mestre)	dep.	0610	1455
2354	1306	dep.	Venice (Mestre)	arr.	0608	1453
0003	1315	arr.	VENICE (S. Lucia)	dep.	0600	1445

Genoa—Pisa—Florence—Rome

IC 612		Cristoforo Colombo		IC 603
1910	dep.	ROME (Termini)	arr.	1025
2049	arr.	Florence (Rifridi)	dep.	0845
2052	dep.	Florence (Rifridi)	arr.	0842

2137	arr.	Pisa (Centrale)	dep.	0800
2140	dep.	Pisa (Centrale)	arr.	0757
2226	dep.	La Spezia	dep.	0712
2256	dep.	Rapallo	dep.	0632
2330	arr.	GENOA (Brignole)	dep.	0610

Rome — Bari

IC 517		Borromini		IC 514
1810	dep.	ROME (Termini)	arr.	1030
1946	arr.	Caserta	dep.	0850
1947	dep.	Caserta	arr.	0849
2026	dep.	Benevento	dep.	0812
2128	arr.	Foggia	dep.	0714
2240	arr.	BARI	dep.	0600

Grand Train Stations
Islands of Order

Italian train stations are islands of order in seas of confusion. Adventuring in Italy takes you through four of Europe's best stations. Use Milan's, Rome's, and Florence's centrally located stations as your bases. Venice's remarkable Santa Lucia station is a scenic vaporetto ride away from the Piazza San Marco.

Milano Centrale

This is the grand station of Europe, a cyclopean complex opened in 1931. The station itself is something of a tourist sight. Its grandiose, eclectic syle has been characterized as "Assyrian-Babylonian," or "Mussolini Modern." Its second-class waiting room is enormous, and its staircases — mercifully equipped with escalators — sweeping.

When you enter the upper hall you see a feature so gracious it is unique. A bubbling water fountain — its sounds fighting the cacophony of the trains — shoots above a polished rose-colored marble floor surrounded by wire-web jump seats and warm pastel mosaics.

The long hall itself is highlighted by the creatively positioned "Gran Bar" at one end and "Informazioni" (for train information) at the other. Luggage checking is deviously located down a hall near the information office. Look for the illuminated suitcase sign.

FS's information office also contains a money change counter. A second bank is located on the long wall next to the sign in four languages indicating the city information office.

The "Self Service" cafeteria is located next to the "Gran Bar," down from a

ISLANDS OF ORDER

MILAN

ITALY

FLORENCE

Mediterranean Sea

-N-

ROME

0   20   100

MILES

place for freshening up called the "Hour Hotel." A post office is outside on the ground level, conveniently tucked into the same edifice.

Once you are through the guarded gates to the platform, you find the largest "Composizione Treni Principali" console in Europe. It wraps around three walls of a stairwell and elevator shaft at the head of track 9.

Near the center of the long wall are the entrances to the first- and second-class waiting rooms. A guard restricts entrance to the upholstered chairs of the first-class lounge, so it is safe as well as pleasant. The second-class room is grand. It is clean with banks of antique, varnished wooden benches. You hear echoes from its marble walls.

Milan's stations include Porta Garibaldi for local trains from Lake Como, Lambrate for trains not intended to serve Milan, Nord (near the Sforza Castle), Greco P., Porta Vittoria, and Porta Romana.

Milan's subway, Metropolitana, is more than just a way for you to get around the city with comfort and speed. It gives you a feeling for the rhythm of Milan and shows you a good example of the Italian flair for contemporary design.

Enter the subway stations at signs with the white letters *MM* (Metropolitana Milanese) in a red field. Milan's two subway lines from the outlying areas in the western and northeastern sections of the city intersect near the Sforza Castle and Piazzale Loreto. Obtain a free system map and helpful guide (in English) at the office of the transit authority (ATM) in the Duomo station, the Provincial Tourist Authority in Cathedral Square, or the Municipal Information Office in the nearby Galleria.

Public transportation is efficient and cheap. A single ticket is good for a trip of up to seventy minutes on any combination of buses, streetcars, and subway (provided the subway is used only once), so be sure to save your ticket when you leave the subway for the free transfers.

Public transportation tickets are sold at vending machines in all subway stations and at many streetcar stops, as well as at newsstands and tobacco stores. Validate them by machine at the beginning of your trip. A day ticket for an unlimited number of trips is a bargain.

Reaching Milan's Centrale station from Milan's Porta Garibaldi station is quite simple. Follow the signs to the subway, buy your subway ticket, and take line 2 (direction: "Gorgonzola") two stops to "Centrale F. S."

Rome Termini

Rome has five train stations. When you ride a through train scheduled to connect two other cities, you stop at Rome's Tiburtina or Ostiense station in Rome's outskirts. Tuscolana and Trastevere serve trains in the direction of Pisa. But your prime destination is Rome's Termini, in the throbbing heart of the Eternal City.

Rome's Termini station is big, modern, and badly signed. You must search for features. It consists of three areas: the platform area where you catch your train, the large inner hall with tables set out for diners, and the outer hall which exits on the taxi stand in front of the station. You must have a train ticket or rail pass to enter the platform area, so the platform area is where the manager has located many valuable functions.

On both sides are luggage-checking counters. There are no lockers. Toilet facilities are by track 1, and in the "Hour Hotel." There are no luggage carts in Rome Termini, but you can find porters easily.

Waiting rooms are comfortable, more so in first class than second, but both have television monitors displaying train arrival and departure times.

The only "Composizione Treni" in Rome Termini is for night trains, at the heads of platforms. Termini is an end station and trains are waiting for you when you arrive to board.

The Provincial Tourist Authority personnel can be found at a small window facing the platform area opposite track 4. They answer questions, make bookings without charge, and give you free maps, but automation has come to the hotel reservations services in Rome.

An aluminum display case in the outer hall lists hotels in categories from one to five stars. Beside the hotel names you see the map coordinates for the adjacent city map, their addresses, telephone numbers, and red/green lights to indicate their availability. Use one of the nearby telephones to determine rates and make a booking when acceptable.

The outer hall also has ticket windows and windows 34-43 for seat and cou- chette reservations ("Prenotazioni VL Posti e Cuccette").

FS's train information office (with signs above the windows indicating lan- guages spoken) is located in the outer lobby, next to FS's change bank. At the other end of the hall you use the Banco di Roma's money change office or, in the inner hall, change your money at the Banca Nazionale della Comuni- cazioni.

In the inner lobby you can enjoy coffee, croissants, etc., at the pleasant tables set out, or go inside (pay the cashier before ordering) for quicker service.

Adjacent, in a cafeteria ("Self Service"), you will find a complete selection of excellent food. It is enough to know that more than 95 percent of the customers speak Italian.

Rome Termini has three levels. You enter both Metro lines, Linea A and Linea B, below the inner hall on the main level. (Look for the white M on the red field.) The middle level is a neglected floor containing an "Hour Hotel" for freshening up and an office for long-distance and international telephoning.

The bottom level, below the "Hour Hotel," is the crossing of Rome's two subway lines. Line A's orange cars take you between Anagnina station and

Ottaviano station near the Vatican City with stops at Roma Nord train station, Spagna (the Spanish Steps, for the American Express office), Vittorio E, and Barberini. Line *B*'s cars run south to the EUR Center, where some hotels are located.

Deposit the correct change in the ticket-vending machines on the walls of the entrance hall or buy Metro tickets individually or in booklets of ten for a 14 percent discount at the transit authority's office. The office is located on the bottom level, between the entrances to the *A* and *B* lines.

Florence S.M.N.

Florence's Santa Maria Novella station is similar to Rome's Termini. Probably the same architectural firm was employed. It is one of the most pleasing Italian train stations because of its long architectural lines and modern layout, and is airy with its inner and outer halls. Because there is no Metro to complicate getting around, it is easy to find your way.

When you leave the tracks the inner hall has first- and second-class waiting rooms, "Ufficio Turismo" tourist information where patient agents make your hotel reservations at the head of tracks 9 and 10, "Ufficio Informazioni" train information, and a "Composizione Treni Principali" board.

In the outer hall you find a change bank, FS change, and domestic ticketing. In a connecting hall you find counters for reservations ("Prenotazioni") and international ticketing ("Biglietti Internazionali").

The "Self Service" restaurant here is the equal of those in other grand Italian stations. It is managed well and offers excellent selections.

You will find the luggage carts convenient at Florence S.M.N. Train calls are made in Italian and English.

Florence S.M.N. is conveniently located near the center of Florence. Hotels surround it, and more hotels are located in the direction of the Arno River, the Duomo, and the Piazza della Signoria, but the city brims with adventurers during the summer so it is best to rely on arrangements by the Tourist Office.

Other train stations in Florence include Castello, Rifredi (where FS's Pendolinos call), Fiesole Caldine, and Campo di Marte, but S.M.N. is your base.

Venice's Santa Lucia

Leaving Santa Lucia is like stepping into a dream. The Grand Canal stretches right before you, crammed with gondolas and busy with vaporetti (water buses) ready to take you through a wondrous world.

Adventurers lured to the City of the Doges will be pleased with their welcome at Venice's beautifully situated Santa Lucia station. Although not a hub like the other grand stations, it provides an appropriate terminal for excellent trains such as Pendolinos and InterCities.

At the head of the tracks you find palm trees and blooming red flowers. Facing the platforms is a restaurant, a sweet shop for take-out items, and a self-service cafeteria area extending to an open-air awning-covered verandah facing the canal where you enjoy dining in one of the most gracious train terminal surroundings. Inside you find a Tourist Office, FS change office, bank, reservations counter open until 10 P.M., ticketing, luggage storage, and post office.

Venice has two stations. Mestre is the stop for the express trains between Italy and Yugoslavia. Santa Lucia is your stop to meet the vaporetti to St. Marks Square. In style it recalls Florence S.M.N. with long marble steps covered with young and old idlers. Across the Grand Canal, visitors lounge on the steps of green-domed Fondamente S. Simeon Piccolo and on the Ponte degli Scalzi soaring over the canal in picture-book Venetian style. Gondoliere mooring their black gondolas across the canal do a brisk business.

Vaporetti require two floating terminuses. On the left as you exit Santa Lucia, line 2 (Diretto) takes a shortcut through a side canal to reach San Marco. Line 34 (Tourist) takes the scenic route.

Compelling Sardinia
Through the Highlands and
beside the Sea

Rome designed fast mainline trains to scamper through Sardinia's easy central valley. They skirt the special, rough terrains and scenic, wild seashores molded by seasonal mistral winds. The stop-and-go FCS local railroad takes you to out-of-the-way, wonderful corners and backwoods.

The FCS (Ferrovie Complementari della Sardegna) is a rough railroad dating from when it was essential to bind together rural towns and shepherds' villages. It is crude. It is remote. It has next to no amenities, one coach per train, and locomotives covered with grime. Inside, passenger space is clean and comfortable.

You may miss convenience and luxury, but there is no finer way for you to discover the gracious, proud feel of Sardinia. After all, you visit Sardinia for the atmosphere, not the amenities.

Riding the narrow-gauge train through remote highlands from Mandas to Arbatax catches the honest spirit of autonomous, feudal Sardinia. This fifty-six-mile trip is a microcosm of Sardinian life and scenery.

Sardinia is Italian now. Sardinians watch mainland Italian television channels and ride mainland Italian railroads, but in their hearts, they know mainland Italians are tourists from abroad.

SARDINIAN RAILROADS

Palau

Porto
Torres

Olbia

SASSARI

ALGHERO

Nuoro

ARBATAX

Flumendosa

MANDAS

- N -

CAGLIARI

0   20   50

MILES

Neither Romans nor Phoenicians, Greeks nor Arabs ever subdued Sardinia, the second-largest island in the Mediterranean after Sicily.

The uncompromised integrity of the Sardinian way of life makes travel through the island personal and compelling. Getting around Sardinia is relatively easy. You use good, cheap trains and buses.

The Mandas-Gairo-Lanusei-Arbatax morning train twists through constantly rugged, varied, lonely, and wild country. This is the kind of countryside to harbor notorious sheep-nappers. Lightninglike zigzags on your road map give clear warning of the extent of your U-turn ascents and steep descents. You pass sweeping, high-altitude panoramas and surprising stone outcroppings.

A second-class ticket costs you very little. No, Eurailpasses are not accepted on the FCS.

For the price, it is surprising that the single passenger car departs from Mandas on time. The diesel locomotive pulling it looks as dated as war-surplus equipment—covered with such an accumulation of dust and railroad grease that it looks like it just returned from battle.

Inside, the passenger coach is swept and dusted. The heating works but you lower the glass to keep close to the rugged scenery to come. Well-padded seats are small, soft, and comfortable, but your carriage is almost empty. The line suffers from such low ridership (because it is so remote) that it loses money and is in constant danger of being replaced by buses.

The first stop on your climb, Villanovatulo, is like an Alpine village, high and remote. Villanovatulo's one-room station house lies below the village at the foot of an unpaved path. The station is complete with a flea-chewing sheep dog and peasants wearing berets.

The air in Sardinia's highlands is light and sweet and the sun is bright. Your mountain site affords wide views, particularly of green Lake Flumendosa, the long, serene, artificial lake created for hydroelectric power. (Sardinia has no natural lakes.)

Soon you hear the engineer screech his whistle and see the train lights come on. You enter the first of frequent black tunnels. In the rear of your carriage, the conductor has placed his cap with gold braid beside him and relaxes on a seat next to an electric switch panel. He reads a newspaper—which is difficult because of the bouncing. Swaying and perusing his jiggling newspaper, he pushes a toggle switch on and off without glancing up from the bouncing headlines. The driver cues him with the screeches. Flip! Lights go on with the alarm. Flip! Lights go off exiting the tunnel. All the time reading the paper.

Silvery-green olive trees on the slopes vary with cork oak trees, almond trees, and small hillside vineyards. The gnarled cactuses growing as hedgerows are sheared to nourish pigs. Sardinia is greener and cooler, especially in the mountains, than one expects.

Soon you reach the pink stucco station house of Esterzili, where idlers trade humor and gossip with a conductor and stationmaster. A pretty young woman, probably from the mountains judging from her billowing pink skirt, kisses her husband goodbye.

Your train roams up and down the valleys and through the fields—the surveyors seem to have been freethinkers—averaging about 10 mph. The brown curtains beside the windows oscillate with the swaying of your coach.

After studying the dramatic, jagged rock formations on your left, it is greatly surprising to see cement-block and brick construction on the rough, rocky plateau. This is Sadali, the village of shepherds and agriculture. The slender-footed merino sheep below are white and glistening, not dingy, so that the black sheep playing among the flocks are very black indeed.

Your train is still climbing. You pass into Seui on a cut through the mountainside at the top of the village, for Seui is a settlement draped precariously down the mountain. From above, Seui looks like a maze of red-tile roofs huddled together. Only the bell towers of the white cathedral rise up to the height of your train.

Here you pause for the return train to Mandas to pass. Some of the passengers get off in Seui and board the waiting bus.

As your train approaches the summit above Seui, still running through a trench in the steep mountainside, sharp outcroppings of wind-carved stone rise next to the track. A creek far below churns round huge boulders. The road at the bottom of the valley winds like a thin gray tape with a white line in its center.

You stop for seven minutes at Gairo, a rouge-colored station with bus connections. A group of six grandmothers in brown, rough, woolen shawls and hoods mount the train. They are wearing mountain clothing—as close to costumes as you see on nonfestival days. Their loose, full aprons and skirts trail to the ground. They have wrapped their hoods/scarfs around their heads so one can only see their wrinkled, weathered, ruddy features and the roots of gray hairs. When they smile they reveal gums only partially toothed.

The red-capped dispatcher waves his baton and several high-school-aged girls come scampering aboard. They wear faddish clothing, the kind worn in classrooms everywhere. They sit across from the veteran women so that the contrast of clothing is vivid evidence of the changes occurring on the island.

Descending, you see more merino sheep mingled with cows clanging cowbells. Closing on Lanusei, you pass a clothesline hung with diverse washing, but your eye is riveted to a blue, boy's-size, "University of Michigan" sweat shirt.

As the tracks begin to parallel the highway, your train passes the road sign: "Lanusei 5 Km." An old woman in charge of the highway right-of-way has halted a string of lined-up Fiats with her red baton.

Scotch broom and gorse turn the hillsides bright yellow on the approach to Lanusei. This is the most thickly wooded part of your adventure. The mountains are newly forested with Canadian pines. You have a long view down on Lanusei, a large village growing larger with busy construction.

Blue buses wait at Lanusei station. You see another postcard view of the prosperous village from the train station. On a good day you see a stretch of sea, seven miles below, at Arbatax on Capo Bellavista, the center of a resort area. Arbatax is the landing for ferries from Genoa, and the end of your fascinating train ride through the Sardinian highlands.

Beside the Sea

Your maroon-and-gray, narrow-gauge diesel railcar is freshly scrubbed and glistening wet. It is now boarding for its convenient run from Sassari, on the Sardinian mainline in northwest Sardinia, to Alghero, the jewel-box port on the Mediterranean Sea.

It gives the lie to the notion that getting around Sardinia is difficult or dull. Railcars take you from Sassari's busy train station, which is seemingly lost in the center of Sassari's sea of red roofs rolling over graceful hills. But looks are deceiving, for Sassari is a bustling commercial city, the second town in Sardinia, and its train station is crowded.

The faded, Roman gold-colored terminus serves both FS (some visitors come by train the whole length of the island from Sardinia's capital city, Cagliari) and the Strade Ferrate Sarde, which has its headquarters here.

First aboard come businessmen with shiny attache cases, then gossiping nuns in black habits, peasants dressed in their Sunday best, and finally northern European adventurers carrying books of poetry.

Your railcar glides south past surprisingly tall olive trees and careful rows of trellised vineyards. Cliffs of Sardinian tufa limestone look as white as the Cliffs of Dover. Small, spiny artichokes for Sardinian antipasto flourish in the rust-red earth. Merino sheep frolic in the brown fields.

Your trip to Alghero, twenty-two miles, takes you forty-nine minutes at a leisurely pace of 27 mph, including nine stops. Your cost is very little, but not covered by Eurailpass.

At the end of your narrow-gauge railroad, Alghero is the highlight of the northwestern coast of Sardinia. Here you discover a hybrid Catalan/Italian culture and a seaside resort offering inexpensive accommodations, food, and drink.

You ride patiently, enjoying the warmth of the sun. Parochial-school children poke one another and lean out the windows. The northern Europeans put down their poetry and doze off.

Five minutes before arriving in Alghero's center, your railcar halts in S.

Agostino station to discharge many of the passengers to the long lineup of waiting regional blue buses. There are two further stops, ending in the center of Alghero.

Alghero lies on a small peninsula surrounded by Aragonese fortifications. Until 1848 the town was locked tightly at night. The former entrance, at the stubby tower of the Porta Terra, is still a good place to begin your walking tour through the narrow streets. The tourist office is nearby, so pick up free color maps for your explorations.

In a sense, Alghero isn't a Sardinian town at all. It started as one, in the early Middle Ages, but Spaniards from Aragon began their Sardinian conquest by annexing Alghero in 1355. The Algherese did not prove to be docile subjects; after two fierce rebellions the Aragonese solved their problem by deporting the entire population to the interior and replacing them with Catalans from the Iberian peninsula.

Everyone enjoys the friendly Catalan atmosphere here — Alghero is now known as "Little Barcelona."

Strolling through the narrow streets of the old town protected by Aragonese fortifications gives you a sense of quiet adventure and colorful leisure. You soon discover the busy quay. Photograph scenes along the dock showing a way of life you don't find at home. Green and blue fishing boats tie up to unload crawling, creeping, and leaping Mediterranean marine-life catches. Fishermen are mending orange-colored nets on the beaches. You admire the raw pink coral destined for the exquisite cameos sold in Rome and try to avoid the leaping lobsters escaping from plastic pails.

An added attraction is Neptune's Grotto, one of Italy's greatest natural wonders, just a boat ride away across the bay to Capo Caccia.

Sardinian Highlands Service

Ferrovie della Sardegna (Cagliari)

0845	dep.	MANDAS	arr.	1210
0917	dep.	Orroli	dep.	1139
0926	dep.	Nurri	dep.	1130
1020	dep.	Villanovatulo	dep.	1112
1028	dep.	Esterzili	dep.	1037
....	dep.	Sadali	dep.	1029
1053	dep.	Seui	dep.	1004
1142	dep.	GAIRO	dep.	0908
1126	dep.	Villagrande	dep.	0851
1211	dep.	Arzana	dep.	0838

1232	dep.	Lanusei	dep.	0818
1241	dep.	Elinia	dep.	0805
1322	dep.	TORTOLI	dep.	0724
1331	arr.	ARBATAX	dep.	0714

Railcar Service between Sassari and Alghero

Ferrovie della Sardegna

dep.	SASSARI	0720	0835	0950	1415	1640	1823	1950	2040
dep.	Molata	0728	0843	0958	1423	1648	1835	1958	2048
dep.	S. Giorgio	0738	0853	1008	1431	1658	1843	2008	2056
dep.	Arcone	0743	0858	1013	1436	1703	1848	2013	2101
dep.	Olmedo	0751	0906	1021	1446	1711	1856	2021	2111
dep.	Mamuntanas	0757	0912	1027	1452	1717	1902	2027	2117
dep.	Punta Moro	0800	0915	1030	1455	1720	1905	2030	2120
dep.	S. Agostino	0804	0919	1034	1459	1724	1909	2034	2124
dep.	S. Giovanni	0807	0922	1037	1502	1727	1912	2037	2127
arr.	ALGHERO	0809	0924	1039	1504	1729	1914	2039	2129
dep.	ALGHERO	0601	0820	0935	1255	1625	1740	1935	2051
dep.	S. Giovanni	0604	0823	0938	1258	1628	1743	1938	2054
dep.	S. Agostino	0607	0826	0941	1301	1631	1746	1941	2057
dep.	Punta Moro	0611	0830	0945	1305	1635	1750	1945	2101
dep.	Mamuntanas	0614	0833	0948	1308	1638	1753	1948	2104
dep.	Olmedo	0620	0839	0954	1314	1644	1759	1954	2110
dep.	Arcone	0627	0846	1001	1321	1651	1806	2001	2117
dep.	S. Giorgio	0633	0852	1007	1327	1657	1812	2007	2123
dep.	Molata	0641	0900	1015	1335	1705	1820	2015	2131
arr.	SASSARI	0648	0907	1022	1342	1712	1829	2022	2138

Appendix A

Train and Tourist Offices

New York and Massachusetts

Austrian National Tourist Office
500 Fifth Avenue, Suite 2009
New York, NY 10110
Tel. 800-223-0284 or 212-944-6880

Belgian Tourist Office
745 Fifth Avenue
New York, NY 10151
Tel. 212-758-8130

British Tourist Authority
40 W. 57th Street
New York, NY 10019
Tel. 212-581-4700

BritRail Travel International
1500 Broadway, 10th floor
New York, NY 10036-4015
Tel. 212-575-2667

CIE Tours International (Ireland)
122 E. 42nd Street
New York, NY 10168-0015
Tel. 800-CIE-TOUR, 800-522-5258
(NY), or 800-331-3824 (West Coast)

Finnish Tourist Board
655 Third Avenue
New York, NY 10017
Tel. 800-346-4636

French Government Tourist Office
610 Fifth Avenue
New York, NY 10020-2452
Tel. 900-420-2003 (50 cents a minute)

FrenchRail, Inc.
610 Fifth Avenue
Rockefeller Center
New York, NY 10020
Tel. 800-345-1990

German National Tourist Office
747 Third Avenue, 33rd floor
New York, NY 10017
Tel. 212-308-3300

GermanRail
747 Third Avenue
New York, NY 10017
Tel. 212-308-3100

GermanRail
625 Statler Office Building
Boston, MA 02116
Tel. 617-542-0577

Greek National Tourist Org.
645 Fifth Avenue, 5th floor
New York, NY 10022
Tel. 212-421-5777

Ibusz Hungarian Travel Company
630 Fifth Avenue, Room 2455
New York, NY 10111
Tel. 212-582-7412

Irish Tourist Board
757 Third Avenue
New York, NY 10017
Tel. 212-418-0800

Italian Government Travel Office
630 Fifth Avenue

New York, NY 10111
Tel. 212-245-4822

Italian State Railroads
594 Broadway
New York, NY 10012

Luxembourg National Tourist Office
801 Second Avenue
New York, NY 10017
Tel. 212-725-2345

Monaco Government Tourist Office
845 Third Avenue
New York, NY 10022
Tel. 212-759-5227

National Tourist Office of Spain
665 Fifth Avenue (at 53rd Street)
New York, NY 10022
Tel. 212-759-8822

Netherlands Board of Tourism
355 Lexington Avenue, 21st floor
New York, NY 10017
Tel. 212-370-7360

Portuguese National Tourist Office
548 Fifth Avenue
New York, NY 10036
Tel. 212-354-4403

Scandinavian Tourist Board
(for Denmark, Norway, Sweden)
655 Third Avenue
New York, NY 10017
Tel. 212-949-2333

Swiss National Tourist Office
608 Fifth Avenue
New York, NY 10020
Tel. 800-223-0448 or 212-757-5944

Texas

Austrian National Tourist Office
1300 Post Oak Blvd., Suite 960
Houston, TX 77056
Tel. 713-850-9999

British Tourist Authority
Cedar Maple Plaza
2305 Cedar Springs Road
Dallas, TX 75201-1814
Tel. 214-720-4040

BritRail Travel International
Cedar Maple Plaza, Suite 210
2305 Cedar Springs Road
Dallas, TX 75201
Tel. 214-748-0860

GermanRail
222 W. Las Colinas, Suite 1050
Irving, TX 75039
Tel. 214-402-8377

California

Austrian National Tourist Office
11601 Wilshire Boulevard,
Suite 2480
Los Angeles, CA 90025-1760
Tel. 800-252-0468 (CA)
or 213-477-3332

British Tourist Authority
World Trade Center, Suite 450
350 S. Figueroa Street
Los Angeles, CA 90071
Tel. 213-628-3525

BritRail Travel International
800 S. Hope Street, Suite 603
Los Angeles, CA 90017
Tel. 213-624-8787

Finnish Tourist Board
P.O. Box 67190
Los Angeles, CA 90067
Tel. 800-346-4636

French Government Tourist Office
9401 Wilshire Boulevard
Beverly Hills, CA 90212-2967
Tel. 900-420-2003 (50 cents a minute)

FrenchRail, Inc.
100 Wilshire Boulevard, Suite 435
Santa Monica, CA 90401
Tel. 800-345-1990

FrenchRail, Inc.
360 Post Street, Suite 606
San Francisco, CA 94108
Tel. 800-345-1990

German National Tourist Office
444 S. Flower Street, Suite 2230
Los Angeles, CA 90071
Tel. 213-688-7332

GermanRail
11933 Wilshire Boulevard
Los Angeles, CA 90025
Tel. 213-479-2772

GermanRail
240 Stockton Street
San Francisco, CA 94108-5306
Tel. 415-362-6206

Greek National Tourist Org.
611 W. Sixth Street
Los Angeles, CA 90017
Tel. 213-626-6696

Italian Government Travel Office
360 Post Street, Suite 801
San Francisco, CA 94108
Tel. 415-392-6206

Italian State Railroads
6033 West Century Blvd., Suite 980
Los Angeles, CA 90045

National Tourist Office of Spain
San Vicente Plaza Building
8383 Wilshire Boulevard, Suite 960
Beverly Hills, CA 90211
Tel. 213-658-7188

Netherlands Board of Tourism
90 New Montgomery Street, No. 305
San Francisco, CA 94105
Tel. 415-543-6772

Scandinavian Tourist Board
(for Denmark, Norway, Sweden)
8929 Wilshire Blvd.
Beverly Hills, CA 90211

Swiss National Tourist Office
222 N. Sepulveda Blvd., No. 1570
El Segundo, CA 90245
Tel. 213-335-5980

Swiss National Tourist Office
250 Stockton Street
San Francisco, CA 94108
Tel. 800-443-5566, 800-633-5566
(CA), or 415-362-2260

Florida and Georgia

British Tourist Authority
2580 Cumberland Parkway,
Suite 470

Atlanta, GA 30339
Tel. 404-432-9635

Danish National Railroads
Scandinavian Seaways Agent
6499 N.W. 9th Ave., Suite 212
Fort Lauderdale, FL 33309
Tel. 800-533-3755 (in USA);
800-247-1587 (in Canada)

FrenchRail, Inc.
2121 Ponce de Leon Boulevard
Coral Gables, FL 33134
Tel. 800-345-1990

GermanRail
Lenox Towers, Suite 1229
3400 Peachtree Road N.E.
Atlanta, GA 30326
Tel. 404-266-9555

National Tourist Office of Spain
1221 Brickell Ave., Suite 1850
Miami, FL 33131
Tel. 305-358-1992

Illinois

Austrian National Tourist Office
500 N. Michigan Avenue, Suite 544
Chicago, IL 60611
Tel. 312-644-5556

British Tourist Authority
625 N. Michigan Avenue
Chicago, IL 60611
Tel. 312-787-0490

French Government Tourist Office
645 N. Michigan Avenue, Suite 430
Chicago, IL 60611-2836
Tel. 900-420-2003 (50 cents a minute)

FrenchRail, Inc.
11 E. Adams Street
Chicago, IL 60603
Tel. 800-345-1990

GermanRail
9575 W. Higgins Road, Suite 505
Rosemont, IL 60018
Tel. 312-692-4209

Greek National Tourist Org.
168 N. Michigan Avenue

Chicago, IL 60601
Tel. 312-782-1084

Italian Government Travel Office
500 N. Michigan Avenue
Chicago, IL 60611
Tel. 312-644-0990

National Tourist Office of Spain
845 N. Michigan Avenue
Chicago, IL 60611
Tel. 312-642-1992

Netherlands Board of Tourism
225 N. Michigan Avenue, Suite 326
Chicago, IL 60601
Tel. 312-819-0300

Swiss National Tourist Office
150 N. Michigan Avenue
Chicago, IL 60601
Tel. 312-630-5840

CANADA

British Columbia

Austrian National Tourist Office
736 Granville Street, Suite 1220
Vancouver, BC V6Z 1J2
Tel. 604-683-5808

BritRail Travel International
409 Granville Street
Vancouver, BC V6C 1T2
Tel. 604-683-6896

FrenchRail, Inc.
409 Granville Street,
Suite 452
Vancouver, BC V6C 1T2
Tel. 800-345-1990

Ontario

Austrian National Tourist Office
2 Bloor Street E., Suite 3330
Toronto, Ont M4W 1A8
Tel. 416-967-3381

British Tourist Authority
94 Cumberland Street, Suite 600
Toronto, Ont M5R 1A3
Tel. 416-925-6326

BritRail Travel International
94 Cumberland Street
Toronto, Ont M5R 1A3
Tel. 416-929-3333

Finnish Tourist Board
1200 Bay Street, Suite 604
Toronto, Ont M5R 2A5
Tel. 416-964-9159

French Government Tourist Office
1 Dundas Street W.
Toronto, Ont M5G 1Z3
Tel. 416-593-4723

FrenchRail, Inc.
55 University, Suite 600
Toronto, Ont M5J 2H7

GermanRail
1290 Bay Street
Toronto, Ont M5R 2C3
Tel. 416-968-3272

Greek National Tourist Org.
Upper Level, 1300 Bay Street
Toronto, Ont M5R 3K8
Tel. 416-968-2220

Irish Tourist Board
160 Bloor Street, Suite 934
Toronto, Ont M4W 1B9
Tel. 416-929-2777

Italian State Railroads
111 Avenue Road, Suite 808
Toronto, Ont M5R 3J8

Netherlands Board of Tourism
25 Adelaide Street E., Suite 710
Toronto, Ont M5C 1Y2
Tel. 416-363-1577

Portuguese National Tourist Office
2180 Yonge Steet (Concourse Level)
Toronto, Ont M4S 2B9
Tel. 416-487-3300

Scandinavian Tourist Board
Box 115, Station "N"
Toronto, Ont M8V 3S4
Tel. 416-823-9620

Spanish Government Tourist Office
60 Bloor Street W., Suite 201
Toronto, Ont M6W 1A1
Tel. 416-961-3131

Swiss National Tourist Office
154 University Avenue
Toronto, Ont M5H 3Z4
Tel. 416-868-0584

Quebec

Austrian National Tourist Office
1010 W. Sherbrooke Street,
Suite 1410
Montreal, P.Q. H3A 2R7
Tel. 514-849-3709

Belgian Tourist Office
P.O. Box 760
Succursale N.D.G.
Montreal, P.Q. H4A 3S2
Tel. 514-489-9795

French Government Tourist Office
1981 McGill College Avenue,
Suite 490
Montreal, P.Q. H3A 2W9
Tel. 514-288-4264

FrenchRail, Inc.
1500 Stanley Street
Montreal, P.Q. H3A 1R3
Tel. 800-345-1990

German National Tourist Office
2 Fundy
P.O. Box 417
Place Bonaventure
Montreal, P.Q. H5A 1B8
Tel. 514-878-9885

Greek National Tourist Org.
1233, rue de la Montagne, Suite 101
Montreal, P.Q. H3G 1Z2
Tel. 514-871-1535

Italian Government Travel Office
1 Place Ville Marie, Suite 1914
Montreal, P.Q. H3B 3M9
Tel. 514-866-7667

Italian State Railroads
1450 City Counsillors Street, Suite 750
Montreal, P.Q. H3A 2E6

Portuguese National Tourist Office
500 W. Sherbrooke Street, Suite 930
Montreal, P.Q. H3A 3C6
Tel. 514-843-4623

AUSTRALIA

Canberra

National Australia Bank
Travel Service
21-23 London Circuit
Canberra

National Australia Bank
Travel Service
Capital Savings Centre
Corner City Walk & Ainslie Avenue
Canberra, ACT 2600

New South Wales

CIT-Australia Pty. Ltd.
123 Clarence Street
Sydney, NSW 2000

Concorde International Travel
Thomas Cook Pty. Ldt.
Shop 34A, Charlestown Shopping
   Square
Charleston, NSW 2290

National Australia Bank
Travel Service
175 Pitt Street
P.O. Box 3590
Sydney, NSW 2000

National Australia Bank
Travel Service
Mezzanine Floor
23 Hunter Street
Sydney, NSW 2000

Queensland

CIT-Australia Pty. Ltd.
131 Elizabeth Street
Sixth Floor
Brisbane, QLD 4000

Concorde International Travel
Thomas Cook Pty. Ldt.
168 Edward Street
P.O. Box 1066
Brisbane, QLD 4000

National Australia Bank
Travel Service
308-322 Queen Street
Brisbane, QLD 4000

South Australia

CIT-Australia Pty. Ltd.
118 King William Street
Third Floor
Adelaide, S.A. 5000

Concorde International Travel
Thomas Cook Pty. Ldt.
45 Grenfell Street
P.O. Box 1383
Adelaide, S.A. 5000

Tasmania

Concorde International Travel
Thomas Cook Pty. Ldt.
40 Murray Street
P.O. Box 306
Hobart, TAS 7000

Victoria

CIT-Australia Pty. Ltd.
500 Collins Street
Ground Floor
Melbourne, VIC 3000

Concorde International Travel
Thomas Cook Pty. Ldt.
541 King Street
West Melbourne, VIC 3003

Concorde International Travel
Thomas Cook Pty. Ldt.
83 Malop Street

P.O. Box 1010
Geelong, VIC 3220

Concorde International Travel
Thomas Cook Pty. Ldt.
159 Collins Street
Melbourne, VIC 3000

Concorde International Travel
Thomas Cook Pty. Ldt.
Shop 13, State Bank Galleria
Corner Elisabeth & Little Collins St.
P.O. Box 775H
Melbourne, VIC 3000

National Australia Bank
Travel Service
271 Collins Street
Melbourne, VIC 3000

Western Australia

CIT-Australia Pty. Ltd.
43 Ventnor Avenue
Second Floor
Perth, W.A. 6004

Concorde International Travel
Thomas Cook Pty. Ldt.
Shop 22-23, Wesley Centre
Hay Street Entrance
P.O. Box L907
Perth, W.A. 6000

NEW ZEALAND

Atlantic and Pacific Travel International
P.O. Box 3839
Auckland

Thomas Cook Holidays
96-98 Anzac Avenue
P.O. Box 3595
Auckland

Appendix B

European Eurail Aid Offices

For sales of Eurailpasses to qualified visitors, corrections of incorrectly issued Eurailpasses, and replacements of lost or stolen Eurailpasses.

Austria

Innsbruck Hauptbahnhof
Tel. (05222) 33633
Open Mon.-Sun. 6:15 A.M. to 7:45 P.M.
Salzburg Hauptbahnhof
Tel. (0662) 1700
Open Mon.-Sun. 24 hours
Vienna Westbahnhof
Tel. (0222) 839-574 or 872-425
open Mon.-Fri. 9 to 4

Belgium

Brussels South (Midi/Sud) Train Station
Salon d'accueil/Service International
Tel. 02-218-6050 ext. 5630
Open Mon.-Fri. 8 to 8;
Sat. 9 to 7

Denmark

Copenhagen Central Station
DSB Travel Agency
Tel. 01-124-122
Open Mon.-Sun. 6:30 to midnight

Finland

Helsinki Main Train Station
VR Lipputoimisto
Tel. 090-664-849
Open Mon.-Fri. 8:30 to 4:30

France

Paris St. Lazare Station
Service International
Tel. 01-4387-1661
Open Mon.-Fri. 8 to 7;
Sat. 9 to 1 and 2 to 5
Paris Nord Station
Bureau Information — Reservation
Tel. 01-4280-6363 ext. 11803
Open Mon.-Fri. 6 A.M. to 11:15 P.M.;
Sat.-Sun. 8 to 8
Paris Orly Airport SNCF Station
Tel. 01-4862-2218
Open Mon.-Sat. 8 to 8;
Sun. 9:30 to 1 and 2:45 to 6:45
Paris Charles de Gaulle Airport SNCF Station
Tel. 01-4862-2218

294 ADVENTURING ON EURAIL

Open Mon.-Sat. 8 to 8;
Sun. 9:30 to 1 and 2:30 to 6:30
Marseille St. Charles Train Station
Billets Internationaux
Tel. 091-95-14-03
Open Mon.-Sun. 4:30 A.M. to 1 A.M.
Nice Ville (SNCF) Train Station
Tel. 093-88-29-54
Open Mon.-Sat. 9 to noon and 2 to 6:30

Germany

Berlin Zoo Train Station
Ticketing (Fahrkartenausgabe)
Tel. 311-02-131
Open Mon.-Sun. 6 to midnight

Cologne Hauptbahnhof
Ticketing (Fahrkartenausgabe)
Tel. (0221) 141-2669
Open Mon.-Fri. 6 A.M. to 11 P.M.;
Sat.-Sun. 6 A.M. to 10:30 P.M.

Dresden Hauptbahnhof
Travel Office near the Train Station
(Verkehrsstelle am Hauptbahnhof)
Tel. 461-3656
Open Mon.-Fri. 6 A.M. to 9 P.M.;
Sat.-Sun. 7 A.M. to 8 P.M.

Frankfurt/Main Hauptbahnhof
Ticketing (Fahrkartenausgabe)
Tel. 069-265-5581
Open Mon.-Sun. 6 A.M. to 10:30 P.M.

Hamburg Hauptbahnhof
Ticketing (Fahrkartenausgabe)
Tel. 040-3918-4313
Open Mon.-Fri. 7 A.M. to 8 P.M.;
Sat.-Sun. 9:30 to 4

Heidelberg Hauptbahnhof
Ticketing (Fahrkartenausgabe)
Tel. (06221) 525-341
Open Mon.-Sat. 6 A.M. to 10:15 P.M.;
Sun. 6:30 A.M. to 10:15 P.M.

Leipzig Hauptbahnhof
Ticketing (Fahrkartenausgabe)
Tel. 724-3368
Open Mon.-Sun. 6:30 A.M. to 9 P.M.

Munich Hauptbahnhof
Ticketing (Fahrkartenausgabe)

Tel. 089-128-6635
Open Mon.-Fri. 7:15 to 6;
Sat.-Sun. 7:15 to 3:30
Stuttgart Hauptbahnhof
Ticketing (Fahrkartenausgabe)
Tel. (0711) 2092-2464
Open Mon.-Fri. 7:30 to 7;
Sat. 7:30 A.M. to 12:30 P.M.

Great Britain

French National Railways
179 Picadilly
London W.1.V.O.BA
Tel. 01-493-9731
Open Mon.-Fri. 9 to 5:15;
From Easter Saturday till end of August,
Sat. 9 to noon

Greece

Athens Greek Railroads Office
Bureau des Voyages et du Tourisme No. 2
1, rue Karolou
Tel. 01-522-4563
Open Mon.-Sun. 8 to 3:30

Thessaloniki Central Train Station
Tel. 031-519-519
Open. Mon.-Sun. 24 hours

Hungary

Kozonsegszolgolati Iroda
(Customer Service Office)
Nep Kos Earsasag Utjah 35
Budapest VI
Tel. 01-228-405
Open Mon.-Wed. and Fri. 9 to 6;
Thur. 9 to 7

Ireland

Dublin International Rail Ticket Sales
Office
35 Lower Abbey Street
Tel. 01-363-333
Open Mon.-Sat. 9 to 5

Italy

Bari Centrale Station
Information Office
Tel. 080-521-3302
Open Mon.-Sat. 9 to 1 and 4 to 8
Florence Santa Maria Novella Station
Information Office
Tel. 055-27-87-85
Open Mon.-Sat. 8 to 3
Milan Centrale Station
Information Office
Tel. 02-67500
Open Mon.-Sun. 7 A.M. to 11 P.M.
Naples Centrale Station
Information Office
Tel. 081-553-4188
Open Mon.-Sun. 7 A.M. to 9:30 P.M.
Palermo Centrale Station
Information Office
Tel. 091-616-4808
Open Mon.-Sun. 8 A.M. to 9 P.M.
Rome Termini Station
Information Office
Tel. 06-4730-6385
Open Mon.-Sun. 7 A.M. to 9 P.M.
Venice Santa Lucia Station
Information Office
Tel. 041-715-555
Open Mon.-Sun. 7 A.M. to 9:30 P.M.

Luxembourg

Luxembourg Train Station
Bureau de renseignements
Tel. 49901
Open Mon.-Fri. 8 to noon and 1 to 5

Netherlands

Utrecht Centraal Station
Information desk in hall

Tel. 030-35-44-80 or 030-35-37-35
Open Mon.-Fri. 8:30 to 4:30

Norway

Oslo Sentral Station
Ticket Office
Tel. 02-36-81-11 or 02-36-80-98
Open Mon.-Sun. 7 A.M. to 11 P.M.

Portugal

Lisbon Santa Apolonia Station
Departmento commercial
Tel. 01-648-303/4/5
Open Mon.-Fri. 9 to 1 and 2 to 5:30

Spain

Barcelona Sants Train Station
Tel. 093-322-2025
Open Mon.-Fri 9 to 1 and 4 to 8
Madrid RENFE Downtown Office
Alcala, 44
Tel. 091-532-5632
Open Mon.-Fri. 9 to 3 and 5 to 7;
Sat. 9 to 1
Madrid Bajaras Airport
RENFE desk
Tel. 091-205-8544
Open Mon.-Sat. 8 to 8;
Sun. 8 to 2
Seville RENFE Office
Calle Zaragoza 29
Tel. (0954) 222-693
Open Mon.-Fri. 9 to 1:15 and 4 to 7;
Sat. 9 to 12:30

Sweden

Stockholm Central Station
Ticket Office
Tel. 08-762-2561
Open Mon.-Fri. 8 to 6:30;
Sat.-Sun. 10 to 6

Switzerland

Basel SBB Station
SBB Tourist Office
Tel. 061-23-67-67
Open Mon.-Sun. 6 A.M. to 8 P.M.
(summers to 10)

Bern Main Train Station
Train Information Office
Tel. 031-211-111
Open Mon.-Sun. 7:30 A.M. to 8:30 P.M.

Geneva Train Station
Train Information Office
Tel. 022-7316-450
Open Mon.-Fri. 8 to 7;
Sat. 8 to 6; Sun. 10 to 6

Geneva Airport Train Station
Reservation Office
Tel. 022-910-250
Open Mon.-Sun. 9 to 7

Lucerne Train Station
Train Information Office
Tel. 041-213-311
Open Mon.-Sun. 6:30 A.M. to 8:45 P.M.

Zurich Hauptbahnhof
Train Information Office (upstairs)
Tel. 01-211-5010
Open Mon.-Sun. 6:30 A.M. to 8:30 P.M.

Zurich Airport Train Station
Train Information Office
Tel. 01-814-2822
Open Mon.-Sun. 6 A.M. to 9:40 P.M.

Index

Selected Pelican Travel Guides

ORDER FORM

____	Premier Hotels of Great Britain: 52nd Edition	$16.95 pb
____	Bulgaria: A Travel Guide	$15.95 pb
____	Polish Cities: Travels in Cracow and the South, Gdansk, Malbork, and Warsaw	$13.95 pb
____	Northern India: Rajasthan, Agra, Delhi	$14.95 pb
____	The Maverick Guide to Hawaii: 1991 Edition	$12.95 pb
____	The Maverick Guide to New Zealand: 8th Edition	$12.95 pb
____	The Maverick Guide to Thailand	$14.95 pb
____	The Maverick Guide to Australia: 8th Edition	$12.95 pb
____	The Australian Bed and Breakfast Book: 1991 Edition	$9.95 pb
____	The New Zealand Bed and Breakfast Book: 1991 Edition	$9.95 pb
____	New Zealand by Motorhome	$11.95 pb
____	A Personal Kiwi-Yankee Dictionary	$4.95 pb

____ Postage and handling: $1.50 for first book ordered and $.50 for each additional book ordered.

____ Jefferson Parish residents please add 8% tax. All other Louisiana residents please add 4% tax.

____ Total enclosed

NAME_____

ADDRESS_____

CITY_____

STATE_____ ZIP _____

TELEPHONE_____

Please make check or money order payable to:

PELICAN PUBLISHING COMPANY
1101 Monroe Street
P.O. Box 189
Gretna, LA 70053
Or Order Toll Free 1-800-843-1724

Please tell us about your Eurail trip.
(This page can be folded to make an envelope.)

Fold here. Fasten lip on front with clear tape.

Fold along dotted lines to make an envelope.

<table>
<tr><td></td><td rowspan="3">Place
first-class
postage
here</td></tr>
</table>

re: 2nd edition, Eurail

ADVENTURING ON EURAIL
Pelican Publishing Company
1101 Monroe Street
P.O. Box 189
Gretna, LA 70053